BEYOND RECIDIVISM

# Beyond Recidivism

*New Approaches to Research on Prisoner Reentry and Reintegration*

*Edited by*
Andrea Leverentz, Elsa Y. Chen, *and* Johnna Christian

*With an Afterword by Shadd Maruna*

NEW YORK UNIVERSITY PRESS
New York

NEW YORK UNIVERSITY PRESS
New York
www.nyupress.org

© 2020 by New York University
All rights reserved

References to Internet websites (URLs) were accurate at the time of writing. Neither the author nor New York University Press is responsible for URLs that may have expired or changed since the manuscript was prepared.

Library of Congress Cataloging-in-Publication Data
Names: Leverentz, Andrea M., 1973–, editor. | Chen, Elsa Yee-Fang, 1970–, editor. | Christian, Johnna, editor. | Maruna, Shadd, writer of afterword.
Title: Beyond recidivism : new approaches to research on prisoner reentry and reintegration / [edited by] Andrea Leverentz, Elsa Y. Chen, and Johnna Christian ; afterword by Shadd Maruna.
Description: New York : New York University Press, [2020] | Includes bibliographical references and index. | Summary: "Beyond Recidivism" explores new approaches to research on prisoner reentry and reintegration"—Provided by publisher.
Identifiers: LCCN 2019029132 | ISBN 9781479862726 (cloth) | ISBN 9781479853885 (paperback) | ISBN 9781479823024 (ebook) | ISBN 9781479877775 (ebook)
Subjects: LCSH: Recidivism—Research. | Prisoners—Deinstitutionalization—Research. | Resocialization—Research.
Classification: LCC HV6049 .B44 2020 | DDC 364.3—dc23
LC record available at https://lccn.loc.gov/2019029132

New York University Press books are printed on acid-free paper, and their binding materials are chosen for strength and durability. We strive to use environmentally responsible suppliers and materials to the greatest extent possible in publishing our books.

Manufactured in the United States of America

10 9 8 7 6 5 4 3 2 1

Also available as an ebook

CONTENTS

Introduction   1
   *Andrea Leverentz, Elsa Y. Chen, and Johnna Christian*

PART I: IMPROVING ON DEFINITIONS AND MEASURES OF RECIDIVISM

1. Beyond Recidivism: Toward Accurate, Meaningful, and Comprehensive Data Collection on the Progress of Individuals Reentering Society   13
   *Elsa Y. Chen and Sophie E. Meyer*

2. Community Capacity-Building and Implementation Advances to Addressing the RNR Framework   39
   *Faye S. Taxman*

PART II: RESEARCHING REENTRY: METHODS OF REENTRY RESEARCH

3. Conducting In-Depth Interviews with Jailed Fathers and Their Family Members   59
   *Kristin Turney*

4. Collecting Social Network Data in Prison and during Reentry: A Field Guide   81
   *Corey Whichard, Sara Wakefield, and Derek A. Kreager*

5. Interviewing the "Rabble Class": Recruitment and Retention in Studies of Prisoner Reentry   100
   *Andrea Leverentz*

PART III: FRAMEWORKS AND CONCEPTUAL CONSIDERATIONS

6. The Promise of Unpacking the Black/White Dichotomy for Reentry Research   135
   *Janet Garcia-Hallett and Kashea P. Kovacs*

7. Prison Experiences and Identity in Women's Life Stories: Implications for Reentry — 151
   *Merry Morash, Elizabeth A. Adams, Marva V. Goodson, and Jennifer E. Cobbina*

8. Does Thinking of Oneself as a "Typical Former Prisoner" Contribute to Reentry Success or Failure? — 172
   *Thomas P. LeBel and Matt Richie*

PART IV: CONTEXT AND CONSEQUENCES OF INCARCERATION AND REENTRY

9. Social Support in Daily Life at Reentry — 197
   *Naomi F. Sugie and Dallas Augustine*

10. Formerly Incarcerated Men's Negotiation of Family Support — 219
    *Johnna Christian*

11. "This Individual May or May Not Be on the Megan's Law Registry": The Sex Offender Label's Impact on Reentry — 235
    *Jamie J. Fader and Abigail R. Henson*

PART V: THE INTERPLAY BETWEEN RESEARCH AND POLICY

12. Running Away: Probation Revocation Programming in St. Louis County — 259
    *Beth M. Huebner and Morgan McGuirk*

13. Education's Failed Promise: How Public Policies "Educate" a Criminal Underclass — 275
    *Keesha Middlemass*

14. Mercy-Oriented Reentry and Reintegration: Lessons from Policy, Research, and Practice — 293
    *Alexandra L. Cox and Reginald Dwayne Betts*

Afterword: Can the Rehabilitative Ideal Survive the Age of Trump? — 315
*Shadd Maruna*

*Acknowledgments* — 321

*References* — 323

*About the Editors* — 369

*About the Contributors* — 371

*Index* — 379

# Introduction

ANDREA LEVERENTZ, ELSA Y. CHEN, AND JOHNNA CHRISTIAN

The United States has experienced a period of unprecedented prison population growth. This growth reflects changes in criminal justice policies, including an increase in the use of prisons and jails as punishment, increases in the length of prison sentences for a broader range of offenses, and adoption of mandatory minimum and repeat-offender sentencing policies (Gottschalk 2015). As a result of these policy shifts, more people spend more time incarcerated. Garland attributes these changes to the cultural and criminological conditions of late modernity—including a decline in belief in the rehabilitative ideal, a return to expressive justice and punitiveness, and emphases on victims and the need to "protect" the public. In addition, the United States and other countries embraced the use of prisons (Eason 2017; Schoenfeld 2018) and emphasized control theories of criminal behavior that lend themselves to control policies (Garland 2001). Crime is seen as normal, and the infrastructure to protect the public and to prevent crime is growing and becoming more and more commercial. In other words, the conditions leading to mass incarceration are deeply social and political, and only partly connected to crime rates or offending patterns.

There have been some signs of reductions in new prison admissions in the last decade; for example, the state and federal prison population declined by 12,600 prisoners, a drop of 1%, and the imprisonment rate decreased from 459 adults per 100,000 to 450 per 100,000 (Carson 2018). Still, the United States has among the highest rates of incarceration in the world (Travis, Western, and Redburn 2014). In spite of signs of a recent decrease, the past few decades of "tough-on-crime" policies have resulted in the incarceration of millions of individuals. Inevitably, most people in prison are eventually released, reentering society, sometimes after spending lengthy periods separated from the community. In addition to individuals returning from prison, many more people enter or exit jails each year or are on community supervision (probation or parole) (Kaeble and Cowhig 2018). In total, more than 2 million people are under correctional supervision in the United States. These people are impacted not only by possible issues that may have led to offending and incarceration, but also by the experience of incarceration and the stigma of a criminal record. In addition, their families and communities are affected by both their absence and their return (Braman 2004; Comfort 2008; Comfort et al. 2015; Wakefield and Wildeman 2013).

Prisoner reentry has been a focus of research for decades (Irwin 1970). It drew greater attention in the early 2000s with work by Jeremy Travis and colleagues at the Urban Institute (e.g., La Vigne and Mamalian 2004; La Vigne, Mamalian, et al. 2003; La Vigne, Thompson, et al. 2003; Travis 2005; Watson et al. 2004). Research about prisoner reentry has advanced significantly in the last decade, incorporating theories of desistance, life course criminology, and inequality, among other areas. This also has corresponded with renewed interest in research on desistance, or why and how people stop offending (Laub and Sampson 2003; Maruna 2001; Sampson and Laub 1993). These bodies of work have continued to grow over the past fifteen years. Reentry research covers a wide range of dimensions of the incarceration and post-incarceration experience. Much of the research focuses on immediate needs of people exiting prison, such as housing and employment, and how efforts to secure housing and employment are shaped by incarceration. This body of research addresses the impacts of incarceration on employment, earnings, and intensified inequality (Pager 2007; Pettit and Western 2004; Western 2018; Western and Pettit 2005); impacts of incarceration on neighborhood, neighborhood attainment, housing, and homelessness (Clear 2007; Harding, Morenoff, and Herbert 2013; Herbert, Morenoff, and Harding 2015; Leverentz 2019; Massoglia, Firebaugh, and Warner 2013; Simes 2018); and neighborhood influences on reoffending or official measures of recidivism (Hipp, Petersilia, and Turner 2010; Kirk 2009; Kubrin and Stewart 2006; Mears et al. 2008). Researchers also address the health consequences of incarceration (Schnittker 2013; Schnittker and John 2016; Schnittker, Massoglia, and Uggen 2011). Some research explicitly addresses the connections between incarceration and post-incarceration experiences (Lopez-Aguado 2018; Schnittker et al. 2015).

Scholars are increasingly mindful of the diversity of experiences with incarceration and reentry. A growing body of work explores the experiences of women and the gendered nature of incarceration, reentry, recidivism, and desistance (Chen and Adams 2019; Cobbina 2010; Huebner, DeJong, and Cobbina 2010; Leverentz 2014). A consistent theme across reentry research is the importance of race in understanding the impact of incarceration on future life chances (Lopez-Aguado 2018; Pager 2007; Western and Sirois 2019). Researchers also have focused on juveniles and how involvement with the juvenile justice system impacts their transition to adulthood (Cox 2018; Fader 2013; Flores 2016; Soyer 2016). In addition, there is growing focus on the ways in which incarceration impacts not only the person who is incarcerated but also the individual's family, loved ones, and children (Braman 2004; Comfort 2008; Turney and Haskins 2014; Wakefield and Wildeman 2013; Wildeman and Turney 2014) and community (Clear 2007).

In addition to a focus on the experiences of people who have been incarcerated and their families and communities, there also has been growing attention to the systems themselves, including how and why policies were developed and how they are embedded in a wider social and political world (Garland 2001; Gottschalk 2015; Middlemass 2017; Schoenfeld 2018; Simon 2007). In addition, recent research addresses a number of key policy areas, including the significance of fines and fees as hurdles to successful reentry (Harris 2016), the ways in which even community-based sentences, low-level charges, and open cases form a web of social control (Kohler-Hausmann 2018; Phelps 2013; Uggen et al. 2014), and how policies like California realignment (Bartos and Kubrin 2018), voter disenfranchisement (Manza and Uggen 2008), "ban the box" (Vuolo, Lageson, and Uggen 2017), and online background check systems (Lageson 2016) continue to control formerly incarcerated people and shape reentry outcomes. Researchers have also begun to consider how reentry organizations have become a site of collusion between social welfare and criminal justice actors to manage marginalized populations (Halushka 2016; Kerrison 2017; Mijs 2016; Miller 2014).

In 2014, the National Academy of Sciences issued a comprehensive report about the causes and consequences of the growth of incarceration in the United States (Travis et al. 2014). The challenges of prisoner reentry figured prominently in the findings, including a discussion of the risk-needs-responsivity framework for prison rehabilitation programming and reference to research on how individuals navigate the reentry process. The report emphasized the need to focus on improved outcomes by assisting returning prisoners with employment, housing, and other transitional needs. It also called for data improvement and standardization. Evidence-based policies and practices are considered the most promising for reducing recidivism, but challenges of implementation and sustainability remain. In addition, political pressures, budgetary constraints, and the tendency for policy areas such as criminal justice, housing, and health care to be addressed as separate "silos" may limit innovative thinking and policy development related to prisoner reentry. The collection and sharing of data on those involved in the criminal justice system also raise ethical issues about how those data are used and secured. These approaches also typically maintain focus on the behavior, risks, and needs of returning prisoners, with less attention to the behavior and attitudes of others, including landlords, employers, family members, and neighbors.

This is a lively time in reentry research, and the contributors to this volume are at the cutting edge of theoretical and empirical advancements. This volume brings together chapters that reflect the range of current work on prisoner reentry, across disciplines, methods, and focuses. While reoffending and recidivism are a concern of researchers and policymakers, throughout the volume we also make a case for the need to expand research and policy attention *beyond* recidivism, to capture other key aspects of people's lives as they leave prison. Theoretically and analytically, we extend reentry research to include the subjective experiences of prisoners, former prisoners, families, communities, and others who are impacted by mass incarceration. How and why do they search for work despite limited job prospects? Which people help or hinder their attempts to reestablish their lives? How do criminal justice policies and practices provide support or present obstacles? In addition to expanding the range of questions asked about prisoner reentry, the contributors to this volume employ original and time-intensive methodologies to uncover answers that provide greater depth, breadth, and nuance to our conceptualization and understanding of recidivism, and extend beyond it. Many of the contributors work successfully with practitioners, policymakers, and correctional professionals to both access data and influence policy. Scholars from fields such as sociology, political science, law, criminology, and criminal justice offer insights that are often not adequately communicated across disciplines, despite the fact that the topic of reentry from incarceration spans academic and policy areas. Our volume joins this conversation, further expanding and deepening our collective understanding of the impact of incarceration and other penalties.

The book is divided into five sections, highlighting different aspects of research on the impact of incarceration and incarceration policies on individuals and communities. In the first section, authors address the state of the field with respect to how we measure and understand recidivism and develop research-informed policies. Elsa Chen and Sophie Meyer discuss shortcomings of current definitions and measures of recidivism and propose more accurate and meaningful ways to measure the progress of returning prisoners. They recommend a shift in data collection practices from the current prevailing emphasis on risks and failure to a focus that considers needs, availability of resources and support, and incremental successes, integrated across policy areas. Their analysis draws on interviews with government and nonprofit employees who have expertise in reentry resource coordination for returning prisoners, data collection, and data sharing and integration. Next, Faye Taxman develops a data collection strategy for a modified risk-need-responsivity framework that takes into account the needs of the population in each community, emphasizing the importance of addressing key needs such as housing stability, food security, substance abuse treatment, and mental health resources. Echoing Chen and Meyer, Taxman redirects the spotlight from returning prisoners' risks and needs to the availability of effective programs appropriately matched to address returning individuals' specific needs; without recognizing and addressing gaps in program capacity, rehabilitation and reintegration goals cannot be adequately fulfilled. In addition to extending beyond criminogenic factors, this approach goes from a personal, individual focus to one that incorporates social-structural factors associated with the specific place where reentry is taking place.

In part II, authors draw on their recent and ongoing research to discuss methodological approaches to collecting data in prisons and jails and among those impacted by incarceration. Kristin Turney writes about a longitudinal, qualitative investigation into the ways paternal incarceration creates, maintains, and exacerbates inequalities among families and children. In her chapter, she highlights the challenges of gaining access to jailed fathers and of interviewing multiple members of the same family. Corey Whichard, Sara Wakefield, and Derek Kreager discuss related studies of prison and post-prison networks. The chapter details their experiences collecting social network data in a prison by providing a field guide to collecting this type of data. They also highlight the potential in using this methodological approach to understanding incarceration and reentry experiences. Finally, Andrea Leverentz details a longitudinal interview study of men and women being released from a county-level correctional facility and discusses the challenges of recruiting and following a highly disadvantaged and unstable population. She draws on multiple sources of data from this study to understand why people may be lost to interviewers along the way, the consequences of this, ways to mitigate it, and some of the ethical implications of this type of research. Together, these three chapters highlight different types of data collection, a range of experiences navigating institutional rules and constraints, and research ethics of collecting data among incarcerated and formerly incarcerated people and their families.

Part III turns to conceptual issues in defining and understanding reentry populations, and the implications of definitions and frameworks on the questions we ask and how we address them. We know that there is a social context to incarceration and reentry. Individuals are embedded in relationships and communities, and broader social forces also shape their experiences. For example, a white man with a college degree returning to a middle-class neighborhood will have a different experience exiting prison than a black woman with a high school degree who is returning to a disadvantaged neighborhood (Western and Pettit 2010). People returning with a history of drug addiction, or with low levels of family support, will have different outcomes than those without these experiences. While prisoners are shaped by their lives in prison, many other broad social forces also shape them. Each of the chapters in this section pushes us to expand and deepen our definitions of key categories and populations. First, Janet Garcia-Hallett and Kashea Kovacs "unpack" the black-white dichotomy. They urge us to take seriously a range of experiences across ethnicity and emphasize that large racial classifications mask a high level of variability in experiences, and therefore also hinder social support efforts. Merry Morash, Elizabeth Adams, Marva Goodson, and Jennifer Cobbina analyze how the prison experiences of women shape their life stories and their narratives of reentry. They draw on narrative interviews with women who discussed the pains of imprisonment as causes of distress in their lives, often discussing the inability to fulfill perceived obligations to family. Thomas LeBel and Matt Richie draw on survey data of formerly incarcerated people to explore how one's identity as a "typical former prisoner" shapes the ability to successfully reintegrate into society and avoid future incarceration. Consistent with earlier research on desistance (e.g., Maruna 2001), they find that identifying as a typical former prisoner may hinder a sense of agency over desistance efforts. Each of these chapters highlights key aspects of a person's identity and how we define and measure them, including race and ethnicity, gender, and a sense of stigma.

Part IV continues the discussion of how social context and position shape one's experiences post-release. Chapters highlight several consequences of criminal justice system involvement and how the experience of incarceration continues to shape the lives of people who have been incarcerated. Naomi Sugie and Dallas Augustine analyze data from Sugie's recent smartphone study, in which she sent participants daily open-ended survey questions about the more important positive and negative points in their day. They unexpectedly found that social relationships were paramount in the immediate months after release from prison and therefore call for greater attention to the importance of emotional support in reentry studies. Johnna Christian continues a focus on social supports in her analysis of interview data from men who had been released from prison. She looks at how these men understood and drew upon support from family members and other members of their social networks, and how they attempted to minimize the burdens they placed on others. Jamie Fader and Abigail Henson present a case study of one of the men Fader initially introduced to us in her book *Falling Back* (2013). Tony pled guilty to statutory sexual assault at age nineteen; Fader and Henson detail the subsequent twelve years as he attempted to navigate the system and how the sex offender label shaped his experiences. Each of these chapters emphasizes the social embeddedness of people, and how social and criminal justice system connections make their experience easier or harder.

In the final section, authors address the importance of the interplay between research and policy, including how each may better influence the other. Beth Huebner and Morgan McGuirk use a case study of probation revocation programming. There is growing attention to the significance of jails, community-based corrections, and the negative impacts of even short periods of incarceration. Given that people serving time for probation violations are a significant portion of jail populations, programming related to probation revocation is an important aspect of prisoner reentry. The authors detail a program designed to mitigate the costs of incarceration while addressing root causes. Keesha Middlemass discusses the limitations and failures of educational programs in prison. She draws on federal and state public policies, along with fieldwork and interviews among returning prisoners, to demonstrate the ways in which "tough on crime" policies prevent currently and formerly incarcerated people from gaining a formal education. Finally, Alexandra Cox and R. Dwayne Betts call for increased use of life history interviews in shaping sentencing practices to better achieve a goal of social justice. They emphasize the value in focusing on mercy-driven sentencing that draws on the social history of the accused. Together this set of chapters demonstrates how research and policy can better inform each other to both understand issues related to prisoner reentry and to develop more effective policies to reduce recidivism, enhance justice, and otherwise improve outcomes for people.

Shadd Maruna concludes the volume, emphasizing the importance of the political climate not only in terms of shaping policy but also in terms of shaping research agendas. Chapters in this volume addressed different aspects and implications of these shifts, with recent shifts to a more humanistic research approach to understanding the lives of those implicated in mass incarceration. Maruna concludes with a call for a social movement of people who are or have been incarcerated or on community supervision, along with their loved ones and supporters, to work toward reversing this punitive turn.

Together, the chapters in this volume present a picture of prisoner reentry as we understand it today. While all of the chapters center on questions related to incarceration and its consequences, they draw on and reflect deeply social and political issues that are relevant to a wide range of readers. They incorporate a range of methodological perspectives and methods, from ethnography to experimental designs, with several authors drawing on mixed methods. In addition to the empirical analyses, the volume also provides a road map of some of the key directions to pursue next in researching criminal justice policies and their consequences and in developing effective policies.

PART I

Improving on Definitions and Measures of Recidivism

1

# Beyond Recidivism

*Toward Accurate, Meaningful, and Comprehensive Data Collection on the Progress of Individuals Reentering Society*

ELSA Y. CHEN AND SOPHIE E. MEYER

There are more than 2.3 million people incarcerated in state prisons, federal prisons, and local jails in the United States (Wagner and Rabuy, 2016). The rate of imprisonment more than tripled from 220 per 100,000 in 1980 to 775 per 100,000 in 2008 and has been slowly declining ever since; yet America continues to incarcerate at a rate five times higher than any other country with similar levels of crime (van Dijk, van Kesteren, and Smit, 2007; Kaeble et al., 2016; International Center for Prison Studies, 2018). More than 600,000 people are released from prison each year, and the number of people who enter and leave jails, including sentenced inmates and pretrial detainees, has been estimated at approximately 9 million per year (Carson, 2018; Wagner and Sawyer, 2018).

On average, 68% of state prisoners will return to prison within three years (Alper, Durose, and Markman, 2018; Durose, Cooper, and Snyder, 2014). That rate increases to 79% returning to prison within five years, and 83% will return within nine years (Alper et al., 2018). At the federal level, about half of federal prisoners will be rearrested within eight years after release (Hunt and Dumville, 2016).

Given these numbers and the budgets required to sustain the American criminal justice system, reducing recidivism has become a pressing state and national concern. States have long been using recidivism, "a person's relapse into criminal behavior, often after the person receives sanctions or undergoes intervention for a previous crime," as an indicator of the success of the justice system (Hunt and Dumville, 2016, p. 7). As the Pew Center on the States (2011b, p. 6) explains, "avoiding future criminal conduct through deterrence and rehabilitation [is] measured by the recidivism rate and has long been considered the leading statistical indicator of return on correctional investment." Recidivism rates are often used as a catchall measure. The success of correctional programs, imprisonment, and reentry programs is couched in terms of their effects on the reduction of recidivism. However, this measure gives an incomplete and sometimes misleading picture of formerly incarcerated individuals' progress in the reentry process. Furthermore, the variables currently included in recidivism definitions vary widely by jurisdiction, making it challenging to compare recidivism rates.

If the justice community seeks a full picture of the effectiveness and community impact associated with our current approaches to criminal punishment, data collection efforts should include information on formerly convicted individuals' access to rehabilitation and reentry programs and resources such as housing, employment, medical care, substance abuse and mental health treatment, and government benefits, along with measures of the effectiveness of these programs and services. Data sharing and integration are also needed, despite the formidable obstacles that currently stand in the way of greater collaboration between agencies.

This chapter seeks to illustrate some of the shortcomings of existing measures of recidivism and to examine why and how measurements of formerly incarcerated individuals' success should be reevaluated, standardized, updated, and improved. It also includes recommendations for both researchers and policy practitioners.

## The Current State of Recidivism Research and Practice

Factors considered in the calculation of recidivism vary from state to state. Measures of recidivism can be based on a variety of different events, such as rearrest, reconviction, reincarceration, or return to prison. This makes "recidivism" an imprecise term at best, susceptible to either unintentional or intentional misuse or misinterpretation. Furthermore, nuances in the definition of each of the events commonly used to measure recidivism create problems for comparison.

Few states consider rearrest by itself a full measure of recidivism, but research on recidivism sometimes cites this statistic (The Sentencing Project, 2010; Alper et al., 2018). A rearrest can entail a new crime or a violation of the terms of supervised release, whether it be probation, state parole, or community supervision (Hunt and Dumville, 2016). It may mean that a new crime has been committed and/or that a former inmate will be reincarcerated. Alternatively, a rearrest can result in a subsequent acquittal, or the sanctions for the offense or violation may not entail jail or prison time.

Reconviction is more often used as a full measure of recidivism. This term is defined as an arrest followed by a court conviction (Hunt and Dumville, 2016; Durose et al., 2014). The new offense is usually a new crime and does not include technical parole violations, but as with rearrest, a new conviction does not always mean jail or prison time.

Reincarceration is also a commonly used measure of recidivism, and among these options, it makes the most sense for representing recidivism. Reincarceration is a conviction or revocation of parole that leads to time in prison or jail (Hunt and Dumville, 2016). Still, like the term recidivism itself, reincarceration is complicated because it lacks a standard composition. Jurisdictions that use this term may separate out new crimes versus technical parole violations or they may give a combined statistic, which can imply a higher number of new crimes than actually occurred. A technical violation of parole or supervised release often does not involve a new crime and can be an event as minor as forgetting a meeting with a parole officer or failing a drug test (Pew Center on the States, 2011b; Council of State Governments Justice Center, 2014). To be fair, not all parole violations are as innocuous as missing an appointment, but in some instances, parole violations may reflect shortcomings in the reentry programs a former prisoner was offered, rather than a relapse into dangerous criminal behavior that will adversely affect public safety. A Pew Center on the States (2011b) study comparing recidivism in 1999 and 2004 found technical violations could in fact account for the majority of a state's recidivism rate. For example, in 2008, California had a total recidivism rate, as measured by reincarcerations, of 58%, but this figure comprised 18% returned to prison for new crimes and 40% returned to prison for technical parole violations (ibid.). At least sixteen states specify that technical violations are included in recidivism rates in their Department of Corrections documents (The Sentencing Project, 2010).

The type of correctional system a state uses also has the potential to skew numbers. If a state has a unified correctional system, in which the state operates both prisons and jails, then imprisonment numbers coming from the Department of Corrections automatically include those in custody in local jails, whereas another state may only count inmates in the prison system (Pew Center on the States, 2011b; Council of State Governments Justice Center, 2014). Six states—Alaska, Connecticut, Delaware, Hawaii, Rhode Island, and Vermont—use a unified system (Krauth, 1997).

Instead of reincarceration, some states use the terms imprisonment or return to prison, which capture the number of offenders who go back to prison but say nothing about those returning to jail. It is important to note that any incarceration-based measures can reflect disparities in enforcement, which can introduce bias into estimates of recidivism. For example, a recent study conducted in San Francisco found that "black defendants are less likely to have their cases dropped or dismissed, less likely to be successfully diverted, more likely to be released to another agency or have a motion to revoke filed against them, and when convicted, receive the longest incarceration sentences and are the most likely to receive a prison sentence" (MacDonald and Raphael, 2017).

Comparison of states' definitions of recidivism can be problematic depending on the components selected to illustrate recidivism, but there are additional complicating factors. The time frame in which states compute recidivism statistics also has an impact on recidivism rates (Pew Center on the States, 2011b). In the federal system, recidivism numbers are computed every three years, but state prison systems can measure recidivism anywhere from six months to nine years after release from prison (Alper et al., 2018; Hunt and Dumville, 2016; The Sentencing Project, 2010). Looking at exactly the same data for different periods of time can yield drastically different numbers. A Bureau of Justice Statistics study found that state prisoners have a 44% rearrest rate within one year, but a 68% rate within three years, 79% within six years, and 83% within nine years (Alper et al., 2018). Thus, to compare recidivism rates for two different jurisdictions, it is essential to compare rates within exactly the same time frame. While a longer time frame might seem preferable in order to capture more potential reoffending, additional years of data collection are likely to yield limited marginal benefits after a certain length of time. Kurlychek, Brame, and Bushway (2007) found that if an ex-offender can avoid reoffending for seven years, she has the same chance of committing a crime as someone who has never offended before.

On a related note, the length of post-release supervision also affects the measurement of recidivism. Terms of parole can considerably restrict everyday life, and closer engagement with parole agents and more structured reentry programming, while potentially beneficial, heighten an individual's risk of parole revocation and possible subsequent incarceration for minor offenses or program noncompliance. States where sentences tend to include longer periods of supervision may therefore report higher recidivism rates than states with shorter periods (Pew Center on the States, 2011b).

Sentencing policy, parole procedures, and departmental differences in recordkeeping or analysis have the potential to make comparisons of recidivism numbers misleading. States that send lower-risk offenders to prison will have different imprisonment and recidivism rates than states that reserve prison sentences for violent offenders (Pew Center on the States, 2011b). This is especially pertinent for drug offenses, as some states attach a jail or prison sentence to marijuana offenses while others have legalized recreational use (Governing, 2018). States that have stricter policies around sending parole violators back to prison instead of imposing other sanctions may report higher recidivism rates than states that prioritize other responses to parole violations (Pew Center on the States, 2011b).

Implementing a more standardized and detailed approach to collecting recidivism data is not a new concept. A 2014 collaborative report by the Council of State Governments Justice Center, the National Reentry Resource Center, and the Bureau of Justice Assistance set forth guidelines for creating an "accurate and meaningful" recidivism measure. The guidelines recommend a common "primary definition of recidivism," such as return to prison for a new offense, along with other measures, such as violations of probation or parole; more information about each "recidivism event"; information about the offender's demographic characteristics, history, and risks and needs; collection of follow-up data at regular, fixed intervals; and annual updates (Council of State Governments Justice Center, 2014). Both researchers and policy practitioners need to be aware of how variations in definitions and data collection practices can mislead. Some states have higher reported rates of recidivism than others without experiencing more reoffending, and apparent changes in recidivism rates may result from changes in reporting processes. These nuances should be considered when recidivism rates are compared across locales and systems, or over time.

In addition to the numerous technical shortcomings of recidivism statistics, a more important and perhaps more challenging conceptual problem is the reliance on measures that focus primarily on reengagement with various parts of the criminal justice system. These measures are insufficient to accurately or thoroughly gauge a former inmate's success or failure at reintegration into society.

The integration of data across policy areas is uncommon, but when it exists, it provides opportunities for cooperation and creative problem-solving. South Carolina, for example, has used integrated data to determine the impact of incarceration on families, gathering data from the Department of Juvenile Justice, Department of Mental Health, Department of Alcohol and Other Drug Abuse, Department of Social Services, Department of Health and Human Services, Department of Education, and the Department of Health and Environmental Control (DeHart, Shapiro, and Hardin, 2017). After using South Carolina's integrated data to investigate that relationship, DeHart et al. (2017) found that "combining data from multiple service systems can harness information in meaningful ways that transcend service silos and allow community members to focus collective attention on important issues across systemic boundaries." Likewise, reentry and recidivism transcend policy boundaries. Helping a reentering individual succeed in society requires addressing her mental health, physical health, employment, housing, and other economic and social needs. The benefits of data integration accrue at both the individual level and the systemic level. Culhane et al. (2010, p. 1) analyzed eight exemplary integrated data systems, including South Carolina's, and concluded that

> building capacities for timely, data-based decision-making across multiple systems will not only result in greater efficiencies in service delivery; it will also benefit policymakers, who can use such integrated data to answer critical policy and program questions: what works, for whom, and at what cost. The integration of administrative data across service agencies

has been identified as the next frontier for generating quality evidence to inform public policy and system reform.

Data integration is highly likely to improve cost efficiency and effectiveness of the entities sharing the data in the long run, but it requires a high level of cooperation among all the actors involved. The creation of an integrated data system, whether it be a data linkage center, a statewide data warehouse, or an online archive, faces legal, ethical, technological, economic, and political challenges, but ways to address these problems have been found (Ball, 2010; Tafoya et al., 2014; Culhane et al., 2010; DeHart et al., 2017; Moore, Youngs, and Ritter, 2006). There even exist a few different manuals on the process of creating an integrated data system (Moore et al., 2006; Culhane et al., 2010).

Collecting data on offenders is subject to state and federal privacy laws, and there are clear ethical standards in place to ensure the security of personal data. Health and education data are protected by the Health Insurance Portability and Accountability Act of 1996 (HIPAA) and the Family Educational Rights and Privacy Act of 1974 (FERPA). Data on federal shelter and housing information collected under the Homeless Management Information Systems (HMIS) are subject to HIPAA and FERPA as well as local privacy laws (Culhane et al., 2010). Usually, the actors involved in integrating data develop memoranda of understanding or agreement on how data will be used and agree to conduct external and internal compliance audits (Culhane et al., 2010; Moore et al., 2006). Some have a review board to determine if a research proposal will be allowed and to evaluate the process for sharing research results (Culhane et al., 2010; Moore et al., 2006; DeHart et al., 2017).

Bellamy and Raab (2005) studied data integration in England in the crime, welfare, and health sectors and found that balancing the tension between data integration and privacy depended on the political contexts, legal histories, and prevalent culture and practices related to privacy and confidentiality in each respective sector, along with assessments of the individual and political risks associated with integrating data or not doing so, and the political power or powerlessness of those whose data might be shared. They determined that "distinguishing better from worse 'balances' [of data sharing versus privacy concerns] is as much a matter of political judgement in each field about what of kinds of evidence and argument will carry greatest local weight, as it is of the application of unambiguous jurisprudential tests in data protection and service-level law" (ibid., 412–13). For better or worse, in comparison to other sectors such as health care, privacy seems less sacred in the criminal justice sector, so data sharing proposals related to recidivism may be less likely to encounter organized resistance and more likely to garner political support.

For the criminal justice community to have an accurate picture of the effectiveness of programs designed to reduce recidivism, data integration is indispensible across state and county incarceration agencies; parole, probation, and other community supervision agencies; courtroom actors; and reentry resource agencies and organizations. Data on criminogenic risks and needs, as well as on programs in which the offender has participated—in and out of prison—do exist in the form of pre-sentence reports and risk-needs-assessments that are used in sentencing decisions and allocation of services in jail or prison, but these measures are neither standardized nor used consistently between agencies (Ball, 2010; Tafoya, Grattet, and Bird, 2014).

Data about what happens once an offender is released from incarceration are even harder to gather but may be even more important to obtain. Services to address reentering individuals' many complex and interrelated needs are provided by a multitude of public, nonprofit, and private sector agencies. Therefore, obtaining a full picture of the reentry experience requires data sharing and integration both vertically, between states, counties, and/or local government agencies or service providers, and horizontally, across counties or parallel jurisdictions and between agencies in different policy domains, such as criminal justice and health care.

Development of a full picture of a returning individual's needs requires county, state, and national systems to define and track data in a way that is compatible to enable sharing. This requirement poses technological challenges because different agencies use different systems and software to record their data and may define similar terms differently (Culhane et al., 2010; Moore et al., 2006). Definitions, the types of data to track, and collection technology would need to be agreed upon, standardized, and updated to ensure transfer between systems.

Along with technical issues, government agencies may lack the appropriate expertise or capacity to create integrated data systems. Both South Carolina's and Michigan's data warehouses contracted with private companies to build the technology to allow data sharing, but data integration does not always require building new technology (DeHart et al., 2017; Moore et al., 2006).

Political factors are an additional major hurdle for proposals to share or integrate data. In choosing a funder and primary coordinator, there is the possibility that if it is a government agency, subsequent shifts in political power could jeopardize the continued functioning or funding of the data system. Getting agencies and partners to work together can also be highly political, regardless of the subject. Analysis of shared data may reveal inefficiencies or ineffectiveness, which actors or agencies would rather not expose to scrutiny (DeHart et al., 2017). Therefore, gaining political will to support and implement an integrated data system can be challenging. Support for data sharing and willingness to direct resources toward integration efforts are likely to increase as the nascent body of research on the effectiveness and usefulness of integrated data systems grows. However, integration may still require a push by an office or agency with political authority and budgetary resources to provide or withhold. In England, the support of influential political actors and a lack of coordinated opposition played a major role in the implementation of data integration in the welfare sector by the Department of Social Security, whose "acquisition of the necessary technology was possible only because the Secretary of State was willing to match anti-fraud rhetoric with solid investment" (Bellamy and Raab, 2005, p. 400).

The analyses that follow provide perspectives and recommendations on the measurement of recidivism and the integration of data from policymakers engaged in criminal justice agencies and nonprofit organizations that serve individuals reentering society from incarceration.

## Data and Methods

This study uses qualitative data gathered from semi-structured interviews with eight city- and county-level employees including professionals working in the areas of mental health, law enforcement, probation, and reentry, a Superior Court judge, and staff from community-based nonprofit organizations in a Northern California county in 2010–2012, and four representatives from county or state research or probation organizations in three different large California counties in 2016. Interviewees were selected for their knowledge of reentering prisoners' needs and risks, recidivism rate calculations, data integration, and reentry resource coordination.

One of us (Chen) conducted all of the 2010–2012 interviews in person, with individuals from public and nonprofit agencies who were involved with two initiatives: (1) a pilot program for "inreach" into jail facilities to connect with jail inmates with housing and other services and programs prior to their release, and (2) an "outreach court" primarily serving individuals involved with the criminal justice system (e.g., with misdemeanor charges, infractions, or outstanding warrants) who are homeless and working with case managers. Questions focused on the services and information needed for successful transition between incarceration and reentry to the community. Some interviewees were also asked about the use of a shared database to coordinate services in custody with those in the community. A second author (Meyer) conducted the 2016 interviews by phone. The interview guide for the 2016 data contained questions on the topics of recidivism, reentry, and data integration.

Interviews lasted from thirty minutes to more than ninety minutes in length. All participants provided informed consent. Interviewees were promised confidentiality, so in this chapter we refer to them using general descriptors rather than names (some of the individuals had unique position titles). Interviews were audio recorded, transcribed, and coded, looking at similarities in responses to questions, common themes, novel answers, and unexpected information. Thematic memos were created around these codes. Prominent themes that arose included concern about differing recidivism measures, the need for more comprehensive and detailed shared data on inmates reentering society, concern about data quality and interpretation, a desire for better coordination regarding services provided in custody and individuals' needs in the community, and discussion of technological issues and political obstacles around data integration.

## Findings and Discussion

*Defining Recidivism: Inadequacies and Inconsistencies*

Many interviewees identified shortcomings and inconsistencies in existing definitions and measures of recidivism. A Probation Department Official from County A discussed the importance of avoiding oversimplification. When asked, "Do you currently have an agency or department definition of recidivism?" she did not give a "yes" or "no" answer, but instead commented, "Well, that's an interesting question... if we do I would say that we shouldn't." Asked to describe a better approach, she explained:

> Sometimes people get hung up on "How are we going to define recidivism?" I've seen counties go in circles trying to come up with an agreed-upon definition for recidivism and my advice has been "OK, recidivism should be anything and everything but let's call everything what it is. Not to try to oversimplify it, but if somebody is arrested for a new law violation for which charges are filed, well that could be one way that we're measuring recidivism. If somebody is arrested and then convicted on a misdemeanor or a felony, well, that could be another way that we're sort of defining recidivism.... [I]f somebody is on some form of supervision and they have a new arrest or a technical violation for which they end up having revocation that results in a termination with sentencing to jail or prison and we call it that. Then there is never any confusion about what we mean by recidivism. We just try to measure everything that anybody is interested in, if you can. And report out on that. Now you usually have to frame it in some big umbrella just so people can wrap their heads around it and I think that's where you get into "recidivism," but my advice has always been and has continued to be what I say here: "just call it what it is."

In other words, the concept of recidivism should be deconstructed into its various possible components, and each should be defined, measured, and discussed with specificity and clarity, to avoid confusion and inaccurate or misleading comparisons. To clearly understand reentry and the setbacks associated with it, it is necessary to go beyond simple measures of recidivism.

Lack of temporal specificity also creates problems. As the Probation Department Official from County A explained, post-release arrest data may capture law-breaking behavior that occurred prior to incarceration:

> Say we're going to measure recidivism based on a new arrest. To me that's too vague. It needs to be more specific. . . . [For example,] if someone had a bench warrant out for them and they were brought in on that bench warrant, that's gonna look like an arrest if you just pull the data out on a certain point and you don't get more detail. [If] you get more detail then you might know that the person didn't commit any new law-breaking behavior, they were just picked on a warrant that could potentially be two or three years old. Is that really a new arrest?

As a State Official who works with collaborative courts described how arrest data can also encompass violations of terms of supervised release that do not entail a new offense:

> [With] collaborative courts, they get arrested quite a bit and the way the DOJ data is set we don't know for sure if they're being arrested on a probation violation which could be just a flash incarceration, etc.—a program compliance arrest, actually. So that is one challenge that we have.

Inconsistencies associated with data that are collected and maintained in a decentralized manner also came up in interviews. As the State Official put it, "The courts don't have a statewide case management system so we all sort of free fall. There's fifty-eight local courts [corresponding to California's fifty-eight counties] and fifty-eight different ways to share data." Because of this, even if researchers and practitioners ensure that definitions are as clear and consistent as possible, comparisons must still be made cautiously.

*Need to Broaden the Focus beyond General Measures of Failures and Risks*

Interviewees acknowledged that reducing recidivism is a legitimate goal, but they also pointed out that it is important to examine the means to that end by examining intermediary indicators of progress toward success. Recidivism statistics have limited value without an understanding of the reasons for variations in outcomes. When asked whether recidivism is a useful thing to measure, the Probation Research Director from County A responded, "I do. I think it is very important because again you know what services, what processes, what people impact your client and that ultimately is the goal, for us to decrease criminal offenses." In response to the same question, the State Official explained,

> There's been a lot of focus on the high-risk recidivism people. I think it's very important, but I don't think it's the only important thing. I think sometimes there is too much emphasis on it but there are other more proximal goals that could be measured as well so that would be like perhaps relapse, you know, that kind of thing.

In other words, recidivism can be a useful measure, but it is rarely sufficient. To understand success and challenges in reentry, with the goal of preventing a return to criminal behavior, it is essential to gather data that shed light on the effectiveness of programs and interventions designed to accomplish that goal.

Reliance on inappropriate or inaccurate data can compromise effective and efficient delivery of programs and services. When information about a client's needs is not sufficiently detailed, probation officials may provide the wrong kinds of services, or even too many services. Asked what kind of data would be useful that are not currently available, the Probation Research Director from County A answered:

> I think two things: one is the service data, we don't really have great service data, but that's being worked on. The second thing I'd like more information on are case plans. We are in the early stages of probation officers doing formal case plans on the adult side. We've been doing it on the juvenile side for a really long time. The adult side just started doing them. Adult probation officers though have fairly high caseloads, so a formal case plan is kind of a struggle to get going because there are kind of constraints on time, but we're moving to a place where we're doing a better job of doing the case plans and I think the case plan information is

> really helpful because it's helped us note the journey of the client. When did they complete this program? How long did it take them to connect to the program? So you're looking at access to programs, engagement in programing, hopefully start collecting information on dosage. . . . I think the reason I'm really interested in the case plan information is I feel like sometimes clients are given a lot of services by the courts that they don't necessarily need or they're not prioritized well, or they're not specific enough.

Data sources such as case plans and associated data could also prove valuable for researchers. While they are certainly more challenging to collect, code, analyze, and compare than more accessible recidivism statistics, they are a rich source of information.

The Probation Research Director from County A offered a short description of a more nuanced approach to assessing success in reentry, with a focus on intermediate goals and progress, that is already in use by her office in practice, but not as prevalent in research.

> When we work with partners . . . nobody really looks at recidivism in a black and white way, which really kind of grew and evolved over the last few decades. We look at things such as violations of probation: are they decreasing? We look at kinds of offense and the amount of time between offenses: is it expanding? Is the severity of the offense decreasing? So our Chief . . . calls it "incremental improvement"—if someone came in and they had a history of more personal offenses [and] maybe they're now only doing property offenses, [it] isn't great, but for public safety is definitely an improvement.

A narrow focus on desistance (or lack thereof) from crime or drugs can overlook other indicators of progress. For drug-addicted individuals, for example, it is usually unrealistic to expect immediate and complete abstinence, but as the State Official explained, drug courts often track relapse while also maintaining program retention as a measurable and more attainable goal. Likewise, research on recidivism should gather not only information about reengagement with the criminal justice system, but also information about the programs a reentering individual had access to, if any; the extent to which that person succeeded in the program(s); and the reasons for failure, if relevant. Measurements like these redirect some accountability from the individual who is expected to succeed regardless of the circumstances, toward the systems that may or may not be providing adequate support and resources to facilitate success.

Furthermore, current measures of recidivism only record a specific type of failure. When a formerly incarcerated person finds and keeps housing or employment, that should be considered an indicator of success. Currently, obtaining this kind of data on ex-offenders is difficult because little data integration exists in the criminal justice system and even less outside of it.

Interviewees also expressed a need for more and better data on clients' needs, rather than focusing exclusively or primarily on risks, as existing tools for assessment and data collection on individual inmates. As the State Official explained when talking about criminal justice data,

> I think they've figured out the risk part. We don't necessarily get enough about the needs. I'd love to know more specifics about where [clients] come on the spectrum in terms of needs that they're exhibiting, you know mental health, substance abuse, and even housing.

A City Housing Specialist, recalling conversations she had had with incarcerated men while participating in a new jail "inreach" initiative, discussed how inmates themselves face uncertainties regarding their needs:

> I would ask them, "Are you employed? Do you have a job?" And they're like, "I don't know that I'll have a job when I get out of here. Like, I have one, but I probably won't have it when I get out of here." The big needs are jobs, housing . . . rehab, a few of them mentioned rehab.

In addition to the aforementioned needs, other needs mentioned by interviewees include education or training; disability benefits, income support, and other benefits; medical care and prescription medications; child care; and transportation.

While reentering individuals share many common needs, there also exist differences in needs across subpopulations that cannot be captured in generalized statistics. For example, a County-Level Homelessness Policy Official discussed similarities and differences between the reentering men and women he encountered: "There was more domestic violence stuff in the women . . . Other issues were very similar." Housing was "obviously" the biggest issue for both men and women this official met. Children's issues were a concern for many women, and "that came up with some of the men too," but there was "more custody-related stuff for the women."

Likewise, a Homeless Shelter Case Manager who worked closely with non-English-speaking Latino clients returning from incarceration discussed how she tends to "oversee the population different[ly] because their needs are different." She explained that her Latino immigrant clients were often reluctant to seek benefits even though they were eligible, and were not as persistent in the face of rejection:

> Resources are there, but they are kinda afraid to go and ask because of . . . the stigma of "me not being born and raised here, I don't have the rights of the people born and raised here" . . . The Latino born and raised here, they don't give up that easy. They go and fight for the rights. [But] the Latino immigrant, you say no and they give up easily . . . when they go to social service and apply for benefits for the first time and somebody tells them no, they get rejected and hurt and they don't go back any more.

According to this Case Manager, the lack of a sense of empowerment to seek and receive necessary help not only results in a greater risk of relapse or recidivism, but it can have intergenerational effects:

> That's part of the victimization pattern . . . they actually tend to be victimized over and over because they don't advocate for themselves, they don't know how to reach out for help. And then guess what? The generation that comes from them tends to be victimized also because it's a pattern that they have not [broken].

While she observed close family ties among many Latino immigrant clients, which can provide a valuable source of support, she also expressed concern that these strong bonds come with high expectations that are difficult for returning inmates to fulfill, leading to pressures that could trigger relapse, which could lead to parole revocation.

> They still have the bond with the family that is gonna support them but they feel a lot of responsibility that they carry on helping their family . . . it triggers them when they get out. The guilty feelings of not being a good daughter or a good mom triggers a lot and regarding the substance abuse, they relapse.

Another issue this Case Manager brought up was literacy—"with the male population of Latino immigrants, language is a barrier, even the Spanish language"—which impedes access to the services and benefits that facilitate successful reintegration. This type of information, while relevant to reentry, is unlikely to be captured in common recidivism statistics, but more likely to be understood using data gathered from case plans.

Furthermore, several interviewees explained, the coordination of services between custody and the community is especially important for inmates who may not be capable of identifying or articulating their needs and seeking the appropriate services on their own, such as inmates who have substance abuse problems, severe mental illnesses, or challenges such as cognitive disabilities. As the City Housing Specialist described it,

> some people need a lot of hand-holding. . . . They get out of jail, they're so overwhelmed . . . people's cognitive levels are different, right? They need direction and support. And it depends on the individual. Some are super smart and they know what to do, but others don't. Maybe they do want it, but they have too much other stuff going on. It's overwhelming for them.

To summarize, interviewees felt that changes in measurements used to track the progress of reentering individuals can be improved by broadening the focus from the reentering individual's encounters with the criminal justice system to the programs and resources provided to the individual; from a single measure of failure to multiple incremental measures of success, inside and outside the criminal justice system; and from risks to needs and whether they are addressed. More detailed information beyond what can be summarized in commonly available recidivism statistics is needed to assess needs accurately and appropriately.

*The Power of Data Sharing and Integration*

Interviewees spoke about the need for integration of data both vertically and horizontally. In California, some individuals who were incarcerated in state prison for lower-level felonies may be released to probation under the supervision of county-level authorities, rather than to parole, which is administered by a state agency. The Probation Manager from County A described the challenges associated with lack of vertical data integration between the state and county:

> I feel like from state prison we don't get all the information all the time and so sometimes we're receiving [probationers] pretty blindly with limited information . . . it would be nice to know "well gosh, they've spent a significant amount of time up there. What have they spent their time doing? What are some of their presenting factors? Are there challenges?" Then we can have a better connection and better landing when they come to us.

According to the Probation Research Director from County A, the lack of data integration across counties may paint an incomplete picture of a person's reoffending: "We only know what happens in our county and because we have people that live really close to other counties, they may be committing crimes in other counties and we don't know about that." Furthermore, an individual can be on probation in multiple jurisdictions, which makes compliance unusually difficult: "If you get two different probations in two different counties then you get two different probation officers. That person is probably never going to be successful if they've got two people they're beholden to try and get them to accomplish their tasks." The lack of information sharing in this type of situation could also present challenges to the probation officers, each of whom may be unaware of the extent of the other's work with the client.

Interviewees also spoke about how data integration is sorely needed between agencies in different policy domains, between custody and community, and across sectors (e.g., between public and private agencies). For example, many of the interviewees who worked in the criminal justice system, including judges and jail staff, spoke about how a high proportion of their clients faced serious challenges related to mental health, substance abuse, and/or homelessness. At the same time, community-based nonprofit service providers, such as homeless shelter directors and county mental health professionals, discussed how a substantial proportion of their clients were on probation or parole, or had recently been released from incarceration. Interviewees from both government agencies and the nonprofit sector discussed challenges that their clients faced around employment opportunities, transportation, medication, drug and alcohol treatment, child care, and government benefits (including Social Security, Supplemental Security Income disability benefits, General Assistance, Electronic Benefit Transfer, veteran's benefits, Medicare, and Medicaid). It became apparent over the course of multiple interviews that many of the public and private sector offices, agencies, and programs whose representatives were interviewed had clients in common. Chronically homeless individuals often cycle through both jails and homeless shelters. The Family Homeless Shelter Director talked about her interactions with inmates when she visited the county jail:

> You're just kind of like (pointing in different directions, as though greeting different people), "Hey! Heeeey! Hey! Aww, what are you doing back here? I thought you'd stopped that!" It's the same crew, like when I go to [another provider's homeless shelter], I'm like, "Hey!" Same thing when I went to [a local food pantry] . . . it's like, "Hey!"

A more reliable and consistent flow of information between homeless shelters and jails could contribute to reductions in recidivism by ensuring that individuals discharged from custody have realistic and sufficiently specific reentry plans, and that service providers in the community are better prepared to receive them. Asked to describe an ideal program for reentering inmates who are homeless, a City Housing Officer imagined highly coordinated services:

> With coordination, there could be reserved beds for mentally ill and homeless released offenders that they can access immediately upon

release, similar to the way that beds are reserved for drug court clients. . . . Someone to meet them at the jail when they are released. . . . Case management, beds, transportation. They should all have a plan.

However, in the real world at this time, it is even challenging to share an individual inmate's release date between multiple agencies and providers so a pre-release agreement can be arranged to coordinate the reinstatement of benefits such as Social Security or disability. As the City Housing Specialist, who was working on a way to develop these types of agreements, explained:

> One of the things that we are trying to iron out is release dates. Release dates are very important because the Social Security Office needs to know their release dates, in order to set up their reinstatement benefits. The Department of Corrections doesn't always know their release dates, because it's a court thing. So that's why it's also important for the court to be involved in the reentry planning. There's so many pieces to the whole thing.

Improvements in data sharing and integration would not only improve the delivery of services to meet the needs of reentering individuals, it could also lead to greater efficiency, effectiveness, and long-term cost savings. As described by the Probation Department official from County A, these benefits transcend political ideology:

> It doesn't matter if you're more liberal, it doesn't matter if you're more conservative. If you can convey to people that you are hopefully having a positive impact on people's lives . . . sometimes people care about that and sometimes people don't. For the people that don't you can share that you're saving the city money or you're saving the county money. I mean, that resonates with people and it is important to measure.

The Family Homeless Shelter Director, describing a pilot program for coordinated reentry planning that had attracted representatives from multiple government offices and nonprofit agencies, suggested that one reason for the high levels of interest was the potential for long-term savings with greater efficiency associated with coordination: "It could be a cost-saver. There is money in saving money, and that's what we're hoping to do."

*Obstacles to Overcome*

Despite compelling arguments for data sharing and integration, the practice remains uncommon for several reasons, including concerns regarding confidentiality and data security; incompatibility of hardware and software technology; lack of budget and staff; and sometimes a lack of motivation. To facilitate data integration, several elements are necessary: the ability to address technical and legal obstacles, political will and support, resources, and coordination between agencies.

The State Official working on collaborative courts explained, "a lot of it is just the technological limitation of keeping data secure, getting accurate data, and then having the data sharing agreements and the confidentiality." In addition, realities and myths exist regarding HIPAA, the Health Insurance Portability and Accountability Act. As the Probation Department Official from County B put it,

> If we're dealing with full offender record information . . . then there's limitations on how and when that can be shared. Then if you're dealing with HIPAA there's limitations on that too. But there's also a lot of myths associated with that. So I think it's really having the right people at the table that can say, "OK, here is what it actually says, here are the times we can't share it and here are the times we can."

HIPAA is designed to safeguard health data that is identifiable by name or social security number while also allowing data to be shared within the healthcare system to improve care, and outside the health system to support statistical research and the use of de-identified information in research that improves knowledge (Culhane et al., 2010). Contrary to some assumptions, HIPAA explicitly not only allows for de-identified data to be shared, but it also permits identifiable data to be shared, with specific and rigorous safeguards and agreements (ibid.).

Privacy is a serious and important concern, and researchers may find it easier to access data where identifying information has been used to match individuals' records across databases, then redacted. However, de-identified data are limited in their usefulness from a practitioner's point of view. As the Probation Research Director from County A explained:

> [For] most clients their two primary needs are mental health and substance abuse, and those are the two areas that we have a really hard time getting treatment data on . . . we do get a lot of data from them stripped of identifiers and [in] aggregate format. But the problem with that is you can't really match it up with clients. . . . One of the county counsels [is] really trying to work out how we might overcome those issues because [the restrictions are due to] federal guidelines from the government.

Possible approaches to sharing semi-de-identified data do exist, but they require clear communication about procedures for compliance with regulations and avoidance of data security risks. The Probation Department Official from County B explained:

> There are, I think, places where we can share data that can be de-identified enough that we can give it to another department who's able, based on some data element, to link it up with their people and then maybe strip out that piece, so that you at least have this connect-the-dots piece from one department to another and . . account for the concern associated with confidentiality and the potential to have the information get into the wrong hands. I think that oftentimes one of the things that people bring up the most is, we can't share identifiable data. We can under certain circumstances and if we do it in a certain way that is thoughtful and so that everybody kind of knows "here's the data that we want to share. Here's the format. Here is the exact data. Here's how we can link up people in one system with another system, but then here's what you need to do if you're reporting it out, so that that information can't be used."

In South Carolina, state agencies have worked together to maintain pre-aggregated records so that pooled data can be filtered down to de-identified individual case histories including health, crime, and education data that can be accessed and analyzed along with the aggregated information (Culhane et al., 2010).

Even when solutions are available to surmount technical and legal obstacles, efforts to share data may still be impeded by budget limitations in public sector organizations. Describing the computing technology in a different jurisdiction, the State Official explained, "I think people just assume it's easy, but we're working with these antiquated systems." The Probation Research Director from County A elaborated, discussing the lack of capacity, staff, and resources:

> There's not really a lot of resources for departments to use the data in a way that really informs practice and that's the hurdle for most probation departments in the county. Especially if you are a really small department in a really small county. They just don't really have the budget for the support staff or to support external researchers, so a lot of times they'll try to apply for grants that might come with an evaluation component but I think that's the biggest problem with probation, generally and within the state. Not having internal support to tackle the work.

In the nonprofit and private sectors, community service providers who are responsible for reentry programming may also lack the capacity to do good data collection and reporting, but the Probation Department Official from County B argued that it is important to motivate them to do it, and pointed out that making funding conditional on it could provide the necessary motivation.

> You know it creates a lot of anxiety among the community-based organizations because frankly some of them are low-scale mom and pop kinds of organizations where they don't necessarily have any staff that can report data and collect it and all this kind of stuff. It's just trying to get them thinking that way and starting to do that and saying "hey we're gonna measure this" so you need to be able to report it to us so we can say, "Yes, we want to keep funding this." We need to have some sort of justification other than "well, it's really great."

Since data integration is a resource-intensive undertaking, it may be most practical for agencies large and small to coordinate plans with other organizations to build improvements related to data integration into their own longer-term plans for eventual upgrades or replacements of database systems or hardware.

The combination of technological challenges and lack of motivation can seem nearly impossible to surmount, but the State Official suggested that an underlying interest in data integration among agency staff could propel efforts forward if concerns about confidentiality, technical obstacles, and costs could be addressed:

> I think there are also attitudinal changes that would need to take place for people to be more open, but I understand the reasons that sometimes they're not open with data sharing because of confidentiality reasons. I think if it was easier, I would never minimize the importance of the actual people involved, their interest in data sharing and their willingness to share. It's hugely important, but if there were sort of more efficient ways and technological fixes to some of it then I think that the attitudes, I don't know, maybe it's a chicken or the egg thing. But I think if it was easy to do and not super expensive then probably people who are kind of the holdouts could go along with it.

Some of the interviewees indicated that the political will to make improvements in data sharing efforts is strong in certain places. Two interviewees from the same jurisdiction described in detail how the mayor of a major city and county supervisors came together to support and advocate for an initiative to develop a comprehensive plan to end homelessness that entailed coordination between housing and homelessness, criminal justice, and mental health agencies, as well as many nonprofit shelter and housing providers. Housing for individuals involved with the criminal justice system was one of the priorities. However, political will alone was not enough; coordination and ample resources were also essential. To move the effort forward, a separate entity, funded in large part through philanthropic contributions, was given the authority to monitor progress toward the plan's common goals. Even then, interviewees from the same county expressed frustration over the lack of compatibility between the database used by the courts and probation and the database used by agencies focusing on homelessness, but progress was occurring.

## Conclusion

Drawing from analyses of qualitative data from interviews of government and nonprofit agencies working with reentering individuals, this chapter highlights and illustrates a number of flaws with current practices in the measurement of recidivism and offers suggestions for improvements in the measurement, collection, and sharing of data related to the experiences of individuals returning to society from incarceration, to make the information we collect and use accurate, meaningful, and useful.

Many methods are currently employed to define and measure recidivism, and each has its own flaws and limitations. At the very least, agencies tasked with measuring and recording recidivism data should attempt to use clearly defined standardized measurements. A statistic such as "returns to prison for a new crime" might be a useful common starting point. Better yet, multiple measures associated with different ways to look at recidivism, with each component uniformly defined, would help to avoid oversimplification.

Moreover, it is necessary to go well "beyond recidivism" in data collection and usage. Even multiple measures of recidivism are not adequate to understand why a person might have recidivated, and a focus on failure may overlook indicators of progress. Measures that focus on reengagement with the criminal justice system are insufficient to gauge a reentering individual's progress, which is likely to be incremental, will probably involve setbacks, and inevitably spans numerous policy areas including employment, housing, mental health, substance abuse treatment, issues related to family and children, government benefits such as income assistance, and much more. Instead of primarily emphasizing reentering individuals' risks of recidivating, however that is measured, more attention should be placed on their needs, and on access to reentry resources to address those needs. This shift would represent a change from what Bellamy and Raab (2005) characterize as a threat-based approach to criminology to an approach that prioritizes rehabilitation and reintegration. Collecting information on the availability of programming and resources would also help hold the system accountable for providing the necessary support for successful reentry. It could even ensure that fewer resources are wasted.

For data on reentering individuals to thoroughly capture their needs and risks, successes and failures, data sharing is needed between different levels of government and policy domains, between custody and community, and across the public and nonprofit sectors. Data integration has been successfully implemented in some states and localities, but it remains rare. Researchers have successfully completed project-based data integration, but a more systematic practice of data sharing could lead to improvements in service delivery and outcomes for reentering individuals as well as long-run cost efficiencies. Substantial obstacles exist, such as concerns about privacy and confidentiality, technological limitations, insufficient funding and capacity, and lack of motivation by some agency employees and political authorities, but they can be, and have been, surmounted. The support of those with political influence, accompanied by allocation of resources, can provide the much-needed impetus to introduce broad and systematic data integration.

More precise, nuanced, thorough, and consistent measures of recidivism are desperately needed, but that is not enough. A shift is needed from a paradigm based on risks and failures to a more productive emphasis on needs, resources, and incremental measures of rehabilitative success. To enable such a change, more widespread implementation of data sharing and integration will be necessary. While this entails formidable challenges, it is possible.

2

# Community Capacity-Building and Implementation Advances to Addressing the RNR Framework

FAYE S. TAXMAN

Recidivism reduction is as much an art as a science. The "what works" movement identifies the programs and practices that reduce recidivism (Aos et al. 2006a, 2006b; Cullen, Jonston, and Mears 2017). But, these programs and practices are not commonly available among justice agencies or community treatment agencies, and there are many unanswered questions about how they should be implemented (Taxman 2018). Such questions often include: what programs/practices exist, how many people can be served to achieve certain outcomes, whether the programs and practices can achieve their goals, whether the programs/practices align with organizational culture, and whether the programs/practices incorporate the "responsivity" factors that affect outcomes, to name just a few. And, there is often drift from what works in the scientific laboratory to the results in the real world. Recidivism reduction may appear as an illusion, or it may be a target goal of programs/practices but there is a need to understand the ability of these programs and services to fulfill this goal. A major part of the illusion has to do with the availability of programs, and programs and services that are geared to prevent crime and/or recidivism. Part of the illusion is the notion of capacity—a measure of the degree to which there exists sufficient "room at the inn" to address the need. Capacity is generally not an area that is discussed, and in fact more attention is given to what type of programming than how much and for whom (Taxman, Caudy, and Perdoni 2013). In this chapter, the issues of capacity are considered as part of the missing piece to addressing the recidivism reduction puzzle.

## Recidivism Reduction in Context

Recidivism reduction essentially means that a program or practice will reduce the likelihood that a person will have further involvement in the justice system. The involvement can range from arrest to conviction to incarceration to technical violations for any type of behaviors. Recidivism, as Michael Maltz noted in 1981, is a very broad concept that refers to any type of behavior as well as any type of decision made by a variety of justice actors. The generality of the concept is unlike other fields where there is more of a specific definition of an event happening—in medicine, an individual who has a disease is considered in remission only when the disease is not active or when a specific disease disappears. If the person gets another disease or condition, this is not considered a recidivist event. This is not the same as offending, where all behaviors from misdemeanors to felonies to violence to shoplifting to drunk and disorderly conduct are often lumped together and considered the same. Since offending is not considered specialized behavior and it is very generic, it is difficult to reduce recidivism, since all types of behaviors fall into this category.

The added difficulty of measuring recidivism, or examining changes in patterns of offending at the individual level, relates to the point in the justice system that is being used to assess recidivism. Recidivism can be measured as arrest, technical violations, convictions, reincarcerations, or revocations. The broader the measure, the more recidivism is likely to occur. Often recidivism focuses on arrest and/or technical violations. A key consideration should be given to the types of behaviors that are included in the measure of recidivism and the point in the system at which the decision occurs.

### The "What Works" Movement

The "what works" movement (or evidence-based practices) is based on identifying programs and practices that are supported by research that demonstrates that the programs/practices can generate reductions in recidivism. The emphasis is on programs and practices that have been replicated using a similar protocol, conducted in multi-site studies where more than one protocol is tested in various sites, or there is a systematic review that synthesizes findings across studies. (Systematic reviews use different research designs, have different sample sizes, serve different populations, use different measures including measures of recidivism, and use different statistical techniques.) The summation processes measure the size of the effect—some are small, medium, or large, which is the degree to which the program/practice will have an impact on recidivism.

The programs and practices that are considered "what works" include: cognitive behavioral programs, therapeutic communities with stronger effects for programs that have a continuum of care, and cognitive processing. Effective practices are: drug courts, risk-need-responsivity supervision, contingency management, and medication-assisted treatments. There are a number of programs that are considered promising (with smaller effect sizes basically due to varying implementation factors that affect the outcomes), such as prosecution diversions, motivational interviewing, moral reasoning, mindfulness, and relapse prevention. Ineffective programs/practices include case management, incarceration, intensive supervision, and a myriad of others. The best resources on these programs are Sherman et al. (1997); Caudy et al. (2013); Aos, Miller, and Drake (2006a, 2006b); and Cullen, Jonson, and Mears (2013).

Landenberg and Lipsey (2006), in a meta-analysis, identified the key components of cognitive behavioral therapy (CBT) programs (one known evidence-based treatment) that are more effective in reducing recidivism. Effective CBT programs tend to: (1) occur in community settings, (2) target higher risk offenders, (3) include an anger management component or a cognitive restructuring component, (4) provide supplementary individual sessions, (5) be of sufficient duration, and (6) be well-implemented. Landenberg and Lipsey (2006) note that CBT treatment elements of interpersonal problem solving, anger control, victim impact, and behavior modification appear to approach or be statistically significant predictors of positive findings for CBT treatment.

Based on findings from the what works literature, a list of principles has emerged regarding how best to reduce recidivism. These principles are found in the Risk-Need-Responsivity (RNR) model: (1) Risk refers to targeting people for intensive services who are at higher risk for recidivism; (2) Need refers to addressing the specific needs that are related to offending specific criminal risk, criminal value systems, antisocial peers, antisocial family, substance use disorders, employment deficits, educational deficits, and leisure activities; and (3) Responsivity refers to factors that progress in treatment such as literacy, motivation, gender, culture, etc. Andrews and Bonta (2010b) specify that general responsivity denotes programming that focuses on social learning, whereas specific responsivity extends to tailoring the programming to individuals. The areas for programming include substance abuse, criminal thinking or decision making, self-management, life skills, interpersonal skill development, and social skills. These different types of programs have been identified based on the criminogenic needs that are drivers of criminal offending. Taxman (2014) extends responsivity to ensure that programming provides sufficient capacity in the community or agency to meet the risk-need profiles of the individuals in the system.

## Modifying Risk-Need-Responsivity to Include Human Frailty

While the Risk-Need-Responsivity (RNR) framework focuses on criminogenic needs, or those needs that have an empirical link to criminal offending, it is also important to note that individuals involved in the justice system have complex issues. Rates of past-year mental health (56%) (Bronson, Maruschak, and Berzofsky, 2015), substance use disorders (66%) (Bronson, Maruschak, and Berzofsky, 2015a, 2015b; Hartwell, 2004; Baillargeon, Binswanger et al., 2009; Jordan et al., 1996; Teplin, Abram, and McClelland, 1996; Lurigio, 2001; Baillargeon, Williams et al., 2009; Crilly et al., 2009; Fearn et al., 2016; Fazel, Bains, and Doll, 2006; Lurigio et al., 2003), lifetime suicide attempts (13–20%) (Hayes and Rowan, 1998; Sarchiapone et al., 2009), lifetime opioid use (15%) and pain medication dependence (11%) (Crilly et al., 2009) are dramatically elevated among justice populations who also tend to be from racial or ethnic minority groups (Kaeble and Glaze, 2016; Minton and Zeng, 2016; Carsen, 2016) and are lower income (Kaeble and Glaze, 2016; Minton and Zeng, 2016). Mental health and substance use disorders are associated with overdose (Baillargeon, Binswanger et al., 2009), suicide (Hayes and Rowan, 1998; Charles et al., 2003; Sarchiapone et al., 2009), disabilities and physical disorders (Bronson et al., 2015; Fazel and Baillargeon, 2011), homelessness (McNiel, Binder, and Robinson, 2005), repeat incarcerations and technical violations (Hadley, et al., 2011), and death (Binswanger et al., 2007) among justice populations.

Criminogenic needs, as defined by Andrews and Bonta (2010b), are directly related to offending behavior based on research studies. Many of them were conducted by Andrews and Bonta using their instrument, the Level of Service Inventory–Revisited, in Canada. They prioritize the needs into two levels: primary (antisocial personality, peers, values, and family) and secondary (substance abuse, education, employment, leisure) needs. As noted by Taxman (2014) and Taxman and Caudy (2015), Andrew and Bonta's priority ranking may not be accurate for other populations using other measures for the same domains. In fact, Taxman and Caudy (2015) found that there were different configurations of risk-need profiles and each had different recidivism patterns. The risk-need profiles comprised multiple domains, not a single domain (i.e., antisocial peers, substance abuse, etc.), that affected outcomes. This is important because it alters the conceptualization of the need principle originally offered by Andrews and Bonta.

Additionally, the RNR framework does not include the social determinants of health, socio-economic status, or behavioral health factors. Given the overrepresentation of individuals of lower economic needs in the justice system, these factors cannot be overlooked in terms of how they affect the behavior of individuals, recognizing that these behaviors are necessarily "criminal" (although under some social construct of the notion of criminal, the behavior may be more of a criminalization of certain behaviors such as homelessness, disorderly behavior, etc.), but these factors affect the cognitive functioning or decisions that individuals make. While the RNR framework focuses on criminogenic needs, there is another dimension that should be considered in terms of human frailty that causes the person to be vulnerable to making inappropriate decisions, engaging in behaviors for survival purposes, or making it difficult for a person to participate in treatment or programming. The latter—engaging in treatment—is covered under responsivity in terms of motivation, but those regarding the impact of mental health conditions, co-occurring disorders, traumatic brain injuries, developmental disorders, literacy, educational deficits, intergenerational poverty, and other conditions are generally not included in responsivity. Given the prevalence of human frailty, these are important conditions in terms of considering which programs and services to offer to different individuals based on their configuration of individual risks, needs, and stability (or destability) factors.

The rationale for including human frailty is based on recent evidence about how much housing, social support, food security, and mental health individually play a role in recidivism. While earlier research focused on single traits of an individual, the studies did not fully investigate complex needs or traits. Although we cannot review the robust literature here, a few studies are worthy of mention. Bruce Western (2018) followed nearly one hundred individuals after their release from prison for one year and found that poverty, homelessness, lack of employment, inadequate social connections, and being preyed upon led to poorer outcomes—not the picture of recidivism or criminal involvement that is typically portrayed. Other studies document that nearly 10% of people reentering from prison do not have a place to live, and that this rate doubles if the person has a mental illness. Housing instability is common, and it is exacerbated by different types of supervision programs and conditions of release (Herbert, Morenoff, and Harding, 2015). The Housing First experiments found that providing transitional housing to those with drinking disorders, instead of requiring sobriety before providing housing, led to reduced consequences from drinking including jail days, emergency room visits, and less drinking to the point of intoxication (Collins, Malone, and Clifaselfi, 2013). Wang and colleagues (2013) found that individuals returning from prison who reported having only one meal a day during the thirty days following release had higher recidivism rates than those who did not have food-related issues. Social supports continue to be noted as important, including the value of having visitors during periods of incarceration and having supports in the community to assist with normal, daily stressors as protectors against recidivism (Taxman, 2018b). While some contend that these human frailty issues could be part of responsivity, there is a larger argument that the criminogenic needs component should be reframed to include a broader range of issues and not be focused on a single domain. In fact, recent studies confirm that individuals with more complex needs have higher recidivism rates and are more likely to engage in programming, and thus it is important to design and develop approaches appropriate for this group.

The RNR-Revised framework needs should be modified to adjust the two levels of primary needs (focused on criminogenic traits) and secondary needs (focused on substance abuse, employment, education, and leisure) since needs are not really single domains neatly organized into categories. In addition, these domains do not represent the way that race and socioeconomic status affect justice involvement, the overrepresentation of substance abusers and mental illness among the justice population, or the problems associated with poverty such as housing or food stability. That is, RNR is based on the individual-level traits, but these traits cannot be separated from social structural factors that affect individuals, including decisions that are made. A revised RNR framework needs to integrate human conditions other than "criminogenic needs."

## Systematic Responsivity as an Unmeasured Factor

RNR focuses on the individual without considering place or capacity of places. Place plays a major role in justice system issues. Cadora (see reference entry) framed this best with his notion of the "million dollar blocks" which represented areas where concentrated numbers of individuals in a community were incarcerated and returning to, and there is a high degree of criminal justice involvement by various agencies (i.e., police, jails, probation, courts, etc.) and churning through the justice system. The "million dollars" represents the amount of money spent on the justice system in a concentrated space. Cadora's characterization is augmented by studies that show places with concentrated recidivism rates consisting of concentrations of probationers or parolees (Kubrin and Stewart, 2006), and geographical areas that have depleted resources due to incarceration-based problems of coerced mobility (Rose and Clear, 1998), or areas that are prone to greater degrees of social disorganization such as teenage pregnancy rates due to higher incarceration rates (Thomas and Torrone, 2006).

The position of place in the context of RNR is an important but understudied area. Place is beginning to "appear" in some individual risk and need assessment tools—one tool has recently introduced the notion that if a person lives in a "high crime area," this increases the risk to recidivate. Place is a double-edged sword—as discussed by Rose and Clear (1998)—certain places have large concentrations of justice-involved individuals but often have limited capacity to address the needs of the individuals in their communities. Taxman (2014) has referred to this as systematic responsivity where capacity to meet the needs of the individuals involved in the justice system should be considered. Using the RNR-Revised framework, this refers to whether appropriate programming exists for substance abuse treatment, improvement in cognitive decision making, interpersonal and social skills, life skills, housing, food supports, and other services needed to be protective factors against justice involvement. The notion is that having sufficient capacity can reduce the need for justice-related services by relying upon community services provided by either government or nonprofit organizations. As noted by Hipp, Petersilia, and Turner (2010), services that are within a two-mile radius of a person can serve as a protective factor to reduce recidivism, which means that the location of service provisions is an important factor to consider when planning for recidivism reduction efforts.

## Case Study Examining Building Community Capacity to Be Systemic Responsivity

St. Louis City continues to have the highest rate of homicide in the United States (US DOJ, 2016). The St. Louis Area Violence Prevention Collaborative (STLVPC) is charged with: (1) reducing violent crime in the region by coordinating and supporting services and interventions; and (2) serving communities at risk of violent crime. As part of this effort, the team used the Risk-Need-Responsivity (RNR) methodology to assess existing programs' capacities and services to address violence and crime reduction efforts. The goals of this study were to: (1) identify programs and services that aim to reduce violence; (2) determine the needs of individuals to reduce violence; and (3) identify gaps in services to allow for a more efficient and effective allocation of resources. The following will discuss the results of an assessment of the capacity of the system to reduce recidivism. (Further information on this study can be found at Taxman et al., 2017.)

The RNR simulation methodology provides a structured analytical approach to understanding the characteristics of the population, both general and justice-involved, and assessing the best approaches to reduce violence and crime. (See Taxman and Pattavina, 2013, for an explanation of the models and how the simulation measures capacity and need.) The emphasis is on identifying and targeting protective factors for violence and/or crime and addressing risk factors.

### Methods

Data were gathered from: (1) the Missouri Department of Corrections (DOC) for risk-needs information about adults on community supervision in St. Louis; (2) various secondary data sources to identify the socioeconomic factors of the general adult population; and (3) information on programs and services offered to adults in programs offered in the St. Louis area. To obtain demographic information on the general public in St. Louis City, data were collected from the US Census Bureau (e.g., 2010 Census Data and the American Community Survey). Primary variables gathered were age, race, educational attainment, poverty, and employment. A variety of questions about Missouri residents' relationship with substances such as alcohol, marijuana, and other illegal drugs were analyzed from the 2014 National

TABLE 2.1. Overview of Programs and Services Available to Address Crime, Violence, and Behavioral Issues

| Program | Description |
| --- | --- |
| Severe Substance Use Disorders (SUD) | Focus on treating severe substance use disorders for drugs such as opiates, opioids, methamphetamine, crack/cocaine, and PCP |
| Decision Making | Use cognitive restructuring techniques to target antisocial attitudes, impulsivity, and antisocial thinking |
| Self-Management | Emphasize developing self-improvement and management skills |
| Interpersonal Skills and Conflict Management | Focus on building social and interpersonal skills; conflict resolution |
| Life Skills, Vocation, Employment | Target life skills such as education, employment, management of financial obligations, etc. |
| Other, Nonclinical | Provide nonclinical interventions (e.g., supervision only) |

Survey on Drug Use and Health (NSDUH, 2016). NSDUH provided information on drug dependence and mental health. Drug dependence in the last year included illicit drugs, marijuana, and alcohol. Mental health refers to any mental health issue.

As part of this effort, the programs and services were grouped by the type of services provided to individuals. These programs are designed to target different types of behaviors that affect factors that affect involvement in crime, violence, and social dysfunction (Crites and Taxman, 2013).

*General Adult Population*

In St. Louis, 45% of the adults are African American and 51% are Caucasian. More than half (54%) of the adult population are female and 46% are male. Close to half (48%) of residents are forty-three years of age and older. Below, we provide an overview of need issues:

- Involvement in Violence: Involvement in violence and cognitive distortions as determined by the percentage of individuals in St. Louis City who engage in gun violence (Rosenfeld, 2016). Less than 10% (7%) of the population was estimated to engage in violent behavior.
- Mental Health Issues: Individuals who reported having any type of mental health issues on the NSDUH survey for Missouri were classified as having a mental health issue. Almost one in five (19%) individuals had

a mental health issue (Missouri Department of Health Mental Health Status Report, 2013–2014).
- Estimated Involvement with Criminal Associates: Rates for family/friends involved in criminal activity were estimated based on the criminal justice involvement from national statistics. For this population, 8% had a friend or family member who engaged in crime.
- Substance Use Dependence: This includes illicit drug dependence (e.g., opioid or cocaine) in the past year based on the NSDUH survey for Missouri, which was 2% for opioid or cocaine and 9% for alcohol/marijuana (Missouri Department of Mental Health Status Report, 2013–2014).
- Poverty or Financial Difficulties: Using the poverty measure from the US Census Bureau, 27% of the population lives in poverty in St. Louis City.
- Unemployment: According to the US Census Bureau, 12% of the population was estimated to be unemployed in St. Louis City.

TABLE 2.2. Needs of the General Adult Population

| Need Factors | % General Population |
| --- | --- |
| Involved in Violence | 7 |
| Has Mental Health Issue | 19 |
| Estimated Criminal Associates | 8 |
| Substance Use Dependence Including Opioids, Cocaine, Methamphetamines | 2 |
| Uses Marijuana or Alcohol | 9 |
| Poverty or Financial Difficulty | 27 |
| Unemployed | 12 |
| Less Than High School Diploma | 16 |

TABLE 2.3. Programs and Capacity for the General Population

| Programs | Number of Programs Serving General Population (Non-DOC) | Estimated Annual Client Capacity |
| --- | --- | --- |
| Severe Substance Use Disorders | 2 | 3,134 |
| Decision Making | 0 | 0 |
| Self-Management | 16 | 12,243 |
| Interpersonal Skills | 9 | 2,006 |
| Life Skills | 17 | 15,813 |
| Other (e.g., nonclinical) | 11 | 2,957 |

Note: Of the 55 programs that serve the general population, 14 also serve DOC populations. This reflects the non-justice-involved capacity for these programs.

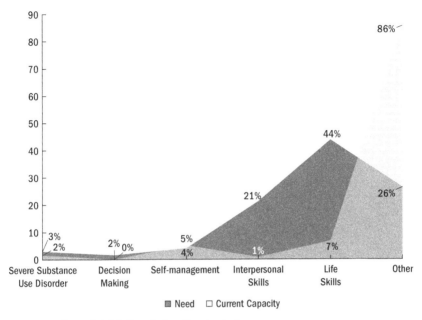

Figure 2.1. General Adult Population Gap Analysis

- Less Than High School Diploma: Slightly less than 20% (16%) of the St. Louis City population dropped out of high school, according to the US Census Bureau.

A review of the programs in the community for the general population found the services available as presented in table 2.3.

As shown in figure 2.1, St. Louis has fairly good capacity for most programming for its citizens except in the areas of interpersonal skills and life skills. Given the high unemployment rate and degree of poverty, there is a need to expand programming and services to address these issues within the general population. Interpersonal skills are needed to manage mental health issues, violence, interpersonal violence, and stress management.

*Community Supervision Population*

Of those on probation or parole, more than 80% (82%) are men, two-thirds (66%) are African American, and close to 30% (29%) are between the ages of sixteen and twenty-seven.

TABLE 2.4. Demographics of Adult Community Supervision Population

| Variables | Probation N (%) | Parole N (%) | Violent N (%) | Total N (%) |
|---|---|---|---|---|
| **Age** 16–27 | 2,595 (35) | 655 (18) | 608 (30) | 3,250 (29) |
| 28–35 | 1,859 (25) | 970 (26) | 459 (22) | 2,829 (26) |
| 36–42 | 1,201 (16) | 732 (20) | 303 (15) | 1,933 (17) |
| 43+ | 1,721 (23) | 1,357 (37) | 689 (34) | 3,078 (28) |
| **Race** African American | 4,699 (64) | 2,635 (70) | 1,571 (76) | 7,334 (66) |
| Caucasian | 2,643 (36) | 1,062 (30) | 481 (24) | 3,705 (34) |
| **Gender** Male | 5,699 (77) | 3,336 (90) | 1,803 (88) | 9,035 (82) |
| Female | 1,677 (23) | 378 (10) | 256 (12) | 2,055 (19) |

DEMOGRAPHICS OF VIOLENT OFFENDERS

Violent offenders on community supervision are mostly forty-three years of age and older (34%), and the second most common age category is sixteen to twenty-seven (30%). A vast majority of violent offenders are African American (76%) and male (88%).

The following is a summary of the needs of the justice-involved population.

- Unemployment: Individuals who did not have any type of employment. More than 40% (41%) were unemployed.
- Marijuana/Alcohol Use: Individuals who used marijuana/alcohol in the past six months. More than 80% (82%) used marijuana/alcohol.
- Opiate/Stimulant Use: Individuals who used opiates/stimulants in the past six months. Fewer than 20% (16%) used opiates/stimulants.
- Criminal Lifestyle: if an individual was unemployed and had a legal need (e.g., being arrested or convicted) or a technical need (e.g., missing an appointment with a probation officer), the individual was classified as having a criminal lifestyle. Approximately one-fourth (24%) were estimated to have a criminal lifestyle.
- Mental Health Issue: The community supervision assessment did not have a stand-alone mental health variable; however, there was a variable labeled social need. Social need is defined as an individual having either a financial, mental, and/or medical issue. The assumption was made that

if the individual had a job and a social need, they would most likely not have a financial need, which left only a mental or medical need. Therefore, this measure was used as a proxy for mental health, consisting of 38% of this population.
- Financial Difficulty: Individuals who did not have a job and had a social need were labeled as having financial difficulty, which represented 37% of this population.

## Adult Community Supervision Population Gap Analysis

The RNR methodology determined that the most pressing treatment need was for Self-Management services (35%), where programs use counseling to manage mental health issues and treat substance abuse (e.g., marijuana and alcohol) and other risky behaviors. There was also a need for Decision Making programming (33%) to address cognitive restructuring and change maladaptive thinking patterns supportive of

TABLE 2.5. Adult Community Supervision Population Need Issues

| Variables | Probation N (%) | Parole N (%) | Violent N (%) | Total N (%) |
|---|---|---|---|---|
| Marijuana/Alcohol Use | 5,963 (81) | 3,122 (84) | 1,703 (83) | 9,085 (82) |
| Opiate/Stimulant Use | 1,096 (15) | 600 (16) | 191 (9) | 1,696 (15) |
| Criminal Lifestyle | 1,723 (23) | 942 (25) | 392 (19) | 2,665 (24) |
| Mental Health Issue | 2,969 (40) | 1,294 (35) | 806 (39) | 4,263 (38) |
| Financial Difficulty | 2,481 (34) | 1,477 (40) | 638 (31) | 3,958 (37) |
| Unemployed | 2,891 (39) | 1,699 (46) | 753 (37) | 4,590 (41) |

TABLE 2.6. Programs and Estimated Annual Capacity for Programs Serving Community Supervision Population

| Programs | Number of Programs | Estimated Annual Client Capacity |
|---|---|---|
| Severe Substance Use Disorders | 22 | 1,503 |
| Decision Making | 0 | 0 |
| Self-Management | 6 | 3,134 |
| Interpersonal Skills | 2 | 280 |
| Life Skills | 7 | 1,033 |
| Other (e.g., nonclinicals) | 3 | 233 |

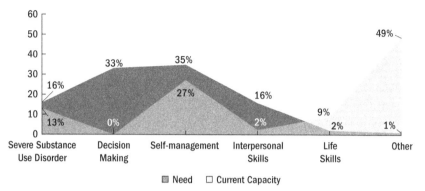

Figure 2.2. Adult Community Supervision Population Gap Analysis

criminal activity. The system currently has no designated Decision Making programs to address violence proneness.

Currently, there is a program deficiency for the following program types: Severe Substance Use Disorders, where 16% of the population needs this kind of programming but the current capacity only allows for 13%; Self-Management, where 35% of the population needs this kind of programming but the current capacity only allows for 27%; and Interpersonal Skills, where 16% of the population needs this kind of programming but the current capacity only allows for 2%. On the other hand, the system appears to have sufficient capacity for Life Skills, where the current capacity allows for 9% of the population when they only need 2%. More of the programming and services available are low-level (e.g., restorative justice or efforts focused on repaying society, Group F) where the need is 1% and the current capacity is 49%.

SUB-ANALYSIS OF NEEDS

Table 2.7 summarizes the primary needs of various adult community supervision populations: probationers, parolees, emerging adults, violent offenders, men, and women. For violent offenders, approximately one-third (34%) have a primary need for Self-Management programming and another one-third (34%) have a primary need for Decision Making. Women have a 19% need for Severe Substance Use Disorders, whereas men only have a 15% primary need. On the other hand, 37% of men have a need for Decision Making programming compared to 19% of the women. Parolees have a 43% need for decision making

TABLE 2.7. Primary Needs of Adult Community Supervision Subpopulations

| Programs | Total Population (%) | Probationers (%) | Parolees (%) | Emerging Adults (%) | Violent Offenders (%) | Men (%) | Women (%) |
|---|---|---|---|---|---|---|---|
| Severe SUD | 16 | 15 | 16 | 12 | 10 | 15 | 19 |
| Decision Making | 33 | 29 | 43 | 40 | 34 | 37 | 19 |
| Self-Management | 30 | 32 | 27 | 30 | 34 | 30 | 31 |
| Interpersonal Skills | 17 | 19 | 13 | 15 | 19 | 15 | 24 |
| Life Skills | 2 | 3 | 1 | 2 | 3 | 2 | 5 |
| Other | 1 | 2 | 1 | 1 | 1 | 1 | 3 |

programming, compared to 29% of the probationers. Nearly 40% of the emerging adults would benefit from decision making programming.

## Moving Forward

Reducing recidivism is embedded in "what works," a research-based foundation that identifies effective programs and practices, which are essentially those that reduce recidivism. The use of a research foundation reinforces a data-driven, empirical approach—instead of polarized "get tough" mass incarceration policies with more rational politics, science can influence our knowledge about the best methods to reduce recidivism. The Risk-Need-Responsivity (RNR) framework emerged as that scientific framework to provide a decision tree to illustrate that recidivism reduction is feasible if criminal justice decisions regarding punishments (including the types of programs offered) take into consideration the static and dynamic risk factors that individuals present. Recidivism reduction is therefore feasible by using appropriate programming and punishments that respond to an individual's risk factors coupled with responding to unique features such as developmental issues, gender, culture, motivation, and so on. The RNR framework provided a scientific model for achieving reductions in recidivism, regardless of how recidivism was defined.

The scientific-driven RNR framework focused primarily on the individual and was viewed through a criminological lens. The framework, in its original formulation, neglected to incorporate: (1) the similarities that exist among justice and non-justice-involved populations on many of the risk factors that are considered "criminogenic"; (2) social structural issues that affect involvement in the justice system such as race and socioeconomic status; and (3) social capital issues that affect availability of evidence-based programs and practices. The case study presented in this chapter illustrates that the RNR framework, while useful, should be further developed to focus more on a sociopsychological interactional model that incorporates structural issues which would adjust the "what works" potential regarding recidivism reduction. These are the issues that will be discussed in this section.

Similarities exist between justice and non-justice populations on risk factors that are considered "criminogenic" (dynamic factors). Wooditch, Tang, and Taxman (2014) in their review of the criminogenic needs noted that many of the needs areas—education, employment, substance abuse, peers association, family, leisure—are not necessarily "criminogenic" (directly linked to offending) but are characteristic of those of lower socioeconomic status and minorities. And, while the justice population has a higher concentration of individuals with some of these needs, these needs may not be the causal factors that affect involvement in criminal behavior. (In fact, because of the "war on drugs," it might be due to the criminalization of certain behaviors.) For example, an average of 84% of high school students graduate, yet this varies by racial groups from 72% (Native Americans) to 88% (Caucasians); the amount of high school graduation (including GED) ranges from 63% to 71% (see Harlow, 2003). Trying to assess whether educational deficits are criminogenic has not been empirically tested—in some areas of high concentrations of poverty, such as St. Louis, the difference between the general and the justice populations may not be that great, and may not be a driver for involvement in the justice system. The definition of factors contributing to criminal behavior is an area that requires further research.

RNR, as noted by the designers (who were psychologists), is primarily focused on the individual and primarily on individual factors that are psychological in nature. Social and social structural factors, including race or economic status, do not play a large role. Increasingly, research is illustrating how individual behavior is influenced by Maslow's hierarchy of needs including food, housing, and psychological security, which are not directly addressed or incorporated into the RNR framework. While some may argue they are tucked into "responsivity," others contend the RNR framework needs to be revised to consider these structural factors. Such revisions might occur in the following way: (1) revise the estimate of recidivism reductions if the programs and services do not attend to food security and housing instability issues that affect longer-term impact on recidivism, and to include these factors in the scientific and policy literatures; (2) incorporate as part of the core features of evidence-based programs (i.e., use of cognitive behavioral programming, use of risk-need assessment tools, etc.) an emphasis on nutrition, food, and housing security as part of the programming; and (3) develop prototype programs and services that incorporate these critical services. Besides food and housing security, similar exercises might be considered for mental illness, racial biases, or other areas where social factors affect individual-level behavior. A close examination of Western's (2018) book illustrates how individuals caught in the cycle of poverty make decisions, and these decisions do not necessarily exhibit criminal thinking but reflect situations that involve conflict, feelings of insecurity, lack of housing, and struggles to obtain basic needs.

The depletion of social capital in communities makes recidivism reduction programming more of an illusion than a reality. As shown in the St. Louis case study, this is a community with insufficient resources for many of the needed crime prevention and recidivism reduction programs for either the general adult population or the justice-involved population (a similar analysis was done for youth which illustrated an even more depleted resource picture). Even with high concentrations of justice populations in certain parts of the city, the appropriate programming is not available that can serve the purpose of reducing violence and crime. St. Louis is known for its long history of violence and having a high violence rate. Yet, as shown in the capacity figures, few resources exist to help mitigate this situation. For the general population, there are insufficient resources to address interpersonal violence issues, a precursor of violence that may end up in the justice system and one that often affects security in the home, schools, and community. In the justice system, resources are not available to address decision making or interpersonal issues. And, given the high rate of poverty in this community, life skills are lacking. Recidivism reduction assumes that these resources are available and that we have the social capital in place to offer appropriate services and programs when needed. Rose and Clear (1998) illustrated that this was not the case. The RNR methodology used in this case study is important because communities need to address this issue if they are going to be successful at the individual-level recidivism reduction efforts. That is, besides knowing "what works," it is also critical to know "what exists." If programs do not exist in the community, then the premise of using the RNR framework is flawed since we are not offering individuals effective programs and services.

The RNR methodology is a technology to provide communities with the ability to examine their capacity to deliver the RNR framework. The social capital-capacity issue is a difficult resource question given how cash-strapped most communities are. Left unaddressed, however, justice and community agencies will merely be following an illegitimate version of RNR, which is to assess individuals on the drivers and risk factors of their criminal behaviors without then offering the best available assistance to address these drivers. This is the challenge before us—to build capacity to truly deliver the RNR framework.

PART II

Researching Reentry

*Methods of Reentry Research*

# 3

## Conducting In-Depth Interviews with Jailed Fathers and Their Family Members

KRISTIN TURNEY

Alongside the rapid rise of incarceration in the United States is a burgeoning literature documenting the challenges faced by formerly incarcerated individuals reentering the community after a jail or prison spell. Indeed, this research shows that formerly incarcerated individuals face substantial difficulties upon release. Formerly incarcerated individuals often confront obstacles to securing a place to live, experience barriers to employment, and encounter challenges desisting from substance abuse (Harding et al. 2014; Leverentz 2014; Western et al. 2015; Western 2018). Formerly incarcerated individuals are often placed under correctional supervision—such as probation or parole—that necessitates an extended and continual surveillance (Phelps 2013).

Though the challenges experienced by individuals reentering the community after incarceration are well documented—particularly in domains of housing, employment, and health—it is less well understood how reentry affects the family life of formerly incarcerated individuals and how it affects the family members of formerly incarcerated individuals. Indeed, currently and formerly incarcerated individuals do not exist in isolation; they are connected to families as parents, current and former romantic partners, and children. Therefore, the consequences of incarceration—and the corresponding processes associated with reentry back into the community—extend to the family members connected to the incarcerated (Comfort 2008). This, in combination with the concentration of incarceration among already socially and economically marginalized families, means that incarceration has profound implications for structuring of social and economic inequality across families (Wildeman and Muller 2012).

Indeed, similar to the growing research on the challenges faced by formerly incarcerated individuals, there has been a corresponding increase in research documenting both the prevalence and consequences of being connected to a currently or formerly incarcerated individual (for reviews, see Comfort 2007; Wakefield and Uggen 2010; Wildeman and Muller 2012; Wildeman and Western 2010; also see Braman 2004; Christian this volume; Comfort 2008, 2016; Goffman 2009; Nesmith and Ruhland 2008; Nurse 2002; Siegel 2011; Turanovic, Rodriguez, and Pratt 2012; Turney 2014a, 2014b; Turney and Wildeman 2013; Wakefield and Wildeman 2013). For example, women who share children with formerly incarcerated men, compared to those who share children with men who have not been incarcerated, report employment difficulties and economic strain (Bruns 2017; Schwartz-Soicher, Geller, and Garfinkel 2011), impaired relationship quality (Turney 2015), poor-quality coparental relationships (Turney and Wildeman 2013), and physical and mental health challenges (Wildeman, Schnittker, and Turney 2012). Furthermore, a parallel literature documents inequalities in the educational, behavioral, and health outcomes between children who do and do not experience paternal incarceration (for reviews, see Eddy and Poehlmann 2010; Foster and Hagan 2015; Johnson and Easterling 2012; Murray, Farrington, and Sekol 2012; Travis, Western, and Redburn 2014; Turney and Goodsell 2018; Wakefield and Uggen 2010; Wildeman, Wakefield, and Turney 2013; Wildeman and Western 2010).

Despite this growing literature documenting the challenges endured by family members of currently and formerly incarcerated men, several important gaps remain. For example, little is known about the processes through which incarceration leads to deleterious outcomes for parents, romantic partners, and children. These processes—though certainly dependent on both the type of connection to the incarcerated individual (e.g., parent, romantic partner, child) and the specific outcome variable (e.g., health, economic well-being)—likely entail some combination of stigma, stress, and strain (Haskins and Turney 2017). Relatedly, little is known about heterogeneity in the family-level processes associated with incarceration and reentry and, specifically, how these heterogeneous processes change during and after incarceration.

Against this backdrop, the Jail and Family Life Study—a longitudinal and qualitative data collection effort that comprises 123 families who have experienced paternal incarceration—was designed to understand the collateral and potentially countervailing consequences of jail incarceration for incarcerated fathers and their family members. The overarching research questions include the following: First, what are the processes through which paternal incarceration affects families and children? Second, how do these processes change during and after incarceration? Third, how do these processes vary across social groups (for example, fathers in pretrial detention compared to fathers serving a jail sentence, or fathers living with their children prior to incarceration compared to fathers not living with their children prior to incarceration)? The Jail and Family Life Study answers these research questions by conducting in-depth interviews with incarcerated fathers; conducting in-depth interviews with the family members of these incarcerated fathers (including but not limited to children, current and former romantic partners, and mothers of fathers); and by conducting in-depth follow-up interviews with fathers and family members after fathers are released.

The purpose of this chapter is to document the challenges—and feasibility—of interviewing jailed fathers and their family members. The chapter proceeds as follows. First, I review literature that documents the prevalence of family member incarceration. Second, I suggest that jail incarceration, in particular (and in contrast to prison incarceration), is an important and understudied aspect of the criminal justice system with unique implications for the well-being of individuals and their family members. Third, I describe the Jail and Family Life Study, paying particular attention to sampling, recruitment, and interview protocols and, more generally, to the feasibility of conducting this type of research. Fourth, I describe challenges to navigating access to jailed fathers, an especially vulnerable population, and their family members, highlighting the similarities and differences in challenges across accessing these two groups. Finally, and relatedly, I discuss challenges associated with interviewing multiple members of the same family. These challenges include the interrelated processes of navigating strained relationships among family members, building rapport with interconnected individuals, and maintaining between- and within-family confidentiality of all participants. Taken together, this chapter provides a road map for accessing a difficult-to-reach and vulnerable population and highlights how this road map may be useful for accessing other difficult-to-reach and vulnerable populations.

## Prevalence of Family Member Incarceration

Incarceration in the United States is a phenomenon characterized by its concentration among already marginalized individuals. The rapid growth, though recent stabilization, in incarceration means that a historically unprecedented number of individuals are exposed to incarceration and, correspondingly, family member incarceration (Patillo, Weiman, and Western 2004; Wakefield and Uggen 2010).

Being connected to an incarcerated family member is not an uncommon event for individuals, particularly women, in the United States. Recent research provides the first nationally representative accounting of connectedness to incarcerated individuals in the United States. Using data from the 2006 General Social Survey (GSS), researchers document the prevalence of connectedness to an incarcerated person, with connectedness being defined as (1) knowing someone who is currently imprisoned, (2) having a family member who is currently imprisoned, (3) having someone you trust who is currently imprisoned, or (4) having someone from your neighborhood who is currently imprisoned (Lee et al. 2015). The findings show that the prevalence of connectedness to an incarcerated person is high for all race/ethnic and gender groups considered, but that black women are particularly likely to experience the spillover consequences of incarceration. Nearly half (44%) of black women are connected to an incarcerated person (a number that is almost certainly an underestimate because the questions about "imprisonment" exclude jail incarceration). This stands in sharp contrast to the prevalence among white women (12%), black men (32%), or white men (6%). Furthermore, other research documents the relatively high prevalence of romantic partner incarceration among urban women. Recent research using data from the Fragile Families and Child Wellbeing Study, a cohort of urban parents who gave birth around the turn of the century, show that nearly one-fifth of mothers shared a child with a father who had experienced jail or prison incarceration in the past two years (Turney 2014b).

Children have also experienced the consequences of the prison boom in the United States. More than 2.6 million children have a parent, usually a father, currently incarcerated in jail or prison, most of them for nonviolent offenses (Pettit 2012), and this number excludes children with parents recently released and under other forms of correctional supervision such as probation or parole. Importantly, paternal incarceration is especially common among children of minority and poorly educated parents. Recent estimates suggest that 4% of white children compared to 25% of black children, and more than 50% of black children born to high school dropouts, had a father imprisoned by age fourteen (Wildeman 2009). Among urban children, about one-third will experience the (jail or prison) incarceration of their father by age nine (Turney 2017). Therefore, for children, especially vulnerable children of poorly educated minority men living in impoverished neighborhoods, paternal incarceration has become a normative and transformative life course event (e.g., Western and Pettit 2010).

## The Importance of Studying Jail Incarceration

The sheer number of individuals affected by family member incarceration, in conjunction with race/ethnic and social class inequality in family member incarceration, provides a good rationale to understand the spillover consequences of incarceration for family life. Though much research on the collateral consequences of incarceration focuses on prison incarceration (e.g., Comfort 2008), or does not distinguish between prison and jail incarceration (e.g., Turney and Wildeman 2013), jail incarceration—and the processes of incarceration and release associated with jail incarceration—is a particularly understudied aspect of the criminal justice system (Turney and Conner 2019; though see Comfort 2016). In this section, I first describe the demographics of the jail population. I then document why it is strategic to study the individuals who cycle through jails and the families connected to these individuals, highlighting how this population is important to understanding the intersection of the criminal justice system and family life.[1]

Understanding the consequences of jail incarceration, and reentry into families and communities after jail incarceration, is important because of the sheer number of individuals who cycle through jails each year. More than 12 million individuals are admitted to jail annually, often but not always for a short amount of time (Wagner and Rabuy 2017).

Currently, 229 per 100,000 individuals in the population are incarcerated in local jails. Therefore, though it is commonly stated that the US incarceration rate hovers around 450 per 100,000 in the population, including jail incarceration raises that figure by nearly 50% (to 679 per 100,000 in 2017) (Carson 2018; Zeng 2018). Furthermore, three-fifths of individuals incarcerated in jails have not been convicted of any crime but are instead awaiting trial. In fact, 99% of the growth in jail incarceration throughout the past fifteen years results from the increase in pretrial detention (Wagner and Rabuy 2017). Though most quantitative data sources that gather information on family member incarceration do not distinguish between jail and prison experiences, there is some evidence that jail stays are quite commonly experienced by families. For example, data from the Fragile Families and Child Wellbeing Study show that about half of incarcerated fathers are in jails (Wildeman, Turney, and Yi 2016).

Examining the collateral consequences of jail incarceration for families and children is strategic for three reasons (Turney and Conner 2019). First, jails serve as the initial point of institutionalization via the criminal justice system. That is, nearly all individuals sentenced to prison spend at least some time in jail (though the length of time these individuals spend in jail depends on whether they have the option to post bail and, if given the option, whether they use it). Second, because individuals generally spend a relatively short amount of time in jail (at least compared to the time they spend in prison), understanding jail incarceration allows one to capture both the consequences of incapacitation (e.g., during incarceration) and the consequences of reentry (e.g., after incarceration) for families and children. Third, the jail population is quite heterogeneous—with some individuals in jail serving sentences and other individuals awaiting trial or sentencing—and examining jail incarceration allows for an examination of how jail incarceration differentially affects these different groups. For example, the uncertainty surrounding pretrial detention may be especially consequential for the mental health of both the incarcerated and their family members. As criminal justice practices and policies have shifted away from a rehabilitative model, literature suggests that increased certainty around term length is associated with less psychological distress among inmates (e.g.,

Goodstein 1984; Goodstein and Hudack 1982; Parisi 1982), which may have implications for how inmates interact with their family members and for the family members themselves.

The Jail and Family Life Study

The Jail and Family Life Study relies on data obtained from longitudinal in-depth interviews with incarcerated fathers and their family members. This qualitative approach is especially appropriate for answering the overarching research questions of the study. First, in-depth interviews provide rich empirical data lacking from much previous research on the intra- and intergenerational consequences of paternal incarceration (though see, for example, Comfort 2008; Nesmith and Ruhland 2008; Wakefield and Wildeman 2013; for research on maternal incarceration, see Siegel 2011). These data document the complex and dynamic consequences of paternal incarceration for children as they are being lived out. Second, these rich data points allow for strong and nuanced assertions about the intra- and intergenerational consequences of paternal incarceration and the heterogeneity in these consequences.

There are both strengths and limitations to focusing on incarcerated fathers and their families. Given gender differences in incarceration rates, paternal incarceration affects a larger number of children than maternal incarceration, so a focus on paternal incarceration allows for an examination of a commonly experienced childhood stressor (especially among children of color and poor children). A focus on paternal incarceration, particularly with in-depth interview data, is also warranted because it further illuminates patterns of intergenerational consequences found in quantitative data (e.g., Geller et al. 2012; Turney 2017; Wildeman 2010). That said, the focus on incarcerated fathers (and their families) necessarily excludes an examination of incarcerated mothers and incarcerated individuals without children. The consequences of incarceration for families may be different when a mother is incarcerated. For example, on average, children's living arrangements differ when mothers are incarcerated compared to when fathers are incarcerated (as, with the latter, most children continue to live with a biological parent) (Turney and Goodsell 2018). The consequences of incarceration for families may also be different when men and women without children are incarcerated, as children tie families together in ways that structure intra- and intergenerational relationships.

*Sample and Recruitment*

The sample comprises 123 families in Southern California that experienced paternal incarceration. I recruited families, with the cooperation of the Oceanside Sheriff's Department (OSD),[2] through three jails in Southern California. Southern California is a strategic site to conduct this study. First, as a practical matter, the three jails are in close proximity to the University of California, Irvine, facilitating recruitment. Second, though Southern California includes notably wealthy cities including Newport Beach and Irvine, the county is racially and socioeconomically diverse. Cities including Anaheim, Fullerton, Garden Grove, and Santa Ana are racially diverse communities with poverty rates above the national average. Third, the incarceration rate in California is similar to the incarceration rate nationally (Walmsley 2013). Fourth, California has been undergoing prison realignment that has altered the way the state handles offenders.[3] Realignment, which began in response to a Supreme Court ruling (*Brown v. Plata*) to reduce the overcrowding in California prisons, shifts the responsibility of those convicted of many non-serious offenses from the state to counties. Therefore, many individuals who would have been sentenced to state prisons, prior to realignment, are now sentenced to jails.

Along with a team of trained graduate student interviewers (seven in total), I collected longitudinal in-depth interviews from incarcerated fathers and their family members [including children (those ages eight or older), mothers/caregivers of children, and fathers' own mothers, as well as occasionally siblings, adult children, and other family members]. Interviewing incarcerated fathers and their family members provides a nuanced picture of the lifeworlds affected by paternal incarceration. Fathers and their family members generally provided information with some commonalities, facilitating triangulation; but, within families, each individual provided unique information. Family members would sometimes provide conflicting information, allowing for opportunities to further unpack variation in individuals' perceptions of experiences.

Fathers provided critical information about their incapacitation and reentry experiences. Children's mothers and father's mothers, who were often children's primary caregivers, provided useful information about family and child functioning (e.g., Lareau 2003). It was also useful to directly incorporate children into the research (Eder and Corsaro 1999; also see Avison 2010), as the children often had different perspectives than parents (e.g., Thorne 1987) and likely provided the most direct accounts of school and peer experiences (e.g., Calarco 2011).

RECRUITMENT OF FATHERS

The research team recruited fathers, with the cooperation of the OSD, between July 2015 and October 2016.[4] First, fathers were recruited through various classes (e.g., classes about parenting, substance abuse, money management, ESL) held across the three jails.[5] In these classes, we provided a brief description of the study's purpose and the interview procedures. Men interested in participating were administered a short questionnaire to determine their eligibility. The questionnaire asked men to report (1) the length of time they had spent in jail during this current stay and/or their sentence length, (2) the number and ages of their child(ren), and (3) the last time they had contact with their child(ren). Men were eligible for study participation if they met the following inclusion criteria: (1) had been in jail for at least two months (or had a sentence length of at least two months), (2) had at least one child under age eighteen, and (3) saw at least one child in the month prior to incarceration. We limited enrollment to fathers with recent contact with a child, as theory and existing research suggests paternal incarceration would be most consequential for these families, though the sample includes substantial variation in father involvement prior to incarceration. We enrolled and interviewed fathers across two maximum-security facilities (40 fathers and 53 fathers, respectively) and a minimum-security facility (30 fathers).

Recruitment occurred across three jail facilities in part to explore variation in policies and practices across facilities. There is some unique variation in both the official and unofficial policies and practices across the three facilities. The biggest differences are between the minimum-security facility and the two maximum-security facilities (though there are also differences across the two maximum-security facilities). For example, inmates in the minimum-security facility had more autonomy to move about the facility (both inside and outside), whereas inmates in the maximum-security facilities had limited freedom of movement. Also, in the minimum-security facility, visitation with friends and families is conducted at a table (compared to in the maximum-security facilities, where visitation occurred through Plexiglas and over the telephone). Furthermore, the research team's interactions with employees across these facilities suggest substantial informal variation in the implementation of policies across the jails.

RECRUITMENT OF FAMILY MEMBERS

The research team recruited family members with the cooperation of the fathers. Before we began the father's interview (though after we had secured consent), we asked fathers to provide us the names and contact information of their mothers, the mothers of their children, and other important adults in their lives or the lives of their children. Therefore, a family member was eligible for study participation if the father provided contact information for him or her (and permission to contact him or her). As soon as possible after the father's interview, we contacted these family members (generally via telephone), described the study purpose and procedures to them, and asked them if they were interested in participation. We enrolled 38 children, 78 mothers of children, and 122 other important adults. The number of family members interviewed varied according to each father's unique family situation (with the number of eligible family members ranging from one to seven). We interviewed at least one family member for 90% of fathers.

*In-Depth Interviews*

Fathers and their family members were interviewed twice: (1) during the fathers' incarceration (which was always the case for baseline interviews with fathers and usually the case for baseline interviews with family members), and (2) ideally within one and two months following the fathers' release. Though many fathers were released from jail relatively quickly after their first interview, others spent months or years awaiting trial or serving their jail sentence, and still others were eventually sentenced to state prison. If fathers were not released from jail within one year of their initial interview, we conducted follow-up interviews with them and their family members at this time. Similarly, if fathers were transferred to state prison within the year, we conducted follow-up interviews with them (in prison) and their family members.

The research team was successful in getting fathers and family members to complete follow-up interviews. For example, we conducted follow-up interviews with 72% of the fathers (89 of the 123). The most common reasons for study attrition included a prison sentence that was not within driving distance (though we did conduct follow-up interviews with fathers sentenced to prison within a four-hour drive driving distance), deportation, and inability to locate the father. We worked to minimize study attrition in a number of ways: by asking fathers at baseline to provide us with contact information for friends and family members who would know where they were staying after release; by sending thank you notes after the baseline interview; by contacting fathers as soon as they were released from jail (to collect up-to-date contact information and remind them that we would be contacting them soon to schedule a follow-up interview); and by keeping in touch with family members.

The first round of interviews with fathers occurred in the attorney/bonds rooms (in the jails). In the first round, we began by asking fathers to tell us the story of their life. This open-ended and broad question elicited a range of narrative information. We then asked questions that centered around the following eight modules: (1) child information, (2) incarceration experiences, (3) economic well-being, (4) romantic relationships, (5) parenting, (6) health and social support, (7) family background, and (8) future. Within each module, we often asked fathers to discuss their lives prior to incarceration and their lives during incarceration. For example, we asked questions about their romantic relationship prior to and during their confinement, probing for changes that occurred over time. We asked similar, mostly open-ended questions of all respondents, but varied the wording and timing of the questions to make the interviews flow as much as possible like a conversation.

The initial and follow-up interviews with family members, as well as most follow-up interviews with fathers, occurred where the respondents were comfortable (ideally their home to provide additional contextual data but often a public space such as a park or fast food restaurant). The interview protocol for mothers and other adult family members was similar to the interview protocol for fathers, as we asked these respondents to describe their family lives prior to and during incarceration. We asked children about their experiences related to the father's incarceration and about their families more generally, their schools, and their peers (for more details, see Turney et al. 2017). The follow-up interviews were most often conducted by whomever conducted the initial interview; for example, 62% of follow-up interviews with fathers were conducted by a member of the research team who conducted the baseline interview. The follow-up interviews followed a protocol similar to the baseline interviews but primarily focused on changes since the first interview. The interviews were conducted in both English and Spanish (depending on the respondent's preference).

Following each interview, interviewers composed detailed field notes (Emerson, Fretz, and Shaw 2011). Field notes included descriptions of the interview context (including location, presence of other people, unusual distractions or noises, and the respondent's disposition during the interview). Field notes also included summaries of the interview modules and, for first-round interviews, detailed tips for the follow-up interview (including unanswered questions, information that seemed contradictory during the interview, and topics for clarification).

The length of the interviews varied based on the type of respondent (i.e., interviews with adults were lengthier than interviews with children) and whether it was a baseline or follow-up interview (i.e., baseline interviews were most often, though certainly not always, longer than follow-up interviews). For example, baseline interviews with fathers lasted, on average, three hours (ranging from a minimum of thirty minutes to a maximum of six hours, with only ten interviews lasting fewer than two hours). To facilitate cooperation, adults were paid with a $50 Visa gift card per interview (for fathers, only after release, as the OSD prohibited paying them while incarcerated) and children were paid $10 (cash) per interview.

## Challenges to Accessing Jailed Fathers

This section discusses challenges to accessing jailed fathers. In short, accessing jailed fathers was initially challenging because it required approval from two institutional gatekeepers: the Institutional Review Board (IRB) at the University of California, Irvine and the OSD.[6]

But, once approved by these institutional gatekeepers, it was relatively uncomplicated to recruit, consent, and interview fathers. That is, fathers overwhelmingly wanted to participate in the study.

*Gaining Access from Institutional Gatekeepers*

As described above, institutional gatekeepers included the IRB at the University of California, Irvine and the OSD. I focus on OSD access here, as IRB access was fairly straightforward and the project received approval from the IRB (via a full committee review that included a prisoner representative) in June 2015.[7] There were two parts to gaining access to the OSD, as the research study first had to receive official administrative approval from the sheriff and then had to receive less official (but certainly no less important) buy-in from the deputies and other employees at the three jails (Fox, Zambrana, and Lane 2011).

Receiving administrative approval from the OSD was time-consuming, as it took a long time to develop rapport and trust with the entity, but was fairly straightforward. The administration was initially supportive of the research project and, for the most part, maintained consistency in their support throughout.

The most substantial challenges posed by the OSD administration revolved around not *whether* I could conduct the research project but *how* I could conduct the research project. One initial challenge involved the OSD's reticence with the research team's interviewing family members of the jailed fathers in the study (as I was always transparent with the OSD about the scope of the entire research project). The OSD was initially resistant to this idea (and further, the idea that we would pay these family members for their participation in the study), as it is against their usual protocol to allow "outsiders" to have contact with both an inmate and those connected to an inmate (as, theoretically, an outsider could pass information between jailed fathers and their family members). Relatedly, the OSD was initially resistant to the research team conducting follow-up interviews with fathers, as they do not usually allow outsiders to have contact with inmates both during their jail stay and after release. The negotiations about the scope of the research project were messy and complicated, as is the case in nearly all original data collection efforts, but the OSD eventually relented on both fronts.

Perhaps the biggest compromise the research team made in these negotiations with the OSD administration was that the OSD would not allow us to record interviews with fathers. This roadblock was unexpected, as it occurred after initial access was granted (though prior to the beginning of data collection), and the research team had to quickly adapt to develop a strategy for collecting high-quality data. This strategy involved two members of the research team conducting each interview, with one researcher doing the interview and the other researcher serving as a transcriptionist (capturing, as much as possible, word-for-word what the father said). After the interview was completed, the interviewers immediately reconstructed the interview by speaking the notes into a voice recorder (with the transcriptionist taking the lead on this and the interviewer chiming in to clarify whenever necessary). The goal was to have the reconstruction of the interview resemble the interview as much as possible (including using direct quotations from the father whenever possible). This compromise was costly on two fronts. First, despite our best efforts to reconstruct the interview word-for-word, and our intensive training and practice doing so, it is inevitable that some data were lost with this approach. Second, using this approach, data collection took at least three times as long as it would have otherwise (as each interview required two interviewers, instead of one, and both of those interviewers had to do the reconstruction, which took, on average, half as much time as the interview). That said, having two interviewers at each of the baseline interviews facilitated rapport with fathers and likely expanded the amount of information collected (as both interviewers had an opportunity to clarify details or probe with follow-up questions).

The second stage of access from institutional gatekeepers, getting buy-in from the deputies and other employees at each of the three jails, proved at least equally as formidable as being granted administrative access. That is, once the project was officially approved by the OSD, the research team still had to negotiate access with those working in the jails directly. We experienced several roadblocks throughout, again not about *whether* we could conduct the research project but *how* we could conduct the research project.

For example, the research team learned early on that the administrative approval for the project did not necessarily correspond to more informal approval from those working in the jails. This administrative approval was not conveyed to those working in the jails, those individuals who would be vital to our recruitment and interviewing efforts (as they were the ones who worked with us to bring the fathers from their housing unit to the attorney/bonds rooms for the interviews). This meant that the research team had to go to great lengths to explain the purpose of the research project, the study protocol, and how the deputies could help us achieve our research goals. I had initially requested a memorandum of understanding (MOU) from the administration, in an effort to avoid some of this disconnect in communication, but this request was denied (as the administration told me it was unnecessary). Essentially, our initial attempts at recruitment and interviewing—and our subsequent attempts, too, as there was relatively frequent turnover in employees who were assisting us—required a lot of explanation. This shows that institutional access is not necessarily something that needed a one-time approval but, instead, was something that needed to be continually negotiated.

As another example, our interactions with the deputies at the jail experienced temporary changes about seven months into data collection, when three inmates at one of the jails engaged (and succeeded) in a high-profile jail escape. The inmates were not participants in our study, and were eventually caught, but this caused the OSD to review their policies regarding outsider access; accordingly, the research study received more scrutiny than it did previously. For example, our usual protocol involved, after completing the interview with the father, handing him our consent document and my business card (that included all of the typical information as well as a handwritten phone number, which was set up to accept collect calls from the jails in the event the fathers needed to get in touch with us after the interview). Soon after the jail escape, a graduate student interviewer handed the deputy this business card for him to pass along to the father, as was common protocol for the prior seven months. However, this concerned the deputies, as they thought the student was giving the father her personal cell phone number. After multiple phone calls to me and additional calls to the project phone to ensure it was not the graduate student's personal cell phone, and a brief hiatus in our research, this was resolved (and I purchased new business cards that included the project phone number formally printed on them).

## Recruiting and Interviewing Fathers

After receiving access from the institutional gatekeepers—namely, the OSD—we had to work to recruit and interview fathers, a stage of data collection that proved to be less challenging than gaining institutional access. The fathers, by the nature of their confinement, are a captive population. By and large, they were eager to participate and were generally available for participation. Occasionally a father who had signed up to participate in the project was released from jail or sent to prison before we were able to interview him. However, as we were able to keep track of fathers' release dates (with assistance from the OSD) and their upcoming court dates (via online search tools that provide this publicly available information), and we were able to prioritize interviewing fathers whom we knew would be released soon, this happened fairly infrequently.

Fathers were overwhelmingly eager to participate in the study, both in terms of the number of fathers who signed up during recruitment and once we showed up to conduct the interview. Throughout the course of the study, only one father changed his mind about study participation between recruitment and when we arrived to interview him. The interviews were quite lengthy (up to six hours, as noted above). We strove to conduct every interview in one sitting but occasionally had to conduct interviews over two or three different days. In one facility, we were only allowed a 180-minute window to conduct interviews each day, which usually necessitated conducting the interview over two days. Across all facilities, we would occasionally have to end an interview if it ran into lunch or dinner times (which we worked to avoid) or if the respondent needed a break (for example, to use the bathroom). In instances where interviews took place over more than one visit, the lead interviewer remained the same (but sometimes the transcriptionist changed). Conducting interviews over multiple days did not harm rapport (and, if anything, increased respondents' familiarity with the interviewers and strengthened rapport). Conducting interviews over multiple days also allowed the interviewers to ask targeted clarification questions during the second or third day (as the interviewers had a chance to reflect on the first part of the interview).

## Challenges to Accessing Family Members of Jailed Fathers

The procedures for accessing jailed fathers is quite different than the procedures for accessing family members of jailed fathers. Accordingly, the challenges to accessing family members of jailed fathers were generally quite different than the challenges to accessing the fathers themselves.

### Fathers as Gatekeepers

While the OSD served as a gatekeeper for the fathers, one with whom we were able to negotiate, the fathers essentially served as gatekeepers for their family members. All fathers had choices about whether or not to provide us with contact information for their family members and, if so, how much information to provide (e.g., names, phone numbers, addresses, Facebook accounts).

Fathers were overwhelmingly willing and able to provide contact information for their family members, including their children's mothers/caregivers and their own mothers (and, sometimes, other important adults in their lives, such as adult children, fathers, or extended family members). They overwhelmingly wanted to give us this information, regardless of whether they were on good or bad terms with their family members. Further, they overwhelmingly *could* give us this information, as they often had it memorized.[8]

Occasionally fathers did not have all of the contact information that they wanted to provide. We had several strategies to retrieve this additional information. One method involved coming back in the next day or two (and telling the fathers that we would be doing this so that they would bring the information when we arrived). We minimized this strategy, though, as the OSD wanted us to minimize our repeated visits with study participants. Another strategy, which we employed when suggested by fathers, was to contact one family member who could put us in touch with another family member that we wanted to interview. An example of this was a father who said that he did not have an address or phone number for his child's mother but instead gave us information for his sister (and told us the sister would be able to provide us information for his child's mother, which she did).

## Connecting with Family Members

Once we received contact information from fathers, the research team had the challenge of connecting with family members. Family members—including children's mothers/caregivers, fathers' mothers, and other adults connected to the father and/or children (e.g., sisters)—can be generally placed into two basic groups: (1) those with supportive and positive relationships with fathers, and (2) those with tumultuous relationships with fathers. Not surprisingly, the nature of the relationship between the father and family member played an important role in how easy or difficult it was to recruit the family member into the study. For fathers who reported positive relationships with their children's mothers/caregivers and their own mothers, it was generally not difficult to track down these individuals, tell them about the research study, and set up a time to do an interview. In many of these cases, fathers would offer—unprompted by us—to vouch for us to their families, sometimes even encouraging us to hold off on contacting their family members until they had an opportunity to vouch for the research team.

Alternatively, it was more challenging to contact family members when fathers reported tumultuous or negative relationships with their children's mothers/caregivers and their own mothers, although our procedures for contacting these family members was quite varied. Importantly, though it was occasionally challenging to gain access to fathers' mothers, it was more often challenging to gain access to their children's mothers/caregivers, as these relationships were generally more conflictual and less stable than fathers' relationships with their mothers. The challenges began with receiving correct contact information. These fathers were more likely to give us incorrect contact information (e.g., giving us a street address that did not exist, transposing two numbers in a phone number). The challenges persisted when we did reach the family member, as these family members were less likely than others to want to participate in the study. In these cases, having interviewed the father could hinder the initial participation of these family members, as they would sometimes report not wanting anything to do with the father, not wanting to relive painful memories related to him, or having moved on to a new partner. These cases of complicated family relationships required delicate discussions regarding participation in the research study (which included reminding the family members that they could choose to not answer any questions in the interview guide and working to make the time and location of the interview as convenient as possible for the potential respondent). The research team worked to encourage participation of these individuals, so that the sample of family members was as diverse as the family relationships themselves.

Finally, maintaining confidentiality within families—and letting potential participants know that we will maintain such confidentiality—sometimes facilitated participation among family members. The research team had to maintain confidentiality for each respondent. This meant that there was no break in confidentiality across fathers, mothers, children, and other adults. For example, when we interviewed family members of fathers, we could not share any information with them that the father disclosed during his interview. When we interviewed children, we could not share any information with them that the father or adult family members disclosed during their interviews. When we conducted follow-up interviews with fathers and family members, we had to maintain the confidentiality of all parties. This often facilitated participation but came with its own set of challenges. For example, occasionally family members would ask us to disclose information about the father, which we could not do (and had to delicately tell the family member in a manner that would not ruin the rapport we had developed).

## Conclusions

The consequences of reentry for family members of the incarcerated are less well known than the consequences of reentry for formerly incarcerated individuals. The Jail and Family Life Study, a longitudinal and qualitative data collection effort, provides an interesting lens through which to understand the collateral consequences of reentry for families. In this chapter, I highlighted the large number of individuals who experience the reentry of a family member and specifically suggested that reentry from jail, as opposed to reentry from prison, is an understudied yet critically important aspect of the criminal justice system with unique implications for family life. I also described challenges to navigating access to jailed fathers, an especially vulnerable population, and their family members. In doing so, I discussed challenges associated with interviewing multiple members of the same family, which include the interrelated processes of navigating strained relationships, building rapport, and maintaining both between- and within-family confidentiality of all participants.

These data collection strategies have a number of strengths. I highlight two of them here. First, interviewing fathers in jail, and again after release, provides a unique window into the challenges that these fathers and their families face during the incarceration period and during the reentry period. This facilitates comparisons over time and allows for an understanding of how processes change over time. Second, interviewing multiple members of the same family provides opportunities to understand comparable and divergent reports of the collateral consequences of incarceration. Fathers' perceptions of the collateral consequences of their incarceration for their families and children are not always in line with family members' perceptions (and, further, different family members sometimes also have different experiences). Having multiple reporters offers an opportunity to understand the complexities inherent in family dynamics. But the data collection strategies employed here also have a number of limitations, one of which is the scope of data collection. For example, the data can only speak to the consequences of incarceration for fathers and their family members and therefore exclude other populations such as incarcerated mothers and men and women without children. The (baseline) data, in particular, can only speak to the consequences of jail incarceration (as opposed to prison incarceration or immigrant detention). Another limitation includes the fact that participation of family members in the study may be contingent upon their relationship with the father. Though the research team made every effort to complete interviews with all nominated family members, some family members chose not to participate because of a conflictual or nonexistent relationship with the father.

Taken together, these data provide an opportunity for researchers to understand these consequences from the perspectives of multiple individuals connected to the incarcerated father and over time. These data collection efforts contribute to the growing literature on the collateral consequences of incarceration by examining how the cycle of jail incarceration and release affects fathers and their family members (including their children, their children's mothers and caregivers, and their own mothers) and, more broadly, how the criminal justice system increases inequality within and between families.

ACKNOWLEDGMENTS

The Jail and Family Life Study has received generous funding from the National Science Foundation, the William T. Grant Foundation, and the School of Social Sciences at the University of California, Irvine. The Jail and Family Life Study has benefited from the excellent research assistance of Britni Adams, Nadine Alsaadi, Natalie Averruz, Belen Barocio, Elisabet Barrios, Jaymesha Carter, Emma Conner, Adrienne Credo, Patricia Delacruz, Ann Fefferman, Gabriela Gonzalez, Rebecca Goodsell, Jessica Kizer, Jesse Garcia, Arevik Gyurjyan, Christopher Hoffman, Payton Huse, Alma Leon-Oseguera, Crysbelle Lopez, Setarah Mahmoudi, Katelyn Malae, Analicia Mejia Mesinas, Carmel Mitchell, Jasmine Morales, Janet Muniz, Katherine Navarro, Hannah Neatherlin, Tiffany Park, Elizabeth Partida, Alexandra Russo, Steven Schmidt, Archibaldo Silva, Desirae Sotto, Breauna Spencer, Luis Vaca-Corona, Alexis Velez, Cara Vermaak, Kanoelani Villanueva, and Jessica Zhu. This chapter has benefited from feedback from Jessica Hardie and Anita Zuberi.

NOTES

1 I do not mean to suggest that it is unimportant to understand the role of prisons in family life. Indeed, prisons—as well as other forms of correctional supervision such as probation or parole—play an important role in family life, and there are a number of excellent studies that examine this (e.g., Braman 2004; Christian 2005; Comfort 2008; Harding et al. 2014; Turanovic et al. 2012; Western et al. 2015).
2 This is a pseudonym.
3 For details, see "Bill Number: AB 109," Committee on Budget, Official California Legislative Information, January 10, 2011, www.leginfo.ca.gov.
4 Interviews with fathers in the two maximum-security facilities took place between July 2015 and May 2016. Interviews with fathers in the minimum-security facility took place between May and October 2016.
5 We recruited in nine classes in each of the two maximum-security facilities and in ten classes in the minimum-security facility.
6 Follow-up interviews that occurred in prison received institutional approval from both the California Department of Rehabilitation and Corrections (CDCR) and the Committee for the Protection of Human Subjects (CPHS).
7 The project also received approval for a number of IRB modifications since June 2015, as occasionally the project developed in ways that required an addition or alteration to the initially approved protocol. For example, I was initially told by

the OSD that the interviews with fathers could be conducted in classrooms at the jail, but I (and the OSD) learned quickly that the jails did not have the classroom capacity to allow for these lengthy interviews; therefore, I amended the IRB protocol to conduct the interviews in the attorney/bonds rooms. Additionally, though the OSD initially told me that interviews could be recorded, they altered this policy prior to the beginning of data collection, and I amended the IRB protocol accordingly.

8 During recruitment, we told fathers that we would want to collect contact information for their children's mothers/caregivers and their mothers. However, most fathers did not remember this when we interviewed them. Furthermore, when fathers were called for an interview with the research team, they did not know what they were being called for (with most fathers assuming the visit was from their lawyer) and it was often weeks or months after recruitment.

4

## Collecting Social Network Data in Prison and during Reentry

*A Field Guide*

COREY WHICHARD, SARA WAKEFIELD, AND
DEREK A. KREAGER

Criminologists have had a long-standing interest in understanding the informal social organization within prisons (for reviews, see Crewe 2016; Kreager and Kruttschnitt 2018). Scholars have also long focused on ex-prisoners' family ties and social capital accumulation to elucidate community reentry processes in the era of mass incarceration (Bales and Mears 2008; Morenoff and Harding 2014; Petersilia 2003; Uggen, Wakefield, and Western 2005; Western 2018). This chapter describes a mixed-method study focused on the social relationships of prisoners from incarceration through reentry. The Prison Inmate Networks Study (hereafter PINS) and its companion, the Reentry Prison Inmate Networks Study (hereafter R-PINS), leverage surveys, qualitative interviews, administrative data, and social network data to better understand the social organization of prisons and how social ties influence experiences upon release. The chapter is focused primarily on the collection of social network data within a prison setting and in the context of a reentry study. Though the process is similar in many ways to conducting ethnographic or traditional survey research in these settings, there are unique challenges associated with collecting network data from prisoners and reentrants. Before addressing these challenges, the chapter begins by describing the utility of network science and providing examples of research findings from the PINS and R-PINS projects.[1]

## A Network Approach

A social network is a way to represent, in visual and matrix form, a set of relationships or a social system (Kadushin 2012; Robins 2015). A key benefit of the network approach is that it provides a means of theoretically and empirically representing interdependent structures. Within criminology, network analysis has been particularly well-suited to investigating peer influence mechanisms as articulated in differential association and social learning theory (Haynie 2001; McGloin and Kirk 2010; Papachristos 2014), as well as examining the interactive processes involved in generating and benefiting from social capital (Burt 1992; Coleman 1988; Granovetter 1973; Lin 2002; Putnam 2000). Examples of research questions that can be addressed with a network approach include: (1) the structural properties of a social system and how these correlate with aggregate behavior; (2) how individuals' positions within a social system correlate with individual-level outcomes; (3) how individuals form social connections (i.e., become embedded in the social structure) and how these connections influence behavior over time; and (4) how resources, behaviors, and ideas flow across a social system.

The PINS and R-PINS projects offer hypotheses and evidence for each of the above research questions within the contexts of incarceration and reentry (Kreager et al. 2016). For example, Schaefer et al. (2017) used PINS data to analyze peer associations among prisoners living on the same housing unit. The authors found that the peer network formed a singular community structure that was characterized by cohesion and social integration. Indeed, the network was structurally similar to adolescent friendship networks observed in school settings. Kreager et al. (2017) also used PINS network data to examine the origins of prisoner social status. Respondents nominated powerful and influential peers, and the resulting network identified a small number of high-status "old head" prisoners who were older, serving longer sentences, and perceived as knowledgeable of the prison and unit. In addition, Haynie et al. (2018) analyzed PINS data to investigate the relationship between health and social integration. The authors found that prisoners in better physical and mental health were more likely to occupy central positions in the peer association network, and the healthiest prisoners tended to cluster together in peer groups organized by exercise behavior, religiosity, and race. Finally, preliminary analyses of the R-PINS data indicate that soon-to-be-released prisoners anchor their expectations for future social relationships based on the other person's kinship status, prior visitation, and perceived involvement in kinkeeping behavior. However, follow-up interviews upon reentry reveal that most of these "expected" relationships fail to become actualized after leaving prison, resulting in additional strain and unforeseen complications that exacerbate the difficulties of reentry.

## Network Fundamentals

There are three fundamental components to all social network studies: (1) the *actors*, or individual social entities that inhabit the network; (2) the *boundary*, or the threshold that determines which actors are included in the network; and (3) the *ties*, or the relationships among actors that link them together and generate the network structure (Wasserman and Faust 1994). This section discusses the essential features of each of these components and how they connect to the PINS and R-PINS projects.

*Actors*: Although the actors in a social network can be collectivities, groups, or gangs, the PINS and R-PINS foci are prisoners and reentrants, respectively. It is straightforward to connect these actors with other actors in the prison context (e.g., peers and staff) as well as outside of prison (e.g., family and friends). Similar to random survey studies, actors are also connected to their individual attributes and behaviors taken from self-report survey instruments or other sources of historical or administrative records (e.g., department of corrections data).

*Boundary*: The boundary defines network membership and identifies actors who will be excluded or included in analyses, with clear implications for the scope of the data collection effort. The main distinction here is between *egocentric* and *global* network designs. Egocentric network designs focus on measuring the relationships of a focal actor (ego) and the members of her immediate network (alters). These studies offer an in-depth view of the local social system surrounding a specific actor (for a comprehensive review of egocentric network methods, see Crossley et al. 2015) and are well-suited for investigating research questions related to social capital (e.g., Coleman 1988; Lin 2002). As described in greater detail later in this chapter, R-PINS focuses on social capital through the reentry process and thus relies on an egocentric network design. In comparison, global network studies attempt to collect relational data from a full census of entities within a given boundary or setting. Such data can be used to map an entire social system. It is the most common form of social network research, and many techniques for social network analysis require this type of data (Borgatti, Everett, and Johnson 2013). The main advantage of this approach is that it enables insight into characteristics of the social system that may not be perceptible to individual actors. Often, social network boundaries may appear unclear or arbitrary, but the physical barriers of the prison and the social separation inherent in the incarceration experience increase the desirability of a global network approach, and this design forms the basis of the PINS project (Kreager et al. 2016).

*Ties*: Ties define a set of relationships between the network actors. Though there are many possible relationships that can be measured as network ties, most ties represent either relational states or relational events (Atkin 1977; Borgatti et al. 2013). Relational states refer to continuous or semi-continuous conditions that connect two actors (e.g., friendship or status deference), while relational events refer to discrete moments of connection (e.g., trading cigarettes or other resources).

To measure relationships between a given set of actors, a label must be applied to the tie that describes the relation. The wording of tie labels can have a significant impact on data quality, particularly with respect to question clarity and sensitivity. Poorly worded or highly sensitive tie labels may discourage respondents from providing honest answers or from answering the question at all. In the prison context, for example, the notion of "friendship" between prisoners is often a contentious issue for prisoners (Crewe 2009). Many express that friendship—with its connotations of trust, support, and social intimacy—is simply not possible in prison and are reluctant to use this word to describe their relationships with other prisoners. The PINS project relies on the more neutral terms of "get along with" to specify prison peer relationships (see Schaefer et al. 2017). The R-PINS project measures more generic ties based on "knowing each other" and frequency of interaction.

## Challenges for Social Network Data Collection

The success of a social network study is directly tied to the recruitment and engagement of a high proportion of respondents within the focal context. For example, studies suggest that system-level network statistics are only robust to approximately 20–30% missing observations (Kossinets 2006; Smith and Moody 2013). There are three primary challenges facing recruitment in prison environments. First, whatever the method eventually employed, a primary difficulty for prisoner data collection is establishing trust while simultaneously motivating prisoners to participate in research (Giallombardo 1966; Jewkes and Wright 2016). Second, researchers are legally and ethically restricted in their ability to encourage participation of prisoners through incentives (Jewkes and Wright 2016; Smoyer, Blankenship, and Belt 2009). Finally, while prison staff will (often grudgingly) defer to written authorization and permit researchers to operate within the prison, prisoner trust is never guaranteed and requires substantial investment, particularly as the prison environment virtually requires incarcerated people to be suspicious of strangers. It can be difficult convincing prisoners to even meet with interviewers, much less persuade them to make a good-faith effort to honestly answer questions.

While low response rates and respondent resistance are concerns for all forms of research, they are exacerbated in prison settings and highly consequential for social network statistics. Moreover, the very nature of social network data collection runs the risk of violating prison norms guiding how incarcerated people talk about each other with third parties. There are powerful sanctions against "snitching" in prison (Irwin 1980; Irwin and Cressey 1962; Skarbeck 2012; Sykes 1958), and the process of collecting network data bears a striking resemblance to this very behavior. In the authors' experience administering network surveys in prison, simply presenting a prisoner with a list of names—a routine procedure for collecting social network data—can provoke a tense reaction. Compounding this problem is the fact that participants in a global network study know each other, and prisoners who initially participate will inevitably talk about the experience with others, quickly diffusing negative perceptions and potentially producing devastating consequences for response rates and prisoner safety. A solution to this issue that was applied in PINS was to focus only on "positive" ties when gathering network nominations, which reduces respondent resistance or "snitching" fears.

Finally, social network data collection within a prison setting presents challenges for human subjects review. Social network data give the appearance of greater invasiveness to respondents for IRB reviewers who are often unfamiliar with the method. The authors' initial IRB review requested that they gain consent from all primary respondents *as well as* every actor named in their network. This would have rendered the study impossible to complete, requiring a 100% response rate, and few social network studies could achieve this standard. It is likely that the request relies on an understandable, but fundamentally incorrect, assumption about the risks of disclosure presented by social network data relative to other common survey methods. For example, PINS and R-PINS asked questions about attributes of actors in the network, as reported by the respondent (e.g., age, race, gender, employment status, legal history). In practice, this is no different from a survey of juveniles who may report on the deviance of their (unconsented) peers or a study of individuals who report on their romantic partners. Neither peers nor partners are consented into the study, but the reports do present a risk of disclosure (if one assumes peers and partners are valid reporters). Network science does much the same thing, but because it takes such ties into account formally, it has the appearance of greater risk. The authors are aware of at least two other cases where network researchers were initially subject to a global consent request by IRBs and therefore caution researchers to address this concern proactively in their initial applications by situating the risks of social network data with comparisons to the more widely understood risks associated with non-network survey research.

Despite these challenges, the authors can attest that it is possible to successfully collect social network data from prisoners as long as researchers acknowledge the constraints of the prison environment and allow these considerations to guide their approach. Drawing on the authors' own experiences conducting network research across multiple prison settings, this chapter discusses the process of designing and administering network surveys for prisoner respondents and suggests potential strategies for avoiding pitfalls and effectively operating within the prison context.

## PINS and R-PINS

The Prison Inmate Networks Study (PINS) is an example of a global network study conducted in a prison setting.[2] PINS collected two waves of survey and social network data from prisoners living in a minimum-security unit (i.e., good behavior or "honor" unit) of a Pennsylvania medium-security men's prison. The unit housed approximately 200 prisoners using a combination of enclosed cells and an array of bunk beds. About 70% (n = 144) of unit prisoners participated in the survey for the first wave, and 60% (n = 120) participated during the second wave. At each wave, a small team of interviewers met with respondents one-on-one in empty office rooms provided by the prison staff. Surveys were administered using Computer Assisted Personal Interview (CAPI) instruments to each respondent over the course of one (PINS wave 2) to three weeks (PINS wave 1).[3] The primary goals of the study were to reveal the network structure of a men's prison unit and correlate this with prisoner health and rehabilitative outcomes.

The Reentry Prison Inmate Network Study (R-PINS) is an example of an egocentric network study conducted in prison and during reentry. R-PINS applied a longitudinal, mixed-method design to collect data from a subsample of PINS respondents who indicated they were parole-eligible and willing to participate in a community reentry study. The department of corrections provided monthly updates on the parole status of the full PINS sample, which allowed members of the research team to identify when a prospective reentry respondent was to be released. These prisoners were interviewed prior to release. Following this first interview, the research team attempted to re-interview all R-PINS respondents two additional times. The first interview typically took place within three weeks of prison release, while the second and third interviews occurred about three and nine months after release, respectively. During every R-PINS interview, respondents provided narrative data during a 60–90-minute semi-structured qualitative interview followed by an egocentric network survey administered via CAPI; all conversations between respondent and interviewer were audio-recorded and later transcribed for qualitative coding and thematic analysis. For R-PINS, forty-five respondents participated in the first interview, thirty-two (71%) were successfully interviewed a second time, and ten (22%) were interviewed a third time.

The egocentric network design helped to resolve ambiguities surrounding the network boundary. The actors in each R-PINS network consisted of one focal prisoner and his social contacts in the community. While the R-PINS researchers knew that they wanted to bound the networks to include both strong and weak ties during reentry, it was not clear at the outset who these people were or what determined network membership. To remedy this, R-PINS researchers used a *name-generator design* (see Bidart and Charbonneau 2011). This design functions by implementing a respondent-driven approach to identifying network actors and defining the network boundary. It allows for greater flexibility in data collection, as it is not necessary for researchers to have a predefined list of actors before starting data collection, and it individually tailors the bounding process to each respondent. R-PINS researchers constructed the survey using EgoWeb 2.0, a free computer program designed for collecting egocentric network data using a name-generator (see EgoWeb 2.0). The name-generator design proceeds in three stages: (1) the name-generator stage, where the respondent responds to a survey prompt with a list of actor names; (2) the name-interpreter stage, where the respondent answers a series of questions about the characteristics of each network actor; and (3) the name-interrelater stage, where the respondent identifies ties among the actors.

During the name-interpreter stage, the survey presents the respondent with a series of questions about each network actor named during the name-generator stage. For reentry research, it is often desirable to measure reentrant exposure to risk factors for recidivism, such as whether they associate with criminally active peers. However, reentrants may be wary of answering questions that amount to tacitly admitting they have violated conditions of parole, such as when they are prohibited from interacting with co-defendants or former criminal associates. In the authors' experience, the crux of the issue is whether the wording of the question requires the reentrant to report that one of their peers is *actively* involved in illegal behavior. As long as the question is sufficiently vague with respect to the timing and type of crime, reentrants appear to be comfortable reporting which members of their network have engaged in illegal behavior. For example, the survey asked respondents: "Since you've known them, has this person ever been in serious legal trouble?" Respondents appeared to provide valid answers to this item, as their responses are stable across multiple interviews, and consistent with narrative accounts where they discuss exposure to antisocial peer influence. Unfortunately, a limitation of this strategy is that it produces relatively crude measures of actor behavior.

The name-interrelater stage asks the respondent to systematically go through the list of actor names and identify every instance where two actors share a tie. It is important to note that this process grows progressively longer for every actor that the respondent initially nominates. Overly long surveys are problematic for interviews with prisoners and reentrants, as institutional procedures often make it difficult for interviewers to have uninterrupted access to prisoners for more than a couple of hours at a time, and many reentrants will have work and family obligations that limit their availability for survey participation.[4] Fortunately, there are design strategies for mitigating the risk of respondent burden. The simplest way to minimize this risk is to limit the number of names that the respondent can provide during the initial name-generator stage of the survey.[5] Other strategies include focusing on symmetrical relationships and using double-barreled question formats to measure relationship strength. The R-PINS survey took this approach by asking about a symmetrical relationship (i.e., "knowing each other") and incorporating a measure of relationship strength (i.e., interaction frequency) into the same item. For example, respondents were asked: "Does [*focal alter name*] know each of the other people that you mentioned? If so, how frequently do you think they will be interacting soon after you leave prison?"

The main disadvantage of the name-interrelater is that it is monotonous for respondents to complete (Hogan, Carrasco, and Wellman 2007; McCarty, Killworth, and Rennell 2007). For example, an R-PINS respondent with ten actors in his network would be asked to describe the relationship status of forty-five pairs of actors. In practice, this requires interviewers to ask the same basic question forty-five different ways. It is important that interviewers have some level of rapport with respondents before initiating the network survey, as respondents who do not feel invested in the study may be unwilling to dutifully complete this section. R-PINS interviewers used data visualization in order to incentivize completing the name-interrelater process. EgoWeb 2.0 automatically transforms the data collected during the name-interrelater stage into a network diagram, and the majority of respondents enjoyed viewing (and discussing) the visualization of their social lives. R-PINS interviewers introduced the name-interrelater as a tedious but necessary process in generating a novel image that visually maps out the respondent's social world. Because respondents were often intrigued by this prospect, they were willing to sit through the name-interrelater.

## Network Data Collection in Prison

Researchers have several options for network survey administration, each with its own strengths and weaknesses (see Borgatti et al. 2013: 55). The authors argue that the face-to-face interview is the best method for collecting network data from prisoners and reentrants. The main advantage of this approach is that it provides the greatest opportunity for prisoners to have a rewarding interpersonal experience, as it maximizes the degree of interaction between respondents and interviewers and it provides the best mechanism for defusing respondent resistance and item nonresponse (Brewer 2000; Johnson and Weller 2002). In contrast, there is limited ability to establish rapport with respondents during survey administration in group settings, and even less interaction when distributing paper surveys for self-administration.

As mentioned previously, it is common for prisoners to exhibit some degree of resistance to network questions, but this can be overcome by a well-trained interviewer. For example, several respondents for the PINS project resisted nominating other prisoners for the "get along with most" network by telling the interviewer that they got along well with everyone in prison. Interviewers were trained to respond to this by nodding and asking, "But who do you get along with *most*?" Simply re-asking the survey item in a nonconfrontational manner was usually sufficient to persuade the prisoner to answer the question. This type of exchange is not possible for self-administration and may be difficult to execute when administering surveys in a group setting.

The primary challenges for face-to-face survey administration of incarcerated people are ensuring (1) respondent confidentiality and (2) interviewer safety. Face-to-face surveys require that interviewers verbally discuss potentially sensitive items with prisoner respondents, and these conversations might be overheard by other prisoners or staff. An obvious solution is to move data collection to private settings. However, such privacy may place the researchers outside of easy observation and activate correctional staff concerns about interviewer safety. There are several possible ways to maximize privacy and interviewer safety, including (1) conducting interviews within view of staff, but outside of hearing distance or behind see-through glass, or (2) providing interviewers with personal alarms. Such decisions are typically outside of the researchers' control, and the PINS team experienced both conditions without incident.

*Question Formats*: The organization and formatting of the survey instrument also influences whether prisoners enjoy participating in the study and feel comfortable providing network information. In particular, network questions can significantly impact survey length and respondent fatigue. It is recommended that, when possible, researchers take a closed-ended approach to eliciting prison network nominations. In PINS, the unit roster was programmed into the CAPI survey so that it appeared on the computer screen with clickable boxes next to each name and respondents were provided with a paper copy of the roster. This allowed the prisoner to search the paper roster while the interviewer recorded nominations into the CAPI.[6]

*Interviewer Characteristics*: There is a robust social science literature on interviewer effects on recruitment and response bias (e.g., Durrant and D'Arrigo 2014; Laumann et al. 1994; Liu and Stainback 2013; Schaeffer 1980; Van Tilburg 1998). The evidence suggests that matching interviewer-respondent race and gender may be useful in some cases, especially when the focal questions involve discrimination experiences (race matching) or sexual assault histories (gender matching). The authors' assessment of this research, however, was that it provided little guidance on how to pair interviewers to respondents or how to approach study recruitment for a prison social network study (but see Crewe 2009; Jenness 2010; Jewkes and Wright 2016; Schlosser 2008). Moreover, the ability to match interviewers to respondents on one or more demographic characteristics (let alone other traits) has several strong assumptions: (1) a large pool of potential interviewers, (2) a substantial research budget, and (3) prior knowledge of the respondent pool and salient traits before entering the prison. In a perfect world, researchers would have the optimal interviewer for every respondent—but a review of the literature on interviewer effects provided no such guidance.

In PINS, the authors noted gendered patterns that were instructive for successfully navigating prison recruitment and network data collection in a male prison. Gender of the interviewer structured interactions within the prison in noticeable ways. Male and female interviewers were equally skilled (or unskilled in some cases) at recruitment and interviewing, but they encountered different challenges. PINS began with a mixed-gender interview team, though heavily tilted toward female (largely white) interviewers as a result of the pool of interested and qualified graduate students to work on the study. In a single-gender setting of involuntarily confined men, the presence of female interviewers had an unmistakable impact on recruitment, and this should surprise no one given the prison deprivation of limited heterosexual contact (Sykes 1958). PINS interviewers consistently observed that male prisoners were much more willing to agree to participate in research when approached by female members of the research team, or when participation involved the chance to interact with a female interviewer during survey administration.

Yet it was also the case that one specific female member of the research team was especially skilled at recruitment. She was also the team member with the most experience in correctional settings. In a context with multiple interviewers with varying levels of experience, having a lead recruiter and interviewer was valuable because she provided onsite training and evaluation for less experienced research staff. While it is the case that the female interviewers in an all-male setting were a clear benefit when collecting global network data in men's prisons, recruitment and experience in correctional facilities or with formerly incarcerated people appeared more important. The authors thus caution readers against adopting an overly simplistic view of gender dynamics in the data collection process or extrapolating from extant research to research conducted inside gender-segregated prisons (Jewkes and Wright 2016).[7]

*Recruitment*: How a research team first presents itself to the prison unit is of critical importance for establishing rapport and situating the study within the polarized environment of staff and prisoners. For PINS, team leaders requested (from staff) a community meeting where prisoners listened to an overview of the research study from the principal investigator. This was the first time that the unit residents came into contact with the research personnel and study. Such community meetings are uncommon in most prison settings, so curiosity resulted in a large turnout. However, it should be noted that PINS interviewers explicitly asked the staff not to make the meeting mandatory as this could make the study appear coercive and in violation of the voluntariness required for study participation (and per IRB approval).

After an initial presentation, members of the interview team were on hand to collect information from prisoners who wished to participate. Where permissible, such recruitment should be distanced from prison staff to avoid perceived coercion and to build trust. There are many different ways to accomplish this, and interviewers will need to adjust their approach to suit the logistical demands of the situation. The main distinction is whether there will be one occasion to opt in to the study, or multiple opportunities for prisoners to participate (i.e., rolling recruitment). Where possible, it is strongly recommended that researchers implement rolling recruitment, as many prisoners may not be available at the community meeting (e.g., for employment, medical, or legal reasons) but choose to participate later, after hearing positive peer perceptions. The easiest way to execute this is by using the "point person" method, where a designated member of the interview team remains available to interact with prisoners while other interviewers are conducting face-to-face surveys.

Upon first meeting the respondent, interviewers should dedicate a few minutes to introducing themselves, completing the informed consent process, and talking further about the study. This is an important moment, as many prisoners are unsure of whether they truly wish to participate until they personally meet with interviewers and learn more about the project. PINS researchers found it effective for interviewers to respond to prisoners' questions by framing the study in a way that appeals to their sense of dignity and authority. For example, it can be helpful to present the project as an opportunity for prisoners to teach researchers about the incarceration experience, signaling that the research team *values their perspective* and *needs their help* in order to understand prison life. Many prisoners responded well to this approach.

*Interacting with Prison Staff*: One of the most significant challenges for collecting network data in the prison environment is learning how to effectively interact with correctional staff. Depending on the culture of the institution and broader correctional organization, this can be the most difficult aspect of data collection. PINS was conducted in a state with a long commitment to evidence-based research and a department of corrections research office staffed by a PhD in Criminology. This increased the likelihood of gaining access and administrative support but did not guarantee that line officers unreservedly supported the project. The essential problem is that while the cooperation of correctional staff is absolutely critical for successfully interviewing a large number of prisoners in a brief period of time, staff members invariably experience this process as inconvenient and disruptive. As a result, interviewers should be prepared for the likelihood that prison staff will be initially resistant to the process and somewhat unresponsive to requests for assistance. In the interest of establishing rapport with correctional staff, it may help to consider their position. For example, many staff members adopt a posture of steady indifference to requests for assistance as a means of managing prisoner claims on their time. By design, prisoners have extremely limited autonomy and are forced to rely on prison staff to accomplish everyday tasks. Because a small number of correctional staff oversee a very large number of prisoners, it is simply not practical for staff members to present themselves as highly responsive to the demands of other people. Unfortunately, this professional orientation is incompatible with the logistical requirements of data collection, and interviewers may soon find themselves in the same position as many prisoners—repeatedly asking for assistance from prison staff who appear reluctant to help. Incidentally, this situation may promote rapport between interviewers and prisoners, as incarcerated individuals are likely to witness the research team's dependence on correctional staff who are resistant to help. For example, it was evident that PINS interviewers had no authority in the prison setting and were regularly ignored by correctional staff, which occasionally prompted sympathetic gestures from prisoners.[8]

There is no getting around the institutional burden of prisoner data collection, particularly when the goal is to interview as many unit residents as possible. Fortunately, there are both interpersonal and logistical strategies for mitigating this burden. It is important for interviewers to be courteous and respectful to prison staff at all times. In addition, interviewers should take pains to avoid exchanges that might be perceived as somehow challenging the staff members' authority or "ordering" them to do something. This is particularly important for interacting with correctional officers in the presence of prisoners. There are few things that will harm a network project more than interviewers who take an imperious attitude toward prison staff.

It is also recommended that interviewers be prepared to succinctly discuss the purpose of the research project with correctional staff, as they are sometimes sensitive to the possibility that researchers will use the study to make them look bad or negatively evaluate their job performance. During this discussion, interviewers should also be prepared for staff members to respond by sharing their own perspective on the research topic, often framed as providing a definitive "answer" to the stated research question. When this did occur, PINS interviewers took an interest in this response and treated it as an opportunity to inform data collection, rather than an opportunity to debate or educate correctional officers. Finally, it is likely that interviewers will be required to interact with a rotating cast of staff members over the course of data collection. Interviewers should be proactive about introducing themselves to "new" staff members and offering a brief explanation of the project.

*Efficiency and Logistics*: The logistics of data collection can also be structured to reduce staff burden. A fundamental principle for prison network data collection is that the level of staff involvement in the process is negatively associated with the efficiency and speed of data collection. Too much interaction or cooperation between researchers and staff also runs the risk of raising suspicions among prisoners. Researchers should thus do their best to design the process so that interviewers are responsible for as many tasks as possible to limit the study's impact on daily operations. By shouldering as much of the work as they can, interviewers minimize the degree of effort that correctional staff must devote to the project, which directly reduces staff burden. For example, PINS researchers initially relied on staff to channel respondents to interviewers. However, the PINS team later shifted this responsibility to a dedicated researcher who independently carried out this task. Some researcher independence also has the benefit of further distancing the research team from the prison administration and alleviating prisoner concerns of non-neutrality.

A central issue for efficient prison data collection is maintaining a constant supply of respondents. Because of scheduled mealtimes and routine "counts" of the prison population, PINS interviewers were only permitted around six hours of guaranteed interview time per day, though this required spending a full 8–9 hours inside the facility. Because intermittent periods of inactivity are imposed by the institution, under ideal conditions an interviewer would finish with one respondent and immediately begin survey administration to a new respondent. Minimizing the total time spent inside the institution reduces the absolute burden of data collection for interviewers and correctional staff alike. Though it is often not possible to meet this standard, it is nevertheless problematic if interviewers must wait for more than a few minutes between interviews. In the authors' experience, the most efficient process is to have the interview team stationed in the same building as the respondents, with one team member in charge of funneling respondents to the other interviewers. For the PINS project, this meant putting three or four interviewers in office rooms on the housing unit, with a designated "point person" positioned on the unit itself. Using this system, interviewers focus exclusively on survey administration, while the point person casually interacts with prisoners and develops a steady queue of respondents who are available to take the survey.

Alternatively, researchers can coordinate with prison staff to schedule interviews for each prisoner using the institution's formal "call-out" system. This involves providing correctional staff with a list of respondents (or prospective respondents), who will then officially schedule prisoners to meet with interviewers at specific times throughout the day. The authors have occasionally been forced to rely on this system while collecting data at different prisons, and it is not optimal. Its main disadvantage is that it forces correctional staff to be heavily involved with the data collection process, which is undesirable for many reasons. For example, the call-out system only works if it is enforced by prison staff. However, staff members are often preoccupied with other tasks, and are also generally unconcerned with how quickly interviewers are able to administer surveys. Moreover, many staff members work on shifts that rotate throughout the day, so there is limited continuity in the composition of personnel responsible for assisting with data collection. As a result, the call-out system tends to be unpredictable and inefficient, often resulting in unnecessary stretches of inactivity between interviews.

## Linking In-Prison Research to Reentry Studies

Finally, the authors wish to underscore the link between in-prison work and reentry studies. Studies of prison reentry commonly begin with a short pre-release interview or an initial interview just after release. They do not often include sustained interactions with respondents while they are incarcerated and typically sample only on those who are soon to be released. Greater investment in reentering prisoners long before they are released would address many of the difficulties encountered by those focused on reentry. Most notably, reentry studies are notorious for high attrition rates (for a discussion of this issue, see Western et al. 2016). In R-PINS, however, interviewers had established rapport with respondents long before the reentry study began. The R-PINS participants had all participated in the PINS study months before their release and none of them experienced negative consequences as a result of their participation. The post-release R-PINS interviews also provided the first opportunity for respondent financial incentives ($25 per community interview), as PADOC does not allow such incentives for currently incarcerated individuals. The PINS team was able to foreshadow these funds during the prison surveys. Rapport and future rewards thus facilitated continued respondent involvement through the volatile reentry process, resulting in a 72% R-PINS response rate over the pre-release and first post-release interviews, with the second post-release interview process remaining ongoing at the time of this writing.

## Conclusion

The obstacles to prison-based research are many and varied, including challenges that precede prison entry (e.g., IRB and prison administrator approval) and follow data collection procedures (e.g., managing interviewer and prisoner emotions: Jewkes and Wright 2016). This chapter focused on the practical considerations, decisions, and recommendations directly relevant for collecting network data in prison and from prisoners upon prison release. Collecting prison network data has similarities with the surveys, ethnographies, and participant observations of prior penal research, and this chapter covers much of the same ground as has been done in past methods chapters. However, there are also unique features of a network design that require forethought to ensure valid results within prison and post-prison contexts. This chapter detailed those in the hopes of providing a road map for future investigations.

The team-based prison data collection presented in this chapter differs substantially from the ethnographies and participant observations common to past carceral research. Specifically, the above approach seeks to build prisoner and staff trust to maximize participation over a relatively short period of time (e.g., 1–3 weeks inside of the institution). This is a distinctly different task than the sole ethnographer who "holds the keys" to the institution and embeds herself within prisoner society (see Crewe 2009 for an excellent exposition of this method). The PINS team was unable to cross over the "outsider" veil and observe the intimate details of daily prison life, nor was this the primary goal of the study. Rather, it sought to connect with as many prisoners as possible over a relatively short time to achieve an aggregate view of the unit's structure and culture. The limitations of the method are the absence of richly detailed accounts of prison's pains and adaptations found in most prison ethnographies, but the benefits are the inclusive and overhead view of the prison social system that may be easily compared to other similar studies.

In conclusion, network studies hold promise for illuminating the social worlds of prisons and previously incarcerated individuals (Kreager et al. 2016). PINS and R-PINS demonstrate the feasibility, efficiency, and comprehensiveness of prison network designs. Moreover, network studies provide results that are simultaneously easy to summarize for criminal justice policymakers and capable of testing long-standing hypotheses using sophisticated network methods. It remains to be seen if future studies can utilize and extend the above methods and build a repository of prison and ex-prisoner network datasets, but the potential for such efforts to inform the prisoner experience in the era of mass incarceration is difficult to ignore.

ACKNOWLEDGMENTS

This research was supported by grants from the National Science Foundation (1457193), National Institutes of Health (NIAAA1R211AA023210), National Institute of Justice (2016-MUMU-0011), and PSU Justice Center for Research. The content is solely the responsibility of the authors and does not necessarily represent the official views of these organizations.

NOTES

1 Interested readers should seek out comprehensive overviews of network theory and research methods (Borgatti et al. 2013; Kadushin 2012; Robins 2015). Readers should also consider the broader ethical and practical challenges associated with prison research (Bosworth et al. 2005; Schlosser 2008; Warr 2017).

2 Prior to the PINS data collection, small-scale pilot studies were conducted in a prison work unit (N=21) and therapeutic community (N=20) (Kreager et al. 2016; 2018). The pilot studies were valuable in demonstrating feasibility and testing many of the discussed survey items and procedures.

3 The Pennsylvania Department of Corrections allowed computers to enter prisons permitted they were wi-fi disabled.

4 Researchers conducting interviews both in prison and after release should be sensitive to how time constraints shift during reentry. R-PINS interviewers were able to conduct relatively long in-prison interviews, with most interviews lasting around two hours. Community interviews needed to be much shorter, as many respondents were unwilling to dedicate more than an hour to the interview.

5 Limiting the number of nominations during the name-generator stage will prevent researchers from analyzing variation in egocentric network size, which may be important for certain research questions.

6 A limitation of the closed-ended approach is that prisoners occasionally go by prison nicknames that will not appear on the nomination roster. PINS researchers devised two strategies for dealing with this issue. The first is to include multiple pieces of information for each prisoner on the nomination roster, including each prisoner's first name, last name, inmate number, and cell number. The second strategy is to include open-ended response options that allow respondents to offer a description of their nominee so that researchers can attempt to identify the nominee after survey administration.

7 Gender dynamics may shift for research conducted in female prisons. PINS researchers recently replicated their study in a women's prison and did not find that female prisoners were equally eager to speak with male interviewers. Due to the frequent history of male-perpetrated victimization in this population, the initial IRB review attempted to prohibit male interviewers from participating in this study. However, PINS researchers resisted this constraint, and female respondents appeared comfortable interacting with experienced male interviewers.

8 To be clear, this is a general observation that does not apply to all correctional staff members. PINS researchers have occasionally encountered staff who were consistently responsive and helpful from day one, and most correctional staff do seem to become progressively more accommodating over the course of data collection. However unlikely, it is nevertheless important for researchers to avoid fraternizing with correctional staff, as this will be noticed by prisoners and may raise suspicions.

# 5

## Interviewing the "Rabble Class"

*Recruitment and Retention in Studies of Prisoner Reentry*

ANDREA LEVERENTZ

I first met Pablo, a Latino man in his fifties, when he was incarcerated on drug possession and assault with a dangerous weapon charges. He had a criminal history dating back twenty-five years, with charges mostly related to a long-standing drug addiction. He explained what happened that led to his most recent incarceration.

> Last time I was here, I was homeless . . . I was living at St. Francis, Long Island, Pine Street [shelters], so umm, you know, you can't use drugs inside those places. So I used to, I would go to, I would go to garages, I would go to restaurants, bathrooms, and I started getting picked up in them places. I started getting stopped coming out, and searched, and I got busted with paraphernalia and drugs and they put me on a year suspended at the BMC [Boston Municipal Court] court . . . I got out of jail and went back to that old lifestyle! That insanity. Thinking it was going to be different. Doing the same things expecting something different. And I got picked up at a garage in Chinatown. Same thing . . . I had about three bags of dope, four bags of crack, and two bags of marijuana on me . . . And umm, I got lucky and I got, I got six months, with a year concurrent, six months concurrent. Something like that.

Pablo was one of a hundred men and women that I, and a team of research assistants, interviewed at the Suffolk County (Massachusetts) House of Correction in the hopes of following them into the community after their release. After Pablo's release, he once again expected to be homeless. He could stay with his father, but he too struggled with drug addiction, and Pablo said, "So I'm thinking of more like a dry shelter. Out in Long Island.[1] 'Cause you know, my sponsor, and everybody that's been helping me with my recovery issues says, 'you've got to be in a safe place your first week out.' You can't be around drugs and alcohol or you have people that's doing them, because it will lead me back into that spiral." After his release, the only way I could reach Pablo was to mail letters to a day shelter that people could use for mail delivery and wait for him to call me from their phone. When he was first released, he alternated his time between the Long Island shelter and staying on the street. Usually, I sent multiple letters before getting a response. Once, a research assistant went to meet him for our arranged interview, to explain that my flight back to Boston was postponed because of a snowstorm and so I couldn't be there; I had no other way to reach him that day.

In spite of the challenges in contacting him, I interviewed him twice in the community and twice in the House of Correction. In our third interview, when he was once again at the House of Correction, he described the intervening months.

> Pablo (T3): Within seven days I'm using, I'm drinking. I'm putting needles in my arms and smoking crack. Soon after that I stopped reporting to probation. I picked up two new charges. Shoplifting and disorderly out of Macy's. Now I'm on the run again. I'm doing all these shoplifting trying to make the outside [i.e., his outward appearance] look good. Like an apple, you see a shiny apple but it got a worm in it. On the inside I was no good. This is why I started hiding from everybody that was trying to help me. You, family, and friends. I was just hiding. I would only come out at night. If I was out in the day, I'm hiding from everybody. I was getting your letters. I was like, wow, I've got to call her as soon as I go to detox. I never made it to detox.

In total, I interviewed Pablo four times. There was a year between our second and third interviews, and our fourth interview was a few months later, shortly before Christmas and shortly after his latest release. While still in custody, he had major surgery and spent time recovering in a secure section of the hospital. After his release he spent a few nights at a halfway house, and then moved in with a girlfriend. He said, "women have that effect on men sometimes." This woman "been drinking. She been using." He went on to say,

> I have drank. I ain't been using, though. No coke and no weed. You know that's just a "yet" with all the New Year's coming up. That's why I saw this is not going to work in the end. I'm not the first man that just jumped. That is something we all do for love. I think it's part of our weakness. It's something in our chromosomes or something. Women have that effect on us.

While Pablo said he moved in with her because of love, he also did not have many options for living arrangements. He regretted leaving the halfway house, but he also bristled at its rules. The director tried to reach out, but Pablo "avoided him, 'cause right now, the guilt, shame." Similarly, he was avoiding the director of the day shelter, "I could [talk to him], but he would make me go to detox." In spite of multiple attempts to reach him over the next ten months, I did not reach Pablo for a fifth interview.

Pablo's experience was not unusual among this group of releasees. As with most incarcerated populations, many of our respondents faced significant challenges and instability upon their release. Many of the people held at the House of Correction met John Irwin's definition of the rabble class. Irwin argued:

> Jail prisoners share two essential characteristics: detachment and disrepute. They are detached because they are not well integrated into conventional society, they are not members of conventional social organizations, they have few ties to conventional social networks, and they are carriers of unconventional values and beliefs. They are disreputable because they are perceived as irksome, offensive, threatening, capable of arousal, even protorevolutionary. (Irwin 1985, p. 2)

These same characteristics that made them vulnerable to arrest and incarceration also made them difficult to stay in contact with. They were arrested for minor offenses, often related to drug addiction and poverty. While some were fairly stable upon their release, many were unstably housed, struggling with addiction, and otherwise dealing with the challenges of being recently released from prison. Interviewing them took persistence and creativity, in addition to the rapport and trust necessary for any interview-based study. In this chapter, I detail the process of recruiting, interviewing, and maintaining contact with a returning prisoner population. It is focused less on the substantive findings, but rather on the methods used and the lessons learned. I illustrate the challenges of conducting research both in a correctional facility and among a returning prisoner population, while being an outsider to both, and provide some insight into how to manage these challenges. Where possible, I draw on interview transcripts, field notes, and official criminal records to document the data collection process and to illustrate these complications and the dynamics shaping the interview process.

Motivating Questions

The goal of this project was to understand the neighborhood context of prisoner reentry.[2] There has been some research demonstrating that returning to disadvantaged neighborhoods increases the likelihood of reoffending, for at least some types of charges (Kubrin and Stewart 2006; Mears et al. 2008). Moving to a new neighborhood can make reoffending or reconviction less likely, particularly when one moves to a new city or county (Kirk 2009, 2012; Sharkey and Sampson 2010). Still, while this may be beneficial, it is difficult to achieve, with most returning prisoners going back to similarly disadvantaged neighborhoods and many relying on family and partner connections to secure stable housing (Herbert, Morenoff, and Harding 2015; La Vigne, Visher, and Castro 2004; Massoglia, Firebaugh, and Warner 2013). In addition, statistical findings fail to take into account emotional and relational connections to places that may make a "bad" neighborhood desirable or preferable because of its familiarity (Leverentz 2010), and which also may make it easier to navigate potentially violent or dangerous situations (Clampet-Lundquist et al. 2011; Harding 2010; Sharkey 2006). Neighborhoods also may be more or less welcoming to people returning from prison (Browning 2009; Leverentz 2012; Pattillo-McCoy 1999).

A second focus was to look at reentry from a county-level facility. Much of our research and policy attention has been on the impact of long sentences and state prison incarceration. While this remains an important focus, there is also growing attention to the importance of jails and shorter periods of detention and incarceration (Apel 2016; Comfort 2016; Subramanian et al. 2015; see also Turney, and Huebner and McGuirk, in this volume). In Massachusetts, county-level incarceration includes a majority of those sentenced to serve time in the state, and county-level facilities hold people sentenced to serve 2.5 years or less per charge.[3] This is in contrast with most states, in which county-level sentences are limited to a year (Subramanian et al. 2015). Key differences from state prisons include both the relatively short sentence length and the placement in the counties from which the prisoners were drawn, which could potentially make it easier to maintain ties with loved ones through less expensive and time-consuming visits.[4]

To address the complexities of the influences of neighborhood context and residential change, I drew on a multipronged data collection strategy. First, the research team (me and several graduate student research assistants) recruited and interviewed men and women being released from a county House of Correction. The goal was to interview people five times—once pre-release and four times post-release—over the course of about a year, to understand their process of reentry, including where they lived, when they moved, and why, among other aspects of their lives and relationships. Interviews were semi-structured, following an interview guide that included some questions that were asked in each interview, and some that were asked in only one. This allowed us to ask new questions as themes and topics emerged in early interviews. In addition, we collected official criminal histories on these men and women, as one measure of their pre- and post-release criminal justice system involvement, and basic information on all people released from that facility during our recruitment, in an attempt to understand how representative our interview sample was of the facility population. These additional data sources also provided important context to understand why we may have lost contact with some participants.

### Research Design, Access, and Recruitment of Men and Women

The target date for the initial interviews was a week or two before release, and for the first post-release interview it was two to four weeks after release. The timing of these interviews was intended to capture the acute experience of being released from prison. During the first interview, the release would feel concrete and imminent, and presumably the participants would have a plan in the days leading up to it. We then gave them time to get settled after their release but would try to talk to them again when their release was a fresh memory. Following these two interviews, we aimed to interview them every three to four months, to capture roughly their first year post-release. This is a period of significant transition and is often a key time marker in studies of recidivism (Durose, Cooper, and Snyder 2014). While this is still a modest time period for a longitudinal study, it does cover the immediate post-release period and often includes significant changes in respondents' lives. The goal was for each member of the team of interviewers to maintain their own interview load, so that the same person would interview a person each time. This was meant to maximize rapport, as the interviewer and interviewee would develop a relationship over time.

Data collection often deviates from the plan, and this project was no exception. In part, we were limited by institutional constraints. When I originally applied for a grant, I discussed the project with the administrative staff at the House of Correction and received a letter of support from the then superintendent of the facility. In the nearly nine months between grant submission and the start of the award, several key members of administration, including the superintendent, had changed. While the new superintendent ultimately honored his predecessor's agreement, thanks in large part to the advocacy of another staff member, this was only after initial resistance and several conversations. This need to negotiate access in an ongoing way exists for all qualitative projects, particularly when relying on institutional access for an extended period of time.[5]

Although we needed the superintendent's approval to gain access, we also needed the support of the line staff who provided information and access on an ongoing basis. This also meant negotiation with multiple staff members of the institution, particularly a few people with key points of access. At the start, the research team met with case management staff of the facility, to introduce the study, explain the goals, and answer any questions. They knew projected release dates, gave us the information on who to interview when, and provided access. Administrative staff members gave us the permission we needed to enter the facility, and to bring in interview materials (including digital recorders). In addition, the security staff at the entrance could make the entry process easier or harder, faster or slower. Over time, we developed relationships with key case management staff and the security staff at the entrance, and became familiar faces at the institution, easing our entry and recruitment.

The recruitment process for men and women differed, because of the nature of the institution. To recruit men, we created fliers, which were posted in the men's housing units. Interested men could sign up, and their information was passed along to the research team by case management staff. We followed similar visitation rules as other professional visitors (e.g., lawyers). We kept most of our belongings in lockers in the lobby, and followed their dress code rules (e.g., no jeans, no open-toed shoes, no revealing clothes). When we got word that there were interested men, a researcher went to the facility. During our first trip there, we met with men one by one in a classroom, with a case manager nearby. After that, in most cases, we met individually with men in the lawyer visiting rooms.[6] Usually one, and occasionally two, researchers went each time, to minimize our occupation of their limited private spaces. All interviews were conducted one-on-one (one researcher and the interviewee). Initially, we had to be escorted by a case manager to this area, but beginning about six months into our recruitment period, we were able to go up to these rooms unaccompanied.[7] Occasionally, there was an issue with missing paperwork to allow us to bring in a digital recorder, but this was usually resolved quickly with a phone call and was a less common problem as they became more familiar with us and what we were doing. We would then give our list of names to the security staff in that area, they would put us in an unoccupied room, and they would call the men down one by one. The room was private, with a window in the door, through which an officer would occasionally peer in, especially if the interview was lengthy. We explained the study, went through the informed consent process,[8] and then started the interview. Initially, we had blocks of about two hours in which we could meet with men, in between counts and shift changes. Over time, staff often let us stay longer without interruption.

Typically, we were told by a primary contact when interested men were about to be released. In several cases, individual case managers reached out directly at the request of a man interested in participating, who had yet to be visited for an interview. I would then call our contact to try to gain access. In one case, I was called in to interview a man the day before his release. When I met with him, I asked him if he had just learned of the study, and he said, "No, I knew about it. I've known about it for about a month and I've been asking them what's going on." In these cases, the men were persistent in making their interest known. Because of our necessarily passive recruitment of men, it is impossible to know if we missed other interested men because we never got their names. It is also unclear what caused these delays or miscommunications, beyond the bureaucratic complications of calculating release dates, with Good Time and other adjustments.

Women are housed on the top three floors of a tower building. Since the female population is much smaller, we were able to go in every few weeks and talk to many of the women who were scheduled to be released soon.[9] We explained the study and invited their participation. This conversation happened either in a common area or a classroom, and sometimes a staff member was present for part of this conversation. For the women who expressed interest, the researcher met with them individually in a private classroom to explain the informed consent and conduct the interviews. A majority, but not all, of the women we talked to consented to be interviewed. As a result, we interviewed a larger percentage of women, given their proportion of the institutional population, than we did men. While 11% of the total release population was women, our sample was 39% women. This fulfilled a project goal of oversampling women, so that we could engage in a more meaningful analysis of gendered experiences, even with a small overall sample.

It took seventeen months to interview our target of one hundred people, among just over two thousand people released during this time period. In spite of the differences in recruitment between men and women, we had a fairly diverse sample that largely reflected the demographics of the institution, with a few notable exceptions. First, our interview sample included few Latinx or Hispanic people, especially women.[10] While 22% of the total release population was Latinx/Hispanic, only 12% of our interview sample was. Only 3% of the women

TABLE 5.1. Recruitment: All Interview Respondents and House of Corrections Releases during the Same Time Period

|  | Men (N = 61) |  | Women (N = 39) |  | Total (N = 100) |  |
| --- | --- | --- | --- | --- | --- | --- |
|  | Sample | HOC | Sample | HOC | Sample | HOC |
| White | 38% | 30% | 72% | 62% | 52% | 34% |
| Black | 44% | 45% | 26% | 26% | 36% | 43% |
| Latinx/Hispanic | 18% | 24% | 3% | 11% | 12% | 22% |
| Asian/Pacific Islander | 0% | 1% | 0% | 1% | 0% | 1.3% |
| Age (years) | 37.7 | 34.4 | 36.5 | 34.1 | 37.2 | 34.3 |
| Time served (months) | 6.3 | 6.2 | 3.9 | 3.5 | 5.4 | 5.9 |

we interviewed were Latina, compared to 11% of the female release population. Table 5.1 summarizes some details of both our interview sample and the total facility release population (i.e., the people who were released during our recruitment period). In addition, on average, our interview sample was 2–3 years older than the release population.

Our goals were sometimes at odds with institutional goals. For example, the institution wanted us in and out as quickly as possible. We often had 1.5 to 2-hour windows to interview people. The first time I went to interview women, the case manager suggested that the women might talk more than men, and so I might only interview one person that day. She suggested I could "push through them faster" to get through more interviews per time block; she also praised research assistants who finished interviews faster. I did not follow this advice, and strongly discouraged research assistants from doing so, as I saw it as a sign of a lower quality and less in-depth interview. The staff wanted us to be efficient and to minimize disruption to them and the institution. My goals as an interviewer were not only to learn more about the participants, but also to use the first interview to make a connection with the person, to establish rapport and increase the chances the person would talk to us again. From an interviewing perspective, "pushing through" was a bad strategy. This did, however, make us more dependent on the cooperation of staff, for a longer period of time. Over time, we did gain some more freedom to stay longer and move somewhat more freely, which also lessened some of the burden on staff.

## Repeated Reentry Interviews

In some ways, interviewing currently incarcerated people is easy once access to the institution is negotiated. Talking to researchers can be a diversion for incarcerated people, and meeting with respondents in private lawyer rooms minimized, but did not eliminate, our association with staff. In addition, prisoners' movements are tightly controlled, and knowing where they were and when they would have time is relatively easy. Once people are released, it becomes much more challenging to keep track of them. Interviewing people repeatedly becomes that much more difficult, as we have to maintain contact with an often unstable population who are dealing with competing demands on their time and attention. For all interviewers, the transition from the House of Correction to the street was the most common time to lose touch with a participant. It also was often not possible to know exactly why someone was unreachable or did not respond to messages. No one explicitly declined to participate in future interviews. Still, we have some evidence to suggest contributing factors to retention. While we did not maintain a perfect record of retention among our participants, we did maintain contact with people with a range of post-incarceration experiences.

In the next section, I detail some of the goals and challenges of interviewing people post-release.

### *Maintaining Contact*

People exiting prisons and jails often experience periods of homelessness, extreme instability, and poverty, all of which can make keeping in touch difficult. Those with a history of addiction face additional challenges and may drop out of contact even with loved ones if actively using drugs. If researchers only maintain contact with the most stable and connected, this skews their findings in important ways. Thus, not only is maximizing retention important, so is understanding, to the extent possible, the reasons that contact is maintained or lost with participants. In this section, I discuss some of the challenges to retention, and the strategies we incorporated to mitigate lost contact. In doing so, I draw on three sources of data. The primary data are interviews, including our

TABLE 5.2. Retention

|  | Pre-release only N = 36 |  | 4–5 interviews N = 39 |  | Total N = 100 |  |
|---|---|---|---|---|---|---|
|  | Men (21) | Women (15) | Men (25) | Women (14) | Men (61) | Women (39) |
| White | 43% | 73% | 32% | 64% | 38% | 75% |
| Black | 29% | 27% | 60% | 36% | 44% | 22% |
| Latinx/Hispanic | 29% | 0% | 8% | 0% | 18% | 3% |
| Age (years) | 34.9 | 35.9 | 40.2 | 38.1 | 37.7 | 36.5 |
| Time served (months) | 6.1 | 3.1 | 6.7 | 4.5 | 6.3 | 3.9 |
| Average length of follow-up |  |  | 14.5 months (9–28 months) |  |  |  |

field notes from those interviews and notes on scheduling attempts. In addition, we have official criminal record data for most participants and basic information on everyone who was released from the House of Correction during our recruitment period.[11] These additional sources of data provide a more complete picture, and sometimes offer additional information on people we lost track of post-release.

From the start, we expected maintaining contact with people would be a challenge, and we built in several strategies to the research design to improve retention. One simple strategy was to originally recruit a fairly large sample for an interview project of this kind. We interviewed one hundred people pre-release, knowing that some would be lost at release and over time. We had sixty-four people in our reentry (post-release) sample, which is still sizeable for a repeated interview study. We also adopted several strategies to maximize retention. For the most part, these strategies parallel other studies of this kind (Harding et al. 2016; Leverentz 2014; Western et al. 2015). For example, we paid respondents for their time.[12] At the pre-release interview, we told them we would give them money for the first and second interviews at the time of the second interview.[13] This served multiple purposes: it simplified the payment to incarcerated individuals. It also was an added incentive to encourage people to conduct a time 2 interview. There are many more competing forces on people's time, energy, and attention once they are released, but it is also a time that most were particularly in need of money. When we interviewed someone who was reincarcerated, we offered to put money for that interview on their books.[14] In a few cases, the person requested that we save it and give it to him or her at the next post-release interview because the money would be more useful then. For example, when I said I would leave a money order on Daniel's books, he said, "I don't care about the $30, man. How about this, I was going to say, you can hold that. And then you just give it to me when I see you."

Another common, and useful, strategy was to gather as many forms of contact as possible. In all cases, we gave participants a copy of the consent form with my name and office phone. Each interviewer also provided a cell phone or Google number at which they could be reached directly.[15] We encouraged participants to contact us when they were released. Some did, but most relied on us being able to reach them. Contacts we gathered included personal phone numbers and addresses, where possible, and the addresses and phone numbers of people who were likely to know where they were, like parents or siblings, current and former romantic partners, and friends. Occasionally, an interviewee had no contact information, either because they did not have any contacts to offer or they did not know a phone number by memory. At each subsequent interview, we again asked for updates on their contact information. We would discuss the best ways to reach them, make sure they were still on good terms with the people whose names they had given us, and that their information was still accurate. Each time, we would take down as much information as they would give us. When we called these numbers, we would explain that the participants had given us their number as a way to reach them. Usually this was sufficient and in many cases, these contacts were used to serving this role for the participants. The most detail that we would provide is that the person was participating in a research project. We only contacted those who the participant had given us explicit permission to contact and we would not mention the participant's recent incarceration (though in most if not all cases, their contacts knew this already).

Associated contacts were incredibly helpful. In addition to potentially reaching our participants, we often learned important things from these attempts. We sometimes learned when someone had started using drugs again or had been arrested. Often loved ones told us this information, in addition to passing along messages or giving us updated phone numbers. Sometimes there was clear tension when we asked for someone.

Over time, many of these people came to know us, and we met some in person during the course of interviews. Still, not everyone had family or loved ones who reliably knew where they were. Many had strained relationships with family, and romantic relationships sometimes ended quickly and badly. Even some of those that wanted to be in touch were dependent on the person contacting them, and often went months without contact, particularly if they were using drugs.

At the beginning of the study, we had no plans to use social media to maintain contact with people. In the course of interviews, many talked about using Facebook to keep in touch with people. Several respondents attempted to connect with me on my personal Facebook account. I then established a separate Facebook account, with higher privacy levels (e.g., "friends" couldn't see "friends" unless they were also connected, minimizing the likelihood of one's identity as a research participant being revealed). In addition, through this account, I reached out to others I could find on Facebook via private message. As Sharpe (2017) thoughtfully details, Facebook can be both a fruitful strategy and an ethically problematic one. Sending a Facebook message is easy and fast, but looking at even publicly available information can feel like an invasion of privacy and it may create an additional opportunity for a breach of confidentiality. In most cases, this led to brief exchanges with people I was still in contact with. In one case, a person I thought I had lost touch with responded to a message, and we resumed interviews. I first interviewed her once shortly after her release. Then, the phone number I had for her went out of service, and her mom said she did not know where she was. Letters I sent to her aunt, where she had been living, went unanswered. Sixteen months after our second interview, I sent her a Facebook message, to which she responded several months later. After we reconnected, we finished the remaining interviews. I learned that during the year and half we were out of touch she violated her probation and spent some of that time incarcerated.

When we interviewed people in the community, these interviews took place in a variety of locations. One key factor is that we met our participants where they preferred to meet, and never asked them to come to us. This was partly for their convenience. While most of our participants lived in the Boston area, several lived up to 90 miles outside of Boston. Even among those who lived in the metro region, few had access to a car and public transit could be time-consuming, expensive, and inconvenient. In addition, meeting them centered their comfort and avoided the power dynamic of having them meet us in our university offices.

I usually offered to go to the person's house as one option.[16] This was often easiest for the person being interviewed and had the added benefit of giving me additional information on their lives. I met family members and friends, saw relationship dynamics play out, and I saw where and how they were living. This included seemingly stable family homes, rooms rented in apartments, and apartments that looked from the outside like they were in abandoned buildings. Others preferred to meet in public places. Interviews in public took place in coffee shops, libraries, and parks. I encouraged the participants to choose a location; again, it was important for them to be in spaces in which they felt comfortable. If they did not have ideas, I usually suggested a nearby public library branch. In these locations, we tried to find semi-private spaces to talk (community rooms in libraries, quieter corners in coffee shops or restaurants). In cafes and restaurants, I offered to buy the participant coffee or food. Here too, the dynamics of the interviews and being in certain spaces provided additional information beyond the interviews themselves. For example, we saw how participants engaged with friends, loved ones, and strangers in public, and also how people responded to them (see, for example, Duneier 2000; Stuart 2016 for two descriptions of similar dynamics). In some instances, we sometimes met people in public and sometimes at their house, depending on their schedules and their current living circumstances. I explained to research assistants my rationale for offering to meet at people's houses, but also encouraged them to meet where they felt comfortable and to leave situations if they ever felt uncomfortable. They typically met with people in public. All interviews were one-on-one.[17]

Participant Motivation

As with previous studies of this kind, some respondents said that they initially chose to participate because of the money (Leverentz 2014). Pablo said, "to be honest, I might need your help financially, so I'm going to definitely get in touch with you." When I asked Kevin, a white man in his twenties, why he decided to talk to me, he said, "First, it was the promise of $60 when I was getting out of jail. Last time when I called you, you pulled a solid by meeting with me and keeping your end of the bargain last time. I figured I'd call you this time and keep my end of the bargain and stay in touch. Today, the fact that I got no job and all that, and money is going to be dwindling soon, an extra $30 can't help. Can't hurt, rather." Others deemphasized that reason and expressed surprise when the cash was offered (though all took the money). Even those who were incentivized by the money often talked about their enjoyment of the process. In most cases, a financial incentive can help persuade someone to participate initially and it is welcomed, but this alone is unlikely to be enough to maintain their involvement over time if the experience is not enjoyable or beneficial.

One key motivation for many participants' continued participation was the ability to talk about their lives and experiences with a nonjudgmental audience (Weiss 1994). For this to be effective, we needed to be perceived as approachable and easy to talk to (Mayorga-Gallo and Hordge-Freeman 2017). Perhaps not coincidentally, people commonly said that the most important thing they wanted someone to know about them was that they are "a good person" and have "a good heart." We needed to create an environment in which they felt like that could come through. Many referred to the interviews as therapeutic. Charles, a black man in his twenties, said he chose to participate to "Get it off my chest. Ever since I sat in jail, I really don't talk to nobody from jail. But somebody just told me in there that I knew that I grew up with, just like, 'Go talk to her. You look like you just need to get it all off your chest.' . . . He was actually the one that told me to talk to you." Often, this is not something that gets them to agree to participate, as it is not a formal incentive and they had not yet experienced it as such, but it did encourage ongoing involvement. Stephen, a black man in his twenties, explained his interest, "The first thing that got my mind to get involved with it was the money, when I seen that they was paying money . . . but then people saying, talking about like, you can go there and it's like, say for instance, you can go there and just figure out who you are. That's what they were saying." Often the money was an initial draw, and a place to talk about their experiences was crucial for someone to keep participating. For example, Lena, a white woman in her fifties, said, "When I talk to you, saying it out loud, kind of helps me go after a goal. Okay, now I just talked to her and now I can do this. It's something that I can work on. I do appreciate you listening." Sometimes the structure of the interview alone was helpful to people. Kevin started our final interview by saying "I'm on an evil, evil tear right now. Lots and lots of drugs." When I later asked why he kept talking with me, he said, "I don't know honestly. I felt good today that I had to be somewhere at a set time, made me feel like I had an agenda today instead of just running around and shoplift for people." Similarly, Kevin, and others, wanted to honor their commitments.

A few participants asked for copies of the interview transcripts, as a record of their lives. Barry, a black man in his fifties, said, "This was intense . . . I mean, if this is how it's going to go, I mean, I'm glad to participate in this. Keeps me fresh. Keeps prison up front, you know? If I could get a copy of that, I'd love to. You could send it to me?" George, a white man in his thirties, first asked for the interview guide, "There is a lot of questions that I've did stuff that you've asked me that I think about." When I offered to send the transcripts, he said, "That would be quite interesting, oh my god! Yeah, if you can send both. Wow, wow. That would be really interesting. I guess that could actually teach you what you want in life, huh? You could see the changes, and wow." While we typically did not offer transcripts, we sent them when requested.

## The Criminal Justice System

We intentionally did not work with probation or parole offices to track people. Conducting interviews in a prison or jail creates an inherent barrier to trust, as researchers will almost always be more closely aligned with the institution than the prisoners. In total institutions, such as prisons, there is a clear line between "staff" and "inmates" (Goffman 1961), and in most cases, researchers are going to be perceived as closer to staff than prisoners. While there are a few exceptions (Hassine 2010; Walker 2016), even self-identified "convict criminologists" (Richards and Ross 2001) and other researchers with past experience with the criminal justice system can choose whether to disclose this to research participants, and participants likely will not assume this experience. While we tried to minimize this as much as possible, some continued to associate us with the institution even after their release. For example, when interviewing Donna, a white woman in her fifties, a second time, she asked me if I was part of aftercare. In the third interview, she asked if I was a correctional officer. In both cases (as I had when we first met), I told her I was "just a researcher" and had no connection to the House of Correction. While Donna did seem forthcoming in our interviews, I also wondered if she tried to put a more positive spin on her current life because of this perceived connection. Even so, she told me about the drug use of her friends and family members and asked for advice on how to intervene in her daughter's drug use.[18]

Because of these inherent barriers, we wanted to avoid as much as possible an association with formal agents of control (e.g., probation or parole officers), and even more so when participants were in the community but could potentially be reincarcerated. Several people talked about their current or former times "on the run," in which they stopped going to court or reporting to probation officers (see Leverentz 2018). Typically, they were not actively sought during these periods, but were arrested when stopped by police. Alfredo, a Latino man in his forties, who had both new charges and a probation violation, was trying to delay a return to prison as long as possible.

> It could be any day. I could be driving with you down the street, you get pulled over and they ask me for my name, I have to give my name and two warrants are going to come out and I'm going to get arrested. It can happen to me every day. I'm living day by day right now. I try to avoid riding in cars. I pretty much stay to myself. If I was to turn myself in, I'll do it in the winter. I'm not trying to go back in the summer. At least finish the summer out here. That's my plans.

In addition to concerns about trust and control, only about half of our participants were on probation or parole after their release. While split sentences (some time incarcerated followed by a period of probation) were common among people incarcerated in the House of Correction, a number of our participants were serving out their probation sentences after a violation. This calls into question the added value of relying on probation or parole officers for information and also raises serious ethical concerns about the risks to participants in these cases (Sharpe 2017).

While we did not work with probation or parole officers, when we heard or suspected that someone might be detained or incarcerated, we did follow up on this where possible. Since the project was originally approved through the Suffolk County House of Correction, this was where we had the greatest access. When we learned someone was detained or incarcerated in Suffolk County, we tried to arrange to interview them there. In a few cases, we learned that someone was being held in a state Department of Correction prison facility. We applied for and received approval to interview several people in state prisons. In some cases, we suspected that someone was incarcerated in another county; we did not pursue these cases, as they would have necessitated establishing individual relationships and permission with each county, and often we had no more specific information than that an individual might be incarcerated *somewhere* that was not a state or Suffolk County facility.

Interviewer Effects

In qualitative research, the researchers are an important part of the data collection process. There is extensive debate among qualitative researchers about the value of being an insider or an outsider, and the complexities of these statuses (Horowitz 1986; May 2014; Mayorga-Gallo and Hordge-Freeman 2017; McCorkel and Myers 2003; Naples 1996; Twine and Warren 2000). On one dimension, incarceration status, we were clearly outsiders (McCorkel and Myers 2003). Over the course of the project, the research team included three white women, one black woman, and one white man. The two primary interviewers, who worked on the project the full time and conducted the majority of interviews, were both white women. One question that arises is the impact of the race and gender of the interviewer on recruitment and retention. Race- and gender-matching may improve recruitment and rapport-building through a presumed sense of closeness, though outsider status may also be useful in fostering an "acceptable incompetent" identity (Lofland and Lofland 1994). In addition, identities are multifaceted and, in part, enacted in the field. Given the nature of our recruitment strategies, the demographic and experiential diversity in the institution, and the available interviewers, matching participants and interviewers along race, gender, or age lines was impractical. As with other studies of diverse populations, it is also difficult to know which dimensions of sameness or difference will be most important in different interactions (Mayorga-Gallo and Hordge-Freeman 2017; Stuart 2016).

Men who participated did not know the race or gender of the interviewer until they had expressed interest and met with the interviewer. No men declined to participate once contacted by an interviewer. Women, on the other hand, first learned of the study through direct interaction with the interviewers, and so may have been influenced by the researcher's race (or other factors) when deciding whether to participate. These exchanges were brief and so provided little opportunity to overcome initial barriers to trust and rapport. When a woman declined to participate, we asked why she was not interested, but no woman who declined to participate offered reasons, and we did not systematically track the race or age of those who said no. I did wonder if there was greater suspicion on the part of black women who were contacted by a white interviewer. The nature of our recruitment and the racial politics of both a correctional institution and Boston made this seem plausible. Still, ethnographic work in women's prisons suggests that the salience of race for female prisoner organization is more subtle and complex and is shaped by characteristics of the institution (Kruttschnitt and Hussemann 2008; McCorkel and Myers 2003). The breakdown of our sample, at least in terms of black and white women and men, was fairly comparable to the total release population (see table 5.1). In addition, we were slightly more likely to lose contact with white participants than black participants (see table 5.2). White respondents were also more likely to have a history of drug or alcohol addiction, which shaped retention success.

Only female interviewers interviewed women. This was at the request of the institution, because of the common history of violence and trauma, often at the hands of men, among women prisoners (Chesney-Lind 2002; Leverentz 2014; Owen 1998). Since most members of the research team were women, women interviewed most of the men as well, though the one male interviewer initially interviewed a few. While this may have shaped what men said and how they talked, they did not seem inhibited talking with women. Occasionally a man was flirtatious with a female interviewer, but our social positionality and the interview context also made it easy to take on an acceptable incompetent role and enact non-sexual roles with the men (Mazzei and O'Brien 2008; Pini 2005;

Soyer 2014). That we were doing one-on-one interviews also shaped this dynamic, as there was less need for the men to publicly display masculinity or intimacy (Orrico 2015) and we could take on more therapeutic roles.

There were several barriers to the goal of maintaining interviewer continuity. All research assistants were first-year PhD students, with limited experience conducting research. While some research assistants came into the project with other research or interviewing skills, including in journalism, social work, and survey research, they had limited qualitative interviewing experience. Their earlier experiences did not necessarily translate into the context of semi-structured interviews, in which their goal was to foster a conversational interview that covered key topics, but they did so as naturalistically as possible (Weiss 1994). Interviewers were trained prior to beginning data collection, and the research team met biweekly to discuss the interview process and dynamics and retention efforts. While they also gained experience over time, the first interview was crucial to establishing rapport and an ongoing relationship, and their limited experience at the start likely impacted their ability to retain participants. As one piece of evidence supporting this, the first person the primary research assistant successfully interviewed five times was the seventeenth person she interviewed. In general, her retention success improved over time.

One research assistant stayed with the project through the data collection period, but three did not. Two of the PhD-level research assistants left the university after a relatively short period of time. An additional student was hired as a master's student and graduated before completing all follow-up interviews. When a research assistant left the project, the principal investigator took over that person's caseload. The original interviewer attempted to contact participants and told them of the change and who to expect to make contact to arrange the next interview, in an attempt to ease the transition. The research assistants who left the project first interviewed twenty-five participants. For nearly half of these (N=11), the research assistants failed to connect with the participants post-release, and so likely the research assistant leaving the project did not impact their retention because the participants were already lost to us, though I continued to try to reach them.[19] In seven cases, the research assistants conducted at least one post-release interview, but they were either lost before the transition or I was never able to make contact with them.

In seven additional cases, I interviewed them and, in all but one case, finished the five planned interviews. Because the research assistants left fairly early in the sequence of interviews, I was able to establish a relationship with their interviewees over three or four interviews. This likely would have been more challenging had the research assistants left later. In the final case, I interviewed Christine, a white woman in her forties, twice post-release, until I lost contact with her. When I tried to reach her for a fourth interview, neither her daughter nor her mother knew where she was, a letter was undeliverable, and a Facebook message went unanswered. Around this time, according to her criminal record, she was arraigned on several new charges and eventually was found guilty and sentenced to serve time in another county.

Continuity of the interviewer and developing rapport with participants is not enough to maintain contact. As with Pablo and others, people often distance themselves from loved ones if they have relapsed into drug use and feel ashamed. Still, the importance of the therapeutic aspect of interviews highlights the importance of a skilled and empathetic interviewer. While this is always important in interview-based studies, formerly incarcerated people are so frequently judged, dismissed, and feared that it is that much more important in terms of both retention and research ethics to not perpetuate this through interview dynamics. In addition, while single-interview studies can withstand occasional bad interviews (and all will have some), the cost is greater in repeated-interview designs. Many qualitative projects are conducted by a single person, and so it is difficult to assess the effect of individual researchers on data collection efforts (see May and Pattillo-McCoy 2000; Miller 2001 for two discussions of qualitative studies with multiple researchers and Soyer 2014 for a discussion of an intrapersonal change that shaped how participants responded to a researcher). This project included five people (the principal investigator and four research assistants) who were involved in data collection for the returning prisoner portion of this study. This allows us to explore some interpersonal dynamics and their impact on data collection.

The original plan was that each interviewer would maintain their own interview caseload and would conduct all interviews with each of their

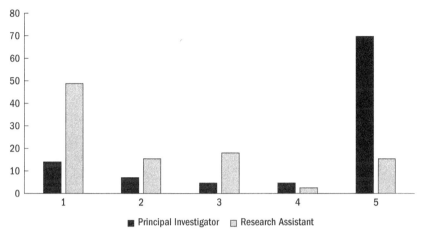

Figure 5.1. Number of interviews per respondent

participants. Rapport grows over time, and maintaining the same interviewer would maximize this, hopefully leading to greater retention and higher quality interviews. There were stark differences in the retention success of the two primary interviewers, suggesting the importance of the interviewer as a tool of data collection, and one that is at least partly in the control of the research team. Figure 5.1 illustrates the retention experiences of the two interviewers (the principal investigator and one research assistant) that stayed involved in the project from beginning to end of data collection. They interviewed roughly the same number of people (N=43 for the principal investigator, including 36 from time 1 and an additional 7 interviewed at least once after a research assistant left the project; N=39 for the research assistant. Time 1 interviews were conducted in the House of Correction and most of the remaining interviews were conducted in the community. For both interviewers, the most common time to lose contact was in the transition to the community. I discuss some reasons for that above, as people wrestled with the challenges of reentry. Even so, there were dramatic differences in retention between the principal investigator and the research assistant. The RA lost nearly half of her participants once they were released, in contrast to 14% for the principal investigator. In contrast, the principal investigator interviewed 70% of her respondents all five times, compared to just 15% of the research assistant's respondents. These discrepancies in retention likely reflected skill as an interviewer (including developing rapport), experience interviewing, and experience interviewing similar populations. It is likely that the relative naiveté of early career researchers can also hinder rapport and retention (McCorkel and Myers 2003). In addition, the principal investigator is likely to be more invested in the project and therefore be more diligent in following up.

## Interviews with "the Rabble Class"

Many of those who are incarcerated in a House of Correction meet Irwin's definition of the rabble class and are both detached from society and disreputable in their personal characteristics or behavior (Irwin 1985). They were arrested for minor offenses, often related to drug addiction and poverty, and their challenges also add to the challenge of staying in contact with them. For example, José, a Latino man in his forties, told us his history. He described himself as "an alcoholic, and a drug addict. And, umm, I need help. I'm homeless." Prior to his incarceration he was "staying with my mother's off and on . . . And umm, you know, I've been in the streets of Boston for the past thirty-eight years." When we met, he was serving time on a probation violation for an assault and battery charge.

> Yeah, I was drunk. Like, all my, all the charges, cases. All my charges are, I have always been drunk, and I don't, I black out. So in the blackout, with the police report said that I was trying to steal some, some liquor out of the liquor store and they caught me, and when they came in, I started arguing with them and pushing them and so they took me in and that was it.

His probation violation was for a similar incident, as were his previous charges. "Yes, they're all kind of similar. Drinking in public and things like that in the beginning." In a later interview he said, "Every time the police arrests me, there's always assault and battery. They always add that to it, because I could have a smart mouth or, once you say something to them they'll put that charge." Others had similar stories involving unruly behavior while under the influence of drugs and alcohol. Sometimes this included assault, often against arresting officers, sometimes shoplifting or other property crimes.

People's detachment, often reinforced and exacerbated by repeated incarcerations and addiction, frequently complicated efforts to follow up with them. If they were stably housed, we could often reliably reach them for an interview. Just over half of those we interviewed four or times times moved no more than once or twice during this follow-up period. For example, Wallace, a white man in his forties, moved back to his family home. While he did get a new cell phone a few months after his release, he maintained the same address, he was easy to reach, and we met on schedule each time. Similarly, John, a black man in his thirties, moved back to his cousin's apartment. He occasionally stayed with his aunt a few blocks away, and his phone went in and out of service, but he had a stable address, a stable contact, and was generally easy to find. It took a bit of time for me to find George, a white man in his thirties, after his release. The old cell phone number that he originally gave me did not work. I sent a letter to the address where he planned to stay, but he wasn't there, "that kind of fell through." Eventually, he got the letter and called me. He couch-surfed with different friends for several weeks before he found an apartment, where he lived the rest of the time I followed him.

Some who might experience instability themselves, but were in close enough contact with loved ones, could also be reached fairly easily. Family members were often forthcoming with information, particularly when they got to know us.[20] For example, Bruce, a black man in his thirties, stayed briefly and periodically with his sister, but would often leave after a fight. When I tried to reach him for a third interview, his sister told me he was locked up, though she wasn't sure where he was or when he would get out. I kept calling, which she said she didn't mind. When her number went out of service temporarily, I mailed a letter to her house. I kept calling as well, and finally reached Bruce 5.5 months after I first tried contacting him for a third interview, and 8.5 months after I'd last seen him. Similarly, Lillian's close friend gave me regular updates on her impending release from state prison and her whereabouts after her release. Without the relative stability of their loved ones, and their friendliness to me, I likely would have lost touch with Bruce and Lillian.

About half of those we interviewed four or five times moved more often or were largely on the street or in shelters. This often made them harder to follow but did not always lead to lost contact. Patience and persistence were necessary to find them again, and this was key to understanding the realities of reentry. For example, Christopher, a white man in his forties, did not have a phone and often stayed on the street. He sometimes reached me on a borrowed phone, and once got my number from another participant whom he ran into on the street and who had my phone number memorized. Since he stayed on the street, his belongings had been stolen and he lost my number. He also reached me via email, which he checked at the public library. Once I ran into him outside of the library. Before our final interview, he stopped responding to the emails. The last time I heard from him, he was out of state. At the time, he wanted to meet, but he did not respond to my attempts to arrange something. Still, we completed four interviews that covered the first eleven months of his release.

Frederick, a black man in his twenties, also was actively struggling with addiction, as were his girlfriend and several family members. His girlfriend was helpful when I could reach her and provided updates about where he was. This included periods of detention and residential drug treatment. While residential drug treatment programs would not confirm that someone was there, they would take a message and pass it along if the person was there (and in one case, Frederick was the one answering the phone). Residents often had restricted movements and also had restrictions on phone possession or use, though sometimes they returned calls and were able to meet. Both Frederick's and his girlfriend's cell phone numbers regularly went out of service or changed. In addition to his girlfriend, a mentor of his from the House of Correction also provided updated information. Initially, Frederick asked me to help him get in touch with this person, and after I did so, he provided information on Frederick to me. In the end, it took two years to interview Frederick five times, with increasingly lengthy delays between interviews. I first connected with him four months after his release. The fourth interview was seven months after the third, and the final interview was nine months after that. Scheduling these interviews involved several months of voice mails and following leads of where he might be and who might be able to reach him. These interviews spanned active drug use, reincarcerations, time in Drug Court, and stays at several residential drug treatment facilities and shelters. During this time, I used about a dozen different ways to reach him.

In other cases, respondents' level of disconnection from all social networks likely contributed to a lack of successful follow-up. Marcos, a Latino man in his forties, for example, had come to Boston a few months before his incarceration to seek out a mother who did not want contact with him. He was arrested and incarcerated with no ties in the area and had no contact information to share. Prior to his incarceration, he was staying at a homeless shelter. At the time of our first interview, he was waiting for a parole hearing to see if he would be released early. He did not know where he would go upon his release or when he would be released. In addition to not being in touch with his mother, he did not know her address. We first interviewed Marcos in July 2014. He had an upcoming parole hearing that could have led to his release, with a maximum release date of May 2015. We had no way to contact him, and so were reliant on him contacting us. According to administrative records, he was not released until May 2015, and, not surprisingly, he did not contact us.

Jackson, a black man in his thirties, was transferred to another facility to serve a short sentence there upon completion of his sentence at the House of Correction. Then he planned to move in with a friend. He described this plan:

> JACKSON: A friend of mine, a woman I met years ago. She's a drug addict. She has a couple of kids. She always has room in the house. I've been staying with her off and on for years. I really don't have to pay her much. Come out of jail, give her a couple hundred bucks a month and I can do whatever I want. Help out with the kids. I love the kids. I'm going to help her with them.
> AL: It's cheap. What else makes you choose that as an option?
> JACKSON: She's an addict. Her being an addict, other people who are addicts are there and they, they're always scamming and that makes the boost, they, credit card scams, stuff like that. So I always come across stuff like clothes or things like that I need. That makes it convenient for me because I need stuff coming out of jail. I can always get stuff on the low for cheap money. Stuff like that. I don't want to

sell drugs again. I'm here for drugs right now. I probably will, to be honest with you, because of the environment I'll be living in, there's money to be made. I don't even have to leave the house. I'll probably dabble a little bit in that.

He described his family: "I have a large family, but they all suck. They're all a bunch of alcoholics, drug addicts, child molesters. I don't want nothing to do with any of them." The only number he could give me was the number of the woman in whose house he planned to stay. While he promised to call me when he was released, he never did. When I tried the number he gave me, it was out of service.

Notably, researchers aren't the only ones who struggle to maintain contact with currently or formerly incarcerated people. As Pablo noted, he was hiding from everyone who cared about him while he was using. Others who felt like they were not progressing may be reluctant to talk about that with researchers (Sharpe 2017). Family members did not always have information about whether their loved one was on the run, detained, or incarcerated. They might know or suspect that their loved one was locked up but did not know where or until when unless the person contacted them. While we managed to meet Maria, a Latina woman in her thirties, once post-release, her mother was our only point of contact with her. When we contacted her mom to try to reach her for another interview, she said that she had no way of reaching her daughter directly. She believed that her daughter was using again, and "she knows to stay away when she is using." Her mother was caring for Maria's children and because of that, Maria was not allowed to stay there. Her mother sounded distraught and talked at some length about her fears. Although she took my message, we didn't hear from Maria. Over the next few months, according to the criminal record information, Maria also was charged several times with new offenses.

Communicating with loved ones while incarcerated is expensive and often difficult. In addition, incarceration was often a source of significant strain in relationships, and people who had been reincarcerated were sometimes reluctant or slow to reach out to loved ones. When I tried to contact Tom, a black man in his forties, for an interview, his phone went straight to voice mail. I tried calling his mother, who sounded abrupt on the phone. She said she wasn't really in touch with him; she also returned the letter I mailed to him at her house. When I found out Tom was incarcerated and talked to him, he said "I don't know why they're [his family] not picking up the phone [when I call]. Maybe they're just tired of dealing with me . . . I didn't do anything to hurt them or anything like that, they were just getting sick of me coming back and forth to jail." When I saw him a few months later, he was back in touch with his mom. He said, "My family has not been able to accept the phone call and I didn't know. When my mother wrote me a letter, she said in her letter that the phone calls are too expensive." Likely both the tension in the relationship, the financial burden of collect calls, and the time delays in letters slowed down their communication, and the tension between them also impacted his mother's willingness to talk to me. While families were often a useful source of information, strains in those relationships could hinder their willingness to help researchers.

Challenges of maintaining contact are not only a result of drug use or addiction. Before his release, Peter, a black man in his twenties, thought his biggest challenge would be his anger. In Peter's case, his history of violence, gang involvement, and incarceration continued to shape his movements and his mind-set. While he thought he had gotten better, "like I used to have like a short fuse and I swear a lot of my fights came from that. And, of course, you know, being gang involved. But if I had it, if I had more control of my anger, I prob-, I probably, I would have probably been in less, less, less fights." Peter was a young man who was incarcerated as a teenager, first in state prison, and then the House of Correction. It took several calls to his father and sister, and several scheduled attempts to meet him for a first post-release interview. He was staying "different places," moving every few weeks, after his release. He was trying to avoid being on the street and couldn't go to one neighborhood because of "an issue." He asked me to pick him up from the place he was then staying, after which he reclined the seat. When we went to a nearby fast food restaurant, he chose a seat where he could face the windows. Still, he kept turning around, because he "had gotten used to keeping an eye out and being alert." The next time I tried to reach him, his voicemail had another person's name in the outgoing message, and messages left with his father and sister and letters went unanswered. In one call, his sister said she didn't know where he was. He was arrested around this time, but bailed out of jail. Those charges were ultimately dismissed, but he received new charges, including gun-related charges, several times in the subsequent few months. Several of these were dismissed, though a few remained open cases at the time we pulled his official criminal record.

Clearly, keeping in contact with Pablo, Frederick, Tom and others was challenging. But understanding their experiences is crucial to understanding the reality of incarceration, addiction, and reentry. The limited contact I had with Peter post-release, and the attempts I made to reach him and others, also provided useful context about their lives, even when we did not complete all of the follow-up interviews. In some cases, follow-up interviews were impossible or impractical. One respondent died, which we learned from family when trying to arrange an interview. Two respondents were incarcerated for lengthy periods. Since the focus on the project was on community reentry, with each of these, we conducted one more follow-up interview and then stopped. A few people were not released when expected. Otherwise, we persistently kept trying, through unanswered messages and missed interviews. Sometimes this resulted in an interview and sometimes it did not. Even then, we gained insight into their lives. Supplementing this information with official criminal records and House of Correction information provided additional details.

## Conclusion

In this chapter, I detailed the factors that seemed to have the greatest impact on recruitment and retention of a returning prisoner interview sample. More than just reporting what we did and our level of success, I detailed what shaped our successes and failures. This sample fit Irwin's definition of the "rabble class," a disreputable and detached group of people who are incarcerated because they are disorderly, more so than dangerous. This made them particularly challenging to follow over time, as many were homeless or unstably housed, poor, and often lacked close connections. Still, maintaining contact with even the most challenging is crucial to understanding the full range of experiences with incarceration, and the ways that even minor contact with the system and short stays can disrupt the lives of those impacted. These individual characteristics shaped the ease or difficulty of interviewing them. Still, several strategies helped us to retain contact, though sometimes sporadically so. "Best practices" of studies of this type include paying respondents, requesting multiple forms of contact, and using all methods at one's disposal to maintain connections. We followed these strategies, with the exception of relying on probation or parole offices to locate participants. In addition, the varying experiences of different interviewers highlight the importance of the experience and skills of the interviewer, the relationship formed between the interviewer and interviewee, and how that translates to a cathartic or beneficial experience for the interviewee. Even so, attempts to maintain contact may skirt ethical lines, and researchers should be careful to prioritize the safety and well-being of their participants (Sharpe 2017). In addition to this relationship, retaining contact requires persistence, as some people may fall off temporarily but remain willing to continue being interviewed. In addition, triangulating data collection, including collecting official criminal histories and talking to family and friends, can add to our understanding, even of those with whom we have less contact.

ACKNOWLEDGMENTS

This project was funded by the National Science Foundation grant # SES-1322965. I thank Sofya Aptekar, Elsa Chen, Johnna Christian, Sarah Mayorga-Gallo, and Leslie Wang for feedback on earlier drafts.

NOTES

1. Long Island is one of the Boston Harbor Islands that was home to a shelter, drug treatment programs, and other smaller health and transitional housing programs. In October 2014, the bridge out to the island was abruptly closed by the city and the services housed there also closed or were relocated to Boston.
2. The larger study also included a "receiving community" component, in which we interviewed and conducted observations in three communities. In this chapter, I focus only on the returning prisoner component.
3. Six of Massachusetts' thirteen counties house women in their House of Correction. County-sentenced women from the remaining seven counties are housed at MCI-Framingham, the state's one women's prison. The Suffolk County House of Correction houses both pretrial detainees (women only) and sentenced women and men. In this study, we recruited only sentenced people.
4. This was often not the case, according to people we interviewed, who resisted visits because of the difficulty they imposed on both prisoner and loved ones and because of their relatively short incarcerations.

5  In addition, they ran background checks on all of the research personnel. They also met with the first group of research assistants, as they did with other volunteers and interns, to ensure that they were "neither too eager nor too afraid" to be in the facility.
6  In one case, the man we were visiting was housed in the worker wing, which was a separate area of the facility. In that case, we met with the man in an empty office in that unit.
7  This involved going through a sally port and up a set of stairs, where an officer met us. We did not go on housing units, nor did we have any more access than regular professional visitors, like lawyers or social workers. We were also, of course, on camera during this short walk.
8  We used a three-stage consent process. The first was consenting to be interviewed. The second was consenting to have interviews recorded, and the third was consenting to allow us to request their official criminal record. The first stage was mandatory to participate; the second two were not, though most people consented to all three. Ninety-three participants consented to allow us to access their criminal histories. To date, we have ninety-one. The last two have some incorrect information, with missing results.
9  In a few cases, the staff determined that a woman was too mentally or physically incapacitated to participate, and so we did not talk to her. Occasionally, it was difficult to see women, especially if they were pregnant or otherwise in need of doctor's visits, which happened during the same time blocks we had access, or if they were in court when we were there. We recruited women for fifteen months.
10  Demographics for both our interview sample and the total release population are based on self-report intake data. It is not clear why our sample included few Hispanic/Latinos, though we did not offer our recruitment materials or interview in Spanish (according to facility staff, most Spanish speakers were in Immigration and Customs Enforcement detention, and were not among those from whom we recruited).
11  The file we received of all releases was stripped of names. We identified our interview respondents using available demographic information. One was released later than expected and so outside of the time period captured.
12  We paid $30 per interview in cash. We paid cash so that it would be a "no strings" payment, with which they could do what they wanted. In a time 2 interview, one respondent, who was struggling with drug addiction, asked for payment half in cash and half in a gift card, so his own use would be limited. We went together to a convenience store to try to buy a gift card, but they did not have any. I offered to hold part of the money to give to him later, but he decided to take it in cash.
13  This idea was proposed by an anonymous grant reviewer and approved by the University's IRB and the House of Correction.
14  We requested, and received, permission to do this at all institutions, including several state prisons where we conducted follow-up interviews. When people were staying in a drug treatment facility or some other semi-secured institution,

we also confirmed with them that they were allowed to have cash. In these cases, we wanted to make sure the incentive did not cause problems for the participant.

15 As principal investigator, my full name was listed on consent forms. Research assistants used their first name and a Google number.

16 At the beginning of the project, we were strongly advised by staff of the House of Correction to not do this, because of their perception of the danger in doing so. Given the work environment of correctional officers and how they are trained and socialized into that environment, this is not surprising (Britton 2003; Goffman 1961; Owen 1998). I never had problems, nor did I feel unsafe, when I did so.

17 While I did not believe the risk level was high in doing these interviews, as a security measure, the research team shared information on where we were doing interviews and communicated with each other when the interview was completed.

18 Occasionally people asked for advice. I tried to provide some answer if they needed information that I could provide or access (e.g., contacts for services). When they asked what they should do, I usually repeated what they had said they wanted and asked if that was a possibility. I tried to avoid overstepping my expertise or passing judgment. This can be a tricky balance to strike as a researcher. In these moments, I did respond to them first as a person and second as a research participant.

19 In one case, I did make contact and had several conversations with the man in question and his girlfriend (with whom he was living and whose phone he used). We scheduled one interview, but he did not respond when I rang his bell. After this, my attempts to reach him failed. I received several angry text messages from his girlfriend asking who I was and why I was contacting him. I attempted, unsuccessfully, to explain. After this, I sent a final letter to his apartment, reminding him of who I was and asking him to call. I did not hear from him, and stopped contacting him, so as to avoid jeopardizing the project or his relationship with his girlfriend (on whom he was dependent for housing). The potential cost to him outweighed my desire to talk with him (see also Sharpe 2017). A male researcher might have mitigated this (and interviewed this man pre-release), but the male RA had left the project.

20 It is worth reminding the reader that we contacted people and used phone numbers and addresses only with the permission of the research participant.

PART III

Frameworks and Conceptual Considerations

# 6

## The Promise of Unpacking the Black/White Dichotomy for Reentry Research

JANET GARCIA-HALLETT AND KASHEA P. KOVACS

The methodological approach to race in reentry research often fails to depict an accurate reentry experience for diverse groups or to represent the true significance of race in prisoner reintegration (Garcia-Hallett 2017; Olusanya and Cancino 2012). Occasionally, race is ignored in reentry research, which suggests the reentry process is experienced similarly by all—irrespective of race (Olusanya and Cancino 2012). Formerly incarcerated individuals, however, "move within a racially-charged symbolic universe" (Martin 2013, p. 502). Thus, examining reentry through a race-neutral lens ignores the challenges experienced by various racial-ethnic groups (Martin 2013). Admittedly, there is increasing consideration of race in reentry research, which is beneficial in understanding the impact of social-structural factors on reintegration.

Criminological research is full of knowledge about prevalent disparities in the criminal justice involvement of black and white offenders. Researchers have found that people of color experience differential treatment by law enforcement as disproportionate policing strategies, and malicious arrest decisions may place them at increased risk of criminalization (Visher 1983; Zatz and Rodriguez 2006). Scholars have also found that once under the eyes of the criminal justice system, racial differences may be further exacerbated while progressing through the system's various stages (Bishop and Leiber 2012; Poe-Yamagata 2009; Snyder and Sickmund 1999). For instance, black individuals are not only overrepresented in arrest rates (Daly and Tonry 1997), but they are also sentenced more harshly than their white counterparts (Mitchell 2005; Steffensmeier and Demuth 2000). Some scholars have attempted to understand and situate these racial disparities within the larger social context of race relations in the United States and to explore how social constructions of race may influence criminal justice policies (James 2008; Zatz and Rodriguez 2006).

While discussions of perceived minority threat often focus on disproportionate arrests and sentencing decisions (see Mitchell 2005), there are serious implications of racial stereotypes, prejudices, and discrimination when black individuals are released from incarceration. For instance, reentry obstacles are particularly detrimental for individuals as job seekers and as workers and are further complicated by racial stereotypes and social status as racial minorities. Research demonstrates that many formerly incarcerated individuals tackle financial challenges prior to their involvement in the criminal justice system (Greenfeld and Snell 1999; Mumola 2000), which may include low income and reduced likelihood of full-time work (Western, Kling, and Weiman 2001). Yet, black individuals are often more economically disadvantaged and less financially stable in comparison to their white counterparts (see Steffensmeier et al. 2010), with unemployment rates twice that of whites (Thompson 2008). Moreover, black individuals in reentry have increased difficulty in securing employment compared to their white counterparts. The penalty for a criminal conviction is double for black applicants compared to similarly situated white applicants (Pager, Western, and Sugie 2009). Employers are least likely to offer job interviews to black applicants with a criminal record compared to white applicants with or without criminal backgrounds (ibid.). Pager and her colleagues (p. 201) found that black applicants *without* a criminal record were a third less likely to be invited to complete an interview than white applicants *with* a criminal record. Thus, while hardship may be common among formerly incarcerated individuals, these hardships disproportionately affect those who are black.

Although there are merits to examining disparities in criminal justice involvement and understanding the barriers to successful reintegration, this research is often conducted under large racial umbrellas. This black versus white outlook shapes numerous limitations in criminological knowledge and in scholars' ability to serve as agents of social change. The following section examines the limitations of a black/white dichotomy and explores the various ways reentry research reinforces racial dichotomies. Though some research comparatively explores racial-ethnic experiences in the criminal justice system, this research largely examines differences in criminal involvement, with less attention to post-incarceration experiences. This chapter briefly reviews this literature to highlight ethnic nuances hidden within broad racial categories. These disparities are discussed vis-à-vis various aspects of reentry such as informal social supports, nativity and language, structural disadvantages, and the positive typification of ethnic groups and their skin tone. Last, this chapter explores the implications of examining racial-ethnic experiences in reentry research and recommends ways to unpack the black/white dichotomy.

## Limitations of the Black/White Dichotomy

Researchers have given little attention to the implications of black/white dichotomies in social science research, except when discussing Hispanics (Piquero 2015; Rodríguez 2000; Steffensmeier et al. 2011; Steffensmeier et al. 2010), referring to biracial individuals (Jackson 2013; Root 1996), or examining how such racial dichotomies may promote racism (see Bonilla-Silva and Zuberi 2008). Yet, a black/white dichotomy reinforces prevalent stereotypes of the black community as being criminal in nature while simultaneously reinforcing notions of the white community as being the innocent victims. As Martínez and Nielsen (2006, p. 109) argue, black/white dichotomies "may result in false conclusions or generalizations based on inaccurate assessments of the racial/ethnic/immigrant makeup of US society." Thus, such a reporting of criminological research along racial dichotomies may be used to fulfill political agendas in a not-so-post-racial society. In addition, broad racial umbrellas limit our understanding of intra-racial nuances in the criminal justice system. Piquero (2015, p. 22), for instance, argues that criminological attention should not be restricted to a black/white dichotomy but must also embrace "all shades in between." This includes the Hispanic ethnic group whose members may identify with a white *or* black racial background, or the West Indian population typically overlooked by racial dichotomies that may be more of a "continuum" in their countries of origin (Waters 1999).

## Reinforcing a Black/White Dichotomy

Criminological research may reinforce the black/white dichotomy in multiple ways. For instance, researchers may be limited in their ability to recognize existing nuances between ethnic groups. This limitation, however, is often due to imposed classifications that may not capture the inter-ethnic complexity of the United States and may conflict with participants' self-identification. Ethnic groups may be lumped into categories such as "Black or African American alone" (see Durose et al. 2014; Minton 2013), which emphasize the presence of African Americans as an ethnic group while simultaneously obscuring the existence of other ethnic groups within a large black racial category. Such classifications become problematic when study participants fall into these categories (according to researcher standards), but do not agree with these labels of their identity. For instance, formerly incarcerated West Indian women believe that members of society "classify everyone who's Black as 'African American'" (Garcia-Hallett 2017, p. 91). In her research on the West Indian population, Mary Waters (1999, p. 65) discovered that the West Indian participants "disliked the term 'African American' because, unlike the term 'Black,' it did not leave room for ethnic distinctiveness within the racial umbrella." Ethnic distinctiveness also goes unnoticed when communities that are predominantly West Indian (as often found in ethnically diverse cities like New York and Miami) are classified under broad racial categories (see Martínez and Nielsen 2006).

Even when data on ethnic groups are available, studies may still reinforce the black/white dichotomy when scholars deem the presence of an ethnic group too small and, therefore, omit the group from analyses or disregard it as an individual group. For instance, Steffensmeier and Demuth (2000) indicate that in past research on race and sentencing, Hispanic defendants were categorized in either the white or the black group due to the relatively small numbers of Hispanics or due to the ambiguity in definition. They argue that, as a result, some research may report small sentencing disparities between whites and blacks, but this could be due to inadequate consideration of the role of ethnicity (Steffensmeier and Demuth 2000). Consequently, scholars may not study these groups independently from others and their experiences become of minimal importance in leading discussions of prisoner reintegration.

Overall, these methods of conducting research may not capture nuances between racial-ethnic groups, limiting our understanding of their experiences in the criminal justice system.

## Racial-Ethnic Experiences and Their Importance for Prisoner Reentry Research

Despite the depth of knowledge on prisoner reentry more broadly, certain questions remain unanswered about potential intra-racial nuances in reintegration. For instance, how might the unique obstacles tied to social perceptions of ethnic groups shape the reentry experience? Do attachments to specific ethnic identities or social interactions with particular ethnic groups function as protective factors? In what ways do cultural meanings of offending behaviors influence familial assistance differently across racial-ethnic groups? Given these questions, it would be useful to understand how reintegration may be shaped by ethnic background as it relates to treatment in the community and values within the family unit. The following examines some of the racial-ethnic nuances, at the group level, hidden within black/white dichotomies, and the importance of understanding racial-ethnic experiences in prisoner reentry research.

### *Informal Social Support Networks*

Social control theories have historically suggested that individuals engage in crime when they have weak ties to conventional society, freeing them to engage in crime (see Hirschi 1979). The stronger an individual's social bonds to society, the stronger the social controls against criminal activity and the less likely the person would be to engage in criminal behavior. Research shows that Hispanics and Latinos often report having strong attachments to family and friends (Landale, Oropesa, and Bradatan 2006; Vega 1995), creating a supportive communal environment that may function as a social control. In fact, the degree and nature of their informal social support networks are theoretical explanations for the lower crime rates in Hispanic or Latino communities compared to African American communities (see Landale et al. 2006). Even though both groups encounter economic disadvantages and other structural adversities within their communities, the strong social bonds partially explain the "Hispanic Effect" (Steffensmeier et al. 2011) or "Latino Paradox" (Steffensmeier et al. 2010) that disproportionately buffers this ethnic group from crime. Scholars have found similar results for Asian communities, which maintain strong social controls that buffer them from crime in spite of existing risk factors like structural disadvantages (Mawby and Batta 1980; Webster 1997).

Once individuals are involved in the criminal justice system, familial and communal reactions may shape their ability to cope with difficulties during the system's various stages, including prisoner reentry. Many of those returning home from incarceration depend on established social connections to learn about available resources as well as potential housing and employment opportunities (Granovetter 1995). Positive familial relationships are often the most instrumental in the reintegration process as family members typically provide emotional support as well as tangible support like financial assistance and housing during the first nights post-incarceration (La Vigne et al. 2009). Though positive family relationships may function as a buffer from crime (Wright et al. 2013) and a constructive aspect for reintegration (La Vigne et al. 2009), groups may be exposed to varying familial responses to their crimes and their incarceration that can affect the support they receive during reentry (Garcia-Hallett 2017; Wakefield and Garcia-Hallett 2017).

For instance, research demonstrates that among the Asian population, criminality is typically perceived as a cultural transgression, which minimizes family prestige (Mawby and Batta 1980; Webster 1997). As a result, Asians may face distinct social exclusion and familial "repercussions" for their criminal involvement (Webster 1997). Similar to Asians, West Indians deemed criminals or moral offenders are subject to a "sanctioning network" within the West Indian community (see Jean-Louis et al. 2001; Kleinman and Lukoff 1978). Such negative familial and community responses may complicate post-incarceration experiences during a time when assistance is crucial to reintegration. Some offenses, however, trigger a larger "sanctioning network" compared to others. Fournier and Herlihy (2006, pp. 170–71) found, "In Haitian culture the worst thing you could possibly be is a thief." They also hinted that prostitution was more socially acceptable compared to robbery. Garcia-Hallett (2017) found some support for this distinction given that prostitution was deemed as sex *work* and, thus, respected as a means of working toward survival during economic turmoil. Though this may not be representative of a viewpoint shared by an entire group, it is worthy of further investigation given the potential implications of these social meanings on the familial and community responses to these crimes.

*Nativity and Language*

Some scholars note a cultural dissimilarity among recent immigrants and the possibility of additional social-structural disadvantages due to their social status (see Steffensmeier and Demuth 2000). Yet, research suggests that large immigrant populations in ethnic communities may buffer criminal activity (Martínez 2003; Martínez and Nielsen 2006; Vélez 2006) and potentially facilitate desistance (Calverley 2013). Specifically, literature suggests that immigrant groups are more likely to overcome social-structural disadvantages through greater group cohesion and solidarity (Aldrich and Waldinger 1990; Bruhn 2011). The solidarity found among immigrant populations can increase their social capital by enabling the sharing of available opportunities as well as creating new opportunities through local and transnational networks (Portes, Guarnizo, and Haller 2002; Sanders 2002). This protective nature of large immigrant groups may account for the incarceration rate of foreign-born males, which is four times lower than the incarceration rate of US-born males (see Rumbaut et al. 2006). Research also shows, however, that this protective component of immigration weakens for the third generation of immigrants and for immigrants migrating at a young age with seemingly more time living in the host country (Morenoff and Astor 2006; Rumbaut et al. 2006). Thus, even in a community with a large immigrant population, there may be generational differences in nativity that can shape individuals' ability to overcome disadvantages.

It is worth noting that some ethnic subgroups may be impacted by imprisonment more than others within the same ethnic group. Within the Asian population, Laotians and Cambodians experience the greatest increase in incarceration rate between the foreign-born and US-born (0.92% and 7.26%, respectively) (Rumbaut et al. 2006). Within the Latino population, Mexicans experience the greatest increase in incarceration rate between the foreign-born and US-born (0.70% and

5.9%, respectively) (Rumbaut et al. 2006). These disparities within ethnic groups may be associated with structural conditions as well as the social treatment and criminalization of particular groups. According to Muñoz, McMorris, and DeLisi (2004, p. 117), sentencing research on "Mexican immigrant communities suggests that powerful business elite and public servants used misdemeanor criminal codes as a means to secure and manipulate a seemingly powerless labor force for Anglo social, economic, and political gain." Regardless of immigration status, Mexican Americans remain particularly criminalized in an anti-immigration social and political climate in the United States (Bobo 2017). Such criminalization may render them (and others perceived to be Mexican) particularly vulnerable to additional discrimination upon their release from incarceration. Although reintegrating into society post-incarceration is difficult amidst social and structural barriers for formerly incarcerated individuals, the heightened criminalization of certain ethnic groups and their subgroups further complicates the reentry experience.

The communities that offenders return to may influence the process of reintegration, given the presence of ethnic enclaves. Concentrated areas of an ethnic group, particularly those with large immigrant populations, can be instrumental to overcome reentry barriers. Formerly incarcerated individuals may benefit from the supportive network in ethnic enclaves sharing knowledge of housing and employment opportunities (Portes et al. 2002; Sanders 2002)—social capital that is valuable for prisoner reintegration. While ethnic enclaves can facilitate the reintegration of formerly incarcerated ethnic minorities, some research suggests that ethnic enclaves may also heighten their visibility and put them at greater risk of hyper-surveillance as "criminals." As previously noted, concentrated areas of a discriminated group may also expose them to heightened criminalization by society and law enforcement—harmful interactions during a period when they are trying to reintegrate back into society. Thus, reentry research should closely examine the role of ethnic enclaves in individuals' reentry experiences.

Another distinction that is overlooked within large racial umbrellas is language and the implications of linguistic barriers on prisoner reintegration. Linguistic barriers, generally, introduce setbacks while interacting with law enforcement officers, gaining information about their involvement in the criminal justice system, and receiving resources to aid in their reintegration (Cheurprakobkit 2000; Culver 2004; Herbst and Walker 2001; Latta and Goodman 2005). Although Spanish is the most dominant non-English language spoken in the United States, and Hispanics/Latinos are the largest ethnic minority in the country (Portes and Rumbaut 2014), they continue to face linguistic barriers communicating and receiving information in social and legal interactions (Davis and Erez 1998; Menjívar and Bejarano 2004; Vidales, Day, and Power 2009). This alludes to the extremity of linguistic barriers for other non-English speakers in the criminal justice system who may have relatively fewer reentry resources in their dominant languages. For instance, languages like Creole and Patois are rarely used in the United States but are commonly spoken by the country's Haitian and Jamaican populations, respectively—groups that are also involved in the criminal justice system (see Garcia-Hallett 2017) but have fewer resources catering to their needs.

*Structural Disadvantages*

Additionally, the structural position of ethnic communities may shape their interactions with the criminal justice system. Criminologists have long argued that social disorganization and structural disadvantages in one's community may weaken social controls and increase the likelihood of offending (Kornhauser 1978; Shaw and McKay 1972). According to this theoretical perspective, communities with fewer structural problems are in a stronger position to avert offending behaviors. As Vélez (2006) notes, compared to African American communities, Hispanic and Latino communities may be disproportionately buffered from crime because they are often less segregated, have relatively less concentrated disadvantage, and have better ties with local officials and law enforcement. In addition, even though conditions of poverty influence crime for all groups, research suggests that the impact of poverty may be less severe for West Indians compared to Hispanics or Latinos (see Martínez 2003). One possible explanation is that West Indian families in the United States have lower poverty rates (12.5%) than Hispanic or Latino families in the United States (18.6%) (US Census Bureau 2016). In addition, the differential impact of poverty on crime within these communities may be linked to perceived strains and relative conditions in their affiliated countries. For instance, the conditions of poverty in the United States may be relatively less severe than the impoverishment in their countries of origin, potentially causing less strain as a crime-inducing factor (Martínez, Lee, and Nielson 2004).

Adverse structural conditions are detrimental to prisoner reintegration, highlighting the importance of stable employment and suitable housing post-incarceration (Visher and Travis 2003). Yet, there are prevalent disparities in employment and housing across ethnic groups and ethnic subgroups in the criminal justice system (HUD 2016; Martinez 2004). For instance, the Department of Housing and Urban Development (2016, p. 10) has recognized, "Because of widespread racial and ethnic disparities in the US criminal justice system, criminal history-based restrictions on access to housing are likely disproportionately to burden African Americans and Hispanics." In addition to the marginalization of particular ethnic groups, there are differential experiences between ethnic *sub*groups. Martinez (2004) found that Hispanic subgroups from Central and South America were more likely than those from the Caribbean to have a job or business prior to their arrest. This suggests differential experiences within ethnic groups that are worthy of exploring, particularly as pre-incarceration circumstances influence individuals' experiences upon their release.

*Positive Typification of Ethnic Groups and Skin Color*

It is widely understood among social science researchers that, historically, whites are deemed and treated as the more dominant, normative group of higher social status compared to those of a black racial background. Stereotypes, prejudices, and discrimination negatively affect people of color and push them into the grips of the criminal justice system. In addition to this, differential experiences between racial-ethnic groups may present some with more protective elements and leave others more vulnerable to destructive treatment and circumstances. African Americans, Hispanics, Asians, and West Indians have historically been minorities in the US context. Still, stereotypes of each group may differ, as will the prejudicial and discriminatory actions directed toward them, contributing to differential treatment in various social contexts pre- and post-incarceration.

Individuals with criminal convictions are often stigmatized and presumed incompetent (Giguere and Dundes 2002; Graffam, Shinkfield, and Hardcastle 2008). Formerly incarcerated individuals battle negative assumptions about ex-offenders, coupled with prevalent stereotypes associated with their racial-ethnic background. Though African Americans, West Indians, and Hispanics are all economically disadvantaged as racial-ethnic minorities, there are varying stereotypes about their work ethics, deservingness of work opportunities, and suitable divisions of labor (Bobo et al. 1995; Garcia-Hallett 2017; Gopaul-McNicol 1993; Model 1995; Portes and Rumbaut 2014; Waters 1999). These stereotypes may arise in the form of positive typification—"when members of an ethnic group or immigrant nationality are viewed as more motivated to work and more reliable than their potential competitors" (Portes and Rumbaut 2014, p. 210). Overall, research has described a positive typification of Asians, Hispanics, and West Indians as ideal employees and preferred workers in comparison to African Americans (de Castro et al. 2006; Garcia-Hallett 2017; Portes and Rumbaut 2014; Repak 2010; Shih 2002; Waters 1999). Yet, Asians have benefited more from positive typification compared to these other three groups (Portes and Rumbaut 2014; Webster 1997). In fact, Portes and Rumbaut (2014, p. 185) argue that certain countries, particularly Asian countries, function as "recruitment targets for firms and institutions in the advanced world and thus sources of a sustained brain drain."

Unique stereotypes and social treatment may complicate reentry experiences for different ethnic groups. In fact, black formerly incarcerated individuals perceive meaningful differences among them in the reentry hurdles they encounter in the labor market and in the workplace due to the positive typification of West Indians compared to African Americans (Garcia-Hallett 2017). After release, some may find themselves pushed into and held in entry-level jobs given their social status as racial-ethnic minorities (Shih 2002). Accordingly, positive typification may act in favor of the preferred ethnic group in question, but it simultaneously presents a detriment to other ethnic groups who are further denigrated. Combined with their status as formerly incarcerated individuals, the positive typification of certain ethnic groups can further influence hiring assessments and income (de Castro et al. 2006; Portes and Rumbaut 2014; Shih 2002; Waters 1999). Additionally, ethnic groups may battle with greater expectations of work productivity without adequate compensation for their work (de Castro et al. 2006; Shih 2002). Yet, Asians remain disproportionately protected in occupational and financial gains compared to other groups like West Indians and Hispanics or Latinos (Portes and Rumbaut 2014).

Together with stereotypes and prejudices of particular racial-ethnic groups, there are differential experiences by skin color—contingent on whether individuals are brown-skinned or lighter-skinned (Alba 2005; Gopaul-McNicol 1993; Hunter 2007; Painter et al. 2016; Waters and Kasinitz 2010). Even skin color is stratified, exposing individuals of the same ethnic group to colorism in which they experience bias because of their skin tone. In addition to the black/white dichotomy during times of slavery, colorism was historically understood among black individuals given that darker-skinned blacks were restricted to outside work as "field slaves" while lighter-skinned blacks worked for slave owners inside their homes as "house slaves" (Davis 1991). Such bias in skin color is fueled by the premise that lighter skin is associated with superiority and graciousness, while darker skin is associated with subordination and violence (Hunter 2007). In contemporary times, such colorism is still prevalent, as Hispanics with darker skin color are associated with lower earnings (Telles and Murguia 1990), less occupational prestige (Espino and Franz 2002), and lower educational attainment in Spanish-speaking neighborhoods (Murguia and Telles 1996) compared to Hispanics with lighter skin. Colorism has also been studied among other ethnic groups like West Indians (Waters 1999; Waters and Kasinitz 2010) and Asian Americans (Rondilla and Spickard 2007). Thus, not only do people experience discrimination along racial categories, but there is also the potential of biased treatment due to ethnic identities and skin color. It is likely that formerly incarcerated individuals battle the intersection of stigma from imprisonment and additional discrimination due to their ethnicity and skin color, but these experiences are overlooked when we rely on a black/white dichotomy in reentry research.

Overall, it is evident that unique experiences in the criminal justice system may have serious implications in the reintegration process but go unnoticed within restrictive black/white dichotomies. Although the structural composition of communities is a greater predictor of crime (Martínez et al. 2004), this chapter has demonstrated how ethnic background and the ethnic composition of communities may be associated with sociostructural and sociocultural circumstances shaping individual narratives and community experiences.

## Resisting and Overcoming the Black/White Dichotomy in Reentry Research

This section provides suggestions for scholars embarking on reentry research, but the points are applicable to other areas of criminology. It begins by introducing ways scholars can resist conducting and reporting research along racial dichotomies. It then notes potential limitations for these suggestions and ways to overcome dichotomous classifications in reentry research when alternative options are less feasible.

As previously discussed, the disparate circumstances and treatment of ethnic groups and subgroups warrant further attention. Racial dichotomies in reentry research can be unpacked through purposeful sampling of racial subpopulations to capture nuances in their reintegration. Yet, researchers should be cognizant of how they gather information on ethnic background and how they convey participants' ethnicity in final reports. For instance, participants should be able to identify their ethnicity without having to choose from a predetermined list that is not inclusive or that may be misleading in final reports. One problematic example includes the "Black or African American alone" classification, which reinforces the interchangeable use of the black race and an African American ethnicity. Although many research reports use these terms interchangeably, researchers should avoid referring to all black participants as "African American" if participants do not specifically identify as such. Doing so overlooks those who identify with another ethnicity within the black racial group and contributes to misleading conclusions about the reentry experience.

In addition to sampling techniques and reporting, researchers can resist racial dichotomies by taking different approaches to data collection and being receptive to exploring aspects that are typically ignored in reentry research. They can better explore narratives by crafting interview guides that capture more nuanced discussions of ethnicity within the reentry experiences. This may consist of interview (or survey) questions that are more direct about post-incarceration circumstances and treatment as they relate to ethnic background. Meticulous research on the reintegration of ethnic groups and subgroups should consider country of origin, generation of US immigrant status, and the racial-ethnic and immigrant makeup of the communities they return to upon release. For example, scholars can examine the reentry experiences of second- and third-generation immigrants and explore the role of ethnic enclaves in their reintegration. Future reentry research should also consider questions that tap into experiences with ethnic positive typification, colorism, linguistic challenges, and sociocultural norms and transgressions. These factors may vary beyond ethnic background but, in conjunction with individuals' ethnicity, they shape social interactions, treatment, and assistance—all essential during prisoner reentry. Regional considerations may also highlight unique reentry experiences since ethnic groups may be concentrated in particular geographical regions of the United States, which can shape the degree and nature of reentry resources catering to certain groups and the criminalization they experience from society and law enforcement in less diverse areas. These are all issues discussed in ethnic studies and sociological literature but seldom integrated into reentry research. Thus, theoretical approaches like Latina and Latino Critical Theory, typically referred to as LatCrit Theory, may be particularly amenable to resist racial dichotomies. This theoretical approach places racial-ethnic nuances between and among Latinos at the forefront of its investigations, highlighting the implications of marginalization and criminalization on the Latino pan-ethnicity—a direct approach applicable to other ethnic groups within reentry research (see Román 1997).

Although these methodological and theoretical approaches may be particularly compatible for scholars embarking on reentry research that explores ethnic groups and subgroups, researchers may encounter some methodological challenges. Resisting a racial dichotomy may not be feasible given the data that are readily available. For instance, existing quantitative data-sets are often limited in their ability to differentiate between black ethnic groups. Additionally, when data are available on participants' ethnic backgrounds, researchers may find that ethnic groups are too small for comparative evaluations and they may combine smaller groups during quantitative analyses. The presence of small sample sizes, however, is likely *not* because these ethnic groups do not offend, but is more likely due to problematic data collection methods (as previously discussed) and potential issues gaining access. As found in empirical research attempting to highlight racial-ethnic nuances in the reintegration process (Garcia-Hallett 2017), scholars may encounter difficulties recruiting diverse participants due to cultural stigmatization of those in the criminal justice system (see Jean-Louis et al. 2001; Kleinman and Lukoff 1978; Mawby and Batta 1980; Webster 1997).

Despite these potential limitations, it remains particularly important to overcome racial dichotomies to best support the reintegration of individuals across various ethnic backgrounds. Even when researchers are limited in their ability to explore reentry experiences across ethnic groups and must report along racial classifications, it is important that they address the limitations of racial dichotomies in their final reports and in any policy recommendations or program implementation. Researchers are in a unique position to enhance programmatic efforts for all groups in the criminal justice system. Thus, a study's methodological challenges to examine ethnic nuances in prisoner reintegration should not dismiss other research demonstrating social and structural inequities between racial-ethnic minorities in the criminal justice system.

Researchers can also support post-incarceration reintegration by incorporating existing knowledge of racial-ethnic nuances into program strategies. For instance, not only is there a need for more employment opportunities receptive to hiring formerly incarcerated individuals, but scholars should advocate for equal treatment of both racial *and* ethnic minorities. As discussed in this chapter, formerly incarcerated individuals may be further excluded from employment opportunities or further restricted to low-wage, entry-level jobs due to discriminatory treatment associated with their ethnic backgrounds or skin color. With greater attention to ethnic nuances in reentry issues, scholars would be better prepared to use this research in advancing policies and pushing for greater accountability when formerly incarcerated individuals are treated unfairly due to their ethnicity or skin tone. This chapter has also demonstrated that, during reintegration, informal support may be disproportionately available among ethnic groups, as West Indians and Asians often experience additional stigma and familial repercussions for their criminal involvement (Garcia-Hallett 2017; Jean-Louis et al. 2001; Kleinman and Lukoff 1978; Mawby and Batta 1980; Webster 1997).

When formerly incarcerated individuals have limited family bonds during prisoner reentry due to cultural transgressions, mentors can function as a valuable asset. Garcia (2016) found that, over time, formerly incarcerated individuals perceived their mentors as fictive kin who protected them from negative influences, provided them with a different outlook about unfortunate circumstances, and ultimately guided them through more constructive behaviors. Scholars can support formerly incarcerated ethnic minorities by advocating for mentoring programs that confront the additional stigma they experience and can offset the diminished social support in their reintegration. Ultimately, by encouraging programs and program personnel to account for racial-ethnic experiences post-incarceration, scholars can aid prisoner reintegration and support equity between racial-ethnic minority groups.

## Conclusion

Although criminologists have emphasized the disproportionate sociostructural barriers faced by certain racial groups, they rarely account for the nuances within racial groups that may also shape reentry experiences after incarceration. Similar to race, ethnicity may also function as an "organizing principle" in society due to social perceptions and responses to groups under certain ethnic classifications (Peterson, Krivo, and Hagan 2006). This chapter argues that reentry research should direct more consideration toward ethnic differences within large, dichotomous racial umbrellas often found within criminological work. Doing so goes beyond merely investigating disparities between ethnic groups in their crime rates or recidivism rates but, instead, exploring how ethnicity functions as an "interactive factor" with other elements, shaping prisoner reintegration. By unpacking the black/white dichotomy in reentry research, scholars can dig deeper into the sociostructural and sociocultural contexts of the reintegration process. As a result, programs can be more sensitive to obstacles that may vary across racial-ethnic groups, accounting for these factors in program strategies and providing more adequate assistance to those in the grips of the criminal justice system.

7

# Prison Experiences and Identity in Women's Life Stories

*Implications for Reentry*

MERRY MORASH, ELIZABETH A. ADAMS, MARVA V. GOODSON, AND JENNIFER E. COBBINA

Much of the research and writing on women's prison experiences highlight negative living conditions and damaging effects on the individual (e.g., Kruttschnitt and Gartner 2005; Kruttschnitt and Hussemann 2008; Owen 2005; Owen, Wells, and Pollock 2017). This emphasis largely reproduces findings from research on men in prison (reviewed by Liebling and Maruna 2005), though there is evidence that incarcerated women experience some pains of incarceration more acutely than do men (Crewe, Hulley, and Wright 2017). For instance, more than incarcerated men, imprisoned mothers engage in frustrating attempts to parent their children as mothers behind bars who are largely out of touch with the outside world (Baldwin 2017; Celinska and Siegel 2010; Enos 2001; Esterling and Feldmeyer 2017). Despite widespread recognition of the negative effects of prison, some scholars (e.g., Toch 1977, 2005) imagine ways that prisons can incorporate programming and even institution-wide reforms to reduce negative effects and increase positive change in prison and thus after release. In the analysis described here, we use an inductive approach to clarifying the pains of incarceration for women who have histories of repeated lawbreaking and a deductive approach to apply two theories of identity change to understand whether and how women experience positive changes in their identity while they are in prison. Knowing the dynamics of positive identity change in prison can provide insight into features of the prison experience that would likely increase women's successful reentry. Alternatively, pains of imprisonment that damage identity and the absence of positive identity development would suggest features of the prison experience that would likely decrease women's successful reentry.

McAdams (2013) developed one theory of identity change, narrative identity theory, which assumes that individuals construct their life stories to reflect how they currently see themselves. In this theory, increases in agency, communion, and ultimate concerns constitute identity development. Themes of agency reflect personal concern for things like power, mastery, and independence, whereas themes of communion reflect concern for things like affiliation and nurturance (Bauer, McAdams, and Pals 2008). Themes relevant to ultimate concerns reflect religious or spiritual growth or well-being (McAdams 2012).

In an application of narrative identity theory, Maruna (2001) examined life stories for a sample of primarily men in Liverpool, England to show how certain themes support desistance from crime. He explained how a negative experience, such as incarceration, can stimulate positive identity development that increases a person's agency, communion, and spiritual resources. Maruna found that ex-offenders were able to desist from crime when they incorporated their negative histories of breaking the law, using drugs, and being incarcerated into a positive identity. For example, some of the individuals whom he studied saw themselves as well suited to helping other people who broke the law because they had themselves stopped a pattern of illegal activity. Providing further support of desistance, this pattern of redemption is related to a script for the future in which offenders see themselves taking on prosocial roles and activities, including giving back to society and contributing to future generations (i.e., generativity). Redemption during incarceration may be related to desistance from crime after leaving prison, because people who tell life stories that contain redemptive imagery tend to self-report well-being and generativity (Bauer et al. 2008), both of which support desistance from illegal behavior (Draine and Solomon 1994; Halsey and Harris 2011; LeBel 2007; McNeill and Maruna 2007; Suldo and Huebner 2004).

In contrast to redemption sequences, contamination sequences are associated with depression, low life satisfaction, and the absence of generativity (Bauer et al. 2008). Contamination events spoil a good, or at least acceptable, state of being or situation and can result in stagnation in identity development. For example, a positive and happy childhood and the related positive sense of self may be ruined by being abused as a teenager, which may be followed by a dependence on drugs stemming from efforts to dull the pain caused by the abuse.

A second theory of identity change, the theory of cognitive transformation, grew out of research on women and men who had been highly delinquent in their youth (Giordano, Cernkovich, and Rudolph 2002). The theory links changes in identity to perceptions of available prosocial roles and agentic moves to grab on to what are called "hooks for change," which enable people to fill new roles. Desistance from crime occurs when individuals come to view themselves in a new way and to assume new roles that are incompatible with breaking the law. This theory led us to examine whether cognitive transformation occurs in prison. If it does, then the prison experience might support avoiding crime after release.

The results presented in this chapter address several questions about women's perceptions of the time they spend in prison and their stories of identity development and contamination during this time. In telling their life stories, what pains of incarceration do women offenders identify, and what do these pains tell us about how they see themselves? Do women's accounts of time in prison reveal redemption and generativity or cognitive transformations? Do they reveal contamination? Although the research that is reported does not link prison experiences to desistance, it does suggest whether and how experiences in prison might influence post-release outcomes.

As shown in the next section, research on women and the more voluminous literature on men has suggested that the pains of imprisonment harm one's identity. We then describe research on narrative identity and cognitive transformation theories in more detail, since they suggest how individuals can move beyond negative experiences such as histories of crime and incarceration and fashion identities that support prosocial behavior.

## The Pains of Imprisonment

Beginning in the 1950s, classic studies that focused on men in prison concluded that the experience of incarceration damaged a person's identity. Sykes (1958) found from his observational study of men in prison that separation from family and friends, deprivations of goods and services, and a total loss of liberty eroded inmates' identities. Another well-known study that placed participants in a simulated prison environment led the researchers to conclude that the individuals playing the role of prisoner seemed to lose their personal identities (Haney, Banks, and Zimbardo 1973). More recently, prison researchers Irwin and Owen (2005) drew on their own and others' studies of both women and men, and concluded that living in tight spaces with prisoners who are often threatening, immature, and ignorant, coupled with close supervision by unsympathetic, even hostile staff make it difficult for offenders to develop a prosocial future script, which is an important element in desisting from crime. Also, based on a review of research, Liebling and Maruna (2005) provided contemporary evidence of how incarceration promoted identity problems that include prisoners' negative attitudes toward themselves and loss of a sense of purpose (also see Crawley and Sparks 2005). Furthermore, they raised the possibility that prison-based interventions with potentially positive effects could be undermined by the damage done by the larger prison context.

Research supports the existence of this undermining effect of the prison environment on prison-based programs. For example, Rucker (1994) compared the outcomes of two programs designed to foster cooperation among program staff and incarcerated women. During the study period of several weeks, in addition to leading group meetings, Rucker carried out participant observation of the interactions among inmates and staff throughout the prison. Both programs led to instances of cooperation, caring, and trust among inmates and group leaders, but these positive outcomes were soon undermined by the institution-wide coercive environment. McCorkel (2013) also studied a program that operated in a coercive women's prison environment, but the general prison environment had its influence through a different dynamic than Rucker (1994) highlighted. In McCorkel's (2013) research, women who participated in a confrontational substance abuse treatment program that was intended to break down their identities described the program as a new kind of punishment. The majority of women resisted program staff's efforts to change their identities, though some did give in and came to see themselves as diseased selves. However, even for those who complied with program expectations, most did not succeed after release. Burnett and Maruna (2004) documented the same lack of effects of prison time on reduced recidivism for men. There is evidence of prison-based programs that do not reproduce the identity-damaging features of incarceration (Collica 2010; Collica-Cox 2018), but the research evidence more fully illustrates the harms of even well-intentioned programs offered in coercive prison environments.

### Narrative Identity Theory and Identity Change

McAdams and colleagues (McAdams et al. 2001; McAdams et al. 1996) developed narrative identity theory and the related Life Story Interview (McAdams 2008). In an application of the theory, Maruna (2001) showed how redemptive episodes and events that transformed a negative history into positive, prosocial activity supported ex-offenders' desistance from illegal activity. For example, people who were formerly breaking the law stopped and turned their attention to assisting other offenders from continuing in a life of crime. However, pertinent to the focus of this chapter on incarceration, for a sample of seventy-five men, Maruna, Wilson, and Curran (2006) found that religious conversion was one of the few available ways that prisoners could make good of past criminal activity. Thus, the development of agency and communion during incarceration may be much less likely than growth in spirituality.

Focusing on women, Stone et al. (2018) studied identity development in the early stages of ninety-three women's parole supervision. The data were women offenders' responses to questions about the incident that resulted in conviction and feelings about justice system responses to that offense, their recollections of parole officers' discussion of common problems, and their actions to make their lives better since the start of parole. Data were coded to produce quantitative indicators of contamination and redemption. A score reflecting contamination was positively related to recidivism, and a score reflecting redemption and generativity was negatively related. Relevant to prison, when women answered questions about how they saw their offenses and subsequent justice system contact, some of them described time in prison as a necessary precursor of their more positive present and future. For example, one woman indicated that prison got her off heroin, stopped her from committing crime to pay for drugs, and allowed her to earn a GED and gain the motivation to do more with her life than she had done before. Providing an example of redemption, she fashioned the negative event of being in prison into a positive opportunity to change her view of herself and her future. Although this research suggests the applicability of narrative identity theory to women's prison experiences, it offers just a glimpse of the connection of prison to redemption and contamination. It only considered redemption and contamination sequences constructed in the first nine months after release from prison, and it did not consider them in the context of a full life story.

In another application of narrative identity theory, van Ginneken (2016) analyzed interviews with six women in prison for the first time. They were selected because they had clear evidence of being traumatized by living in prison, but then they experienced post-traumatic growth through identity development. They coped with incarceration by finding a silver lining, such as coming to view prison and its programs as reasons they were able to get off drugs or prepare to break off abusive relationships. They made good of the trauma of prison by pointing to the positive benefits, including increased agency because of help they received in prison. The benefits affected their vision of life after prison, including their view that they would have increased control over their lives. Van Ginneken's study suggests that despite the trauma of being in prison for the first time, some women find their way into prison experiences that they feel improve them. However, the small and purposively selected sample provides no sense of how many women experience this positive outcome, and thus the generalizability of findings is quite limited.

## Cognitive Transformation Theory and Identity Change

As noted above, according to cognitive transformation theory, when women offenders become aware of prosocial roles they can fill, they take a step toward change (Giordano et al. 2002). Alterations in identity are further facilitated by hooks for change, but only if women are open to change, see it as desirable, and act with agency to take advantage of them. Hooks for change in prison might include job training, educational opportunities, and substance abuse treatment programs. They also might include isolation from the demands of a criminal lifestyle and time to reflect on life circumstances and goals. Further identity change occurs when women see continued lawbreaking as incompatible with their emerging interest in a prosocial replacement self. This replacement self is incongruous with antisocial behavior, and for some people, it further evolves to include negative views of lawbreaking and a criminal lifestyle.

Like all settings, prison imposes constraints on and offers opportunities to change and to enact alternative repertoires. Giordano et al. (2002) provided an example of a prison-related cognitive shift in the description of one woman's rejection of a group leader's depiction of her as ready to jump into a fight. The woman noted that she was tired of that life, was through with it, and had outlived it. She went on to explain that the last time she did substantial time for a minor parole violation, it woke her up, in part because she had a child to care for. Exemplifying how prison can wear a person down, another participant in Giordano et al.'s (2002) study talked about being too old for the penitentiary because her body could not handle it. Although incarceration acted as a catalyst for identity change in these cases, this sequence of events was not inevitable and was relatively rare (ibid.). Instead, influences outside of prison, especially children and the marital/intimate partner, predominated in the stories of change. Also, some women pointed to religion or treatment programs as catalysts for change. For a small number of participants, religion seemed to have an especially profound effect because it provided a total blueprint for behavior and an extremely prosocial replacement self. However, additional longitudinal quantitative research on the same study participants revealed that religiosity was unrelated to sustained desistance; analysis of qualitative narratives showed that despite mechanisms through which spirituality and religious involvement were linked to positive changes, life experiences and realities that were unrelated to spirituality or religion resulted in continued illegal behavior (Giordano et al. 2008).

## Connections between Narrative Identity and Cognitive Transformation Theories

Narrative identity and cognitive transformation theories are distinct. Narrative identity theory highlights contaminating events that impede positive identity change, and the alternative process of making good of negative events that promotes identity development. In contrast, cognitive transformation theory describes a change process that begins when a woman who is open to change and sees it as desirable envisions taking on prosocial roles. Change is promoted when she takes advantage of hooks for change and is buttressed when she sees illegal activity as incompatible with her new prosocial self and roles. Moreover, in narrative identity theory, agency is gained when an individual makes good of a bad event or episode; however, in cognitive transformation theory, agency enables an individual to take advantage of hooks for change.

Turning to similarities between the theories, both conceptualize identity as constructed by individuals and as influenced by events, episodes, and opportunities. Narrative identity theory identifies increased spirituality as a gain in identity development; cognitive transformation theory identifies religion as a hook or catalyst for change and a blueprint for a prosocial replacement self (Giordano et al. 2008). Future scripts in narrative identity theory are similar to the replacement self that changing individuals fashion in cognitive transformation theory. Recognizing these similarities, Giordano et al. 2002 pointed out that Maruna's (2001) application of narrative identity theory to offenders was compatible with cognitive transformation theory. These similarities make it reasonable to use both theories to suggest themes that characterize the prison experience and that are relevant to identity change (or lack thereof) and thus ultimately relevant to women's experiences after they leave prison.

## Methodology

### Sample

Analysis focuses on a subsample of 44 women from a larger study of 402 women who in 2011 or 2012 had recently been placed on probation or parole for a felony offense in Michigan. Since substance abuse is a problem in the lives of a large proportion of women in the justice system (Daly 1994; Morash 2010; Mumola and Karberg 2006), the sample was restricted to women with some indication of substance involvement. Of the 402 women, 75.9% ($n = 305$) were on probation and 24.1% ($n = 97$) were on parole. Most women on probation (94.4%, $n = 288$) had not been to prison at the beginning of the research, but 17 of them had spent between 3 and 223 months in prison before the study started. Of course, all women who began the study on parole had been in prison at least once.

Approximately five years after the study began, we selected and reinterviewed 118 of the 402 women to elicit their life stories. This group was selected to enhance understanding of the desistance of repeat offenders. Thus, the selection criterion was that the woman had five or more convictions before the start of the larger study of the 402 women. Of the 118 women, 75 were on probation and 43 were on parole. Ten women who began the study on probation had official data indicating they had spent time in prison, and all of them talked about the prison experience as part of their life stories. A slightly smaller proportion of the women who began the study on parole, 79.1% ($n = 34$), included prison experiences in their life stories. In total, 44 of the 118 women, 10 (22.7%) who began the 2011–2012 data collection period on probation and 34 (77.3%) who started out on parole, described time in prison as part of their life stories. These descriptions were the focus of the present analysis.

The women on parole were on average older ($M = 40.12$, $SD = 8.12$) than those on probation ($M = 35.90$, $SD = 11.83$), but the difference was not statistically significant ($F = 1.68$, $df = 1,42$, $p = .202$). Women self-identified as white ($n = 19$, 43.2%), black ($n = 19$, 43.2%), multiracial or Hispanic ($n = 5$, 11.4%), or did not specify race or ethnicity ($n = 1$, 2.3%). When the largest minority group, black women, was compared with non-black women, both groups had 50% on probation and 50% on parole. Of the 43 women with available official data, 5 (11.6%) had not been in prison before the start of their participation in the study, 19 (44.2%) had been incarcerated once, 7 had been incarcerated in prison twice (16.3%), and 11 had been in prison 3 to 10 times (28%). Some women spent time in prison after they began participating in the study.

*Life Story Interview*

Extensive qualitative data were collected with the Life Story Interview (McAdams 2008). According to the Life Story Interview protocol, the interviewer first guides the study participant through the identification of the various chapters of her life. Once the participant has key parts of her life in mind, the interviewer asks for detailed descriptions of the high point, the low point, a negative childhood memory, a positive childhood memory, an experience with an ultimate or broader (e.g., the universe) force, a turning point, a vivid adult memory, and a wisdom event. The interviewer then asks for a detailed description of each event or episode by posing questions about what happened, who was involved, when it happened, the participant's thoughts and feelings at the time, and what the entire scene or description says about "who you are as a person." Interviewers did not suggest chapters of women's lives and did not insert their own ideas about important events. More specifically, they did not ask women about their experiences in the criminal justice system, though some women volunteered this information. The life story method of data collection is well suited to understanding an individual's assessments of the meaning and importance they attach to key life events (Giordano et al. 2002).

*Units of Analysis and Themes Relevant to Time in Prison*

Agreement on the number of passages in which women talked about prison when they told their life stories was established for 30 of the 118 women. Two authors examined the qualitative life story data for the 30 women and identified passages that pertained to time in prison. Guetzkow's U (Guetzkow 1950) was calculated to be .06, which indicates coder disagreement regarding 6% of passages, which is considered an acceptable level. Therefore, the first author completed the identification of units for analysis. As noted above, 44 of the 118 women talked about an experience in prison in the course of recounting their life stories.

A codebook for 12 themes was based on the first author's repeated reading of the 44 women's life story content relevant to time in prison. She worked inductively to identify the range of pains of imprisonment women mentioned and was guided by narrative identity and cognitive transformation theories to identify themes relevant to identity change. For the passages in which the 44 women talked about their prison experiences, two authors followed the written codebook to code passages in 30 of the women's narratives for 12 identified themes. The five themes relevant to pains of incarceration were: negative experiences that included bad living conditions and day-to-day hardships (e.g., guards yelling at inmates); distress from events outside of the prison (e.g., a relative's death); separation from children; material loss and loss of contact with living people who were outside of the prison; and the study participant's attribution of a deterrent effect to the pains of incarceration. Very few women (5) described loss of tangibles (e.g., furniture, clothing) or of contact with specific people as a result of incarceration, so detail is not provided below for this theme. The two themes relevant to narrative identity theory included evidence of identity development through redemption and/or generativity in the prison setting and of contamination by prison experiences. Redemption through spirituality occurred frequently, so it was coded as a separate theme. The themes relevant to cognitive transformation were indications of hooks for change and cognitive shifts in perceptions and behavior. One theme, explicit mention that prison or an episode or event in prison affected identity, was relevant to both theories. A final theme, support from friends and family while incarcerated, was coded but was not considered in the present analysis. Two of the authors achieved intercoder reliability in coding the 12 themes for 30 of the cases that had some content pertinent to prison (Cohen's κ = .94) (Cohen 1960), and then the first author completed the coding for these themes.

## Results

Of the 44 women who included prison time in their life stories, the highest proportion (72.2%, $n = 32$) described one or more pains of incarceration. Smaller but still sizeable proportions described redemption or contamination sequences (47.7%, $n = 21$) and/or elements of the cognitive transformation process (43.2%, $n = 19$). Sixteen women (36.4%) noted that prison experiences led to a change in their identities, and 18.2% ($n = 8$) said that the negative experience of being in prison did or would deter them from doing anything that would lead to their return.

### The Pains of Imprisonment

Quite a few of the 44 women described distress from dealing with situations and people (usually relatives, rarely intimate partners) outside of the prison while they were inside (40.9%, $n = 18$). Most commonly, these situations involved the death of a significant female relative—a grandmother, mother, or aunt—or a close unrelated female friend. The women typically regretted not being there to support and help the individual who died. For example, Jolene's grandmother passed away.[1] She explained, "It's something I have to deal with for the rest of my life. You know, I chose to be in prison when I knew that she was sick and I knew that she was getting ready to die. And I chose my lifestyle over being there for her and I am going to have to deal with that for the rest of my life." Similarly, Wendy talked about her mother's death, "She's gone. Nothing I can do. I think about her and have her in my memory—keep her close to my heart. I was in prison at the time of her death so there wasn't much I could do." Several other women who wanted to address major life events—such as a loved one's death or a relative's serious health problems or a child who tried to commit suicide—felt they failed to fulfill their obligations to loved ones. This is often an overlooked negative aspect of incarceration for women.

Sixteen women (36.4%) highlighted the upsetting experience of separation from their children, and in some cases they noted the resulting harm to their children. For instance, relatives acted as foster parents for Yolanda's children. Contrary to the relatives' promises when she signed over custody, Yolanda did not hear from the children. She explained:

> At that time, it was a point in my life where I tried to kill myself. Why? Because I didn't think I had nothing to live for. As I said, I didn't never hear back from my kids, I didn't know what was going on. You know, I knew the state had them, and I knew who had my children. I tried to call them. They changed the phone number on me so I could never, you know, you know, talk to my children, this and that. They wouldn't even allow my mother and them to come see my children, you know, none of that.

Yolanda further noted that the relatives had hidden money, cards, and other items that Yolanda sent to the children, and until the children found these items, they were antagonistic toward her. Yolanda's situation was more complicated than that of many other women, who described suffering from separation from children even though they maintained some contact and were certain they would be reunited after release. Some women felt they had "walked out" of their children's lives when the children needed them. When asked about the greatest regret of her life, Carly summed up common feelings about children when she answered, "Leaving my children. Even though I didn't think it was gonna affect them because they had my family. They wanted me. And that hurt and made me feel like a failure as a parent."

After being cut off from relationships with close family and being separated from children, the next most common pain of incarceration the women mentioned was the living conditions in the prison. Just under one-third (13, or 29.5%) of the 44 women who spoke about prison mentioned a negative experience. Examples varied, but many involved prison staff. Abby described an early release option, boot camp, where sergeants screamed at her. She said it was "crazy" and "insane that she was punished for not eating all of her food by being forced to stand for hours wearing handcuffs." She ended her comments saying, "Maybe something is going to come along later in life that I really needed that experience to happen. That's all I can think." Wendy, who was almost 50, resented having to ask a "20-something" year old correctional officer if she could go to the bathroom and then being given just one tissue to use. A few mentioned the lack of medical and mental health services or the overuse of medications. One of these, Misty, said, "The health system here needs help—improvements in dental, health, and mental health. I mean they just dose people here—it's like everyone is bipolar—when everyone really isn't. When they give meds here it sounds like running with the bulls." Kirsten said that she and the other women called health care "death care."

Eight women (18.2%) were adamant that, because of what they faced in prison, they would never do anything that would lead them to return. Lynnette said she would "never go back to prison" because she was different from other "people that are there for raping children, killing their babies, and stabbing their husbands to death at the dinner table." Some expressed fatigue after multiple stays in jail and prison. Sally asserted, "I jailed too much through my teenage years and my early twenties. I didn't want to keep goin' through it." Similarly, Bree said, "When you go from having freedom to having limited freedom that alone can just make a person go crazy, and so coming home from that, I guess, that would have to be a major turn because I didn't want to go through that again."

*Redemption, Generativity, and Contamination in Prison*

Fourteen women (31.8%) gave examples of how they made good of negative prison experiences by developing or deepening a connection to God. They typically made this change by repeatedly reading the Bible, praying, and, less often, attending religious services. Relationships with God sometimes resulted in messages from Him, insights into the purpose for their lives, prayers being answered, recognition that God protected them by removing them from the streets, and comfort. For instance, Louisa coped with being in prison by spending much of her time reading the Bible. She stated that she was "learning more about God's Word and what was His purpose for me." When people told Louisa that the change in her would not last after release, she emphasized the connection she had to God by saying, "God and myself, not me, not me, not me." During the life story interview, she attributed being out of prison and free for seven years to her connection with God. When the interviewer asked her why getting close to God in prison was such an important turning point, she said, "I think it was because I had nowhere else to turn to."

Very few of the 44 women who talked about prison in recounting their life stories (15.9%, $n = 7$) specified prison as a place where redemption through gains other than increased spirituality occurred. Of those who did, some built on their own negative experiences to help other inmates. Patricia, who had suffered when her own mother died, consoled a cellmate whose mother had just died by reading her a Bible verse that indicated that there would be a place in heaven for her and her mother. Sue talked another inmate out of committing suicide, and more generally she described how, while incarcerated, she connected with "a lot of hurting women" and comforted them. She wanted to be a counselor because helping women in prison gave her a reason "to be here." Vicki was planning to go back to the prison "and give my testimony and my talk and tell them there's life—there's life behind these walls and outside these walls." She was making good of both her time in prison and her prior dealing, stealing, and crack use. As a final example, Cristy planned to write about prison to "tell the world, teenagers, what it is in life and how hard it is and how you can overcome obstacles and how you can overcome using drugs if you become someone better, and how from prison that you can change your life."

Another small proportion of the 44 women (15.9%, $n = 7$) specified that contamination sequences began in prison. Yolanda's fighting with other inmates extended her maximum sentence of four years to ten years served because of new charges for assault. She explained, "I was in prison fighting this and that. So when you fight, you get tickets, you know, this . . . you know, major tickets, this and that. You see the parole board, they might flop you." Carmen said that after she used profanity when she addressed the parole board, they required her to serve the maximum 36-month sentence.

> My minimum was 18 months. I was pregnant when I went to prison, and I ended up having a stillborn so I was mad about that, you know? And then I went and seen the parole board, and they told me that I wasn't gonna go nowhere in life again, so that made me angry. And they told me that I deserved to lose my daughter, which is wrong. So I told them to "fuck off" and I walked out, so I ended up doing the other 18 months.

Carly's fighting in the prison caused a miscarriage that still haunted her years later, as shown by her comment, "And I blamed myself for that for a long time . . . Like, if I wouldn't have gotten in trouble, then I wouldn't have been in prison, and then she'd be here today." Two women felt hopeless because of multiple returns to prison. One of them (Wendy) named a chapter of her life "Old Fool." She said this chapter was about "violating parole and going back and forth to prison . . . , being robbed of years and having time taken away, repeating the same behavior while expecting different results." The remaining two women felt that prison itself was contaminating, because, as Mary said, it made her "worse," and as Andrea said, it made her "crazy." Andrea went on to describe her numerous symptoms of anxiety and bipolar disorder.

### Cognitive Transformation

The number of women who provided examples of cognitive transformation while in prison varied for the different stages of the change process. Just a few (15.9, $n = 7$) described prosocial roles they were motivated to fill, and except for one woman who wanted to care for her ailing sister, they all wanted to be more involved as mothers or grandmothers.

Slightly more talked about grabbing onto hooks for change in the prison. A few explained how prison experiences contributed to their assessment of antisocial behavior as inconsistent with their new prosocial identities.

Of the 10 (22.7% of the 44) women who said they grabbed onto hooks for change while in prison, taking advantage of programs predominated. Yolanda, whose daughter and son were in prison during her incarceration, wanted to be a better mother to her adult children. As a result, she acted with heightened agency to grab onto multiple hooks for change in prison. She explained, "That last time, I really took it serious, you know. I did life things with my life, you know, I accomplished many certificates, you know, that I never, you know, accomplished in my life before, you know. And as I was cooking in the microwave, I was always trying different things, you know." Yolanda, who identified herself as a graphic artist, had discovered how to create crafts in prison from microwaved candies, and she was writing a book to teach children to make the crafts. Kirsten also was on the high end of taking advantage of prison programs. She depicted her life as a "long journey . . . [with] about 23 years of drugs, in and out, back and forth, you know, in and out of jail." The last time in prison, she immediately sought out and obtained a job in the kitchen, and then was accepted in a custodial maintenance program. Shortly after she began that program, the GED program accepted her. She made an unofficial arrangement with the two instructors to participate in both programs by leaving one early to take part in the other. She described her feelings of pride and "loving it" when she talked about the programs.

Also relevant to the process of cognitive transformation, seven (15.9%) of the women expressed dissatisfaction and rejection of a criminal lifestyle, with their repeated cycling in and out of prison, and with prior criminal friends. After other inmates questioned why she was putting meth into her body, Carla came to see her substance use in a much more negative light than she had before:

> I started thinking, like yeah why the hell would I do that, that's some nasty shit. Like I'm just putting battery acid with this and that and I'm putting that into my body. And then I got to where I was shooting that into my body, like who does that? And then I'm, you know, that's not

cool! . . . It literally changed the way I thought about stuff. Like before I thought, oh getting high was cool and you know I was doing the, doing good stuff. Well, shit no. So it like completely changed my process about things.

Lena changed her thinking about a criminal lifestyle after she was arrested for the offense that brought her to prison. She was tired of running, of not having an address she could use, of not being able to get food stamps or work at anything but an under-the-table job, and of not being able to use her real name. All of these actions would put her at risk of being discovered and arrested. She said that thinking about these challenges before and during incarceration made her "realize and smell the coffee, make me think that I can't keep doing this, and I was just tired."

*Changed Identities*

Fourteen of the 44 women (31.8%) who included prison experiences in their life stories explicitly described how time in prison changed their identities, and two additional women explained that while they were in prison, their former "good selves" replaced a temporary criminal self. For instance, Tova had a history of handling violence in her family through her own violent interventions, but she felt that prison had changed that, "because [in prison] you grow, you learn, you humble." After release, instead of reverting to her typical behavior, grabbing her pistol and staging a violent intervention to break up a fight between her sister and the sister's partner, she just talked to them and calmed them down. She commented on the change in herself, "That's why I'm like, somebody gotta be civilized, and it felt good because I swear to God I couldn't see that in a million years coming. Me being who I am now I couldn't see that coming in a million years you know." Other women said that after the prison experience they were "totally different" individuals, which made them proud of what they accomplished, and showed them they were strong enough to change their lifestyles. Because she received help and counsel from an older friend in prison, Rosa felt she was "ready to go home . . . [and] ready to start a new chapter in my life."

## Discussion

Relationships with children and other family members stood out in the data as highly relevant to how women experienced prison and how they saw themselves. The most frequently noted pain during incarceration emanated from women's perceived inability to fulfill important roles as granddaughters, daughters, or mothers, and from their separation from children. Moreover, women's imagined prosocial future roles were nearly exclusively as mothers and grandmothers. In a study of mostly formerly incarcerated women who were living in a halfway house, Leverentz (2014) similarly found that family relationships were central to women's identities, and their role as mothers was very important. Giordano et al. (2002; also see Barry 2007 and Rumgay 2004), also found that compared to men, women's desistance more often revolved around family responsibilities and identity as a mother. Prison-based hooks for change may have broadened some women's identities as students and workers, but these aspects of the self were much less prominent in the parts of their life stories that touched on prison time than the emphasis on identity as a family member. These findings show the importance of programs and prison protocol that enable women to maintain contact with family members, or that substitute community corrections for incarceration.

Consistent with literature on the pains of incarceration, a fair number of women presented evidence of their suffering, especially suffering caused by being cut off from relationships, by virtue of being in prison. Smaller proportions gave accounts of positive experiences in prison. Some women told the interviewer about redemption sequences that unfolded in prison, especially those that left them with increased spiritual resources (narrative identity theory). Some talked about leaving or avoiding prison with the aim of filling available prosocial roles in their families, grabbing hooks for change in prison, and coming to see a criminal lifestyle in a negative light at least in part because of prison time (cognitive transformation theory).

A few said they were deterred from future crime by the negative experience of being in prison. Relevant to both theoretical frameworks, several women reported positive identity changes as a result of being in prison, but a few said they "got worse" due to incarceration or that prison was the site of contaminating episodes or events. Despite some evidence that women perceived some positive effects of prison time, in women's life stories the pains of prison were more common than the benefits. Yet, it did not seem that women felt that they always lost their identities in prison, or that they thought that the prison context always undermined any positive effects of available programs.

Does this mean that despite the pains of incarceration, the US justice system has reason to continue incarcerating women at the rate it does? The answer to this question is no. Narrative analysis reveals how people make sense of their lives and how they construct their identities. Our findings about this process of identity construction do not negate empirical evidence of the harm of mass incarceration to individuals, families, and communities (Clear, Waring, and Scully 2005; Clear 2007) and of the overrepresentation of women of color in prisons due to factors other than their levels of illegal behavior (Mauer and Chesney-Lind 2002). Van Ginneken's (2016) research helps us draw meaning from our findings of some positive prison-based events, episodes, and programs. Recall that van Ginneken purposively selected a sample of six women who were traumatized by their first incarceration, but who responded with positive identity development. Though the women's response was positive, the initial trauma was not, and no doubt there are women who do not cope well with traumatic prison experiences. The positive identity development and change that we documented seems modest in that positive effects on identity were reported by a minority of women.

Similar to findings of Maruna et al. (2006) about men in prison, much of the women's positive identity development in prison involved gains in spirituality. Although Giordano et al. (2002) did not focus on cognitive transformations in prisons, our finding is consistent with their discovery about identity change, that more than men, women described religious transformations. Giordano et al.'s (2008) further analysis led them to conclude that although spirituality may be an important hook for change, needs for a steady income, a neighborhood with some resources, and prosocial partners and companions may undermine its effect. The life story interview that we used to elicit women's narratives was designed to gather evidence of gains not just in spirituality, but also in agency and communion. Consistent with prior criticisms that correctional programming for women places relatively limited emphasis on psychological and vocational gains (Buffard and Taxman 2000;

Morash 2010), in women's life stories, prison was only rarely the site where women described those other types of gains. Gains in spirituality may help women feel that they are supported, but gains in agency and communion may more directly benefit women in addressing challenges such as poverty, stigmatization, and needs to make positive contributions to other people. This possibility may account for Giordano et al.'s (2008) finding from quantitative analysis that offenders' spirituality was unrelated to desistance because of problematic life circumstances. Future research in the narrative identity theory framework should explore whether identity developments that reflect agency, communion, and spirituality are similar in their associations with desistance from crime.

For two reasons, we purposely did not directly examine the link of desistance to pains of imprisonment or identity change in prison. First, our data allowed us to examine pains, identity development, and cognitive transformations that women described as happening while they were in prison. However, we cannot link these dynamics to a subsequent shift toward desistance. Some of the 44 women who talked about prison had been released for several years, others had entered prison after they became study participants, and some were in prison when we conducted the life story interview. We therefore could not establish that identity development while in prison was followed by a period of desistance. Second, based on the literature, we did not expect that what happened in prison would be the predominant influence on the desistance process. Indeed, 9 of the 43 women who began the study on parole did not even mention prison when they told their life stories. Given that the life story is a construction that reflects one's current identity, it is possible that experiences in prison were not connected to how some women saw themselves when they told their life stories.

For the sample of repeat offenders considered in the present analysis, there are pains of imprisonment, but also some opportunities for redemption and cognitive transformation in prison. Consistent with Toch's (1977, 2005) argument, at least in the contemporary Michigan prison, there were ways for agentic women to take steps toward desistance. However, positive identity change may occur even more often in community settings. Both a will to reduce incarceration and research evidence are needed to compare identity change across prison and community-based interventions. For women who are in prison, it is also important to explore ways that programs and the general prison environment can increase opportunities for change, whether they be through more opportunities to develop agency and communion, narrative therapies that promote envisioning prosocial roles and making good out of negative histories, or increased attractive hooks for change. Especially if they are coupled with resources to overcome structural realities and constraints, these types of efforts may increase women's capacity to leave prison and avoid substance use and other illegal activity.

NOTE

1 Pseudonyms are used to refer to participants and to demonstrate the variety of women who provided quoted material.

# 8

## Does Thinking of Oneself as a "Typical Former Prisoner" Contribute to Reentry Success or Failure?

THOMAS P. LEBEL AND MATT RICHIE

It is now generally understood that formerly incarcerated persons are stigmatized and discriminated against in society (see, e.g., LeBel 2012; Petersilia 2003; Travis, Western, and Redburn 2014). Several researchers have assessed the "ex-con" stigma from the perspective of formerly incarcerated persons (see, e.g., Gunnison and Helfgott 2013; Harding 2003; Irwin 2005; LeBel 2012; Uggen, Manza, and Behrens 2004). Moreover, there is increasing acknowledgment that not only being labeled "ex-con," but also the perception that one is stigmatized by society, may make prisoner reintegration more difficult (LeBel et al. 2008; LeBel 2012). For example, Hlavka, Wheelock, and Jones (2015) conclude that "overcoming the master status of the felon label is an essential step on the path towards successful reentry" (p. 411). Maruna's (2001) research indicates that persisters and desisters from crime differ in how they view themselves (i.e., social identity) and in their optimism in the ability to "go straight." This chapter examines formerly incarcerated persons' level of agreement with the statement "I am a typical former prisoner." The relationship between thinking of oneself as a typical former prisoner and a variety of variables previously found to be related to desistance from crime and/or successful reintegration is examined. Implications of the findings for desistance from crime and prisoner reentry research, policy, and practice are discussed.

## Literature Review

### Identity and Membership in a Stigmatized Group

Tajfel (1982) argues that a person's identity, at least in part, is based on their membership in various social groups. Moreover, he argues that this membership is based on three components: cognitive, evaluative, and emotional. The first component is cognitive, meaning that an individual is aware that he or she is in said group. The second component is evaluative and concerns the status of the group within society. The third component is emotional, or how much attachment a member of the group feels toward the group (ibid.). Individuals who identify more strongly as a typical former prisoner may be more committed to the group of former prisoners, meaning that they are still committed to a criminal lifestyle and do not wish to change their ways. Another possibility is that these individuals perceive themselves to be "doomed to deviance" and do not see a way out of the criminal lifestyle or into a more prosocial lifestyle (Maruna 2001). On the other hand, individuals who do not identify as a typical former prisoner may be in the process of establishing a prosocial identity and thus may be further on the road to desistance from crime and successful reintegration into society (see, e.g., Paternoster and Bushway 2009; Paternoster et al. 2016). In contrast, formerly incarcerated persons may identify with their peers, but have a helper/wounded healer/professional ex orientation with a desire and commitment to assist similarly affected/stigmatized individuals in living a pro-social life (LeBel 2007; LeBel, Richie, and Maruna 2015).

Considerable research evidence indicates that stigmatized persons who do not identify with the group (low group identifiers) prefer individualistic strategies such as attempting to leave the group (Branscombe and Ellemers 1998). For formerly incarcerated persons, leaving the group may involve the process of desisting from crime. Many disadvantaged group members may classify themselves as relatively unique individuals and instead of describing themselves as prototypic group members, may indicate that the group as a whole is heterogeneous as opposed to homogeneous (Jost, Burgess, and Mosso 2001, p. 382). For example, Johnson (1971) argues that a person in prison "usually does not see himself as an enemy of society" (p. 39). In this regard, Goffman (1963) posits:

> The stigmatized individual exhibits a tendency to stratify his "own" according to the degree to which their stigma is apparent and obtrusive. He can take up in regard to those who are more evidently stigmatized than himself the attitudes the normals take to him. . . . It is in

his affiliation with, or separation from, his more evidently stigmatized fellows, that the individual's oscillation of identification is most sharply marked. (p. 107)

Wills (1981) noted that, in general, people tend to use downward social comparisons and compare themselves to others who are worse off. Maruna (2001), in his study of ex-prisoners, also found that many desisters made downward social comparisons with their counterparts deemed to be "true criminals" and insisted that "they were not one of them" (p. 136).

## Desistance from Crime and Agency, Hope, and Optimism

Paternoster and Bushway (2009) argue that the first step on the path to desistance is the desire to avoid becoming the "feared self." Then, the development of a more positive and prosocial "good" self-identity is thought to be a key component in the process of desistance from crime (Maruna 2001; Paternoster and Bushway 2009; Paternoster et al. 2016). In addition, Paternoster and colleagues argue that their identity theory of desistance (ITD) "places human agency at front and center of the theory by asserting that desistance is brought about by the decisions and actions of offenders" (Paternoster et al. 2016, p. 1221). Many researchers note that one's sense of self-efficacy, optimism, or hope may be a necessary, if not sufficient, condition for an individual to be able to succeed after prison and desist from crime more generally (see, e.g., Farrall et al. 2014; LeBel et al. 2008; Maruna 2001; Visher and O'Connell 2012). For some former prisoners, the perceived stability in how they are stigmatized and negatively treated by society may influence them to lose hope. For example, persistent offenders tend to lack feelings of agency, experiencing their lives as being largely determined for them in a fatalistic mind-set which Maruna (2001) refers to as being "doomed to deviance" and finds to be similar to the "learned helplessness" theory of depression described by Abramson, Seligman, and Teasdale (1978). The negative impact of this belief system gains credibility from Maruna's finding that "[t]he active offenders . . . seemed fairly accurate in their assessments of their situation (dire), their chances of achieving success in the 'straight' world (minimal), and their place in mainstream society ('need not apply')" (2001, p. 9). Maruna (2004) posits that the understanding that one's outcomes are due to external, stable, and uncontrollable factors may be partly responsible for former prisoners' continued involvement in crime.

LeBel and colleagues (2008; see also Visher and Courtney 2007) found that soon-to-be-released prisoners' positive mind-set was a significant predictor of post-imprisonment outcomes. In particular, an individual's sense of self-efficacy (hope) contributed positively to the reintegration process. Similarly, Woldgabreal, Day, and Ward (2016) found that persons under community supervision with higher Positive Psychological States (PPS) (i.e., self-efficacy, optimism, and hope) had lower rates of recidivism. Moreover, Lloyd and Serin (2012) found that "those who endorse belief in an ability to desist from crime also endorse positive beliefs about desistance," and "that higher agency was related to lower risk to re-offend" (p. 555).

The literature on the "better-than-average" effect (Alicke and Govorun 2005) and "positive illusions" (Taylor and Brown 1988, 1994) suggests that formerly incarcerated persons may view themselves as different from the typical former prisoner. In general terms, people view themselves in a more positive light than others (Alicke and Govorun 2005). Moreover, Taylor and Brown (1988) assert that these positive views of self may promote more beneficial coping and psychological well-being as well as "higher motivation, greater persistence, more effective performance and ultimately, greater success" (p. 199). Based on the negative stereotypes of felons, it is likely that formerly incarcerated persons will perceive the "typical" former prisoner pejoratively, and thus be less likely to see themselves in this way. Thus, we hypothesize that most of the participants in this study will disagree that they are typical former prisoners. Based on this research, and the other literature discussed above about desistance from crime and prisoner reentry, we hypothesize that those who believe more strongly that they are a typical former prisoner will have more antisocial attitudes toward crime, feel worse about themselves (i.e., have lower self-esteem), express less satisfaction with their life, and show less optimism for the future (i.e., indicate a higher likelihood of rearrest).

*Other Factors Related to Desistance and Successful Reintegration*

The geographic concentration of returning prisoners in inner-city minority neighborhoods has become an important topic for prisoner reentry researchers (Travis et al. 2014). Several researchers suggest that incarceration may have lost much of its stigmatizing capacity due to the normalization of the experience in inner-city communities (see, e.g., Clear 2007; Western et al. 2015). The literature supports the view that former prisoners living in inner-city communities where incarceration rates are high are cognizant of their lower position in society. Consequently, we hypothesize that individuals who grew up in neighborhoods where the prison experience is more common will view themselves as more typical former prisoners.

It is generally accepted that the more time one serves in prison, the more disconnected one becomes from the outside world (see, e.g., Irwin 2005). Similarly, Maruna (2001) argues that conviction and imprisonment often serve to reinforce a person's negative worldview and detachment from society. In addition, antisocial attitudes are consistently shown to be one of the major risk factors for recidivism (Bonta and Andrews 2017). The criminal justice literature is replete with examples of how unjust America's criminal justice system is, especially with regard to people of color (see, e.g., Tonry 2011). Former prisoners themselves often articulate that the system is unfair and unjust (Ross and Richards 2003). In a similar vein, Laub and Sampson (2003) conclude that "most persistent offenders (as well as ex-offenders) see society as a whole as corrupt" (p. 186). Consequently, it is hypothesized that stronger feelings that the criminal justice system is illegitimate will be related to thinking of oneself as a typical former prisoner.

Social bonds to conventional society are important for successful prisoner reintegration (Harding et al. 2014; Petersilia 2003; Western et al. 2015) and desistance from crime (Laub and Sampson 2003). The strength and quality of one's family relationships are of central importance (Boman and Mowen 2017; Harding et al. 2014; Visher et al. 2009). These findings suggest that stronger social bonds might act as a protective factor that supports reintegration. The lack of formal education, especially being a high school dropout, has consistently been found to be related to becoming incarcerated at some point in a person's lifetime (see, e.g., Western 2006), and limits one's chances to succeed post-release (Duwe and Clark 2014).

Research on narratives of desistance has found that a characteristic that distinguishes between successfully and unsuccessfully reformed ex-prisoners is the individual's engagement in mentoring, parenting, and other "generative" activities designed to "give something back" to others in his or her community (Maruna 2001; see also LeBel et al. 2015). The analyses to follow will examine if/how these factors often associated with desistance from crime and successful reintegration are related to thinking of oneself as a typical former prisoner.

*Study Objectives*

The main objectives of this study are to examine the strength of agreement in thinking of oneself as a typical former prisoner and the factors related to these beliefs, and to assess the relationship between these beliefs and psychological well-being and potential behavioral outcomes. The main objective of this study is to address three research questions: (1) To what degree do formerly incarcerated persons perceive themselves to be a "typical former prisoner"?; (2) What characteristics account for any differences in thinking of oneself as a typical former prisoner?; and (3) How is thinking of oneself as a typical former prisoner related to psychological well-being, criminal attitude, and potential behavioral outcomes such as the forecast of rearrest?

Methods

*Sample and Data Collection*

In this study, a formerly incarcerated person is defined as: *someone who has served a prison sentence for a felony conviction*. A purposive and targeted sampling technique was used to recruit male and female formerly incarcerated persons from New York City and Upstate New York. Sampling was aimed at recruiting adults, aged eighteen and older, who were currently receiving prisoner reintegration services of some kind. Participants were recruited from six organizations providing a variety of services (e.g., counseling, drug/alcohol treatment, education, and employment services) to former prisoners who come to them both voluntarily and due to parole and court mandates. The recruitment of participants from more than one organization provides a sample from different settings and avoids the possibility of having the findings skewed by the biases of one specific group or the idiosyncrasies of a particular location or program. A total of 228 formerly incarcerated persons are included in this study.

This is a cross-sectional study and the method of data collection is a self-completed questionnaire that was delivered to groups of former prisoner clients at each organization. Data collection was completed between April and September 2004. The questionnaire asked about a variety of topics concerning life as a formerly incarcerated person, including: perceptions of stigma, social identity as a former prisoner, coping strategies, psychological well-being, demographics, and criminal history. The questionnaire primarily utilized a fixed-choice "closed" format with response sets ranging from five to eight items. The majority of participants completed the questionnaire in thirty minutes or less. Approval for the study was obtained from the University's Institutional Review Board and senior-level personnel (e.g., executive director) at each of the organizations.

*Analytical Strategy*

Ordinary Least Squares (OLS) regression analysis (using SPSS version 22) is used to determine how well a set of variables explains thinking of oneself as a typical former prisoner. The mean substitution method is used to account for missing data, and following the suggestion of Cohen et al. (2003), a missing-data dummy variable is included in the OLS regression equation. The OLS regression equation was checked for outliers (using regression diagnostic statistics) and for problems of multicollinearity among the independent variables (using Variation Inflation Factor [VIF] statistics), and the results presented are for the equation with two outliers removed.

Correlation analysis is used to examine the relationship between thinking of oneself as a typical former prisoner and psychological well-being (self-esteem and satisfaction with life), the forecast of rearrest in the next three years, and criminal attitude.

## Measures

### TYPICAL FORMER PRISONER
Participants were asked to respond to the statement, "I am a typical former prisoner," using a 7-point Likert-type response set ranging from strongly disagree to strongly agree.

### DEMOGRAPHIC AND BACKGROUND CHARACTERISTICS
Demographic information including age, sex, and racial/ethnic identity was collected. Age is a continuous variable in years, and for sex, males are coded as 1 with females coded as 0. Racial/ethnic identity is operationalized with Black, non-Latino as the reference category, and categories for White, non-Latino, Latino, and Other, non-Latino. The location where the participant completed the interview is coded with 1 = New York City and 0 representing all others from Upstate New York. To provide a better understanding of the participants, formerly incarcerated persons were asked the reason for attending the reentry program. This variable is coded with 1 = came to this program voluntarily and 0 representing those who were mandated to attend the program.

### CRIMINAL HISTORY
The criminal history of participants was measured in three ways: number of felony convictions in lifetime, prison time served in lifetime, and age at first felony arrest. Each of these measures involves self-report. The variable for number of felony convictions is continuous with a range of 1 to 10. For the analysis to follow, the time served variable has been log transformed in order to account for positive skew. In addition, participants were asked, "How long have you been out of prison?" This variable is measured using a 6-point scale with 0 = less than 30 days and 5 = more than 24 months. This "time out" of prison variable is included to assess if thinking of oneself as a more typical former prisoner is related to more or less experience with the reintegration process.

### SOCIAL BONDS TO CONVENTIONAL SOCIETY
A 4-item scale was developed to measure the quality of respondents' social bonds to family and friends. Participants were asked to indicate

"how you feel about": the way things are in general between you and your close relatives, you and your children, the relationship with your partner, and the amount of friendship in your life. These measures are answered using Andrews and Withey's (1976) D-T scale from 1 (terrible) to 7 (delighted). Education level is operationalized by the highest level of formal education completed and is a 7-item scale with those reporting eighth grade or less coded as 0 and those who have engaged in post-graduate study coded as 6.

### NORMALIZATION OF THE PRISON EXPERIENCE

Three items (i.e., "In the neighborhood where I grew up, going to prison is like a 'rite of passage'"; "A kid growing up today in the neighborhood where I grew up will probably end up in prison someday"; "In the neighborhood where I grew up, there is no shame in going to prison") were combined to form a normalization scale where higher scores indicate that serving time in prison is seen as a likely occurrence, and is not considered shameful in the neighborhood where the respondent grew up.

### ILLEGITIMACY OF THE CRIMINAL JUSTICE SYSTEM

In this study, former prisoners' attitudes and beliefs about how fair, just, and legitimate they perceive the criminal justice system and laws to be are assessed. Four items were used to address the issues relevant to a population of formerly incarcerated persons. The specific items include "Unjust laws have put many people in prison" and "The law represents the values of the people in power rather than the values of people like me." In addition, two reverse scored items are included in this scale: "All in all, I think the criminal justice system treats people fairly" and "All people receive the equal protection of the laws." A 7-point Likert-type scale with a range from strongly disagree to strongly agree is used, and higher scores indicate stronger agreement that the criminal justice system and laws are unfair and unjust. Therefore, this is a scale of the perceived *illegitimacy* of the criminal justice system.

### HELPER/WOUNDED HEALER ORIENTATION

The four specific helper/wounded healer orientation indicators include: I often share my past experiences to help others avoid making the same mistakes I made; I am a good role model for other former prisoners who are trying to go straight; I act as a mentor of sorts for prisoners and former prisoners that need help to get back on their feet; and, I plan to pursue (or am currently pursuing) a career where I can give back and help other people such as former prisoners, youth in trouble with the law, or people with drug/alcohol addictions. This orientation emphasizes an informal role to make it a possibility for former prisoners with only a few months (or weeks) back in society. A 7-point Likert-type scale is used with a range from strongly disagree to strongly agree. Higher scores indicate stronger agreement for sharing one's experiences, strength, and hope; acting as a role model; mentoring others; and, for some, making a career of helping others who are not as far along in the recovery and/or reintegration process.

## PERSONAL STIGMA

Respondents were asked for their perceptions of what "people" think about them personally because of their status as a former prisoner. Items were modified from Link's (1987) devaluation-discrimination scale for persons with mental illness and Harvey's (2001) scale concerning stigma and race. In addition, several new items were developed (see LeBel 2012). The 9-item scale includes many stereotypes of formerly incarcerated persons (i.e., dangerous, dishonest, untrustworthy), as well as indicators for being feared, discriminated against, looked down on, negative attitudes toward them as a former prisoner, and employers' unwillingness to give them a chance to prove themselves. A 7-point Likert-type scale from 1 (strongly disagree) to 7 (strongly agree) is used for the personal stigma scale.

## PSYCHOLOGICAL WELL-BEING AND BEHAVIORAL OUTCOMES

The psychological well-being of respondents is measured with the Rosenberg Self-Esteem Scale (Rosenberg 1965). This 10-item scale has five positively worded items (e.g., "I feel that I have a number of good qualities") and five negatively worded items (e.g., "I feel I do not have much to be proud of"). Negatively worded items are reverse scored so that higher scores reflect feelings of positive self-worth. A single question from Andrews and Withey (1976) was used to measure former prisoners' "global" well-being or life satisfaction, "How do you feel about your life as a whole?" This variable is scored using Andrews and Withey's (1976) D-T scale. Research findings suggest that prisoners and former prisoners tend to view their chances of successful reentry with "rose-colored glasses," that is, forecasting that it will be fairly easy to avoid a return to prison (see, e.g., Burnett and Maruna 2004; Dhami et al. 2006; Visher and O'Connell 2012). Respondents were asked, "Realistically, how likely or unlikely is it that you will be arrested for a new crime in the next three years?" A 5-point Likert-type scale from 1 (very unlikely to be rearrested) to 5 (very likely) was used to assess respondents' forecast of rearrest. Similarly, participants were asked to forecast the arrest for "the average person who was formerly incarcerated." Finally, pro-criminal attitudes are measured with a scale of three items (i.e., "To get ahead in the world you may have to do some things that are illegal"; "It's alright to get around the law if you can get away with it"; and "To make money, there are no right and wrong ways anymore, only easy and hard ways"). A 7-point Likert-type scale from strongly disagree to strongly agree is used for the criminal attitudes scale.

## Results

### Descriptive Statistics

Descriptive statistics are presented in table 8.1. The sample of formerly incarcerated persons has a mean age of 36.18 years, is 84.7% male, and is 57.7% Black, non-Latino, 26.9% Latino, 12.3% White, non-Latino, and 3.1% Other, non-Latino. Nearly three-fourths (72.8%) of the sample completed the questionnaire in New York City. In comparison, the cohort of 24,921 inmates released from prisons in New York State in 2004 had a mean age of 34.5 years, was 93.2% male, and 59% were originally committed to prison from one of the five counties of New York City. Gonnerman (2004), however, reported that about two-thirds of the persons released from prisons in New York State return to New York City. The 2004 release cohort as a whole was 49.6% African American, 29.6% Latino, and 19.0% White (State of New York Department of Correctional Services 2009). In the current study, an effort was made to over-sample female former prisoners in relation to their percentage of the population released each year in New York State. The mean score on the education measure is 2.49 (SD = 1.50), with the median = 2.00

TABLE 8.1. Descriptive Statistics

| Variable | Description | Mean | (SD) |
|---|---|---|---|
| Age | Years. Median = 36.00. Range = 18 to 62. | 36.18 | (9.68) |
| Sex | Male | .847 | (0.36) |
| Race/ethnicity | Black, non-Latino | .577 | (0.50) |
|  | White, non-Latino | .123 | (0.33) |
|  | Latino | .269 | (0.44) |
|  | Other, non-Latino | .031 | (0.17) |
| Education | Formal education completed. 0 = 8th grade or less; 6 = post-graduate study | 2.49 | (1.44) |
| Location (NYC) | Location in which questionnaire was completed. 0 = Upstate New York; 1 = New York City | .728 | (0.45) |
| Voluntary | How did you come to be in this program? 0 = Had to attend a program; 1 = Came to this program voluntarily | .463 | (0.50) |
| Felony convictions | Number of felony convictions (lifetime) | 2.37 | (1.55) |
| Time served | Prison time served in months (lifetime) | 87.38 | (71.55) |
| Arrest felony | Age at arrest for first felony | 21.00 | (7.94) |
| Time out | Length of time elapsed since release. 0 = less than 30 days; 5 = more than 24 months | 2.65 | (1.80) |
| Typical | "I am a typical former prisoner." 1 = strongly disagree; 7 = strongly agree | 3.23 | (1.79) |
| Social bonds | Quality of bonds to family and friends. 1 = terrible; 7 = delighted. 4-item scale. α = .74. | 4.74 | (1.23) |
| Normalization | Normalization of prison experience in the neighborhood where the respondent grew up. 1 = strongly disagree; 7 = strongly agree. 3-item scale. α = .690. | 4.30 | (1.50) |
| Stigma (personal) | Perceptions of personally being stigmatized due to status as a former prisoner. 1 = strongly disagree; 7 = strongly agree. 9-item scale. α = .872. | 3.80 | (1.31) |
| Illegitimacy | The belief that the criminal justice system and the laws are unfair and unjust. 1 = strongly disagree; 7 = strongly agree. 4-item scale. α = .516. | 5.53 | (1.01) |
| Wounded healer | Orientation involving desire and commitment to "reach back" and help other similarly stigmatized people make it in the world. 1 = strongly disagree; 7 = strongly agree. 4-item scale. α = .722. | 5.32 | (1.21) |
| Self-esteem | Rosenberg's Self-esteem Scale. 1 = strongly disagree; 7 = strongly agree. 10-item scale. α = .781. | 5.43 | (0.94) |
| Life satisfaction | "How do you feel about your life as a whole?" 1 = terrible; 4 = mixed feelings; 7 = delighted | 4.38 | (1.19) |
| Forecast of rearrest (You) | "Realistically, how likely or unlikely is it that you will be arrested for a new crime in the next three years?" 1 = very unlikely to be rearrested; 5 = very likely to be rearrested. | 2.09 | (1.09) |

(continued)

TABLE 8.1. *Continued*

| Variable | Description | Mean | (SD) |
|---|---|---|---|
| Forecast of rearrest (Average former prisoner) | "Realistically, how likely or unlikely is it that the average person who was formerly incarcerated will be arrested for a new crime in the first three years after release from prison?" 1 = very unlikely; 5 = very likely to be rearrested. | 3.91 | (0.80) |
| Criminal attitude | Measure of pro-criminal attitudes. 1 = strongly disagree; 7 = strongly agree. 3-item scale. α = .647. | 2.65 | (1.39) |

Note: N = 228. SD = Standard deviation.

for having a GED/HSED. On average, participants served 87.4 months in prison during their lifetime with a median of 60 months. The mean for number of felony convictions in their lifetime is 2.37, while the mean age at first felony arrest is 21 with a median of 18 years old. For the 2004 release cohort, 33.4% had no prior felony convictions, while 30.4% of formerly incarcerated persons in the current study reported having only one felony conviction. Close to half (46.3%) the sample reported attending the reentry program voluntarily. Table 8.1 shows that the elapsed length of time since release from prison (M = 2.65, SD = 1.80) has considerable variation, with 33.0% indicating being out for less than 90 days and 24% indicating being out for more than 24 months.

The social bond scale for the quality of relationships with family and friends has a mean of 4.74, where 5 indicates "pleased." For the helper/wounded healer orientation scale the mean is 5.32 (SD = 1.21) with a Cronbach's alpha coefficient of .722. Overall, many of the formerly incarcerated persons agreed or strongly agreed with each of the four indicators. The mean of the normalization scale (4.30) is significantly above the midpoint (neither agree nor disagree) of the scale, but has a substantial amount of variation, suggesting that some participants grew up in neighborhoods where a person going to prison was a common occurrence, while others did not. The mean of the personal stigma scale (3.80) was significantly below (at $p < .05$) the midpoint, and the alpha coefficient for the scale is .872. The mean of the illegitimacy scale (5.53) was significantly above the midpoint, indicating that the former prisoners in this study generally think that the criminal justice system and laws are unfair and unjust.

For the psychological well-being measures, the mean of 5.43 on the self-esteem scale was quite high, and the mean of 4.38 for life satisfaction was closest to the response of 4 for "mixed feelings." For the forecast of rearrest for the participant him- or herself, the mean was 2.09 (SD = 1.09) where 2 indicates "unlikely to be rearrested" in the next three years. In contrast, the mean for the average former prisoner was 3.91 (SD = 0.80) where 4 indicates "likely to be rearrested" in the next three years. The criminal attitude measure was relatively low (M = 2.65), indicating that respondents disagreed that it is permissible to do something illegal to get ahead in the world.

*Typical Former Prisoner*

Table 8.1 shows that the mean for the measure for agreement that one is a typical former prisoner is 3.23 (SD = 1.79), significantly ($t$ 1, 227 = −6.48, $p$ < .001) below the neutral score (4). More than half (53.1%) of the sample disagreed at some level that they are a typical former prisoner.

*Explaining the Perception of Oneself as a Typical Former Prisoner*

Table 8.2 displays results for the ordinary least squares (OLS) regression equation explaining the level of agreement that one is a typical former prisoner. The table reports the unstandardized coefficients, standard errors, standardized coefficients (Betas), and the statistical significance for each of the independent variables. The multiple regression analysis revealed that the independent variables contributed significantly to the model ($F$ (18, 224) = 3.06, $p$ < .001) and accounted for 21.1% of the variation. Formerly incarcerated persons who more strongly agree that they are a typical former prisoner have higher scores for perceptions of personally being stigmatized due to their status as a former prisoner, have lower scores on the scale for illegitimacy of the criminal justice system, and completed less formal education. Two additional variables have marginally statistically significant (at $p \leq .01$) relationships with thinking of oneself as typical: stronger agreement that going to prison was normal in the neighborhood where they grew up and having fewer felony convictions.

TABLE 8.2. OLS Regression Model for Thinking of Oneself as a Typical Former Prisoner

| Variable | B | SE B | Beta |
|---|---|---|---|
| Age (years) | 0.001 | (0.015) | 0.006 |
| Sex (Male) | −0.055 | (0.361) | −0.011 |
| White, non-Latino | −0.015 | (0.407) | −0.003 |
| Latino | 0.223 | (0.268) | 0.056 |
| Other, non-Latino | 0.699 | (0.653) | 0.069 |
| Education | −0.228** | (0.082) | −0.183 |
| Location (NYC) | 0.246 | (0.297) | 0.063 |
| Felony convictions | −0.145# | (0.083) | −0.126 |
| Time served | 0.077 | (0.170) | 0.037 |
| Arrest felony | −0.013 | (0.018) | −0.057 |
| Time out | −0.018 | (0.065) | −0.018 |
| Voluntary | 0.098 | (0.241) | 0.027 |
| Social bonds | −0.132 | (0.098) | −0.093 |
| Normalization | 0.151# | (0.080) | 0.130 |
| Stigma (personal) | 0.246** | (0.093) | 0.182 |
| Illegitimacy | −0.485*** | (0.121) | −0.274 |
| Wounded healer | −0.013 | (0.101) | −0.009 |
| Missing data dummy | 0.085 | (.362) | .016 |
| Constant | 5.607*** | (1.231) | |
| $R^2$ | .211 | | |

Note. Results shown are for the regression equation with outliers removed (n = 225). Mean substitution is used for missing data. *** $p \leq .001$ ** $p \leq .01$, * $p \leq .05$, # $p \leq .10$.

## Relationship between Thinking of Oneself as a Typical Former Prisoner and Psychological and Behavioral Outcomes

In the next step, an assessment is made of the relationship (correlations) between thinking of oneself as a typical former prisoner and respondents' self-esteem, life satisfaction, forecast of rearrest in the next three years, and criminal attitude. Table 8.3 displays the correlations (Pearson's *r*, two-tailed) and statistical significance level of each of these relationships. Not surprisingly, the results show that stronger agreement that one is a typical former prisoner is negatively related to self-esteem ($r = -.209$, $p \leq .01$). However, although the relationship is negative,

TABLE 8.3. Relationship between Thinking of Oneself as a Typical Former Prisoner and Psychological and Behavioral Outcomes

| Characteristic | Typical Former Prisoner |
| --- | --- |
| Self-esteem | −.209** |
| Life satisfaction | −.093 |
| Forecast of rearrest (you) | .189** |
| Forecast of rearrest (average prisoner) | −.125# |
| Criminal attitude | .081 |

Note. Correlations are shown (two-tailed). Pairwise deletion is used for missing data. N ranges from 223 to 228. ** $p \leq .01$, * $p \leq .05$, # $p \leq .10$.

current life satisfaction is not significantly related to thinking of oneself as more typical. The more a formerly incarcerated person forecasts the likelihood of getting rearrested in the next three years, the more that person agrees that they are a typical former prisoner ($r = .189, p \leq .01$). In contrast, the greater likelihood in perceiving that the average formerly incarcerated person will be rearrested is negatively related to thinking of oneself as a more typical former prisoner ($r = −.125, p = .060$). Finally, although the relationship between thinking of oneself as a typical former prisoner and higher scores on the criminal attitude scale is positive, the correlation is not significant.

## Discussion

This study had three main objectives: to measure the belief that one is a typical former prisoner in a sample of formerly incarcerated persons; to determine the factors most strongly related to thinking of oneself as a typical former prisoner; and to ascertain if thinking of oneself as a more prototypical former prisoner is related to factors considered important to successful reintegration and/or desistance from crime more generally.

As hypothesized, the majority (53.1%) of formerly incarcerated persons disagreed at some level that they are a typical former prisoner, with 20.6% of the total sample indicating that they strongly disagree. In contrast, only 25.5% agreed at some level, and 21.4% neither agreed nor disagreed that they're a typical former prisoner. These findings about perceptions as a typical former prisoner support the notion that formerly incarcerated persons may see their stigmatized group as more heterogeneous.

A regression analysis examining the characteristics associated with stronger agreement that one is a typical former prisoner indicated that three variables were significantly related to this belief. A comparison of the standardized coefficients indicates that perceiving the criminal justice system as more legitimate (i.e., *less* illegitimate) (Beta = −.276) has the largest impact on thinking of oneself as a more typical former prisoner, while the completion of less formal education (Beta = −.173) has the next largest impact, followed closely by perceptions of personal stigma (Beta = .182). The finding that participants who perceive themselves to be more typical former prisoners in this sample view the criminal justice system as more legitimate was unexpected. Perhaps these individuals have internalized their guilt and shame (Braithwaite 1989) to a greater degree than those espousing that they are atypical former prisoners, or they accept their fate. Based on the unexpectedness of this finding involving perceptions of illegitimacy of the criminal justice system, more research is warranted to examine the relationship of these beliefs with desistance from crime and prisoner reentry more generally.

Formerly incarcerated persons who have completed more formal education reported less agreement that they are a typical former prisoner. This finding makes sense, as many prisoners and former prisoners have not completed high school (Western 2006), there is self-selection in the decision to go to college, and respondents who have done so may be more likely to use downward social comparisons with their peers with less formal education. Also, formal education may be understood as a significant factor that differentiates former prisoners from one another, as well as being related to improved employment and recidivism outcomes (Duwe and Clark 2014).

The set of indicators in the personal stigma scale includes many of the stereotypes of formerly incarcerated persons (i.e., dangerous, dishonest, untrustworthy) (LeBel 2012). Consequently, it was expected to find that formerly incarcerated persons perceiving higher levels of stigma see themselves as more typical former prisoners. As part of this study, respondents were also asked about having a visible stigma—"I think that people can tell I've been in prison because of my tattoos, scars or the way

I talk," and 31.2% agreed with this statement at some level. Importantly, the correlation of having a visible stigma with thinking of oneself as a typical former prisoner is statistically significant ($r = 237$, $p < .001$). Perceiving oneself as being a more prototypical former prisoner and facing intense stigmatization from society appears to be similar to learned helplessness (Abramson et al. 1978) and possibly a lack of hope and optimism that successful reintegration is possible (Maruna 2001). Halsey, Armstrong, and Wright (2017, p. 9) argue that researchers "should focus less on 'the will to crime' and more upon factors which undermine *the will to desist*" (italics in original).

Growing up in a neighborhood where the prison experience has become more normalized was marginally significantly related (at $p = .062$) to thinking of oneself as a typical former prisoner. Many released prisoners return to their old neighborhood (see, e.g., La Vigne, Shollenberger, and Debus 2009), or to a similarly disadvantaged community with high rates of crime and relatively few services and support systems to promote successful reintegration (see, e.g., Clear 2007; Travis et al. 2014). Moreover, released prisoners themselves appear to recognize that their chances of success are diminished by returning to the same old neighborhood, as many report that drug dealing is a major problem, that it is difficult to avoid crime, and that their neighborhood is not a good place to find a job (see, e.g., La Vigne, Shollenberger, and Debus 2009; Visher and Courtney 2007). Thus, the relationship between normalization of the prison experience and being a more typical former prisoner also appears to fit Maruna's (2001) view of being "doomed to deviance."

It is also important to briefly mention the characteristics of formerly incarcerated persons not significantly associated with thinking of themselves as typical former prisoners. In particular, the unrelated variables include the following: age, sex, race/ethnicity, having a wounded healer or helper orientation, elapsed time since release from prison, reason for attending the reentry program (voluntary vs. mandated), location of the interview (New York City vs. Upstate New York), and criminal history. The extent and seriousness of respondents' criminal history is, at most, only weakly related to thinking of oneself as a typical former prisoner. Having fewer felony convictions has a marginally significant (at $p = .083$) relationship with perceiving oneself as more typical. Based on the extant literature, and the similarity (by age, race/ethnicity, having only one felony conviction) of this sample to the 2004 prison release cohort in New York State, it is somewhat surprising that demographics and the background of formerly incarcerated persons are unrelated to their perception as a typical former prisoner. Moreover, there was no difference in perceptions of being a typical former prisoner based on the (voluntary vs. mandated) reason for attending the reentry program and for the length of time that a participant has been out of prison and living in the community.

A stronger agreement of typicality as a former prisoner was significantly related to lower self-esteem. Although self-esteem is not seen as an important risk factor or target for intervention to reduce recidivism (Bonta and Andrews 2017), low self-esteem often manifests itself in interaction restriction, marginalization, and concealment (Rosenberg and Owens 2001). Therefore, the link between lower self-esteem and thinking of oneself as a more typical former prisoner does not bode well for the successful reintegration.

The stronger one agrees that they are a typical former prisoner the higher their reported prediction of the likelihood that they will be rearrested in the next three years, but the lower they perceive the likelihood that the average prisoner will be rearrested. In fact, the results reported in table 8.1 indicate a better-than-average effect (or self-enhancement bias) as the formerly incarcerated persons in this sample forecast that they personally ($M = 2.10$, $SD = 1.09$) are significantly less likely to get rearrested in the next three years than the average prisoner ($M = 3.91$, $SD = 0.80$), $t(224) = 20.35$, $p < .001$ (see Dhami et al. 2006).

Moreover, the forecast of rearrest difference score, calculated by subtracting the self-assessment from the average or peer assessment score (Alicke and Govorun 2005), is negatively related to thinking of oneself as a typical former prisoner ($r = -.231$, $p < .001$). This strong negative relationship indicates that the more one thinks of him- or herself as a typical former prisoner, the smaller the difference between the forecast of rearrest for the average former prisoner and themselves. Thus, those thinking of themselves as more typical appear to be more realistic, or pessimistic, concerning their chances to remain arrest-free and possibly to desist from crime and successfully reenter society more generally. As this sample, overall, was found to disagree that they are typical former prisoners, these findings support the notion that many are making downward social comparisons with their peers (Goffman 1963; LeBel 2012; Maruna 2001). That is, the respondents appear to perceive being a "typical" former prisoner pejoratively and are less likely to identify themselves in this way.

Thus, a more "typical former prisoner" may have in a sense "given up" or lost (or lacked) hope on remaining arrest-free and/or going straight (see, e.g., LeBel et al. 2008; Lloyd and Serin 2012; Maruna 2001; Visher and O'Connell 2012), and resigned themselves to either a life of involvement with the criminal justice system or perhaps living on the margins of society, similar to Merton's retreatists (1938). These findings also support Halsey and colleagues' (2017) assertion that "the phenomenon in need of explanation is not a 'will to crime' or 'repeat offending' but rather, dissipation of the will to desist, grounded in a sense of moral exclusion" (p. 13). Although this study has focused on the mindset of formerly incarcerated persons, it is important to note that the actual structural impediments to desistance and successful reintegration are extensive and need to be lessened and removed as well (see, e.g., Farrall et al. 2014; Healy 2013; LeBel et al. 2008).

*Implications for Policy and Practice*

Research findings suggest that one's sense of hope and agency may be a key factor for an individual to be able to succeed after prison and desist from crime more generally (see, e.g., Farrall et al. 2014; LeBel et al. 2008; Lloyd and Serin 2012; Maruna 2001; Paternoster and Bushway 2009; Visher and O'Connell 2012). In a similar vein, there is growing interest in strengths-based assessment and interventions for individuals involved in the criminal justice system (see, e.g., Serin, Chadwick, and Lloyd 2016; Ward and Fortune 2013). Thus, interventions that enhance one's sense of optimism, hope, and agency may be beneficial. In fact, in utilizing hope as an intervention target with sexual offenders, researchers found that increasing levels of hope enhanced engagement in treatment and led to reductions in recidivism (Marshall et al. 2008; see also Huynh et al. 2015 concerning the use of positive psychology interventions with prisoners). The assessment of strengths and focus on agency and hope complements other interventions used with criminal justice involved individuals, such as motivational interviewing (National

Institute of Corrections 2012). Stinson and Clark (2017, p. 28), in their book *Motivational Interviewing with Offenders: Engagement, Rehabilitation, and Reentry*, argue that "the spirit of MI . . . calls you to draw forth their aspirations, values, and competencies" in order to more effectively enhance their opportunity to succeed. Likewise, there is increasing interest in the assessment of, and interventions applying, the concept of "grit," which has been defined as having perseverance and passion for long-term goals (Duckworth 2016). Moreover, Duckworth (2016) claims that grit may be teachable and that interventions may be able to enhance this aspect of agency, which may be especially applicable to incarcerated and formerly incarcerated persons.

Cognitive behavioral treatment is increasingly popular as an intervention for correctional clients (Feucht and Holt 2016). However, perhaps more focus is needed on the cognitive restructuring aspect of these approaches, such as Ellis's (1973) Rational Emotive Behavioral Therapy. That is, the results discussed above suggest that those believing that they are more typical former prisoners may have negative (or possibly irrational) beliefs (e.g., overgeneralization, catastrophizing, all-or-nothing thinking, etc.) for which there are interventions (see, e.g., Van Voorhis and Salisbury 2016). Similarly, researchers have noted that individuals suffering from depression exhibit diminished better-than-average effects (Alicke and Govorun 2005; Tabachnik, Crocker, and Alloy 1983), and may display learned helplessness as well (Abramson et al. 1978). Thus, in order to impact successful reentry outcomes, more attention may be needed to address mental health issues as well (Visher and Bakken 2014; Rose and LeBel 2017).

*Limitations*

Some limitations should be considered when interpreting the results of this study. The use of a purposive and targeted sampling technique (i.e., a nonrandom convenience sample) of formerly incarcerated persons who are currently attending (i.e., clients of) prisoner reentry programs poses a threat to the validity of the study in that these participants may not be "typical." However, the recruitment of both voluntary and mandated clients at reentry programs, and similarities to the 2004 prison release cohort in New York State, allay some of these concerns. In addition, the analysis is limited to a single state, and the data were collected in 2004. That is, these results cannot be generalized to those in other states or to formerly incarcerated persons who are not currently attending reentry programs. This study employed a cross-sectional design, and as a result, it is not possible to establish causal direction for the relationships between thinking of oneself as a typical former prisoner and other variables of interest. Research on desistance suggests that identity beliefs vary over time. Therefore, although this study included a measure for elapsed time since release from prison, longitudinal research designs combining qualitative, quantitative, and more interdisciplinary work are needed to better examine and document the process of how and why formerly incarcerated persons' views about themselves as typical, as well as their chances to succeed, may vary due to the structural challenges associated with reentry. The measure utilized to assess typicality among formerly incarcerated persons in this study is fairly limited, and future research should also consider the use of more extensive measures of group identification.

## Conclusion

To the extent that respondents in this sample are similar to the much larger population of formerly incarcerated persons, this study suggests that hundreds of thousands of individuals released each year perceive themselves to be "typical former prisoners." There appears to be little hope among formerly incarcerated persons who identify as more typical former prisoners that they can "earn redemption" (Bazemore 1999) and rejoin society as accepted conventional members of the community. Thus, thinking of oneself as a typical former prisoner appears to have an individual "off-track" and not on the road to successful reentry and desistance. As Farrall and colleagues (2014; see also LeBel et al. 2008) suggest, "[p]erhaps the principal lesson to be drawn is that those working with people trying to desist should recognize the need to engender hope first and foremost" (p. 215).

PART IV

Context and Consequences of Incarceration and Reentry

# 9

## Social Support in Daily Life at Reentry

NAOMI F. SUGIE AND DALLAS AUGUSTINE

The central role of social relationships and social support in daily life is well established across a variety of fields and disciplines. For people experiencing stressful situations and life crises, social relationships and support serve as buffers, which mitigate potentially harmful mental and physical health consequences (Cobb 1982; House, Umberson, and Landis 1988). During the reentry period, which is a stressful time of instability and readjustment, social support from friends and family is considered key to prevent recidivism and to promote social integration (Berg and Huebner 2011; Cochran 2014; Naser and LaVigne 2006; Western et al. 2015).

Social support is a broad term that refers to different types of assistance and caring; however, it often encapsulates two general categories: instrumental support and emotional support (Caplan 1982; House et al. 1988). Instrumental support includes material aid, such as housing, transportation, and financial assistance, as well as informational resources, such as job referrals and social service information. Emotional support refers to relationships and interactions that make a person feel valued and loved (Cobb 1982). Spending time with others, communicating concerns and anxieties freely, and feeling respected and cared for are all aspects of emotional support. Reciprocity and mutual obligation are also central dimensions of emotionally supportive relationships, such that emotional caring is a two-sided, relational interaction. Although instrumental and emotional supports overlap substantially, emotional support is often considered more integral to esteem, well-being, and overall health in scholarship on stress and coping (Cobb 1976; House et al. 1988).

Within the reentry literature, as well as broader criminological scholarship, social support is widely acknowledged as a central factor for integration and desistance. Within reentry research, however, studies generally emphasize the instrumental or transactional aspects of social support, pointing to the types of resources family and friends provide at reentry and how these resources then contribute to reentry success. Though many scholarly works mention that these resources generally entail both instrumental *and emotional* support, they often direct empirical examination to material, financial, and informational resources, such as housing, food, transportation, and employment information (for exceptions, see Martinez and Christian 2009; Nelson, Deess, and Allen 2011; Wyse, Harding, and Morenoff 2014). Consequently, reentry research tends to highlight the role of material aid and resource provision relative to emotional support.

In this chapter, we analyze novel data—e.g., daily open-ended survey questions via smartphones about the most important high and low points of the day—to understand people's perceptions about social support at reentry from prison. Through this experience sampling method (ESM), or the collection and analysis of self-report experiences in real time and in everyday contexts, we document four main findings. First, people often report social interactions as the most positive experiences of their day. These interactions rarely refer to instrumental aid and instead often suggest that people most value simply spending time with friends and family. Second, social interactions are not uniformly positive sources of support, and people sometimes report social relationships and situations as the most stressful issue of their day. Notably, reports of stressful situations include death, as well as health issues and illness, of close friends and family members, suggesting that this is a significant source of strain and stress for some people at reentry. Third, people refer to a range of different sources of emotional support, including parents and friends; however, they most often describe spending time with their children, romantic partners, and "family" more generally. Fourth, over time, the frequency of people's daily reports about positive social relationships decreases, and the frequency of reports about negative interactions remains stable.

Overall, our methodological approach provides insight into the types of social support that people value in their everyday lives. Our findings—and particularly, the central role of emotional support in everyday experiences—are consistent with broader empirical work outside of reentry on the buffering role of support in times of transition, stress, and crisis. We suggest that more attention be paid in the reentry scholarship to the function of emotional support for moderating key reentry outcomes, including recidivism and social integration.

## Social Support

The central role of social support—including both emotional and instrumental support—is most developed in research on mental and physical health (House et al. 1988). In the stress process paradigm, for example, social support is a buffer that moderates the potentially deleterious health consequences of stressors (Caplan 1982; Cobb 1982; Patterson 2002; Pearlin 1989). Social support systems, such as close friends and family, provide individuals with validation and esteem, which in turn equip individuals to handle stressful situations and crises. Through communication, cooperation, and mutual respect, social support systems provide a source of respite and retreat, as well as provide coping resources (Caplan 1982). In this literature, transitions and crises are typically described as unexpected macro-level events such as environmental and financial disasters or personal life transitions, such as divorce; however, reentry from prisons and jails can be conceptualized as a relevant crisis within this framework.

### Social Support at Reentry

Although social support comprises two interrelated aspects—instrumental and emotional support—reentry scholarship generally focuses empirical attention on instrumental support, including the provision of housing, food, transportation, and income (Harding et al. 2014; Nelson et al. 1999; Visher, LaVigne, and Travis 2004; Western et al. 2015). This scholarship finds that material support and resource allocation help people achieve economic stability in the years following prison (Harding et al. 2014) and facilitate other dimensions of social integration (Western et al. 2015). The emphasis on instrumental support, and its relationship to reentry success, is understandable given the context and challenges of reentry. Indeed, recent qualitative studies describe the extreme financial and material hardship faced by many people after they leave prison (Harding et al. 2014; Western et al. 2015). Within this context, instrumental support provides tangible and immediate benefits.

Emotional support is a dimension of social support that is less often empirically studied but is nonetheless considered a key component of reentry success. Indeed, emotional and instrumental support are often overlapping constructs, such that the provision of material aid and informational resources is often an indication of emotional warmth and caring (House et al. 1988). These distinctions between instrumental and emotional support are further blurred when considering a person's interpretation of the social relationship and of specific exchanges. For example, Martinez and Christian find that family members (as providers of social support) define certain transactions differently from people returning from prison (as recipients of support). Providers of support report the provision of informational resources while recipients interpret the resource exchange primarily through the lens of emotional support (2009). This suggests that empirical measures of instrumental support may be capturing both transactional support and emotional support, depending on the interpretation of recipients.

Notwithstanding the correspondence between instrumental and emotional support, the focus in reentry research on instrumental support raises a larger point about the importance of reciprocity in supportive relationships (Cobb 1982). Material and informational resources represent unidirectional transactions that can reinforce a person's feeling of dependence and threaten a person's sense of self-efficacy (Wyse et al. 2014). Martinez and Christian explain the discrepancy in interpretations described above as a strategy to preserve feelings of autonomy, such that emotional support can be more easily reciprocated than informational exchange during reentry (2009). A focus on instrumental support within social relationships emphasizes the forced reliance on social ties that is often experienced by people during reentry, a condition of material and informational dependence that is also reflected in their relationships with third parties, such as parole officers, reentry organizations, and academic researchers (Miller and Stuart 2017). Moreover, when feelings of self-efficacy and autonomy are diminished, formerly incarcerated people may find it difficult to leave behind their "criminal past" and establish personal narratives of redemption (Maruna 2001; Miller 2014). Reliance on material support from family and friends may impede a person's transformation narrative, particularly if rehabilitative transformation is seen as synonymous with economic self-sufficiency (Miller 2014). Focusing on instrumental support, then, potentially overlooks the importance of reciprocity in social relationships, with regard to both recidivism prevention and integration.

## Social Relationships as Sources of Stress

Another dimension of social support to consider is the negative aspect of interpersonal relationships, or the conflict, lack of reciprocity, and lack of stability that characterizes some relationships. Instead of buttressing coping skills and resources, negative social relationships can be sources of depression, stress, and dependence (Coyne and Downey 1991). Negative relationships can therefore not only be stressors themselves but also can exacerbate stressful experiences and transitions during reentry.

Relationships may convey both beneficial support and harmful tension, which change over time and within different contexts. Romantic partnerships, for example, are often central as sources of both emotional closeness and instability and strife (Comfort 2008; Leverentz 2014; Wyse et al. 2014). At reentry, partners provide instrumental resources, such as housing, food, transportation, and income, and give emotional support, which increases feelings of confidence and self-efficacy (Wyse et al. 2014). Romantic partnerships, however, can also be sources of stress and tension. Navigating romantic relationships, as well as other close relationships, during reentry often entails addressing prior conflicts, revisiting painful memories, and making amends for past wrongs (Leverentz 2014). The emotional work involved in strengthening these partnerships takes place within an already difficult context of material strain and emotional readjustment. Like romantic partnerships, friendships are also likely to be sources of both positive support and negative strain. Although close friends often offer valuable material and emotional support during reentry, they also may expose people to risky or tempting situations, which may in turn cause strain and lead to relapse or a return to "old ways" of criminal behavior (Nelson et al. 1999; Wyse et al. 2014).

*Sources of Social Support*

At reentry, social support systems involve an array of people, including close family members, romantic partners, friends, and even third parties, such as reentry service providers. Family members, and particularly female family members, have been identified as primary sources of social support during reentry (Leverentz 2014; Malik-Kane and Visher 2008; Martinez and Christian 2009; Western et al. 2015). Consistent with the broader literature on social support, relationships with women are often found to be the most beneficial for both resource allocation and emotional closeness (House et al. 1988; Visher et al. 2004; Western et al. 2015; Wheeler, Reis, and Nezlek 1983). Indeed, women are often considered "kinkeepers" or individuals who actively work to maintain consistent communication with family members, strengthening feelings of closeness and solidarity (Rosenthal 1985). During reentry, female family members play a key supportive role by organizing celebratory cookouts and other "rituals of release," as well as by providing ongoing emotional and material support (Western et al. 2015: 1534).

Consistent with the central role of family during reentry, relationships with children are presumably important sources of support. Although children, particularly young children, are not providers of instrumental support, they may be key sources of emotional support. Indeed, reconnecting with children is often a stated goal of those leaving prison and jail (Nelson et al. 1999) and the roles of mother and father are central emotional and psychological resources for individuals striving for reintegration and reentry success (Braman 2004). Indeed, as Maruna (2001) finds in his study of people who have desisted from criminal behavior, rebuilding relationships with children helps to restore self-respect and self-esteem. As one of Maruna's study participants describes, "I mean, my kids are starting to call me 'Dad' now, whereas years ago, they used to just say, 'Who's he?'" (123). Although children are not often described as central providers of social support in the reentry scholarship, this may be due to the tendency of research to focus on instrumental support, as opposed to emotional closeness and mutual obligation.

*Changes in Social Support over Time*

Reentry research consistently finds that most people receive considerable social support in the immediate time period after release from prison and jail. The first week is characterized by post-release celebrations and reunions with family and friends. People spend much of their time during this period with family and spend little time alone (Western et al. 2015). However, after the first week after release, time spent with family decreases (ibid.). As the weeks and months pass after release, relationships with family and romantic partners may become strained, exacerbated by the pressures of needing to find a job, of locating housing, or achieving other markers of independence and self-sufficiency. As a person's desired status as a breadwinner or provider continues, over time, to differ from his or her actual situation of material and financial dependency, strain and stress increase (Wyse et al. 2014). This "role strain" suggests that the correspondence between instrumental and emotional support may change over time, such that individuals may continue to receive instrumental support but in a way that is less aligned with emotional resources and that may even be at odds with any emotional benefits that increase perceptions of self-efficacy and independence. These considerations suggest that reentry research should investigate timing in social support, in addition to distinguishing between instrumental and emotional support.

Data and Methods

We use data from the Newark Smartphone Reentry Project (NSRP) in order to understand daily experiences of social support. The aim of the NSRP was to study job seeking and employment during reentry; however, the study examined a variety of other issues at reentry, as well. From April 2012 to April 2013, the NSRP recruited potential study participants by randomly sampling individuals from a complete census of men on parole who were recently released from prison in Newark, New Jersey. Individuals were eligible to participate if they were male, were not convicted of a sex offense and were not gang-involved, were searching for work, and were conversationally proficient in English.[1] Parole officers contacted those potentially eligible to meet with the researcher about the project and the researcher held group meetings with potential participants. During the meetings, which lasted from one to two hours, potential participants were informed about the study, learned about the types of data that would be collected via phones, and were given the opportunity to ask questions about data privacy, security, and any other concerns. People who were interested in participating then scheduled one-on-one meetings with the researcher, during which they could ask additional questions about their participation, sign the consent form, complete an initial interview, and receive a smartphone and data collection application (for more details on recruitment, see Sugie 2018). In total, 152 people were initially contacted and 135 people (or 89%) participated in the study. In this chapter, we restrict the analysis sample to the 133 individuals who completed daily surveys via smartphones.

Over the next three months, participants received brief twice-daily smartphone surveys, which asked about a variety of reentry experiences, including job search and work, emotional well-being, and other activities. During this time, they received a service plan and weekly gift cards for completing at least 75% of smartphone surveys each week.[2] At the end of the three months, participants completed a final interview and were allowed to keep the phones. Those who left the study early were also allowed to keep their phones, as a condition of their participation. Compared to many longitudinal reentry studies, the retention rate was relatively high, as 70% of participants completed all parts of the study, and the use of smartphones enabled the collection of real-time experiences at reentry.[3]

In this chapter, we focus on smartphone survey answers that were collected daily from an evening smartphone survey ("daily survey"). The daily survey was sent at 7 p.m. each night and asked about activities that occurred that day. This method of surveying individuals in real time, while they are in their everyday environments, is often referred to as an experience sampling method (ESM). Although ESM has been around for decades, it is increasingly being used, as smartphones become more common as tools of scientific inquiry (Mehl and Conner 2012; Stone et al. 2007). There are several strengths of ESM over traditional interview methods. First, ESM is conducted in real time, which helps prevent bias associated with retrospective reports that are affected by people's contemporaneous feelings and experiences (Torelli and Trivellato 1993). Second, the contextual setting of ESM reports—e.g., people are in their normal environments instead of a lab or interview office—describes experiences in situ, while people are navigating the realties of their daily stresses and successes (Bolger and Laurenceau 2013). Third, the repeated collection of daily answers facilitates the study of processes and experiences as they unfold over time. Overall, ESM enables a rich, descriptive understanding of the daily experiences of individuals over time.

We combine ESM with another unique approach: the use of open-ended questions about participants' most positive and negative aspects of the day. Typically, surveys—and often, brief smartphone surveys—use closed-ended questions, which are more cost-effective and easier to analyze (Converse 1984; Roberts et al. 2014; Salganik and Levy 2015). However, closed-ended questions can deter the collection of new and unanticipated information, and they may even bias information by suggesting answers to respondents (Salganik and Levy 2015; Schuman 1966; Schuman and Presser 1979). In order to solicit information about participants' perceived daily high and low points, the NSRP's daily survey asked two open-ended questions: *What was the most important positive event or issue of the day? What was the most important problem or stressful event or issue of the day?* Our analysis of social support and relationships at reentry is based on these answers, which participants volunteered on their own, without any prompts or predetermined answer choices. In total, we received 6,513 answers about positive issues and 6,506 answers about stressful issues.

Although these approaches—particularly, ESM with open ended questions—provide new, bottom-up insights into types of daily social support that individuals value most, these approaches are often characterized by higher amounts of missing data on any given day (e.g., Mehl and Conner 2012; Schuman and Presser 1979). Data may be missing at random, such as when a participant simply overlooks a survey prompt, or data may be missing more systematically, in ways related to social interaction and social support. Our sample represents approximately 54% of total possible days, such that missing observations are due to incomplete or unanswered survey questions during participation as well as to right censoring when participants leave the study early. Because of these challenges, we view the findings as descriptive accounts of social support, as opposed to generalizable estimates of social support at reentry. We return to this issue in the discussion.

*Analytic Methods*

We did not initially approach this chapter as a study of social support and relationships. Instead, we coded participants' answers to the daily open-ended questions using an inductive approach, in order to allow themes and patterns to emerge from the data (Glaser and Strauss 1967; Patton 1990). As part of this process, two researchers each coded the data and we continually revisited codes and participants' answers to refine themes and conceptual categories (Glaser and Strauss 1967). Based on participants' answers, it was quickly apparent that social relationships and support were often participants' most positive aspects of the day.

Through the inductive coding approach, we identified four primary considerations related to social support. Using this approach, first we distinguish between instrumental and emotional support, categorizing the latter as any references to positive social relationships or social interactions that did not involve material or information exchange. This is admittedly a broad view of emotional support; however, we think that participants' own categorization of these situations, as the highlight of their day, is consistent with the types of activities and interactions that undergird the concept of emotional support. Second, we examine participants' daily reports of stressful interactions and relationships, or the converse of emotional support. Third, we identify the source of both beneficial and stressful interactions, in terms of whether the person is a romantic partner, child, parent, or other type of family member or friend. Fourth, we analyze how participants' reports of positive and negative relationships change over time. Specifically, we look at reports, aggregated by week, over the study's twelve-week duration.

Participants' answers ranged from lengthy descriptive accounts to very short statements. In some of these latter cases, we had to make decisions about the most appropriate code. For example, sometimes it was unclear whether a social interaction was also characterized by resource allocation. In these instances, we did not infer that participants received resources and instead coded answers as "instrumental support" only if participants specifically stated that they received something. This issue characterizes open-ended questions more generally, which risk soliciting unclear or ambiguous responses (Geer 1988; Schuman 1966). In these more general situations, researchers attempt to address ambiguity with follow-up probes; however, in our case, we were unable to administer follow-up smartphone survey questions. We return to this issue in the discussion.

## Findings

First, we examine the types of social interactions that people report, in terms of instrumental and emotional support. Even though the broad aims of the NSRP concerned job seeking and employment, reports of positive social interactions not related to employment were not uncommon. Of the 6,513 daily answers about high points of the day reported by the 133 participants, 983 (or 15%) of these were instances that involved social interactions.

Given the emphasis in the reentry literature on material and informational exchange, we were somewhat surprised to see that participants' reports of transactional social interactions were rare compared to reports of more general emotional support, such as spending time with others. Of 983 instances of positive social interactions, only twenty-five (3%) were transactional interactions in which the participant stated that they received resources (see figure 9.1). These patterns, which are based on overall counts of responses across participants, are similar to findings when considering whether a person ever reported instrumental or emotional support. Specifically, of the 106 participants that ever reported the highlight of their day as being social interaction, only twelve people (or 11%) ever reported that they received resources.

Within these twenty-five resource transactions, the exact forms of material and informational support varied. Generally, most involved receiving help with their job search in some capacity. For example, one participant's daughter helped him with a resume for a prospective position. Another participant received a ride to work that day, and another reported that a peer told him "where to check out a job." Some of these highlights were actual offers of work from someone the participant knew, though most were potential opportunities for future work. One participant stated that an "individual came by to inform [him] that they

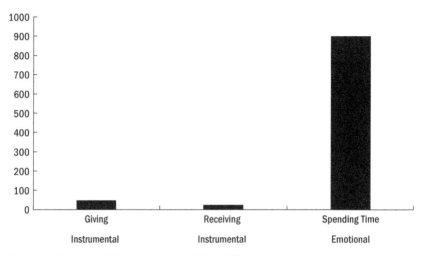

Figure 9.1. Reports of Social Support, by Type of Support

talked to their employer about getting a position at ShopRite," while another participant explained that he "spoke [to] a childhood friend and it's possible that we are gonna work on a few things." Similarly, another participant stated, "my brother talked to me and when I have my license back I'll have a job with him." Though these were not concrete offers for hire, participants still reported these possible job opportunities as the highlights of their day. Beyond these employment-related transactions, participants also received a variety of other resources from people in their lives, including obtaining information on reentry programs from a former romantic partner, accepting food from a church, or receiving a gift from a friend.

Though these twelve participants described twenty-five instances of receiving resources from others, the remaining 958 reports of positive social interactions did not reference receiving material or informational support. In fact, comparatively more participants reported that the highlight of their day was *giving back*, rather than receiving something. Twenty-five participants described forty-nine instances (5% of total positive social interactions) in which the most positive experience that day was one in which they helped someone. While some instances were simply general reports of helping ("helping family" or "helped out a brother"), others specified the way they had given back. It was common for participants to report assisting ill family members; for example, a participant "helped [his] sis, who's on dialysis" while another went with his "grandma to the doctor." Some reported what might otherwise be commonplace acts of helping family as the highlights of their day, such as "helping mother with whatever needed to be done around the house," "helping kids with homework," or "walking niece to school." Three participants even reported going beyond their immediate family to help in their community. One participant volunteered at a local shelter, while two participants helped community members who had been impacted by Hurricane Sandy, the 2012 hurricane that affected much of the Eastern seaboard.

Beyond these exchanges, the majority of reports (901 observations or 92% of total positive social interactions) described the highlight of the day as simply spending time with someone else. These counts, which are aggregated across participants, reflect similar patterns when examining the number of participants that ever reported spending time with others as the highlight of their day. Indeed, the vast majority of participants (96% of participants who reported positive social interactions) reported a social interaction that indicated that the most meaningful part of the day was simply *being with* other people. Although some reports were very specific, such as one participant's reported highlight being that his wife told him she loves him, most reports of positive social interactions tended to be fairly general ("spent time with my wife").

## Social Relationships as Stress and Strain

Just as social interactions were often the most positive part of people's days, they were also sometimes the most important notable problem in a participant's day. Of the 6,506 times participants reported a day's problem, 446 of those (7%) were reports of negative social interactions with others. Importantly, participants reported only approximately half as many negative social interactions as they did positive social interactions (446 and 983, respectively). Consistent with the literature, many of these negative reports referred to current and former romantic partners. When participants described their negative interactions with partners, they often referenced their relationship in general, or spoke more specifically about breakups or arguments with their significant others.

Although these reports tended to be periodic, spread across people and days, several participants consistently reported relationships as sources of tension. Beginning in the second week after release, one participant proceeded to list his "baby mama" as the main source of stress every day through the conclusion of the research period.

Importantly, incidences of death, illness, and loss were alarmingly common themes in participants' reports of their most important problems of the day. Within the study period alone, there were twenty-two instances, spread across fourteen participants, in which the person reported the death of a loved one. In addition, there were sixty-five reported instances where the greatest stressor of the day was a sick loved one, including hospitalizations of a close family member or friend. There were also an additional nine instances, across six participants, in which they reported missing a loved one.

*Sources of Social Support and Stress*

Across participants' reports, sources of positive social support came primarily from family, including romantic partners and children (see figure 9.2). There were 361 instances (40% of all reports of spending time together) in which people were spending time with "family" generally, and there were 343 instances (38%) in which reports specifically referenced spending time with children. In addition to family generally and children specifically, people also reported spending time with their romantic partners (82 instances by 29 participants), friends (30 instances by 21 participants), parents (27 instances by 20 participants), siblings (13 instances by 10 participants), and grandparents (6 instances by 5 participants).

Spending time with children was central to many participants' reentry experiences, and the happiness associated with both reconnecting and bonding after release was conveyed most strongly when participants discussed their children. For fifty-one participants, being with their children was the most positive part of their day, and some even mentioned their children nearly daily. When participants reported spending time with their children, they often referred to seemingly mundane activities, which people often take for granted, as their most positive aspect of that day. For example, family activities like helping children with homework,

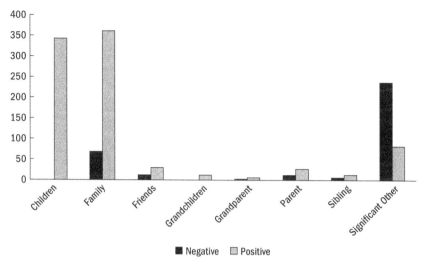

Figure 9.2. Sources of Support, by Positive and Negative Reports

going shopping with kids, or walking children to school were reported as daily high points. In addition to these everyday activities, participants also often listed important milestones in their children's lives, indicating the importance of being able to share these momentous occasions with them. For example, reports of this type included: "my little man graduating to second grade at school"; "spending the holidays with the family"; and seeing "kids' progress" in school. One participant even reported, "today my wife gave birth to my daughter. She weighed 7 pounds. I am so happy, thank God she is healthy and so beautiful. This is what keeps me motivated and out of trouble." Another participant more succinctly expressed this same joy; when asked about the most positive part of his day, he simply wrote: "being a father!"

Interestingly, although participants mentioned their sons, their reports more often were about time spent with daughters. For example, when participants talked about reuniting with family members, they almost exclusively reported this reunion narrative occurring with their daughters. One participant described such a reunion: "My daughter and I talked on the phone. We haven't spoken to one another in about two years." Others were more brief, but carried the same sentiment: "daughter is back in my life!"; "I got 2 talk 2 my daughters 2day"; "reconnecting with my daughter"; "got in touch with my daughter"; and "bonding with my daughter." The central role of daughters, and perhaps specifically adult daughters, in participants' daily lives aligns with social support scholarship and the role of women as primary providers of emotional support and closeness (House et al. 1988; Wheeler et al. 1983).

Children were also sometimes, although less frequently, mentioned as sources of stress or strain. Participants reported eighty instances where their primary problem of the day involved their children. However, when people reported social interactions as the most negative part of their day, they more often referenced their current or former romantic partners. Indeed, there were 237 instances of negative interactions with partners (53% of all negative social interactions). These reports spanned across twenty-six participants. Interestingly, only a minority of these participants ever reported their romantic partner as the most positive aspect of the day (only ten of twenty-six people). This suggests that participants do not necessarily have partnerships that provide sources of both support and stress that vary over time; instead, participants who find their partnerships beneficial and those that find them stressful appear to be relatively distinct from each other, at least over this time period.

*Changes in Social Support over Time*

Over time, the number of reports of positive social interactions decreased, and this pattern remained even when we accounted for participant attrition over time by calculating rates per daily total responses (see figure 9.3). However, despite this decrease, reports remained relatively high, even at the end of the study period and even when compared to reports of stressful social interactions. In some ways, this pattern of beneficial and stressful social interactions over time is consistent with reentry scholarship. Indeed, we expected to receive reports at the beginning of the project, soon after release, about parties and cookouts celebrating a return home, as well as activities to reconnect with family and friends. However, over time, we expected that mounting stress and strain associated with reentry would spark more interpersonal conflicts. And yet, this is not the pattern that emerged from the data. Celebrations of all kinds were scattered throughout the observation period, not simply in the first week or so following release. Further, these festivities

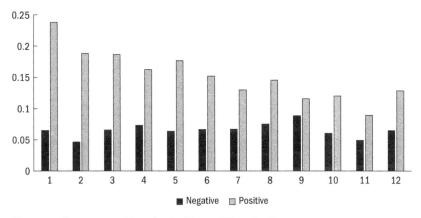

Figure 9.3. Support over Time, by Positive and Negative Reports

made up only a small portion of participants' reported positive social interactions, which were instead mostly reports about simply spending time together.

Discussion

Social support—and particularly emotional support—is widely acknowledged as a central resource to help cope with stressful experiences and life transitions. In reentry research, however, emotional support is less often studied compared to the provision of material and informational resources (but, see Martinez and Christian 2009; Nelson et al. 1999; Wyse et al. 2014). In this chapter, we used open-ended responses from individuals about the high and low points of their day to underscore the important role of social interactions, social relationships, and emotional closeness in daily life.

Through a ground-up, smartphone-based data collection method, we highlighted the types of social support valued by individuals. Specifically, we document four main findings. First, people often report that spending time with others is the high point of their day. As opposed to resource allocation or other types of support, people place a high value on emotional closeness and reconnecting with friends and family. One possible explanation for this finding is that people's networks tend not to have material supports to offer. In additional analyses, we examine this potential explanation by comparing people's daily reports and their answers about instrumental social supports from the initial interview; we find no correlation between measures of perceived material supports from the initial interview and the likelihood of reporting receipt of instrumental support on the daily smartphone surveys.[4] Another potential explanation is that people receive instrumental supports (e.g., information about potential job openings, financial help, etc.) but interpret receipt as a form of caring and emotional closeness (Martinez and Christian 2009). This latter potential explanation emphasizes the perceived importance of emotional support in people's daily experiences at reentry.

It is important to note that when reports of instrumental support were mentioned, participants often described *providing* help to others (and not receiving assistance). Other scholarship suggests that helping (in the form of giving back to one's community, mentoring other criminal justice-involved people, etc.) plays a role in rehabilitation and desistence (LeBel, Richie, and Maruna 2015). More specifically, helping others functions as a means of "rebiographing" or the creation of a redemption narrative (Maruna 2001), as a form of stigma management (Maruna and LeBel 2009), or as a means to realizing one's imagined "positive possible self" (Paternoster and Bushway 2009). In line with this research, we suggest that this finding points to the importance of reciprocity in social support (Martinez and Christian 2009; Miller and Stuart 2017; Wyse et al. 2014). Unlike emotional closeness and support, instrumental support is a unidirectional transaction that can counteract a person's feelings of self-efficacy. Within the reentry context, when people already feel dependent on a variety of people and organizations, emotional support may be a more beneficial asset for integration than specific material and informational exchanges.

Second, participants also reported social relationships and interactions as the most important problem of their day, albeit much less frequently compared to positive reports. Notably, some of these reports referred to death and illness of close family and friends. This finding highlights the various types of stressors experienced by men at reentry, where individuals must navigate not only their own reentry-related issues but also experiences and situations related to broader contextual disadvantage and hardship. Indeed, the frequency of death and illness in men's everyday lives—even in this relatively short three-month period—emphasizes the high rates of mortality and morbidity experienced by the low-income, racial/ethnic minority groups in the United States that are overrepresented among incarcerated and reentering populations (e.g., Deaton and Lubotsky 2003; McLaughlin and Stokes 2002).

Third, participants report an array of different sources of social support, but they most often mention spending time with children, romantic partners, and "family" more generally. In particular, the central role of children in men's daily lives underscores the importance of fatherhood among formerly incarcerated men. Although research on parental incarceration tends to study the consequences of parental imprisonment for children's outcomes, our findings call for more research geared toward understanding the other side of the relationship—i.e., the buffering role of parent-child relationships for parents' outcomes, including recidivism and social integration. These findings also reinforce the importance of various policy and program initiatives aimed at fathers, for benefiting both children and their fathers at reentry (Bronte-Tinkew et al. 2007). In addition, apart from children, men at reentry often reported the importance of their relationships with women (specifically, romantic partners and daughters). The primary role of women is also evident in other reentry and social support literature (House et al. 1988; Western et al. 2015). Because of their central role in providing social support, women may experience increased costs (e.g., health or financial) and may benefit from additional resources that support their health and well-being.

Fourth, positive reports of social interactions and relationships decrease over time; however, they are still frequent—particularly compared to reports of stressful relationships—at three months after release from prison. Notably, the frequency of negative reports of relationships is fairly stable over this period and does not increase, despite some evidence that the stress and strain of reentry transitions may eventually take a deleterious toll on relationships (Leverentz 2014; Wyse et al. 2014). Because this study examined only the first three months following release from prison, it is possible that the frequency of reports of negative relationships would increase over a longer time frame.

This chapter contributes several insights about the central role of social relationships and social support in daily life at reentry; at the same time, however, there are methodological limitations that must be considered. First, as with other data collected via experience sampling, there are higher amounts of missing or illegible data on any given day. In the case of missing data, participants may miss survey prompts and auditory alerts or may be too busy to complete surveys. This could bias estimates, particularly if missed surveys result from factors related to social relationships and social support. For example, individuals who spend more time alone may have more time to complete surveys. In this case, our findings about the central role of relationships and support may be underestimated.

With regard to incomplete data, incomprehensible answers on the open-ended questions may be the result of a variety of different factors. Individuals may have used these shortcuts in lieu of a "don't know" answer or because they perceived that entering a longer answer would be too time-consuming or burdensome. They may also have experienced survey fatigue with the repetitive nature of the daily questions. Unclear or ambiguous answers are common considerations in open-ended questions more generally; however, these issues are exacerbated in our study because of our inability to follow up with clarifying questions (Geer 1988; Schuman 1966).

Because issues related to both missing data and incomprehensible answers likely have differential influences on participants' answers, we suggest that the findings reported here are not interpreted as generalizable estimates of social support at reentry. Moreover, because of these issues, we are unable to test potential explanations or mechanisms, such as participant characteristics or network resources, which might explain variation across participants. Rather, we view the chapter's contributions as underscoring the central—and generally positive—role of social relationships and emotional support in the daily lives of men at reentry. Future research, such as qualitative work or survey questions with closed-answer choices, could fruitfully examine questions related to generalizability and potential mechanisms.

Another limitation is that the study focused on the first three months after release from prison. Although the immediate period after release is considered a key time in reentry scholarship and intervention (e.g., Redcross et al. 2012), it is likely that the primacy of social support in everyday life might be different over a longer trajectory. Indeed, even over the three-month period, participants were less likely, over time, to report social relationships as their foremost positive experience of the day. Even so, the central role of relationships—and the emotional support that they offer—during these immediate months after release is notable.

In conclusion, this chapter used a novel data collection and analysis method to draw attention to the primacy of social support in the everyday lives of men at reentry. By combining experience sampling methods via daily smartphone surveys with open-ended questions about high and low points of the day, we employ a ground-up analytic approach to study reentry. Consistent with reentry and social support scholarship, these findings underscore the role of social support systems for helping individuals cope with the stressful transition of leaving prison. Even though the importance of social relationships and support is well acknowledged in reentry scholarship, we suggest that future research place greater emphasis on measuring and analyzing support—and particularly emotional support—as a key factor for successful integration.

ACKNOWLEDGMENTS

Thank you to the NSRP study participants, the New Jersey Parole Board, Wade Jacobsen, and Elizabeth Lian. The NSRP was supported by the National Institute of Justice (2013-IJ-CX-0007), National Science Foundation (SES-1228333), National Institutes of Health (P30AG024361), Fahs-Beck Fund for Research and Experimentation, and the Horowitz Foundation for Social Policy, as well as the Center for Information Technology Policy, Center for African American Studies, and Office of Population Research at Princeton.

NOTES

1. In practice, restricting the sample to those searching for work excluded only a few individuals, such as those with restrictive health constraints or those who planned to enroll in school full time.
2. Participants picked up weekly gift cards from the parole office or day reporting center. If they were no longer supervised by parole (or were not in compliance with their supervision), participants received gift cards through the mail at an address that they provided to the research team.
3. One potential concern of using smartphones to study reentry is whether phones will be lost or stolen. In the NSRP, only three people (of 135 people, or 2%) reported their phones stolen to the research team. One person recovered their phone from the perpetrators and another person purchased the same phone

model to continue his participation. The third person was unable to recover his phone, unfortunately (Sugie 2018).

4   A scale of perceived social support (modified from the Fragile Families and Child Wellbeing survey) was asked in the initial interview and is the sum of the following five questions: if you needed assistance during the next three months, could you count on someone to loan you $200? Loan you $1,000? Provide you with a place to live? Help you get around if you needed a ride? Help you when you're sick?

# 10

## Formerly Incarcerated Men's Negotiation of Family Support

JOHNNA CHRISTIAN

As a recent National Academy of Sciences report concludes, mass incarceration in the United States has been a long and costly endeavor with questionable benefits and substantial costs (Travis, Western, and Redburn, 2014). The reintegration of formerly incarcerated men and women into their families and communities is a pressing concern for the individuals who are directly and indirectly affected, political officials, government agencies, public and nonprofit service providers, and the public. Nationally, more than two-thirds of state prison inmates are rearrested within three years of their release (Durose, Cooper, and Snyder, 2014). Numerous scholars have studied "collateral consequences" of mass incarceration, including effects on family relationships, civic and political participation, health outcomes and employment prospects (Clear, 2007; Wakefield and Wildeman, 2013; Wildeman, Schnittker, and Turney, 2012). Moreover, it is imperative to identify best practices for the reintegration of the formerly incarcerated into their families and communities, in the furtherance of their well-being and public safety at large (Taxman, 2008; Travis et al., 2014).

Prior research about prisoner reentry has identified an assortment of needs for formerly incarcerated men, particularly in the areas of employment, education, health, treatment for addiction, and family reintegration (Travis et al., 2014). In addition to these concerns, they must navigate complicated family relationships that may have been strained or fractured prior to incarceration and are further challenged by the separation imposed by confinement. The reentry period presents additional challenges, as the formerly incarcerated may be under probation or parole supervision, with the attendant regulations, restrictions, and requirements. Paradoxically, the family relationships that help provide important supports also present challenges in and of themselves, at the same time that they hold great promise to mitigate some of the other hardships posed by reintegration (Martinez and Christian, 2009; Western et al., 2015). These relationships are especially important for men re-entering society after a period of incarceration because family members often provide support and assistance that is not readily available through other channels: a place to sleep, transportation, job leads, meals, and encouragement. Yet, the provision and receipt of support require substantial negotiation of fluid and shifting relationship dynamics, and family often takes on broad definitions to include extended and fictive kin, friends, and acquaintances (Desmond, 2012).

Through analysis of twenty-four in-depth interviews with formerly incarcerated men in an urban, Northeastern city, this chapter examines how formerly incarcerated men identify potential avenues of familial support, how they maximize resources gained from family members, and how they manage strains in family relationships that potentially jeopardize their access to support. Implications for understanding both the benefits and limitations of family support for formerly incarcerated men will be discussed.

Related Literature

A rich body of literature has expanded our focus beyond the individual incarcerated person to encompass a broader network of family members and community (see Comfort, 2007 and Sampson, 2011 for in-depth discussions of evolutions in this research, as well as Travis et al., 2014 for extensive analysis of the causes and consequences of mass incarceration). Researchers have highlighted the multiple ways family members of those who are incarcerated "do the time" with the incarcerated individual (Braman, 2004; Comfort, 2008; Fishman, 1990) and encounter "secondary prisonization" as they venture into prisons to visit and are subjected to regulations and degradation ceremonies that criminalize their relationships with incarcerated individuals.

By examining the impacts of incarceration on family members, research may also inform our understanding of former prisoners' social ties and networks with family and friends, and how prison enhances or diminishes such relationships (Braman, 2004; Naser and LaVigne, 2006). For example, in a study of 247 individuals in Chicago who had a male family member released from prison, Naser and Visher (2006) found that families provided a great deal of emotional and tangible support to the formerly incarcerated, but that contact during incarceration was often difficult. Prison may, therefore, attenuate ties to family and neighborhood at the same time that prisoners rely on family members for support both during incarceration and upon release from prison (Braman, 2004; Martinez and Christian, 2009). Research has also found that family members' own access to support may suffer because of their ties to incarcerated men (Turney, Schnittker, and Wildeman, 2012).

In conjunction with understanding family members' lives, we know that individuals released from prison have a wide range of needs that stem from the broader goals of limiting violence and criminal or antisocial behaviors, forming or strengthening pro-social attachments and engaging in behaviors and activities that foster a crime-free life (Travis et al., 2014). When individuals who have been incarcerated are released from prison and return to their communities, their family members are called upon to provide a range of supports including a place to live, help finding jobs, pocket money, and assistance with child care (Brown, Killian, and Evans, 2003; Naser and Visher, 2006; Western et al., 2015). Indeed, to be released from prison onto parole supervision, an individual must provide information on securing a residence (i.e., an address), indicating where he or she will be living. At the most base level, this requirement means that someone in the to-be-released prisoner's life—likely a female relative such as a grandmother, mother, aunt, wife, or romantic partner—becomes part of the official release plan. Individuals who are not on parole receive a range of supports from family members as well, and there is a need for more expansive definitions of family to include fictive and extended kin networks and friends.

Undoubtedly, some social ties contribute to a resumption of offending, and renegotiating family relationships is a complicated aspect of the reentry process. Criminological research highlights the social control functions enacted by social support networks, or the potential criminogenic influence of peers (Horney, Osgood, and Marshall, 1995; Sampson and Laub, 1993), but we have a limited understanding of the specific mechanisms and value, for people released from prison, of the support exchanged through such relationships. Informal social supports may serve a range of functions for people released from prison. For example, in a study of men returning from prison to Baltimore and Chicago, researchers found that, in a pre-release survey, 69% of prisoners expected to live with family members after release, and that, in a post-release interview, 86% of respondents indicated they were living with at least one family member (Naser and LaVigne, 2006). Moreover, although 55% of prisoners anticipated that family would be an important component of their success after release from prison, in post-release interviews, 80% reported that this was actually the case (Naser and LaVigne, 2006). Other researchers have found that residential context is an important factor in the type of support people released from prison and their family members exchange (Martinez and Christian, 2009) and that family relationships become stronger upon release from prison (Shollenberger, 2009).

Yet, family reunification presents specific challenges, which are shaped by pre-incarceration relationships (Visher and Travis, 2003), the demands of maintaining family connections with incarcerated individuals (Christian, 2005; Comfort, 2008), and shifting family dynamics upon a prisoner's return to the family and community (Arditti, 2005; Fishman, 1990). In addition, many individuals released from prison must draw on support systems other than immediate family members. As several scholars have suggested, it is essential to move beyond traditional family definitions and expand them to include friends, extended family, and kin networks in order to provide a more realistic view of the many forms of families that assist individuals as they cope with the harsh realities of the world around them (Braithwaite et al., 2010; Jarrett, Bahar, and McPherson, 2015; Stack, 1974).

Informal social ties, therefore, have the potential to build crucial support systems that serve specific and immediate instrumental functions for released prisoners as family members' efforts in the desistance process likely overlap with the steps taken by criminal justice officials (Mills and Codd, 2008; Western et al., 2015; Wolff and Draine, 2004). Similarly, Wolff and Draine (2004) emphasize the dynamic nature of informal social support systems and delineate four ways that these supports, offered in the form of social capital, are an important aspect of the prisoner reentry process. They say that the driving factors in the use of social capital in the reentry process are: "(1) the willingness of the prisoner's social relations to provide assistance; (2) the ability of the prisoner to motivate help from these social relations; (3) the resource endowments of the social relations; (4) and the social context of these relationships" (465). The varying nature of these resources means that the supports available to a person prior to entering prison may not be available upon release, and that it is likely that some aspects of the pre-incarceration networks contributed to offending and must be modified or severed during the reentry period. Incarceration itself may attenuate some connections and strengthen others (Arditti, 2005; Hairston, 1988; Mills and Codd, 2008; Shollenberger, 2009), requiring a reconfiguring of support systems during the reentry period.

For some former prisoners, then, the sources of social capital and informal support mechanisms are likely to be damaged, or perhaps missing entirely, leading them to draw upon expanded networks of support such as family broadly defined, faith-based communities, and other community resources (Shapiro and Schwartz, 2001). Drawing from what has been termed a "strengths-based" approach to reentry, there is always a potential support available for a person released from prison, provided agents of the criminal justice system are willing to shift their perspective from a focus on deficits to strengths and work to identify appropriate resources (Maruna and LeBel, 2003). The current research also fits into broader lines of inquiry examining sites of resilience (Payne, 2011).

Matthew Desmond (2012) describes how the urban poor utilize "disposable ties" to get them through periods of economic instability such as eviction. Such ties are formed quickly and intensely, often with new acquaintances, rather than family members who may be absent, unable to provide help, or unwilling to do so, especially when the recipient is frequently in need. Desmond identifies three distinct phases in which people form, use, and then burn ties. In some cases, a tie is no longer needed because circumstances have improved, but in other instances the tie dissolves after a disagreement or betrayal. Extant research about formerly incarcerated people has emphasized familial support, but Desmond's work suggests the value of looking more broadly at other sources of support, as well as identifying dynamic and temporal aspects of support exchanges.

In summary, while we know that former prisoners rely on family members for support upon release from prison, we also know that support exchanges are contextualized by residence (Martinez and Christian, 2009), the former offender's perceptions of the future (Maruna, 2001), and the nature of the relationship prior to (Visher and Travis, 2003) and during (Christian and Kennedy, 2011) incarceration. Moreover, evidence about prisoners' expectations for life upon release from prison indicates that those recently released from prison have high expectations of receiving a range of supports from family members, including assistance finding employment, pocket money, and a place to live (Martinez and Christian, 2009; Naser and LaVigne, 2006). Less is known about how, specifically, formerly incarcerated individuals navigate the shifting availability of support from various people in their familial and extended networks. Examining these processes provides a lens for an agentic view of the reentry experience, while highlighting potential avenues to enhance the availability of support systems.

Research Strategy

The research described in the current chapter is part of a broader study conducted from 2016 to 2018 about prisoner reentry in an urban Northeastern city. The research entailed twenty-four face-to-face, semi-structured, in-depth interviews with formerly incarcerated men who were recruited through a reentry services center, which provides employment training and referrals. Recruitment occurred through case managers who work at the office, as well as direct contact between researchers and clients. Despite the fact that the office provides employment services, not all of the individuals who come to the office are unemployed. Some are seeking additional work, or job changes. The case managers at the office also provide a range of assistance and referrals beyond employment, such as securing identification, housing, and addiction treatment services.

Interview questions probed key life domains, including: (1) neighborhood connections such as public and civic engagement, interactions with local bureaucracies and organizations, mentorship and community-building; (2) experiences during incarceration and after release; (3) family relationships, such as roles in fictive kin networks, parenting (including noncustodial relationships and parenting of non-biological children and extended family members), sibling and parental relationships, and relationships with adult children; (4) engagement with support networks such as faith communities, substance abuse treatment communities, support groups and mentoring relationships; (5) reentry challenges; and (6) resilience strategies and practices. Two researchers were present for interviews, one conducting the interview and the other typing notes of responses and offering follow-up questions where relevant. When consent was given, interviews were audio recorded and transcribed verbatim. Interviews were conducted in a private office at the reentry service center, and participants were compensated $40 for their participation. Typically, interviews lasted 1.5 hours, with a range from one to three hours.

Eighty-eight percent of the participants were men of color (African American and Hispanic Americans), with the average age being thirty-eight years old. Only 54% of the men had obtained their high school diploma or GED. Further, 95% of the participants self-reported charges of aggravated assault, drug distribution, and/or possession of weapons. Last, there was variance in the men's release date. While 50% of the men interviewed had been released for less than a year, 33% of the population had been reintegrated into society for at least three years.

The examples described below were selected to show the diversity of family support situations and illustrate how formerly incarcerated men negotiate social support from family members as broadly defined. Participants were asked a number of different questions to generate information about relationships and potential support networks, including how they define family, who they consider a part of their family, who they go to for advice, and who comes to them for advice. Other questions, such as "how have things been going for you lately," often elicited responses connected to family relationships and interactions. I was interested specifically in how people navigate limited support options, make decisions about which members of support networks might be willing and able to provide support, and reconcile feelings of dependency when receiving support.

## The Negotiation of Family Support

Formerly incarcerated men rely heavily on family support, but their family members may be limited in the amount and type of support they have available to give, requiring men to have expansive and evolving definitions of who constitutes family. The examples below illustrate the broad range of support situations formerly incarcerated men encounter, and strategies they employ to activate, sustain, and protect their support options.[1] The men are mindful of the amount and types of support family members have available and are willing to provide, as well as their own limitations in being able to reciprocate support. In addition, their experiences show how a broad range of relationship types (i.e., mother, wife, siblings, cousins, acquaintances) can serve as resources in the reintegration process.

### Support Available, Offered, and Accepted

Malcolm, a thirty-five-year-old African American man, had been released from prison for eight months after serving a fifteen-year sentence and had a strong foundation of support, primarily provided by his wife Renee. Malcolm and Renee were legally married two weeks after his release from prison, but they had maintained a solid and steady relationship during his fifteen-year incarceration after being "high school sweethearts." They had a sixteen-year-old daughter and a fifteen-year-old son. Renee and the children had visited Malcolm in prison weekly for his entire incarceration and planned carefully for his release. When asked how things had been going for him since his release, Malcom responded:

> Great, I'm marvelous, and I'm appreciating everything else. Everything is sweet. I mean because I make it easy for me. I don't put no hardship on myself. If one door close another one open up. That's how I look at it so. It's really not too much to really complain about because I just was in the three by three by three cell [laughs], you know, with a bunky and it's like, it's beautiful out here. I got my own house. I'm working, taking care of myself. I just got married. I'm good, like I love it.

Malcolm relished his freedom and was hopeful about his life. He worked at a full-time job he "loved," performing inventory control. He often worked fifty hours per week and earned $14 per hour. He started the job, which Renee helped him secure, two days after his release from prison, and he also worked part time at a local stadium. Malcolm said that after his release there was a period when he thought he and Renee "weren't going to make it." They had an argument and he left the house, considering switching his approved parole address to his grandmother's house. He explained that they reconciled two days later, and that his departure was because he didn't like "arguing."

Malcolm's situation shows the emotional attachments, love, aspirations, and need that become entangled with family support. Malcolm explained that his children were getting to know him again since they were infants when he was incarcerated. Their interactions inside of prison had been very different from those now that they were living together as a family unit. Despite the consistently high levels of contact between Malcolm, Renee and their children while he was incarcerated, they had to adapt to shifting circumstances such as learning how to resolve disagreements once outside of the prison.

Tony, a twenty-two-year-old African American man, had been released from prison for three and a half months after serving two years of his sentence, and also described receiving support from family members. Though he had been incarcerated in a neighboring state, he explained, "I transferred my parole . . . 'cause I got more family out here and stuff so I feel as though there's more help out here. Since I got out I just been lookin' for a job and try to take care of my daughter." Both his aunt and mother were supportive of his efforts, demonstrating the benefits of multiple sources of support offered in a variety of domains. Tony was living with his Aunt Susan and described his situation:

> I feel as though she, she been asked me to move with her since I was incarcerated. She said she help me with a lot of things. Help me find a job, help me get on my feet. At first I ain't want to when I first got out, and I feel as though I could do everything on my own, that I ain't need no help with some things, like and then I feel as though I was surrounding myself with the same people when I first came out so I just feel as though I needed to get away.

Tony was able to remove himself from potentially negative influences because he had the buffer of support from multiple family members.

Further, he said, "I know it's good to ask for help, but I wanna try it myself, put my effort. I wanna try myself before anybody else can help me." In line with his desire for independence and self-reliance, he said of his Aunt Susan:

> She helps me, takes me where I have to go, and she just helps me a lot, and she offers. I don't have to go to her or ask her. She offers, asks me do I need anything, do I? She the one that dropped me off down here (job assistance center). She been there when I was incarcerated. Both of my aunts and my mom. That's why I could rely on them.

It was important to Tony that his aunt offered assistance rather than him having to ask for it. Susan not only offered the support to Tony, proactively, but she had been doing so from the time of his incarceration and recognized that he needed support in multiple areas of his reintegration. Tony also acknowledged that while he wanted to "try it myself," he needed assistance.

### Marshaling Support Options

Dante's negotiation of family relationships and support was framed by the fact that he had only been released from prison for two weeks after being incarcerated for seven and a half years. He acknowledged his vulnerability during his early reentry period because he had no stable residence and no job. Dante also felt he was limited in his ability to give back to people who helped him and acknowledged that one-sided support was not sustainable for the long term. When describing his living situation, he explained:

> I'm staying here, and I staying there. I'm not stable right now. I'm staying at a friend's house, sister, relative houses, like that. I'm back and forth. It's only been two weeks, so they ain't tired of me yet. Once you get thirty days, sixty days, they like "oh, you ain't find a job yet?" You know how it go.

Dante expected to wear out his welcome, particularly if he did not find work. He explained, "Can't keep feeding a grown man for free, right? Or staying there without helping no bills, right?" Such awareness of his precarious situation led Dante to develop a strategy that would essentially prevent any one person from being overburdened by his needs, or feeling taken advantage of:

> Couple guys took me shopping to get clothes and stuff like that like yeah, couple outfits from him, couple outfits from him. I got a brother from my father's side, he took me to get a couple outfits, like that, a little you know, just a mean, just a gift. That's why I leave that over there. If you buy me something I'ma leave that over there, like that. So when I come over there, "Oh, what's up?" Take a shower, change clothes, boom, dip off, like that. If you hang out with, you take me out go eat and you take me to the mall, go buy me something, what? I'ma walk around with the bags? Nah, I'ma leave it here cause you my peoples. If you take me out and buy me something I'ma leave that there. When I come over and spend the night I shower, like that, put something on, dip off.

Dante notes that people buying him clothing indicates "you my peoples," and he shows gratitude for the support by leaving items with the people who purchased them, which also allows him to have a reason to visit them and in essence take up temporary residence. In addition to having places to sleep and clothes to wear, Dante had a cell phone a friend from childhood had purchased for him, agreeing to pay the first month's bill.

Mark too, had an array of family members to provide different types of support. He is a forty-seven-year-old African American man who was paroled to his niece's house for three months after spending eight months in a transitional housing facility (after time in the county jail, he was transferred to the state prison reception center and sent to the transitional facility). He ended up residing at his niece's house by a combination of chance and an assumption that parole would find the address suitable. He explained:

> Well, during the holidays, of course, I been goin' to, you know, family comes together, and they're asking, "Oh, this person or that person," and started asking about me so it got to the point where it was explained where I was at, and concern went out so my niece was concerned about, you know what can she do to help, you know, "Where is he?" I got my

niece number, and thank god her ex-boyfriend or whatever was uh at her address on parole, and one thing led to another. They not together, so I just, you know, "Hey, let me, let me use your address just." "Sure." "Well, yeah. Okay." So as I submitted it, it, it kinda made sense because being that her ex was there, her address was approved in their system already so it's not like if I, you know, use your address, hypothetically, they gotta come and look at what's goin', it's already in the system so they could just, "Oh, okay. He's gonna go there." So thank God she was able to help me with that, and um I'm looking forward to, like how I explained, it's short-term. I'm the kinda person don't just lay around and, and just don't do anything. So she's, she understands it, and she works. No children, thank God, and helping me out so I'm just, I'm just blessed.

When the interviewer noted that Mark sounded surprised that his niece was willing to allow him to live in her home, he explained, "Yeah, cause nowadays, people don't just open they doors like to a person. . . . the fact that a person can come to your house, ask you to stay there with no strings attached, but now I'm comin' to stay at your house, and I'm on parole, which means the parole officers may come there . . . Thank God she's allowing me to do that." Mark reported being selective about whom to ask for help and being grateful for support that is offered rather than requested. In addition to the housing support he received from his niece, Mark's mother was taking care of his two-year-old daughter and three-year-old son. Mark expressed a desire to "transition" from his niece's house, to a room or transitional center, and finally to a three-bedroom apartment he could share with friends.

Family members and friends do not always know what the men need, and they may be hesitant to ask. After his phone rang several times during the interview, Dante explained how a childhood friend came to buy him a cell phone:

> Oh yeah, a friend of mine bought it for me cause they, they was like I was calling like, "Yo, where you at?" I said, "Yo, I'm over here." So then as the, the next day I didn't call them or the next two days I didn't call them, and then I called, and they're like, "Yo, where you at?" I'm over here, yo 'cause they come pick me up. He said, "Man, we gonna get you a phone, man 'cause we don't know, never know where you're at." So they got me

a phone. They said they gonna pay the first bill, which is the 26th of this month they gon' pay that, and then the rest of them um then I gotta pay my own or whatever.

Adam, a thirty-seven-year-old African American man who had been out of prison for two and a half years after spending eleven months in a county jail initially thought he would be homeless after his release. He was asked, "how did that work out that you ended up with a place to stay?" and provided the following explanation:

One thing about me, I'm a very independent person, very independent man, period. I don't like to depend on anyone, and when it came to it, I could either stay with a family member, and I had already started the relationship (with his wife). It started prior to the incarceration. I could either take this further or move with a family member, and I chose the lesser of the evils.
INTERVIEWER: So being with her was the lesser of the evils?
I don't wanna put it like that, but I'ma put it like this. Family could be not family sometimes, and you know, yeah, she's uh, she's been with me through a lot, you know, so I seen it as that's somewhere I really should be versus anything else. And not only that, we definitely share a good connection, stuff like that so.

Adam made the decision to stay with his wife rather than other family members, because he saw it as a way to preserve his sense of independence.

Eddie, twenty-nine and African American, was born in the Northeast and lived with his biological mother until he was three years old, when she sent him to Louisiana to live with his paternal grandfather. His mother was under the oversight of the child protection system from the time of his birth, and Eddie described it as a "tough time for my mother she was staying from pillar to post." After living with his grandfather, he was eventually placed in the child welfare system and adopted by a family who were not biological relatives. This backstory is relevant to Eddie's current situation because he served his prison time in Louisiana and had his initial years of reentry there. Seven years after his release from prison he was living in the Northeast in a very precarious situation. He used all eligibility for welfare benefits when he first relocated with his wife and two children. The family was under the oversight of the child protection system, and his wife, who still retained custody of their children, eventually asked for a divorce, but allowed him to stay in the apartment they were renting with Temporary Rental Assistance. Once the financial assistance for the apartment expired, Eddie was given temporary, ninety-day placement in a shelter, explaining, "I have ninety days to get myself together, to get me a job, secure that job, and stack up some money so I can have me a stable place to stay when it's all over."

Further, Eddie said, I have "nobody in my corner except for a reentry program (a local job placement program). I have nobody. I, my, my wife took my children and now I have a restraining order against me that restrains me from my children and her so now I really got nobody." His wife, six-year-old son and two-year-old daughter were living with Eddie's sister, who did keep in contact with him. Eddie credited his sister with his son's recent advancements, indicating he had been a "slow learner" and "slow developer" until his wife and children moved in with his sister and she helped his son. He said of his sister, "She makes sure my kids are terrific, you know, and that, an that right there I can, I, I, I'ma owe her for that." He also spoke of his cousin and said, "he always, he's been having my since, you know, since I got out uh here, and he give me, he lets me hold money. He's letting me hold my clothes at his house." Eddie explained that he was unable to store his belongings at the shelter where he was residing:

> And I had one of them little carts, no big cart, one of them big carts, you know. You see people carrying around their groceries or whatever, and it's filled with stuff, you know, I got, you know, I got my TV in there, my laptop, and speakers, and all this kind of stuff that I've accumulated, you know, after stayin' in my apartment or whatever, and I'm like I don't want this to be in the shelter because somebody unzip this bag and see what's in it, they goin', they gonna go on and get paid. You know what I mean?

Speaking of his cousin, he said:

> He lets me hold my stuff over there. I come over. I talk to him, you know, you know, he, if he got some food, he let me eat, you know, give me some food to eat, you know, and you know, he's just, he just, good friend. And

then if I, if I say like I say somethin' that, you know, like, "Yo, man, I plan on goin' to do this, man. You know what I'm sayin'? If a nigga get wrong I'ma bust him in his head." "No, man. You don't bust him in the head, man. You just let it go, dog." He always tells me something, you know, 'cause he's been to prison.

Eddie's estrangement from his wife troubled him greatly, and he was uncertain about the future of the relationship. He was grateful to his sister for the support she provided his children. His cousin not only provided support by giving him a place to store his belongings, but also provided feedback about how to avoid trouble, which was more readily received because his cousin had been incarcerated himself.

## Conclusions

The investigation of social support for formerly incarcerated men indicates they recognize their need for support, as well as the potential burden it places on their family members. In order to maximize support options, they make decisions about which family members are able and willing to provide support at different points in time. In addition, they work to preserve their sense of independence at the same time they accept help. There are indications the availability of family support is contextualized by a person's history of family connections both before and during incarceration and is also dependent on situational needs and the availability of resources. Investigating the navigation of support provides a more agentic view of the prisoner reentry process, with insight on how people negotiate the challenges of reentry.

One limitation of the research is that family members' perspectives might be quite different than those of the formerly incarcerated men, especially regarding whether support was offered or requested. It is possible that in order to preserve a sense of independence and autonomy, men overreport the offering of support, to downplay the frequency of their requests for support. In addition, support processes and exchanges may be particularly challenging for family members when they have multiple incarcerated family members, particularly given the disproportionate experience of familial incarceration for African American women (Braman, 2004; Western and Wildeman, 2009).

Some men reported that family members providing support were formerly incarcerated individuals themselves. These family members might be considered particularly insightful about the needs of formerly incarcerated men, and thus, various types of support, such as advice about managing stigma, might be better received from them (Maruna and LeBel, 2003). Prior research has differentiated between types of support (emotional, instrumental, informational, companionship, and feedback) and distinctions between perceived support, "available if needed," and received support "recently provided" (Wills and Shinar, 2000: 88). In addition, reciprocity may be a critical factor in sustaining support, as well as allowing men to receive support and maintain a sense of independence and self-reliance (Martinez and Christian, 2006). In addition, family members' own support networks, and how their connections to formerly incarcerated men may enhance or diminish their own resources, are important (Desmond, 2012).

By mapping relationships and social support possibilities and opportunities, we gain a holistic perspective of the reentry experience. Support is contingent on both the capacity and willingness to offer it, as well as the capacity and willingness to receive it. It is part of a dyadic exchange situated in the broader context of family history and dynamics, individual agency, and structural factors. Examining formerly incarcerated men's negotiation of support provides important insight into underexplored aspects of the reentry process.

NOTE

1  In the examples that follow, pseudonyms have been used for all participants, and potentially identifying information, such as the name of a business where a person is employed, has been changed to a general description. Interview excerpts have been edited to remove verbal repetition such as "umm," "you know," and "like."

## 11

# "This Individual May or May Not Be on the Megan's Law Registry"

*The Sex Offender Label's Impact on Reentry*

JAMIE J. FADER AND ABIGAIL R. HENSON

There is good reason to believe that the reentry challenges documented in this volume are particularly difficult for returning offenders with sexual offense charges, who carry the double stigma of criminality and "sexual deviance." In 2006, the Sex Offender Registration and Notification Act (SORNA) was signed into legislation, mandating states to post personal information and photos of registered sex offenders online (Winters et al. 2017). Some states also require residency restrictions and electronic monitoring (Hipp, Turner, and Jannetta 2010). As a result of notification requirements, research has found that returning sex offenders have difficulty securing housing and employment and lack social supports (Mercado, Alvarez, and Levenson 2008; Tewksbury and Lees 2006).

For sex offenders returning to states that prohibit them from living within close proximity to schools, parks, playgrounds, and daycare centers, approved housing is very difficult to find, especially for those returning to urban settings (Inyang 2010; Levenson and Hern 2007). Russell, Seymour, and Lambie (2013) interviewed nine sex offenders in New Zealand prior to their exiting prison and twice post-release and found that participants experienced considerable difficulty finding "appropriate" housing. One participant stated, "Got to move out of this flat up here that I've spent two days in. Got the place checked out and then come Monday, and I've moved all my stuff and paid the $1400 and find out I can't live there. I must have seen 100 houses, but oh shit there's a park down the road. I can't live there. Oh, there's a school just down the road, aw, so starting to do my head in you know" (p. 64).

Similarly, in a survey study of 148 returned sex offenders, conducted by Levenson and Hern (2007), respondents stated that housing restrictions disrupted stability and forced relocation, thus creating transience, financial hardship, and emotional volatility. The authors also found that the zoning laws pushed sex offenders out of metropolitan areas and into rural communities with limited services, job opportunities, and social supports.

Notification laws and sex offender stigma also make it increasingly difficult to secure housing (Inyang 2010; Tewksbury and Copes 2012). A participant of Inyang's (2010) study on the reentry experiences of returned sex offenders stated, "Most apartment complexes and landlords won't rent to SOs [sex offenders] . . . For a while, I lived in an apartment that was very run-down and drug infested because the owner didn't care who lived there. . . . Actually, quite dangerous, but no real options of where to live . . . no decent place will rent to a SO" (p. 99). This experience is in line with previous research that has found that sex offenders are more likely than non-sex offenders to reenter into neighborhoods with higher levels of social disorganization and fewer resources due to discrimination and neighborhood watch petitions (Hipp et al. 2010).

Obtaining employment is also a difficult task for most returning citizens (Travis 2005); however, the compounded stigma of being labeled as an offender and a "sexual deviant" often exacerbates this difficulty and results in high rates of rejection and unemployment (Inyang 2010; Russell et al. 2013). Russell and colleagues (2013) found that many available jobs were not flexible enough to allow adherence to parole conditions. Participants from Tewksbury and Lees's (2006) study of twenty-two registered sex offenders lamented that those available jobs that were flexible enough were often below their skill level. Many returned sex offenders who secure employment lie to their employers during the hiring process, either about the type of offense, or about having a criminal record, regardless of the fact that they are publicly listed on the registry. A survey study of 153 registered sex offenders in Virginia conducted by Robbers (2009) found, through the survey's open-ended questions, that the risk of being discovered was worth the lie because the truth often resulted in rejection or termination. However, some participants discussed receiving threats and harassment at work once coworkers discovered the respondent's criminal history through the registry or some other type of community notification.

Finally, both qualitative and quantitative studies of returned sex offenders have found that social support in the community is particularly hard to find. Inyang (2010) found that many returned sex offenders longed for social interaction but felt unable to relate to their families, community, and old friends, and felt rejected by their local church. On the other hand, some respondents actively avoided their family and friends in order to avoid discussing their offenses and the feelings of shame and rejection that often stem from the discussions (Inyang 2010). Levenson and Hern (2007) found that residence restrictions push sex offenders into rural areas with few opportunities for social connections, which often leads to feelings of isolation.

As is evident here, the vast majority of research on reentry experiences of sex offenders focuses on the direct effects of SORNA and other registration, notification, and residency restrictions. Little attention has been paid, however, to the broader application of sex offender parole restrictions beyond those who are registered sex offenders (i.e., to those with sexual offense charges that were not serious enough to qualify them for their state registry). One important feature of the moral panic over sexual offenders has been the overbroad application of the "sex offender" label to individuals who engage in non-serious offenses such as public urination. Moreover, US states vary widely in both what legal definitions distinguish registered and non-registered offenders and what qualifies as "statutory rape" in the course of an otherwise consensual relationship (often defined as some combination of a minimum age for victim and an age gap between those involved). All states, however, possess a low-end tier of offender that is judged to be non-serious enough to disqualify one from the registry. We could find no study that documents this experience.

The present study aims to fill this gap and to describe the experience of carrying the stigma of a sex offender label over time with an intensive case study of "Tony," who pled guilty to statutory sexual assault more than a decade ago and whose trajectory of parole violations and reincarcerations has been profoundly affected by decision-makers' failure to distinguish him from a child predator.

## Research Design / Methodology

Intensive case studies have a long history within criminology, and their value has been highlighted within the ascendance of the life course paradigm. Readers of classic texts have come to know the lives and criminal careers of real-life "characters" such as Stanley (Shaw 1930; Snodgrass 1982) and Sam Goodman (Steffensmeier 1986; Steffensmeier and Ulmer 2005). Longitudinal case studies allow scholars to represent structural, cultural, and agentic forces as they operate simultaneously in one person's life over time, and within specific social contexts (Fader 2013).

"Tony" was one of fifteen black and Latino young men who were part of a longitudinal, ethnographic study of youth incarceration and reentry beginning in 2004 (Fader 2013). The sample included young men from Philadelphia who had been committed by the juvenile court to "Mountain Ridge Academy," a residential treatment facility targeted toward drug users and drug sellers (all those studied were the latter). Respondents were age 17–19 at study intake, as they would be expected to assume adult roles upon their return to the community; moreover, black and Latino youth were sampled because of their overrepresentation in the juvenile justice system, especially institutional facilities (Hartney and Silva 2007).

Using participant observation and periodic in-depth interviews, the first author followed the young men intensively for three years after their release from Mountain Ridge Academy. She began by recruiting them inside the facility, conducting pre-release interviews, exchanging letters, and conducting monthly visits. Upon their return to Philadelphia, she conducted observations in a variety of settings, accompanying them as they searched for employment, provided child care, participated in court-mandated programming and regular meetings with probation officers, and got to know family members, children's mothers, and members of their male peer groups. She documented their struggle to "fall back," or desist from drug selling as a means of making ends meet, as well as their efforts to secure masculine dignity through providing for their families or being good fathers.

After the completion of the first study, the first author continued to stay in contact with Tony as he wended his way through a ten-year prison sentence on a robbery charge, with lesser included charges of statutory sexual assault and corruption of a minor. We exchanged letters and spoke on the phone; she contributed small amounts to his commissary account; and she did informal reentry case management and advocacy during spells when he returned to Philadelphia on parole supervision. During the twelve years that she has followed him, she had contact with his entire social support network, including two girlfriends, his sister, mother, his public defender, and two probation/parole officers.

As the well-known ethnographers, Patricia and Peter Adler (1987) have noted, all field researchers must consciously adopt a field membership role that guides their own level of participation in participant observation. Contrary to the traditional positivist stance of objectivity, the first author's body of work adopts a post-positivist stance that problematizes the notions of value neutrality and objectivity (Harding 1995). Instead, we choose to forge close relationships with those we study with the goal of developing a strong sense of subjectivity and empathy, allowing us to render respondents' motivations as embedded in their actions. Practically, this often means engaging in helping or advocacy activities as part of the research participants' support networks, which can strengthen the validity of findings. For example, when the first author communicated directly with Tony's parole agent, she was able to confirm Tony's claims that the agent was treating him no differently than the registered sex offenders on his caseload. Nevertheless, those who adopt close relationships with those they study must constantly engage in reflection about the degree to which their involvement has shaped their data and analysis.[1]

## Tony's Story

### The Offense

Tony's account of the scenario leading to his sexual offense charge involved a fifteen-year-old girl who he met on the street and whose name and age he didn't know. Being fresh out of a juvenile facility, Tony was perhaps even more interested in sexual contact than a typical nineteen-year-old young man. The young woman promised sex in exchange for a $100 pair of boots, "like it was basically like a contract. You get what I'm saying? Like prostitution or whatever they called it." He explains that the period of time he spent incarcerated prevented him from being exposed to new, adult norms around sexual interactions with girls. Still in the "high school mindset" even though he was now nineteen and out of school, he and his buddies sought out potential partners at high school "let-out," and he felt that this group of girls was his appropriate sexual peer group. He admits to being naïve about statutory rape laws, failing to pick up the nuances of legal consent.

> JF: And you assumed she was your age?
> TONY: At least in her teens—like 15–16, 'cause at this time I'm really clueless like that, not clueless . . . I always knew of like rapists and stuff like that and baby-touchers but I never knew [long pause] high school was off limits to like another teenager—you know I never made that transition—17 to 18 . . . Cause we were still going to high school let-outs—you get what I'm saying? . . . We was still going to their [school] . . . talking to different females like and it was okay so . . . my peers, we never made that transition.

He describes his sense of disbelief when presented with the statutory assault charges:

> I see the public defender, they was like well . . . the bad news is that she was only fifteen. So I'm like "alright." So I'm like "and . . ." and they're like, "well you was nineteen" and I'm like "right," so they said, "that's illegal" so I'm like, "what is you saying, that I'm raping? I'm a rapist?" Automatically I go there. [Note: his original lengthy list of charges for this incident included forcible rape.] He's like, "no what happens is, she's fifteen, she can't give consent . . . Her mother have to give consent." [I said] Son, that don't even make sense! That's how I'm talking, I'm talking just like, "how does a mother have to tell someone to have sex with her daughter? . . . Like it just doesn't make sense." But they was like, "This is the law. *You don't have to do no time, we ain't going to put you on no registration, nothing like that.* All you have to do is sixteen months' probation and anger management . . . that's a good deal."

By comparison to the robbery charge he was facing, which carried a much more substantial penalty (5–10 years in prison), pleading to "statutory sexual assault" seemed relatively low risk, especially because he was promised that it would keep him from being on the registry.

## Application of the Sex Offender Label

Despite being sentenced on the robbery charge, the sex offender charge became the dominant theme in the decision-making process, almost from the start of his sentence. At his first state correctional institution (SCI), he was placed on a treatment unit with other sex offenders.

> When they first told me, I was shocked and confused and real angry because all I can say was, they never ordered me to do *this*, they only said anger management. I'm up here for a robbery [a separate incident and set of charges]. . . . I'm really frustrated and I'm angry and all of that that I have to do this. And not only that, I'm feeling like really misplaced. . . . I think they could have put me in a place that I could relate to, you know what I'm saying? Don't get me wrong, I learned a great deal. Just like if you put somebody in anything with information, they gonna learn something. As far as a sex offender I learned a great deal [about] relationships and stuff like that but I really was frustrated about the stories that these guys was actually touching their niece and nephews and stuff like that. And I don't think that I should be in that.

When I asked if he felt compelled to take responsibility for things he didn't think he had done, he said no:

> Like I'm not no rapist, I didn't rape the girl . . . but, um, I was wrong. Cause if I was responsible as a nineteen-year-old, if I transitioned as I was supposed to from like 17–18 or whatever I would have knew better, I would have knew to ask this girl her age, her name, and really get to know her. I knew that I was in the wrong because I was dysfunctional at that time. So I admit to things like that, you feel me? But I don't have to lie and say that "oh I did it" just to please them.

Here, Tony makes several references to what psychologists call "arrested development" (Dmitrieva et al. 2012), or the temporary halting of psychosocial development that occurs during a period of incarceration during adolescence. This period of time would typically be where adolescents learn appropriate norms around sexuality and romantic relationships, but Tony missed that opportunity while he was at Mountain

Ridge Academy on drug charges. Nevertheless, to this day he has never internalized the label of sex offender, even when receiving clinical treatment for sex offending. The members of his social circle have never treated him like a sex offender, either, which may be one important difference between registered and non-registered sex offenders.

*Reentry: Parole Conditions and the Revolving Door*

Tony was being held in a local jail for a separate robbery charge when he became aware of the sex offense charge, which had been brought by the girl's mother. The next decade involved stints in two jails, five different prisons, four secure stepdown / community corrections facilities, and a local halfway house. His movement through the system was largely a function of his status as a sex offender, even though he was not on the registry. See table 11.1 for a timeline of Tony's progress.

A defining feature of his parole status involved assignment to the state sex offender probation / parole unit, which was reputed by other system agents like public defenders and county probation/ parole officers to employ the most mean-spirited parole agents in the system. This was entirely consistent with Tony's experience, as his parole agent refused to acknowledge his status as a non-registered sexual offender. Tony reported that his agent called him "a rapist," and I noted that the agent seemed to go out of his way to thwart Tony's reentry plans. This agent notified Tony's landlord of his status as a sex offender and did the same at a halfway house I had arranged (losing him his spot there), as well as informing an employer, and his girlfriend.

Having worked for three years as a probation / parole officer, my husband got involved. He phoned the agent and confirmed that he used a standard script for all of his clients: "This individual may or may not be on the Megan's Law registry." Undeterred, my husband asked him to look again at Tony's file and confirm that he was, indeed, not on the registry. The agent acknowledged that he was not, but he wouldn't agree to stop using this language. Afterward, Tony reflected about the problems caused by notifying landlords and others that he "may or may not" be on the sex offender registry. "Why is you [the parole agent] implying it? . . . 'Oh, he may or may not be a killer.'"

TABLE 11.1. Timeline of Tony's Movement through the Criminal Justice System

| | |
|---|---|
| Summer 2005 | Released from Mountain Ridge Academy, juvenile facility for drug sellers<br>Sexual contact with underage minor occurs<br>Arrested, incarcerated (jail) for drug sales (made bail) |
| Spring 2006 | Incarcerated (jail) for failure to appear (2 months) |
| Fall/ Winter 2007 | Arrested, incarcerated (jail) for robbery—learns of sex offense charge |
| 2007–Spring 2008 | Still detained / awaiting trial, pled to / sentenced for robbery and sexual offense charges |
| Spring 2008 | Transferred to classification facility (6–7 months) |
| 2009–2011 | State correctional institution, sex offender unit |
| 2011–2012 | State correctional institution, therapeutic community for drug users |
| 2012 | Returned to Philadelphia, halfway house (3 months)<br>Home plan never identified, returned on SO parole violations |
| Fall 2012–2014 | Parole board determines he "hasn't learned his lesson"<br>State correctional institution<br>Paroled |
| 2014–2015 | Secure step-down facility outside Pittsburgh<br>Conflict with PO, reincarcerated for "threatening" behavior |
| 2015 | State correctional institution, 4 months |
| 2015 | Secure stepdown in central PA, 2 months |
| 2015 | Secure stepdown in Philadelphia, 2 ½ months<br>Parole violation after release for creating Facebook page, reincarcerated |
| 2015–2016 | State correctional institution, 9 months |
| Spring 2016 | Released—begins living in own apartment |
| Fall 2016 | Parole violation for positive drug test, photos of nephews on cell phone<br>Secure stepdown in Philadelphia, 30 days |
| 2016–2017 | Returns to apartment in Philadelphia |

In the twelve years since he pled guilty to the sexual offense charge, Tony has violated multiple conditions of parole, most of them sex offender–specific. These include: possessing a cell phone, spending time on a block with children or with friends who had children, setting up a social media account, having photos of his nephews on his phone, or having porn sites in his browser history on his phone. Tony reports that his agent regularly asked him to turn over his phone during impromptu home visits or at the parole office, which Tony's public defender later said was illegal. Throughout this process, it seemed that he did not have any due process rights whatsoever. On their own, most of the above-named "offenses" appear to be harmless practices carried out by most Americans on a daily basis. However, since Tony was viewed by his parole agent as a sexual predator, these were used as evidence that he refused to stay away from children and to justify further sanctions. They locked him into a cycle of violation, reincarcerations, and return for long after he served his time. As Tony points out, his time served in prison would have ended in 2012, if not for the sex offender–specific parole violations.

> TONY: Yep . . . for this robbery I would have just came home in 2012 and never been arrested again if it wasn't for the . . . every time I been arrested, it's been for Facebook or something like that.
> JF: It's for a technical violation related to a sex restriction.
> TONY: Yeah, a sex restriction—for a crime that no longer exists once I came home in 2012. I was no longer on probation for it, I was no longer—I was never on Megan's law or anything. This crime was done and over with but I continued to went to jail for it.

It should be noted that violations for technical infractions are a common experience for any returning citizen on parole supervision, but sex offender supervision involves a much longer list of conditions that potentially can be used as justification for violation (e.g., restrictions on use of social media and contact with children).

Another aspect of Tony's supervision, both while confined and in the community, was mandated participation in treatment programs. He completed several treatment programs for sex offenders, anger management classes, and was part of an in-prison therapeutic community (TC) for substance abuse, which he says was ordered for all offenders whose past charges involve drug sales. Moreover, one community provider for sex offender treatment conducted an intake procedure that recommended substance abuse treatment, despite the fact that Tony hadn't regularly used drugs since he was a teenager. I reviewed the treatment paperwork in disbelief, as they had diagnosed him with "Cannabis Use Disorder, Extended Remission." After confirming that this diagnosis really existed in the latest DSM, we talked about his plans to "fake it to make it" through the program, which had become an additional parole requirement (Fader 2013). Although Tony has never read Garland

"THIS INDIVIDUAL MAY OR MAY NOT BE ON THE MEGAN'S LAW REGISTRY" | 245

(2001), he knows first-hand that responsibilization is a key component of earning one's way to graduation in the context of neoliberal corrections, and he is a savvy consumer of the system.

Because of his level of first-hand understanding, Tony has developed an angry, oppositional stance to the system and its actors, which is not unreasonable, given the numerous disappointments he experienced. In fact, the first case study featuring Tony documented how a five-year-old warrant for disturbing the peace (generated when he was fourteen) prevented him from being enrolled in Job Corps, an opportunity to receive no-cost training to become a nurse. His juvenile probation officer who did his reentry planning had been unaware of the warrant because the Family Court computer system didn't interface with the adult civil offense system, leading him to miss a potentially life-changing opportunity. On countless occasions, we anticipated his release and had hopes dashed because no sex offender beds were available, or no legal home plan was possible, or secure supervision was required because of his status.

One particularly egregious instance of the discretion afforded to the system because of Tony's sex offender status came after he was successfully paroled and told he would return to Philadelphia. Instead of being released as we expected, he remained in prison for several months while waiting for next steps and was then instead transferred to a facility for parole violators, where he stayed on a special sex offender wing. His family and the first author repeatedly phoned the facility-based parole agent to ask about his case. According to him, she threatened to begin issuing "hits" (delay in release) if she received another phone call from any of us. This didn't seem legal, but we stopped anyway because we couldn't afford to hire a private attorney to threaten litigation. As he neared release from this facility, he earned a hit for manipulating the soda machine to give him two cans instead of one. Finally, he began to take a demanding stance about his release and—according to Tony—she accused him of threatening her and calling her a bitch.

> They didn't give me that long for the soda. She try to make up another thing why [they] giving me the extension. And it . . . it couldn't be more than 14 days. So whatever it was, it made me mad. But I didn't call her a bitch, I didn't threaten—say "I'm gon fuck you up." It was only 7–14 days,

I'm not going to go through for all that. But she lied, she said "get out my office" bang. But then she screamed, the lieutenant guy came in. . . . And it was like she got real hype once he came—and just started goin' on all this stuff and they put me in cuffs . . . and then she said something, I know I said, "dang, you gon' let her lie like this?" and then they said, "your word against hers."

Since the agent refused to speak with the first author by phone, she was never able to get her side of the story, but Tony's account didn't seem out of step with her approach. After this incident, he was reincarcerated in Western Pennsylvania, told he would be released to Philadelphia and—again because of the shortage of sex offender beds in the city—was placed in a jail in central Pennsylvania for several months while he waited. In the time he was followed through these periods of incarceration, the first author saw him become fairly well adjusted, indeed savvy, to life inside prison, running a sophisticated scheme in the last secure stepdown facility where he had friends toss cigarettes and pills into the backyard exercise enclosure, which he and an associate sold to other inmates to keep their commissary accounts full.

*Housing*

Although Tony faced multiple, overlapping barriers to reintegration, the most fundamental obstacle was finding a place where he could legally reside, given the residency restrictions accompanying his sexual offender status. Since he was not a registered sex offender, these restrictions did not impose a specified geographic distance (e.g., 2,500 feet) from sites where children congregate, such as schools, daycares, and playgrounds; rather, his parole conditions specified that he could not live with or spend time with children, date a woman with children, spend time on a block that appeared (in the parole agent's judgment) to have a lot of children, or keep photos of children (e.g., nephews) on his phone. These are collectively known as "no contact" parole conditions, which prohibit sex offender parolees from having contact with any individual younger than seventeen, including their own children (Brett 2012).

Tony's initial encounter with these restrictions was his first time being paroled after serving his minimum sentence of five years, in 2012; he returned to a halfway house in North Philadelphia. While he was incarcerated, his older sister had become the mother of two small children, which disqualified her household as a suitable place for Tony to live. Given that his sister was his closest source of social support and ran a stable household with regular routines and income, this was an especially difficult setback. Tony's girlfriend lived on a block with many children, so her house was off limits.

Reviewing his mental list of possibilities, he submitted a home plan with the name of a stepfather never mentioned previously, who was apparently willing to allow him to stay. He moved into the halfway house with the intention of staying a few days while his parole officer did a home visit and cleared the plan as being in accordance with the conditions of parole. The stepfather met the agent at the house and gave him a tour. There was some confusion about sleeping arrangements and the home plan was rejected. Tony languished at the halfway house for three months, after which his parole was revoked because he left his job and was found to be spending time at his girlfriend's house on a block with children.

In 2015, nearly ten years after being incarcerated, Tony finally was approved for a home plan. A friend who was single and had no children was willing to share his apartment. The landlord was consulted, and Tony's PO made sure he was aware that a sex offender was living under his roof. Miraculously, he agreed that Tony could stay there for six months. Tony was violated and reincarcerated the next day for the Facebook account he had set up while in the local stepdown facility. Tony was not a savvy user of social media and had friended many people he didn't know, one of whom posted pornography to his page.

The turning point in Tony's trajectory came a year later, after he was released from yet another prison and secure stepdown facility. His sister had found a room in a row house around the corner from her home where Tony could stay for $130 a week. He had found a rare block in Philadelphia where there were not very many children, possibly because it was too grim. The room was tiny and didn't have a kitchen, but it was clean and allowed Tony to live independently for the first time in his life. Importantly, the house was owned by a friend, which came in handy many times in the next several months, when Tony's employment was unstable and hours and income were irregular. The landlord gave him a break on several occasions, most notably holding the place for him while he was briefly reincarcerated on another parole violation.

The room was both a source of stability and an incredible financial burden. Tony rarely was able to work enough hours to make the weekly rent. Philadelphia was ranked in 2015 as the twelfth most expensive city in the United States to rent an apartment, with an average price for a one-bedroom of $1,350 per month (Rooney 2015). Although Tony hardly lived in a pricey neighborhood, his rent took more than 100% of his income. He had no savings to put down a security deposit and month's rent on a place that was less expensive on a monthly basis, and sharing costs with a roommate would have added to the scrutiny by his parole agent. Correctly identifying the apartment as the key factor in preventing him from being reincarcerated, he fought fiercely to retain it and was willing to do anything to keep paying the weekly rent. He tapped his sources of support when he could, but eventually needed to resort to a more reliable way to make rent.

*Employment*

When the first author documented Tony's reentry from the juvenile facility where she met him, she noted that, at age nineteen, he was "not an attractive job applicant and very sensitive to rejection" (Fader 2013, p. 80). Being in prisons for the next decade hardly made this less true. With a criminal record and no established work history, Tony was relegated to the temporary labor market in a series of unstable and exploitative jobs. Since being released from Mountain Ridge Academy more than a decade ago, all of his formal labor market experience came through ManpowerGroup, a temporary agency that places 600,000 workers per day (ManpowerGroup 2017). At nineteen, he had spent two days formally employed under Manpower, one packing roast beef in a meatpacking facility ("the blood splattered on my face") and another packing heavy, wet cotton in a sweltering clothing factory. This time, he worked more stably at the Cheesecake Factory for more than two months before quitting after a conflict with one of the other kitchen staff members. Eventually, being unemployed was one rationale used by his parole agent to reincarcerate him. "So that was on the Tuesday and that Friday I was back in incarceration."

After maxing out his ten-year sentence, employment and good standing on parole presented a double-bind. Since the cornerstone of his continued freedom was his ability to pay $130 per week in rent, employment was crucial. However, he was locked into an unstable segment of the labor market. He tried for several months to make ends meet working for a third-party company that provided nighttime cleaning services to office buildings in Center City, but they rarely gave him enough hours to make his rent, let alone support himself with food, clothing, and cell phone (Hallett 2012). Moreover, his nighttime work schedule was rarely compatible with his mandated curfew, putting him in a position to either go to work or be present when his PO did random spot checks of his residence at night.

Importantly, the positions he occupied in the legal labor market were exploitative in nature. In December 2016, about eight months after returning home, Tony had a phone conversation with the cleaning company's owners, where he explained that he was owed back pay for four weeks of work. He had not carefully documented his punch-ins and -outs, and appeared to have been subject to some unscrupulous practices by the supervisor. He demonstrated an impressive level of resourcefulness in tracking down the owner's contact information. The owner actually seemed sympathetic, but Tony didn't appear to have the soft skills needed to recognize someone who was willing to work with him rather than against him. The owner promised to investigate, but Tony was still very rude to him. We talked later about attracting more flies with honey than with vinegar, but this was a natural reaction to years of exploitative treatment in prison and part of his oppositional stance toward "the system," broadly defined.

After giving up on the cleaning company, Tony got another temporary job at a clothing order fulfillment center in central New Jersey. With his work located more than an hour away in a remote location, he and his colleagues paid $8 per shift to a third-party company for a van ride to and from the facility, which represented nearly one hour of labor (he earned $9.25 per hour). This was in addition to the cost of public transportation to and from the van pickup location. Eventually, Tony and most of his agency-placed coworkers were let go from the fulfillment center because they were no longer needed.

Making his weekly rent with these unstable jobs was very stressful (Western et al. 2015). When he came up short, he either had to rely on his landlord-friend to give him an extension, or ask his sister or the first author to cover the balance. Eventually, he moved to selling small quantities of marijuana, which he noted was extremely low risk, since police were looking for bigger players. (Philadelphia has decriminalized possession of marijuana so that being caught with less than 30 grams would result in a $25 fine). He had a small network of friends he sold to, always indoors and away from street surveillance. This is consistent with prior research on drug sellers who become more risk-averse after arrest or incarceration and continue to sell drugs, only in "smarter" ways (Fader 2016).

> JF: And what's your thinking about your risk associated with doing this, being that you're on probation?
> TONY: I had nightmares about this, like getting booked or something like that. [But] it's either that or homeless.

When asked to elaborate on his assessment of paid employment versus drug sales, he said:

> I'm stuck! If I have a job it's going nowhere. Who wants to work all these hours [in] just a job that's so draining and get so little? I barely pay the rent, I'm barely making the $130 a week. If I'm getting $180–200 a week, now I got $70 to last me through the whole week. So now we gonna say $25 for car-fare [public transportation]. So we gon' say now I got $50, and be realistically, now I'm gon' have to eat and stuff like that, . . . it just not happening, so then you like "what is I'm doing this for?" I'd rather sell my bud and I . . . don't really need transportation cause I'm at my own [place]. And I look at it like it ain't that harsh of a drug.

In April 2017, Tony filed taxes for the first time in his life (at age thirty-one) and looked forward to a tax refund through the Earned Income Tax Credit, a meaningful source of income for low-wage workers (Mendenhall et al. 2012). He was stunned to learn that his entire tax refund, however, was garnished because he owed the Department of Education for loans he took out in 2005 to attend a technical school for nursing.

As he became more stable over time and began planning for his future, this and other legal financial obligations needed to be cleared up in order to make any progress (Link 2017). He had fines for traffic violations, which required $70 that his network provided. After his tax refund was garnished, he still owed $170 for school loans, which prevented him from enrolling in a program to become an electrician at a local community college. Again, his support network helped him clear up that debt. During this period, he was motivated not only by a desire to make some progress in his life, but to establish a positive record to be considered for alleviation of the sexual offense restrictions associated with his probation.

*Sources of Social Support*

Existing research has documented the critical role of social support in the success of returning citizens (Shinkfield and Graffam 2009). As Tony noted, he began his lengthy period of incarceration and reentry with a wealth of supporters, including his "homies" (male friends) who sent him commissary funds to purchase a TV and "sneaks" to make his daily life more palatable. After several years, however, this support dropped off and he "lost a lot of people." By the time he and the first author began corresponding in his second prison stint, she was his lone supporter, occasionally depositing funds onto his books and sending him words of encouragement.

Being confined, particularly in community corrections, is expensive in the age of offender-funded justice (Evans 2014). Many facilities do not offer more than small meals and the most basic hygiene products (Chammah 2013; Klas 2017). Tony needed everything: deodorant, toothpaste and brushes, laundry detergent, food, and clothing. Those without support either went without or borrowed small amounts from their more fortunate comrades. On countless occasions, Tony's supporters had to mail "release" clothing for the many times he returned to Philadelphia. Besides providing material forms of support, the first author tried to harness her position as a university professor and professional knowledge of prisoner reentry to help, but this resulted in limited impact. She found Tony a halfway house and his PO squelched it by telling them he "may be" on the registry. She found him a job at a church, but they ran out of funding soon afterward and had to let him go. She reached out to multiple parole agents, all of whom seemed to view her support as interference.

During his period of incarceration, Tony began to date a woman who he met through another inmate. She sent letters, photos, and deposited money on his phone account so they could get to know one another. When he returned to Philadelphia, they dated, although he openly admitted that he wasn't attracted to her. He described this relationship as "crap," as a "you help me, I'll help you situation . . . I knew I need the emotional support and all that stuff like the financial little things like that so I kept, you know, like leading it on. . . . I knew she like to say that she has a boyfriend or take pictures and stuff. I knew deep down it was never going to be nothing." He started seeing another woman concurrently and drew on her for complementary and supplementary support.

He juggled various sources of support—the two girlfriends, his sister, the occasional male friend, and the first author—walking a tightrope of trying not to tap them so often he permanently exhausted them. Calling in favors also brought unwanted family involvement and judgment for not being able to act like an adult and be more independent. Miller and Stuart (2017) note in this regard that:

> These practices endow caregivers, employers and other third parties with inordinate power. This is because third parties represent one of the few resources that carceral citizens have access to, introducing a new kind of vulnerability where the carceral citizen is subject to the whims of the people they encounter in everyday life—even those whom they are closest to. . . . This combination of precarity and derision creates a power imbalance, altering even the most intimate exchanges between the formerly incarcerated and the most important people in their lives. (p. 540)

Tony also recognizes that the influences in his present environment are not conducive to becoming a productive citizen:

> I know that I should be around people that don't have my problems so that I can get accustomed to their problems—problems of, like, coming to work late. Or I lose a job. Selling drugs to [make ends meet] should

not be in the vocabulary; the vocabulary should be to get another job. Some people don't even have that in their vocabulary, "oh, I gotta hustle or I gotta rob something, or I gotta take something" if they lose a job. No, some people say, I gotta get another job. It don't even cross their mind that they're going out there hustling.

Here, he acknowledges how his view of problem-solving has been affected by those around him.

## Conclusions and Implications for Policy

At the time of this writing, Tony is in a holding pattern while he awaits a judge's decision about whether to continue his sex offender restrictions during his five-year probation stint after he maxed out his ten-year parole period. He remained on the rolls in the state sex offender parole and probation office, but he wisely capitalized on some administrative confusion about whether the sex offender restrictions were still enforceable. His PO asked him to sign a document mandating additional sex offender treatment in the community and he refused, demanding a hearing with the judge to request to lift the restrictions. The first author of this chapter wrote a letter of support and gave it to his public defender to pass along to the judge. The case has been continued several times over the last several months, while the judge defers the decision, perhaps to see how Tony performs on probation.

In the meantime, Tony has taken steps to move forward and do more than just subsist. His new girlfriend is pregnant with his baby and they are planning to make a go of it, despite his stated intentions to wait until he was financially stable (the pregnancy wasn't planned, but they hadn't planned for contraception either). With his school loans paid off, he can enroll in community college in the hopes of becoming an electrician. Despite these apparent gains, Tony—now thirty-two years old—has some substantial deficits to overcome. He has difficulties consistently maintaining an adult schedule and has missed several appointments at the college. It's hard not to think about how he will respond to regular assignment deadlines and complete written assignments without a computer, and he has not considered the cost of textbooks. He has missed many adult lessons about the way the world works, including how to function online and how to deal with people in positions of power. He is sometimes manipulative, and not in a particularly subtle way.

According to his public defender, the Defender's Association is planning a lawsuit against Pennsylvania State Parole for their overbroad application of sex offender restrictions. She has empowered Tony to challenge his sex offender restrictions, leading him to give up his apartment and move in with his girlfriend. His PO immediately went to his new residence, asking his new landlord and girlfriend to sign a paper saying they were aware he was a sex offender. Both refused to comply out of principle, and Tony now faces a precarious situation. Going back to his old apartment is no longer an option, but if it is determined that he cannot live with his girlfriend because of "no contact" parole conditions, he may have nowhere to go but a halfway house. In the past, this has led to heightened surveillance and additional conditions, which have led to repeated spells of reincarceration.

The case study developed in this chapter highlights some common themes surrounding the challenges of reentry and reintegration, including barriers associated with housing, employment, and substance abuse. Perhaps a more critical common thread, also featured here, is the criminal justice system itself as a hurdle to navigate. As can be seen in Tony's story and elsewhere, the current system of plea bargaining deserves greater scrutiny by policymakers. With disproportionately high sentences as the likely alternative, the vast majority of defendants plead guilty, regardless of their innocence or guilt. A high degree of discretion and disparate outcomes play out at every step of the process, from whether treatment is mandated (and for what), to parole decisions, the conditions of confinement, and how probation / parole agents determine what conditions of supervision must be satisfied. Offender-funded justice practices, especially in community corrections facilities, take a toll on family members and supporters to provide basic necessities for inmates. In every stage of the process, a lack of resources (e.g., to hire private attorneys) diminishes individuals' abilities to fight due process violations and can result in confinement before adjudication of guilt in most jurisdictions, where cash bail is required.

Tony's case is an example of the system's overly broad application of the sex offender label and of how the "criminal justice system [has] virtually separated the sexual offender from every other type of criminal" (Huebner and Bynum 2006, p. 962). Despite a growing body of literature demonstrating that sex offender laws do not reduce recidivism (Bonnar-Kidd 2010) and create unnecessary barriers for those with the sex offender label (Mercado et al. 2008), policymakers have been slow to reform these laws. Treated like a child predator, Tony has been subject to coercive treatment for pedophilia and restrictions preventing him from having contact with any child in his life, including his family members. It remains to be seen how far these "no contact" parole restrictions might be extended; in other jurisdictions, they have been used to prevent parolees from having any contact—in person or by phone—with their own children (Brett 2012). This, of course, runs counter to the research on the critical role of family support in healthy reintegration of former offenders (Visher, Bakken, and Gunter 2013) and collateral consequences of incarceration for children (Wakefield and Wildeman 2013). Moreover, for Tony, it has created a revolving door of violation and re-incarceration, where the contradictions involved in meeting supervision conditions (e.g., having a job but being available for evening curfew checks, needing a stable place to live but not making a steady enough income) have resulted in a situation where he views low-level offending as the optimal solution.

There are no known estimates of the prevalence of applying sex offender parole restrictions to non-registered parolees with sexual offense charges. If this is a common practice, it could challenge due process provisions and represent an even wider net of social control resulting from sex offender legislation than previously imagined. At every turn, the judges, parole board members, and parole agents in Tony's case have been risk-averse, apparently believing that the broadest possible application of restrictions is the best way to reduce risk of recidivism. An implied argument herein is that the charges and circumstances surrounding Tony's case should have resulted in his being on a regular supervision caseload and the distinction between him and "real" sex offenders be made by system actors. It seems true that different handling of his case—as well as others who have committed offenses of a sexual nature not deemed serious enough to be placed on a state sex offender registry—would have substantially eased Tony's reintegration after a stint in prison. However, research on the stigma of a sex offense label, the myriad unintended consequences of sex offender restrictions (e.g., housing, employment), and the ineffectiveness of these policies for reducing serious sex offending suggest that they should be revisited on a large scale. Tony's story serves as a lesson about how these practices can backfire and lock individuals into a cycle of offending and criminal justice system involvement.

Finally, probation and parole supervision reform create a critical step toward reducing the high rates of failure among returning citizens (Petersilia 2003). Although this fact has been long argued by experts, the current momentum surrounding criminal justice reform in the United States may present a fruitful opportunity to examine the unnecessarily long lists of supervision requirements, the discretion allowed in applying them, and the use of confinement for technical violations. At the time of this writing, the Columbia Justice Lab just released a scathing report on the "indefensible" rate of citizens on probation or parole in Pennsylvania, which has the third highest proportion of residents under supervision in the country (Schiraldi 2018). As mass incarceration's drivers (e.g., cash bail, harsh sentences for low-level drug offenses) are targeted by policymakers, the degree and nature of parole and probation supervision must not be neglected in reform efforts.

NOTE

1 Because of the sensitive nature of information shared by participants in the course of this research, many precautions have been taken to protect their identities and data. The study has been approved by three university Institutional Review Boards, and the National Institute of Drug Abuse (NIDA) granted a federal Certificate of Confidentiality to prevent having research materials subpoenaed or researchers being forced to testify against respondents who revealed illegal activity for which they were never prosecuted. All names, including the name of the facility where the study began, are pseudonyms, and locations are changed slightly to protect the identities of human subjects.

PART V

The Interplay between Research and Policy

# 12

## Running Away

*Probation Revocation Programming in St. Louis County*

BETH M. HUEBNER AND MORGAN McGUIRK

Extant correctional research and public policy have focused largely on the growth of prison populations. The outcry over the sentencing of rap artist Meek Mill to prison following a probation violation highlighted the importance of considering the role of probation violations in correctional growth. Convicted in 2008 at the age of nineteen for possession of drugs and guns, Meek Mill served eight months in prison and was then placed on probation for five years. His probation was extended numerous times for technical violations. In November 2017, the prosecutor and probation officer overseeing the rapper's case recommended prison time for the rapper, who, now age thirty, had violated his probation (Bromwich, 2017). The judge sentenced Meek Mill to two to four years in prison, sparking protests from hundreds in his hometown of Philadelphia and many more on social media (Jay-Z, 2017). This case exemplifies the long reach of a term of probation and the import of considering the mechanisms that lead to a violation of a term of probation.

The reach of community corrections is broad and deep. As of 2015, it was estimated that one out of every fifty-three adults in the United States is currently under community supervision, totaling more than 4,650,900 individuals (Kaeble and Bonczar, 2016). Individuals on probation comprise 81% of the total community corrections population, four times more than the population on parole (ibid.). In addition to mass incarceration, we are also in an era of mass probation, as the population of probationers grew fourfold, from one million to four million, between 1980 and 2007 (Corda and Phelps, 2017).

Individuals who violate the terms of probation and face revocation are often remanded to jail while their cases are being processed. Yet, jails have largely been ignored in the policy debates over mass incarceration until recently. The jail population is a critical cog in the criminal justice system and is rife for reform. Nationwide, the local jail population has grown from 184,000 in 1980 to 728,200 in 2015, a 296% increase (Zeng, 2018). Communities spent approximately $22.2 billion on jails in 2011, four times more than in 1983 (Henrichson, Rinaldi, and Delaney, 2015). Jails continue to be overcrowded (Subramanian et al., 2015). Jails also are unique from other forms of correctional control in that they can be operated at the municipal or county levels by local law enforcement or correctional agencies. Jails detain a variety of individuals, including those awaiting trial, serving time for a conviction, and probation and parole violators waiting for their judicial hearings. Finally, jails can also house individuals serving time due to overcrowding in prison facilities, a practice that has been used significantly in California (ibid.).

The current work outlines the growth of jail as a punishment for probation violations throughout the past decades and highlights the need for more research on probation violators incarcerated in jails. We focus on the jailing of individuals for probation violations. We also detail a unique program designed to mitigate the costs of jail incarceration for individuals incarcerated for new technical violations, while addressing the root causes of recidivism. In addition, we offer some potential avenues for reform.

## Mass Probation

There has been exponential growth in the probation population over the past three decades, from 1 million in 1980 to a peak of more than 4.2 million in 2007 (Corda and Phelps, 2017). Probation is the largest correctional sanction, with 3,789,800 individuals on probation as of 2015, equating to one in sixty-six US adults (Kaeble and Boncazar, 2017). The growth of the probation rate mirrors that of the incarceration rate (see figure 12.1).

Scholars have tied the growth in probation populations to several key political and social factors. First, a political shift from rehabilitative to punitive punishment beginning in the 1970s due to a lack of successful outcomes for rehabilitative practices, as many of these practices were inadequately implemented (Feeley and Simon, 1992; McCorkle and

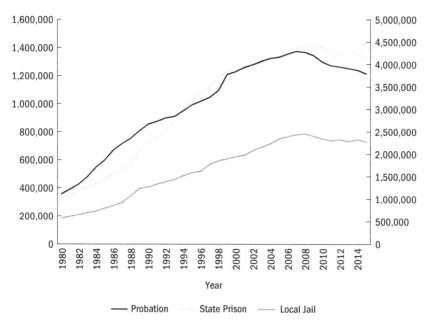

Figure 12.1. Change in National Jail and Probation Populations 1980–2015. Source: Bureau of Justice Statistics.

Crank, 1996; Garland, 2001). Second, the dramatic rise in incarceration strained correctional budgets, resulting in a greater use of community sanctions, including probation (Phelps, 2013; Goodman, Page, and Phelps, 2015; Phelps and Pager, 2016). In several states, in response to the exponential growth in prison populations, legislation was passed mandating an increase in spending on probation and incentivizing judges to sentence more defendants to probation rather than prison (Pew Center on the States, 2009; Phelps, 2013). Additionally, some state statutes expanded which cases were eligible for traditional and intensive probation (Phelps, 2013).

This shift from institutional corrections to community supervision has many potential advantages. Advocates of probation, scholars and practitioners alike, assert that it is a more effective form of punishment. In contrast to prison, probation provides structure to a sentence and creates incentives for compliance, particularly for low-level offenses such as drug crimes (McCorkle and Crank, 1996; Petersilia, 2003; Phelps, 2013).

Individuals on probation can receive social services in the community while maintaining social relationships and employment. Probation also costs substantially less than incarceration (Phelps, 2013).

Conversely, scholars contend there are unintended consequences of the growth in probation as it has widened the net of carceral control (Phelps, 2013). In particular, the expansion of probation has increased the punitive nature of punishments for low-level offenses (Wodahl and Garland, 2009; Phelps, 2013; Corda and Phelps, 2017). Offenses that traditionally would have resulted in a fine or community service now result in a probation term (Phelps, 2013). This increased use of probation enhances the population at risk for subsequent imprisonment in jail or prison, in what Phelps (2013) deems the probation-prison link. Individuals who violate their probation, in most states, are detained in jail before a violation hearing can be held. Nationally, the average jail stay is twenty-five days, which has the potential to greatly disrupt individuals' lives (Zeng, 2018). Despite the growth in probation revocations, there is little evidence to suggest that incarceration for these violations reduces the likelihood of recidivism (Wodahl, Boman, and Garland, 2015).

Additionally, there is evidence that substantial discretion exists in the decision to write a probation violation report and to ultimately revoke one's probation. Probation officers and prosecutors guide the revocation hearings, the majority of which are for technical violations, not new crimes (Kingsnorth, MacIntosh, and Sutherland, 2002). At revocation hearings in some jurisdictions, it is determined that individuals violated their probation and they are then sent to jail, even for missing a scheduled appointment (Subramanian et al., 2015). There is also evidence that race may play a role in the revocation process. Research suggests that individuals of minority races are more likely to have their probation revoked and be incarcerated than their white counterparts (Rodriguez and Web, 2007; Janetta et al., 2014).

*Jails*

Jails remain an understudied part of the criminal justice system. Like prison, there has been a substantial growth in the jail population over the past three decades (see figure 12.1). The number of individuals admitted to jail annually almost doubled, from 6 million in 1983 to 11.7

million in 2013, and the average length of a jail stay increased from fourteen days in 1983 to twenty-three days as of 2013 (Subramanian et al., 2015). Jails house a diverse population, including individuals detained awaiting trial or for a probation or parole violation hearing, those sentenced to a term of less than one year, or those waiting to be transferred to another facility. Jails are managed at the local government level and are most often operated by the county government or an elected sheriff. There is little oversight or systemization of local jails; hence, great variation in the day-to-day practices of each institution exists (Henrichson et al., 2015; Bales and Garduno, 2016).

Jails can have negative consequences for the lives of detained individuals. Jails serve a diverse population, yet many institutions are not equipped to address the needs of individuals who enter the facility. Jail programming and services are constrained for several reasons. Structurally, jails serve individuals for short periods, making services and programs less of a central focus. Jail staff also serve a diverse population. Staff are often not equipped to address the needs of a population that frequently turns over (Bales and Garduno, 2016). Many jails, particularly those in disadvantaged or rural communities, rely on funding from a small tax base, further limiting the availability of effective programs and services (Copp and Bales, 2018). Also, jails often subcontract educational and medical services, further reducing the systemization and potential quality of these resources (Henrichson et al., 2015).

Additionally, jails are often unable to provide individuals with reentry needs before their release. A national assessment of medium-sized jails reports that 23% of jails offered no programming, even when the definition of programming was construed liberally to include laundry and janitorial service, and food preparation within the facility (Miller, Applegate, and King, 2013). Instead, jails also often depend on the assistance of community-based organizations to provide services, training, treatment, and case management (Solomon et al., 2008). Finally, individuals in jail often struggle with mental health challenges, but research suggests assessments for mental health are rare and many struggle with co-occurring substance abuse addictions (Bales and Garduno, 2016).

Jail stays create new stressors for those serving time and for their families. Researchers have long suggested that prison can have negative effects on marital unions (Huebner, 2005; Lopoo and Western, 2005) and families (Wildeman and Wakefield, 2014). There is emerging evidence to suggest that even short terms for jail incarceration, with time incarcerated averaging a month, significantly decreases the likelihood of a resolution in a marital or cohabitating relationship (Apel, 2016). Comfort (2016) argues that probation and short jail stays can have unique effects on families that are different than what is observed in a prison stay. She observed that the churn of multiple jail stays, even those of short duration, and frequent contact with the criminal justice system cause strain and instability among family groups, often leaving families feeling hopeless under the strain of constant supervision. In their study of women returning from a jail stay, Van Olpen and colleagues (2009) found that most reported that even relatively short jail stays affected their lives. The women expressed experiencing cumulative stress after their release, including concerns over child care, housing, and employment. Only a few women reported having a plan for release, further heightening the level of stress in their lives.

Incarceration can also reduce earning potential. There is a rich body of literature that documents the negative effects of imprisonment on employment and one's long-term earning potential. There is evidence that longer terms of incarceration can permanently damage employment prospects. New research suggests that short-term stays can also hamper employment. Harding, Siegel, and Morenoff (2017) observed the employment outcomes of individuals on parole in Michigan. They found that short terms of jail incarceration, resulting from a technical violation, suppressed the earnings of individuals during the quarter in which they were imprisoned. Even more, individual's earnings had decreased by about 13% in the nine months after short-term custody.

In addition, there is evidence that the public perceives jail as a more punitive punishment compared to alternative sanctions including prison. May and colleagues (2014) found that the public views serving a twelve-month jail sentence as the second most punitive sanction next to boot camp, and more severe than electronic monitoring, probation, or prison. Individuals with felony convictions were also more likely to believe jail is a more severe punishment as compared to prison. This belief is likely due to those surveyed having more direct experience with jail or indirectly through neighbors or relatives who have served jail time (ibid.). Although this study is limited in scope, it does highlight the negative effects of jail incarceration.

Finally, there is evidence that jails may increase the risk of recidivism as compared to less punitive sanctions. Cochran, Mears, and Bales (2014) compared the likelihood of recidivism for a matched jail and probation sample. The study found 35% of those sentenced to jail time recidivated as compared to 31% under probationary supervision. The findings suggest that harsher punishments, i.e., those receiving jail time instead of probation, can potentially increase the likelihood of offending. In addition, Gainey, Payne, and O'Toole (2000) contrasted the outcomes of individuals with electronic monitoring to those sentenced to jail. Although the amount of time served in jail was not found to be a statistically significant predictor of recidivism, electronic monitoring reduced the likelihood of arrest. Additionally, De Jong (1997) found that a jail stay is particularly criminogenic for individuals who have not had prior contact with the criminal justice system. A jail term did delay offending for individuals with prior convictions, but the long-term recidivism rates are similar. The author asserts that incarceration fails to deter future criminal behavior. Overall, the current research suggests that jail incarceration has negative and potentially long-term consequences for individuals if not used properly, and more effective alternative strategies should continue to be explored.

Policy Interventions

As the rate of probation violations has increased due to the state's broadened net of carceral control, state and local agencies have implemented policies and practices to try to reduce probation revocations (Hawken and Kleiman, 2009; Campbell, 2018). Some states have made systematic changes to community supervision, while others have focused on changing the ways in which agencies respond to probation violations. An overview of interventions is provided.

Several state policymakers have passed legislation mandating changes to the way in which probation violations are addressed, particularly for individuals who are convicted of nonviolent crimes. In Michigan, county probation departments are given state monetary incentives for improving probation services and reducing the probation failure rate. The department of corrections increased funding for treatment programs including employment, substance abuse, education, and cognitive-behavioral therapy. From 2001 to 2014, the probation revocation rate decreased from 69% to 52% (Phelps, 2017). Similarly, in Arizona, the state pays counties for successfully keeping individuals on probation and out of prison. Arizona has increased staffing for high-risk cases and uses shorter probationary time periods for those maintaining compliance, which has resulted in a 48% decline in probation violations (Pew Center on the States, 2011a). Finally, Kansas passed legislation to fund community treatment services in lieu of jail or prison for individuals who violate probation and has since seen a decline in the number of probation violations (Greene and Mauer, 2010).

Many states have also adopted a swift-and-certain (SAC) approach to addressing probation violations. The most prominent approach is Hawaii's Opportunity Probation with Enforcement, known as Project HOPE (Campbell, 2018). Project HOPE was conceived in 2004 to address Hawaii's consistently high rate of probation revocations. This pilot program was developed for individuals who violated their probation for drug-related violations. Project HOPE is centered on a deterrence model, focusing on swift and certain sanctions for probation violations (Nagin, 2016). The program's model strives to consistently apply simple and straightforward tenets by providing participants with clear guidelines they are expected to follow and punishments that are not unnecessarily severe. Any probation violation, including a positive drug test, is immediately punished consistently with certainty and swiftness. The sanction for a violation is a short jail stay of a few days, and continued violations result in longer stays.

These SAC programs were initially heralded as successes, but more recent results have been mixed. For example, in an older study using a randomized controlled trial by Hawken and Kleiman (2009), they found those assigned to HOPE probation were much less likely to use drugs, miss appointments, and be arrested over the course of the one-year study. Those on HOPE probation spent only one-third of the number of days in prison as compared to those on standard probation for either revocations or new convictions. Additionally, in a quasi-experimental study, Hamilton and colleagues (2016) found that compared to non-participants, SAC participants spent less time incarcerated after a violation, were more likely to participate in treatment programs, and less likely to recidivate.

More recent research calls into question the efficacy of SAC programs. O'Connell, Brent, and Visher (2016) conducted a randomized experiment in a small city in Delaware to test whether the Decide Your Time (DYT) program's SAC method was effective for those on probation who chronically use drugs. The study found no support that those on DYT probation were less likely to use drugs or recidivate compared to those on standard probation. Lattimore et al. (2016) conducted a randomized experiment of the SAC policy in four sites across the nation and found that HOPE probationers did not differ significantly from standard probationers in terms of recidivating. Overall, the research raises considerable concerns over using jail stays as a deterrent, which is consistent with the literature suggesting that even short stays can have deleterious effects for citizens.

## A Case Study: St. Louis County Safety and Justice Challenge

Many communities in the United States are challenged with large jail populations, yet there are few best practices to address the needs of this population. The following section outlines a new program implemented in St. Louis County, Missouri. The program was designed as part of the MacArthur Safety and Justice Challenge, launched in 2015, with the goal of changing the way the justice system thinks about jails. Each funded agency was asked to develop a comprehensive program to reduce jail incarceration, while addressing racial and ethnic disparities in the system. In 2015, St. Louis County received funding to identify the key drivers of the jail population, and individuals on probation emerged as a key population for intervention.

This case study describes an innovative program implemented in one community with the goal of highlighting potential reforms to jail systems overall and the population of individuals under supervision for probation violations more specifically. This work adds to the literature in several ways. First, Missouri is a unique context for research and policy as the state has seen an increase in incarceration, during a time when most states have seen a decline (Carson, 2018). Most probation, or justice reinvestment reforms overall, have been the result of legislative changes, but Missouri has not made similar structural changes observed in other states. Therefore, it is important to explore the role that individual jurisdictions can take in reducing incarcerated populations and potentially mitigating the cost of a criminal record. Second, there is little research on effective jail programming, and less that considers the unique needs of individuals jailed for a probation violation. This chapter highlights one program model that is designed to address the needs of individuals remanded to jail for a probation violation. Detailed information on jail incarceration and probation violations in St. Louis County, data that are often not available in official reports, is included to gain a comprehensive understanding at this local level.

*Scope of the Problem*

Missouri faces substantial challenges in managing its probation and parole population. Missouri has the eighth highest incarceration rate in the nation, at 526 per 100,000 (Carson, 2018). Probation revocations have driven the recent growth in the prison population. More than half (51%) of all new admissions to the Missouri prison system are for probation or parole revocations (Missouri Board of Probation and Parole, 2017). Out of the 18,872 probation revocations for 2016, half were for technical violations, not new arrests. Missouri has the highest female incarceration rate in the nation, and this population of women has increased 33% in the past five years (Carson, 2018). In total, 46% of women in Missouri prisons are incarcerated for a probation violation, and 58% of these revocations are solely for technical violations. In addition, individuals on probation comprise a majority (67%) of the felony community corrections population (Missouri Board of Probation and Parole, 2017).

The growing rate of probation revocations in Missouri has also affected jail populations. In St. Louis County, 29% of the jail population is awaiting a hearing for a probation violation, and 61% of these individuals were revoked for a technical violation. Individuals on probation serve an average of ninety-nine days awaiting a violation hearing, which places a significant strain on the near-capacity jail. There are also racial disparities in the probation population. The sentenced jail population is 50% black, but the probation violation population is 64% black. In St. Louis County, blacks, on average, spend an additional twelve days awaiting a violation hearing. In fact, individuals in jail for a probation violation spend nearly as much time in jail awaiting trial as the individuals who have been sentenced on a state charge.

## *St. Louis County Probation Violation Program*

### PROGRAM MODEL

In response to the growing population of individuals in jail for probation violations, St. Louis County developed a Probation Violation Program. The program has two primary goals: reduce the time spent in jail for individuals detained on a probation technical violation, and encourage long-term success of clients by addressing the root causes of recidivism, including lack of housing, employment needs, substance abuse, mental illness, and outstanding legal challenges. All individuals detained in the St. Louis County Jail for a probation technical violation are eligible for the program and are screened within twenty-four hours of entering custody. Individuals are not eligible for the program if they have a new felony arrest or outstanding warrants. Individuals with a severe mental health diagnosis are also ineligible for the program.

The program model includes several components and is implemented in four phases. The model was developed after traditional transitional release planning projects often implemented with individuals in jail with co-occurring disorders (Osher, Steadman, and Barr, 2003) and reflects the risk needs responsivity model for assessment and rehabilitation (Bonta and Andrews, 2007). First, the needs of the individuals are assessed. The Missouri Department of Corrections' supervision/risk instrument is used to assess all potential participants. Individuals from all risk levels are included in the program, but the instrument is used to guide treatment provision. In addition, an extensive screening tool is completed that identifies housing, treatment, and employment service needs. Next, a plan for treatment is developed and the community agencies responsible for treatment identified. A weekly case management review/treatment team meeting is held with the jail case manager, service providers, and probation and parole. The weekly meetings are used to develop treatment-informed supervision plans for individuals accepted into the program. Efforts are made to ensure that programming is trauma- and gender-informed.

Finally, the program requires detailed coordination to ensure that clients receive a continuum of care. There are several members of the supervision team, including probation officer, jail case manager, and community treatment staff. The jail case manager maintains regular contact with the client, probation officer, community treatment partners, and the courts. The probation officer is responsible for day-to-day community supervision. The Missouri Department of Corrections has dedicated two officers to serve the needs of individuals in the program. In addition, each treatment provider employs a dedicated outreach coordinator/treatment facilitator who facilitates the jail-to-community transition. The outreach coordinator is also responsible for facilitating wrap-around transition services, including job skills and employment training, and building linkages to family and other social supports.

Coordination is also a key element of the program as it facilitates efficient case processing. The goal of this program is to have individuals evaluated by a judge and released within ten days of revocation. Emerging research suggests that even short periods in jail can reduce the chances of long-term success (Lowenkamp, VanNostrand, and Holsinger, 2013). It is critical that individuals are detained for as short a period as possible to begin the process of reintegration. The fast-track processing is also a critical advantage of the program, as most programs of this type have worked to provide transition services to jail detainees and have not concurrently addressed the need to reduce the length of jail stays overall. The case managers are responsible for setting probation revocation hearing dates, communicating case progress to the judge, and filing violation reports if needed.

Several key elements are set in place to enhance the likelihood of success. First, electronic monitoring is used for some probationers to increase the probability of compliance and increase community safety. This supervision modality has been shown to be a best practice with high-risk clients (Padgett, Bales, and Blomberg, 2006). In addition, the team has developed a behavioral response matrix that outlines sanctions for noncriminal behaviors while in the program and provides outlines for positive responses to programmatic achievements (i.e., attending treatment, employment, maintaining sobriety). Utilizing this more nuanced graduated sanctions model assists staff in providing effective supervision of clients with the goal of maintaining individuals under community supervision where feasible. There is emerging research that small incentives, like positive praise from a probation officer, can increase the likelihood of success in the community and reduce recidivism (Mowen et al., 2018).

OUTCOMES

Although a final systematic outcome evaluation of the program has not been completed, there is emerging evidence that the program model can reduce recidivism among participants and contribute to the reduction in jail populations. The program was implemented in 2016 and during the first year of the program, 273 probationers were enrolled. Nearly all participants are classified as high or moderate risk by the Department of Corrections. The population in the program mirrors the total probation population, and the population is predominantly black (60%) and male (66%). Additionally, substance abuse is the most prominent need among the population. In total, 85% of the sample had some form of substance abuse history. Of the 265 individuals released to date, 105 individuals (40% of the sample) have been classified at intake as opioid-dependent.

After one year of follow-up, 33% of the enrolled population has failed to complete the program. The rate of probation violations varies widely. A recent study of probationers in Pennsylvania had an incarceration rate of 55.3% during the first year (Hyatt and Barnes, 2017). The average recidivism rate for individuals on probation in Missouri is 45% (Missouri Board of Probation and Parole, 2017). Recidivism is characterized by a new crime or failure to complete program requirements that were resultant in a return to jail. In total, 34% of the sample was returned to the community after the violation—18% with credit for time served and 16% continued on probation. Individuals released for time served averaged eighty days in jail, and the probation reinstatement group averaged forty-five days in jail before release. An additional 20% of the sample was remanded to the Department of Corrections and averaged fifty-eight days before transport to prison. The remainder were in jail pending further action; this group averaged seventy-six days of waiting time in jail. Individuals were returned to jail for a program violation.

In addition to improving the outcomes of people who entered the program, a secondary goal is to reduce the number of people in jail, overall, for a probation violation. If the processing time for individuals in jail for a probation violation is reduced, it is anticipated that the average daily population and average length of stay for this population will decline. In fact, the average daily population for this group declined 13% after the implementation of the program. The intervention has also reduced the length of stay for this group. Before program implementation, the average length of stay for this group was ninety-nine days. After implementation, the average length of stay was reduced to forty-nine days, a 50% decline. The length of stay has also declined for persons of minority races, with the average length of stay being identical for blacks and whites.

Overall, the program has shown promise in the first phase of implementation, but the rate of technical violations among this population remains a concern. Probation violations perpetuate the cycle of incarceration, and individuals who did not complete the program spent a considerable amount of time in jail after the violation. Although the violation rate is lower than most recidivism models of this type, there is a substantial need to continue to reduce processing times for individuals who fail while in the program and to match treatment needs with services. In the next phase, the program will include a new risk and needs instrument. The program is designed to reflect risk-need-responsivity principles; however, the current risk assessment only includes three levels, and most participants rank in the highest risk group. A new risk and need instrument has the potential to detect the heterogeneity in the population. Treatment services will be reserved for high-need individuals, and individuals who are of lower risk could be returned to the community quickly, without added probation stipulations. Currently, all members of the program receive recommendations for enhanced treatment and supervision. Research suggests that individuals with a low risk of recidivism placed in a highly structured treatment setting have higher risks for recidivism, an increase of 17%. In contrast, matching high-risk individuals to high-intensity programming lowers the risk of recidivism of this population by 19% (Bonta, Wallace-Capretta, and Rooney, 2000). Continuing to develop programming that matches risk and need to services is an essential part of any correctional reform.

## Conclusion

The use of probation has increased dramatically over the past few decades and it is now the most implemented correctional sanction (Kaeble and Boncazar, 2017). Important changes to the criminal justice system have widened its net of carceral control, especially for low-level offenses. Individuals who traditionally would have been sentenced to community service or fines now receive probation, increasing the close monitoring by the system. This greater use of probation has led to an increased chance of an individual violating probationary terms and subsequently being remanded to jail time (Phelps, 2013).

The use of jail as a sanction for a probation violation can have multiple, negative consequences (Corda and Phelps, 2017). As Apel (2016) denotes, short sentences are common in corrections, yet there is only limited research in this area. There is a body of evidence that suggests that jail can have negative effects on families (Comfort, 2016), marriages (Apel, 2016), and employment (Harding et al., 2017). In addition, research using samples of pretrial populations suggests that even very short stays of incarceration can affect recidivism in the short and long term (Lowenkamp et al., 2013). High rates of probation violations can also have deleterious effects for communities. In Missouri, the increase in technical violations costs the state community corrections system $75 million annually. Each of the 3,477 individuals who have their probation revoked each year for a technical violation costs the state $57.76 a day while incarcerated and has an average length of stay in prison of one year, as compared to remaining on probation at a cost of $6.04 per day (Allen et al., 2017; Missouri Board of Probation and Parole, 2017). In addition to the human cost of jail, there is great fiscal incentive to reduce the probation violation rate. Overall, it is imperative to continue the work that documents the unique effects of jail incarceration, particularly for individuals who have been remanded for a technical violation.

Given the consequences of incarceration, it is essential to mitigate the effects by keeping sentences short and by providing more services that address the core needs of this population. The chapter provides an example of one potential program implemented in St. Louis County. Most probation reforms of this type have been conducted at the state level and are centered on fundamentally restructuring the way probation has been implemented (Phelps, 2013). This program serves as an example of an intervention that can be used to respond to probation violations in a swift manner that mitigates the costs of jail, while at the same time addressing the criminogenic needs that lead to a probation sentence and subsequent violation.

Although the program shows promise, there remains much to learn about the needs of individuals who violate probation, and individuals who are jailed, more generally. The work by Solomon and colleagues (2008) suggests several policy changes to help improve the reentry process, primarily developing procedures to better prepare individuals for their release. They argue that reentry plans should be developed for all individuals leaving jail, just as similar plans are now the norm in prisons. Jail has not been the focus of most reentry reforms, and the best practices that do exist are based on research that is a decade old. The goal of the St. Louis County program is to improve the outcomes of individuals jailed for probation violations, but there are critical needs among the jail population that could be addressed. Identifying and treating needs in jail has the potential to break the cycle of incarceration.

In conclusion, it is essential to broaden the scope of work on jails as this institution touches more people than any other correctional sanction. Jails have unique effects on individual lives, yet, most of the work to date has focused on prisons. As Copp and Bales (2018) argue, jails must be a critical element of the decarceration discussion. It is essential to continue to develop programming, like the model described here, that has the potential to mitigate the effects of contact with the criminal justice system while addressing the root needs of criminality.

ACKNOWLEDGMENTS

Professor Huebner serves as the Principal Investigator and Research Partner for the St. Louis Safety and Justice Challenge grant. The project described in this chapter was created with support from the John D. and Catherine T. MacArthur Foundation as part of its Safety and Justice Challenge initiative. More information on the challenge can be found at www.SafetyandJusticeChallenge.org.

13

Education's Failed Promise

*How Public Policies "Educate" a Criminal Underclass*

KEESHA MIDDLEMASS

Reentering society after serving time in prison due to a felony conviction is challenging because of an intersecting set of individual-level characteristics, community and social conditions, and public policies. Individual-level characteristics include a lack of social capital, unreliable and varying types of family support, mental illness, substance abuse, the type of criminal conviction (e.g., violent, drug, property or financial crime), and the conditions of post-release supervision (e.g., parole or probation), while community and social conditions can include overburdened nonprofit organizations and communities experiencing institutional abandonment (Middlemass 2017; Petersilia 2003; Lynch and Sabol 2001). Public policies related to a felony conviction are numerous, and disproportionately shape prisoner reentry experiences. Such policies, laws, statutes, and regulations are often hidden in state and federal statutes outside of the criminal justice system (Middlemass 2017). These "secret sentences" (Chin and Holmes 2002) and "invisible punishments" (Travis 2002) are used to revoke and deny a range of public benefits and social rights to anyone convicted of a felony. As a result, men and women returning home after serving time in prison must contend with how a felony conviction operates like a petite penal institution that entangles them in its grip during the entire post-prison experience (Russell-Brown 2004; Russell and Milovanovic 2001).

Individuals who have been incarcerated tend to be under- or uneducated and functionally illiterate (Nally et al. 2012). A high percentage of former prisoners lived in and return to communities experiencing institutional abandonment, low-performing public schools, and high rates of poverty (Lynch and Sabol 2001; Mallach 2010), and only 25–32% of prisoners earn a GED while they are incarcerated (Durose, Cooper, and Snyder 2014). As a result, while incarcerated, prisoners do not earn formal diplomas and many return to society without the necessary educational foundation to start a degree program. Further, participants shared how they knew that a formal educational degree or certificate would not remove a criminal background check when applying for a job. Therefore, many participants felt that going to school was an unrealistic option (Middlemass 2017).

An additional stressor is related to family reunification; many people returning home after release from prison are not welcomed by their families (Martinez 2006); instead, individuals receive vastly different levels of family support (Middlemass 2017). In many instances, when a family member allows their returning loved one to live with them, the former prisoner is pressured to contribute financially to the family's well-being and is told to "step up and take care of things" (78). The expense of education and a lack of resources in the home are additional reasons why many reentering adults do not pursue formal educational programs (Middlemass 2017). Due to the poor educational opportunities outside of prison and the reduction or elimination of educational programs inside prison, a vicious cycle develops as men and women convicted of a felony remain locked out of educational programs.

Current public policies deny men and women convicted of a felony from securing public funds needed to pay for educational and vocational programs inside prison and upon release. The following analysis reveals how education policies at the state and federal levels deny individuals convicted of a felony the ability to become literate and educated. Despite understanding the important connections between education, employment, and successful reentry, participants admitted to having low educational attainment and limited, if any, legal work experience (Middlemass 2017). Without a minimum of a high school diploma or its equivalent (e.g., General Educational Development, GED), and limited prior legal work experience, men and women are ineligible for most entry-level jobs, which keeps convicted felons out of the labor force (Middlemass 2017; Pager 2007).

## Methods and Data Collection

In order to understand what it means to reenter society as a convicted felon, how some public policies shape reentry, and to capture the individual, community, and societal factors associated with reentry, I incorporated an interdisciplinary research design using four distinct data collection techniques: ethnography and unobtrusive observations, participant-observations, in-depth interviews, and archival review of publicly accessible documents (Middlemass 2017). I engaged in hundreds of hours of ethnographic research and participant-observations over twenty-nine months in the field at a nonprofit organization specializing in prisoner reentry. From February 2011 to June 2013, I conducted research at a reentry organization located in downtown Newark, New Jersey, and I kept extensive written records. My field notes include descriptions of individuals and how they carried themselves, what I witnessed, overheard verbal exchanges between participants, conversations I had with staff, volunteers, and participants, and all of my interactions with men and women convicted of a range of felonies (ibid.). Additionally, I conducted fifty-three semi-structured in-depth interviews with key participants. The IRB approved interview protocol focused on participant's experiences in three policy areas—housing, education, and employment—before and after prison, and included questions to gauge participants' level of knowledge about public policies, their life before and after their last felony conviction, family relationships, and their personal reentry experiences. When participants agreed, interviews were recorded and then transcribed by me. When a participant did not want to be recorded, I took detailed notes during the interview.

Based on previous research, I knew reentering society was hard (Boxer, Middlemass, and Delorenzo 2009), and as a participant-observer of prisoner reentry in real time, I witnessed first-hand the difficulties individuals encountered while attempting to reconstruct their lives, but I did not always understand what was going on and why. Therefore, throughout my time in the field, I re-read interview transcripts and ethnographic notes, examined and reexamined archival data, and as new data were collected, I analyzed them against previously accumulated data. This iterative process allowed me to learn the language of reentry.

The iterative and inductive approach was purposeful, as it focused on finding patterns and themes within the data and exposed some of the challenges related to individual deficits. Often, individual deficits, such as physical and mental illnesses and substance abuse, go unaddressed inside prison and/or are exacerbated due to being incarcerated (Visher and Travis 2003), while public policies and "invisible punishments" hinder reentry efforts (Travis 2002, 2005).

The iterative method is reflexive as the reading and re-reading of data sparks new insights and understanding about participants' lived experiences (Srivastava and Hopwood 2009). As insights emerged, they were refined based on an analysis of public policies, and then externally validated with archival research, participant-observations, formal and informal conversations with staff, appropriate theoretical frameworks, and in-depth interviews. I continuously repeated the process of reexamining past data with new data until I completed data collection and reached data saturation.

Politics and Public Policies

Historically, the American prison system has attempted to combine the Quaker belief in reformation and the Puritan belief that criminals cannot be rehabilitated (Gottschalk 2006). As a result, prisons reflect a theoretical paradox of mixed intentions that are not wholly compatible—incapacitation, control, deterrence, punishment, and rehabilitation—resulting in limited results based on current recidivism rates. The existence of competing aims and poor outcomes is the result of public policies and the politics of punishment that have elevated the practice of punishment and control over rehabilitation. The decline in the "rehabilitative ideal"—the concept that prisons should serve as places to reform prisoners in preparation to return to society—was replaced with the "culture of control" (Garland 2001).

Incarceration policies and rehabilitation programs took a pivotal turn in the 1970s when there was a critical shift toward more punitive policies. The original view was that there was a realistic opportunity for some offenders to be rehabilitated, but based on the concept that "nothing works" (Martinson 1974) and rehabilitation being an unattainable goal for most offenders (Allen 1978), rehabilitation programs were defunded. A 1983 Senate Report (S. Rep. No. 98–225, 1983) reinforced this belief and referred to the outmoded rehabilitation model for federal sentencing, recognizing that the federal criminal justice system had failed at rehabilitation and was not working. As a result, prisons became places to warehouse hundreds of thousands of men and women across the country in state and federal prisons, while a larger number of individuals were put under correctional supervision (e.g., parole, probation, halfway houses, and local jails). The scale and nature of the correctional population is a result of a series of political decisions and policy changes that ratcheted up punishment (Phelps 2011).

The political and policy assault on rehabilitation programs was effective, and the long-standing rehabilitative penological theory and possible reformation of criminals collapsed under the weight of pessimism (Cullen 2013; Martinson 1974), and public policies followed shortly thereafter. For instance, the 1984 Sentencing Reform Act had two main purposes: reduce serious disparities in criminal sentencing in the federal courts, and ensure that criminals were "adequately" punished through long and longer periods of incapacitation. The 1984 Sentencing Reform Act accelerated the passage of other laws, such as the Anti-Drug Abuse Act of 1986, which changed the rehabilitative federal system of supervised release to a system that was punitive, particularly toward African Americans and the policing of crack cocaine (Middlemass 2014). Fighting the "war on drugs" became an urgent political focus and led to "tough on crime" policies, "zero tolerance," and "three strikes you're out." As violence associated with crack cocaine was splashed across major and minor news outlets in the late 1980s and early 1990s, the crack epidemic led to a strong policy response from politicians. Elected officials focused on incarcerating black crack users but not white cocaine users by framing the drugs as two different types of cocaine requiring separate criminal justice responses (ibid., 90). During this time period, harsh sentences took precedence, as rehabilitative educational programs inside prison and prisoner reentry programs on the outside were not considered of vital importance.

The change in policy was supported by a transformation in racialized politics. The most obvious occurrence was the overt use of race in political ads during the 1988 presidential election between Governor Michael Dukakis, the Democratic nominee, and then Vice President

George H. W. Bush, which set the tone linking blackness to criminality. Such a move made for "good" politics, and the story of William Horton forever altered political calculations about race and crime (Anderson 1995). Scholars argue that the "Willie Horton" political commercial is the *most* notorious example of the politics of criminality (ibid.). Politicians' fear of being labeled "soft on crime" changed their political calculations when discussing crime policy, and the politics of crime has forever been racially tinged (Middlemass 2017, 2014).

Politicians wanted to be viewed as being "tough on crime," so they continued to pass laws that elevated punishment over rehabilitation (Stuntz 2001; Chambliss 2001; Simon 2007). The Violent Crime Control and Law Enforcement Act of 1994 focused on public safety, crime prevention, but also incarcerating violent offenders and increasing the length of prison sentences. Under the 1994 Act, states were eligible to receive grants if they provided assurances that they would incarcerate violent offenders for a substantial period of time and that punishment, including for violent juvenile offenders, was sufficiently long to protect the public's safety. The debate leading up to the bill's passage also focused on decreasing funding for educational programs.

Prior to 1994, prisoners were able to use Pell grants to support their educational pursuits due to a 1972 amendment to the Higher Education Act of 1965 (HEA); Pell grants were designed to fulfill a critical financial need to increase the number of low- and middle-class students who could access higher education (Stoll 2006; see Higher Education Act of 1965), but the grants were also used by prisoners for accredited educational programs. The 1994 Act allowed "tough on crime" politicians to argue that prisoners were taking financial aid from "worthy" students (Middlemass 2017). Leading the charge to remove prisoners from Pell grant eligibility was US Senator Kaye Bailey Hutchison (R-Texas). She offered Amendment No. 1158 to the Violent Crime Control and Law Enforcement Act of 1994 directing the US Education Department to deny prisoners Pell grants (ibid.). Senator Hutchison's argument was based on falsehoods and political theater; she argued on the US Senate floor that money was being taken away from "good" students and given to "bad" students, when in reality Pell grants are noncompetitive, needs-based federal funds for accredited educational programs for all students who apply and are eligible (Fine et al. 2001). Students do not compete for a limited number of Pell grant dollars because when one person is eligible for a Pell grant, the funding does not reduce the likelihood of another eligible student getting a Pell grant (Middlemass 2017). Before the statutory change in 1994, less than 1% of the Pell grant annual budget was used by prisoners (Mauer 2006). Yet, Hutchison's amendment won bipartisan support and was signed into law by President Clinton. The immediate impact of eliminating Pell grants was the cancellation of educational programs for incarcerated adults, and states did not replace federal funds to support state educational programs inside prison (Klein et al. 2004; Middlemass 2017).

The political climate of the 1990s allowed state and federal politicians to pass additional "tough on crime" laws, such as mandatory minimums for a host of different crimes, and funding decisions that further dismantled educational programs inside prison. State officials significantly decreased state funding streams for educational programs (Davis et al. 2013). Many scholars believe that the punitive criminal justice policies of the 1980s and 1990s are the primary reasons why incarceration and recidivism rates are so high (Petersilia 2003; Martinez 2006). When people are incarcerated for long periods of time, they come out of prison unprepared for the "new" world, and this has a disproportionate impact on minority communities (Alexander 2010; Lynch and Sabol 2001; Middlemass 2017).

## Prisoner Reentry

Leaving prison and reentering society is hard, and studies demonstrate high recidivism rates, defined as reoffending, re-arrest, and/or reconviction for a technical violation of the conditions of their release (e.g., failing a drug test, missing a parole appointment, failure to look for a job) or because of a new arrest and conviction for a new crime (Hepburn and Griffin 2004; Kubrin and Stewart 2006). The Bureau of Justice Statistics estimates that 67.8% of state prisoners were rearrested within three years of release and 76.6% were arrested within five years of release (Durose et al. 2014), though rates vary between states and by type of conviction (e.g., violent, drug, property, and financial crimes; Pew Center on the States 2011b).

Multidimensional issues and personal risk factors contribute to making reentry difficult (Middlemass 2017). Although the literature tends to group reentry into multiple stages, including the programs offered inside prison, the development of a pre-release reentry program, and community integration (Taxman, Young, and Byrne 2003; Travis, Solomon and Waul 2001), the reality is that formerly incarcerated men and women are largely left to figure out how to reenter on their own (Middlemass 2017). Parole was designed to help men and women reenter, but participants described parole in punitive terms. Participants spoke about how parole emphasized getting a job, any job, and did not put a priority on educational attainment to assist in getting a job. Further, parole officers are overburdened and have multiple parolees to supervise, and do not provide a lot of direction or assistance; as a result, participants had to navigate disconnected public service agencies, nonprofit organizations, and family dynamics with little direction, a lack of social capital, varying types of family support, and limited financial resources (ibid.). Consequently, reentry is an individualized process based on whether a man or woman can access hard resources, such as a place to live, weather-appropriate clothes, and a legal income.

From a policy perspective, reentering society is challenging. Public policies are predominantly focused on punishing criminals by incarcerating them for long periods of time (Stuntz 2001). This achieves multiple political goals for elected officials, including being "tough on crime," which provides a platform for reelection but fails to consider what it means in terms of rehabilitation and reentry. The focus on retribution and deterring criminals from future crime via long prison sentences has allowed legislators to ignore the concept of rehabilitation (see Middlemass 2017).

## Education as a Reentry Tool

Education as a rehabilitative tool is not perfect, and has its limitations; however, those who are self-motivated and able to access accredited programs inside prison and/or upon reentry have better rates of reentering successfully than those who do not. The "Golden Age" of prison and correctional education was in the 1970s, when valid and accredited educational programs were offered inside prison as a basic part of rehabilitation, and prisoners were able to take a variety of courses leading to a GED, and associate and bachelor degrees; by accessing Pell grants, prisoners could afford to pay for the academic curricula and supporting materials (Ryan and McCabe 1994). During this period, education was thought of as the most important rehabilitation tool (ibid.). Courses taught through "inside-out" and other educational programs were an important part of the prison experience until the early 1990s (Middlemass 2017). These programs were supported by research. The Federal Interagency Reentry Council (2016) argues that education is a core resource for successful prisoner reentry and is proven to reduce recidivism rates. A 2013 report argued that correctional education improves prisoners' chances of not returning to prison, that prisoners who participated in correctional education programs lowered their chances of recidivating by 43%, and that having an education improves prisoners' chances of securing legal employment after release from prison (Davis et al. 2013). Research also shows that college-in-prison has a positive effect on the prison population, state budgets, and prisoners' children (Fine et al. 2001; Blackburn 1981). Educational attainment is also known to reduce recidivism rates (Burke and Vivian 2001; Burke and Tonry 2006).

Prior to 1994, more than forty states offered prison educational programs leading to certificates and diplomas that were accepted outside of prison. By 2002, only twenty-two states had mandatory accredited educational programs for prisoners (Davis et al. 2013). Despite data supporting the positive effects of accredited educational programs (Ainsworth and Roscigno 2005), including reducing criminal propensity and lessening future criminal activity, educational programs for prisoners and funding for those reentering were cut at the federal and state levels. The penal politics of punishment makes it hard for politicians to support funding for accredited educational programs for correctional populations. Accordingly, the programs that are offered inside prison are not well funded.

Currently, New Jersey state prisons offer educational programming in line with their institutional mission; however, a survey of those programs demonstrates that they are not universally offered at every prison, and many programs do not lead to an accredited degree or certificate (Stephan 2008). Due to the decline in the availability of such programs inside, and compared to the 1980s, participation rates have declined further, so more prisoners are leaving prison without a GED (Middlemass 2017).

Although educational programs inside prison are an important rehabilitative feature, education upon release is equally critical. After exiting prison, convicted felons were once able to use Pell grants, but "tough on crime" politicians passed additional amendments to the Higher Education Act (HEA). In 1998, amendments to the HEA changed Pell grant eligibility for those reentering society and made most felons ineligible for Pell grants, even after they had completed their criminal sentence (Coley and Barton 2006). The amendments were specifically directed toward drug convictions, and stated that anyone convicted of any offense under any federal or state law involving the possession or sale of a controlled substance was not eligible to receive any grant, loan, or work assistance for one year for the first offense, two years for the second offense, and indefinitely after the third drug-related conviction. Therefore, if someone is convicted of the sale of a controlled substance, the person is ineligible for one year after the first offense and is indefinitely ineligible after the third offense for selling a controlled substance. To prove that a convicted drug felon is rehabilitated, and therefore eligible for a Pell grant, they have to complete a drug rehabilitation program, "pass" two unannounced drug tests, or have their conviction reversed by the courts.

In practice, however, most former prisoners are denied a Pell grant. A 2005 Government Accounting Office (GAO 2005) investigation showed that about 35,000 students were denied a Pell grant based on a specific drug conviction or a felony conviction, and it was noted that the number of denials was actually underreported because many people may not even apply for a Pell grant because they assume they will be denied. Additionally, the Anti-Drug Abuse Act of 1988, as amended, allows federal and state judges to deny all or some federal benefits to individuals convicted of drug trafficking or drug possession (GAO 2005). This means that the implementation of the law was inconsistent depending on which jurisdiction someone was convicted in and what the particular sentencing judge ruled during sentencing (ibid.).

## Educational Programs Inside New Jersey Prisons

In order to understand prison education, I contacted each prison in New Jersey to find out what educational programs were offered; the two most common programs are the Adult Basic Education (ABE) and the General Equivalency Development (GED). Participants agreed that the ABE and GED were offered on a regular basis, but the problem was that when the accredited courses were offered, there were more prisoners who wanted to take the courses than there were resources, such as the required books and study materials needed to do the course work, and certified instructors. If study materials were available, the books were so heavily used that it was impossible to do the exercises without seeing the answers. Another problem participants shared is that there were few certified and proficient teachers who came into the prison, and if they did come there was always something that kept them from teaching the entire course (e.g., prison lockdowns or security issues). A few participants said that the problems were usually caused by prisoners fighting or being locked down for an undisclosed security issue. Being locked down and unable to attend classes on a regular basis is not a new phenomenon inside prisons; what has changed over the last two decades are the types of classes offered inside prison.

In New Jersey, once politicians eliminated funding for a "real" educational curriculum that is valued on the outside, prison administrators had to create programs to replace the hours of classroom time. The programs that were developed focused on earning a certificate for completing a set number of classes or a predetermined number of hours in an assigned topic. The certificate programs described by participants included addiction recovery, such as "The Big Book," the informal name for the twelve-step program used by Alcoholics Anonymous (AA) that guides participants through a series of prayers and meditation, anger management, humanity and kindness, character-building, journal writing, setting goals, budgeting, reuniting with family, and changing one's criminal mind set (Middlemass 2017, 128). While incarcerated, prisoners would attend the certificate classes, and after completing the program they would earn a certificate. "Much like appreciation awards granted for perfect attendance, certificates are printed on heavy golden ivory paper with elegant black text describing the topic [with] dignitary signatures confirming its importance, all framed in a decorative swirly black ink border with an ornate gold sticker attached" (ibid.).

Certificates were highly valued inside prison; participants described that when family members came to visit them, they would show their certificates in an effort to demonstrate that they were working on improving themselves. Individuals newly returned home talked about how many certificates they had earned and would advocate for themselves that they were changed, and then show their certificates as proof that they were ready to reenter society as a better person and were ready to secure a legal job (Middlemass 2017, 128). The reality of the certificates on the outside would come soon after someone visited the nonprofit organization. Regrettably, newly home former prisoners' hopes were dashed when they found out that the certificates held no value on the outside. Someone who had been home for a while would tell them to put their certificates away because they were not going to help them earn credits toward a GED, take college or vocational courses for credit, or secure legal employment. As an almost daily visitor to the nonprofit organization, it was easy to recognize who was newly home based on how they talked about their certificates, and seeing individuals' hopes crushed was hard to witness. As one male participant said, "I got all those certificates, but ain't got no job" (Field Notes, April 18, 2011).

Some participants talked at length of completing the entire set of certificates, and did many of the same classes over again, earning multiple certificates for the same class because they did not have a choice. This was the case because when prisoners are not locked in their cells, prison administrators are responsible for scheduling how prisoners spend their time, and certificate classes can be scheduled every day for several hours a day to create a type of "busy time" (Middlemass 2017, 133). Participants shared how they had no control over how they spent their days, so they spent a lot of time simply waiting for their cell door to open so they could go to a class (Field Notes, several days). The classes offered a place for prisoners to go but did not offer a "real" education.

Based on interviews and conversations I had with participants, it became obvious that the vast majority of them were uneducated. During each interview, I asked each of the fifty-three interviewees what was their highest grade completed; two had a high school diploma and one had some college courses. The remaining fifty had not completed high school. Another indication of the lack of formal education was the language participants used; it was simple, and participants used the phrase, "you know what I'm saying," numerous times in a row; I sensed that when this phrase was used it was to cover for times when they did not have the language to respond to a question or it was an attempt to explain their response when they did not have the language to elaborate on their thoughts. When I asked participants during interviews and at other times if they wanted to go back to school to earn a GED or vocational certificate, most participants said "no." I asked why, and participants offered several different reasons; most often it was due to the lack of funds, pressure from parole to get a job, and insistent family members demanding that they contribute financially to supporting the family. A small number of participants shared that they had a lack of desire to go back to school because they would have to "start all over again, at the very beginning, and who wants to do that?"

Certificate programs inside prison, as described by participants, were taught and facilitated by "good" prisoners who followed the rules and did not get into fights. In the words of participants, the good prisoners were institutionalized to the ways of prison and had adapted a mind-set that they were never going to leave. Known as "reformed lifers," these prisoners were sentenced to life in prison, and for them, becoming a facilitator for a certificate class gave them something productive to do and a small amount of control over their classroom activities (Middlemass 2017, 132). For those with little control over their lives, becoming a facilitator was also a way to serve their time and have a minimal amount of control over their lives (Middlemass and Smiley 2016). Originally, being a facilitator offered a tangible way for prisoners to earn "good time" credits that were used toward an early release date. But New Jersey state legislators terminated the "good time" credit program when the No Early Release Act of 1997 was passed; the law mandated that prisoners had to serve a minimum of 85% of their sentence before being eligible to even be considered for early release (McCoy and McManimon 2004).

The No Early Release Act had unintended consequences within the prison population. For one, participants described that when they found out that they were not eligible for early release consideration, their incentive to "be good" and not fight or "cause stuff" was removed (Field Notes, many days). As a result of not being able to earn "good time" credits, participants said they started to think about being "good" only when their 85% was coming up, but not before. "Why be good?" was the collective refrain when the topic of "good time" credits came up in conversation. "We ain't getting out 'til somebody in Trenton does the calculation we close to 85%" (Field Notes, July 11, 2012). "When that time got close, I was good" (Interview with Tyrone, February 27, 2012).[1]

Participants voiced genuine concerns about the related challenges of trying to make education an integral part of their reentry process, but all of them voiced some agreement that education was important for their reentry success. In an ideal world, instead of waiting around for 85% of their sentence to be served, prisoners would have had the opportunity to earn their GED and other accredited educational degrees. Instead, most participants were returning home lacking a formal education, older (e.g., average age of participants was 43½ years), and with a felony conviction on their record, which created an abnormally high barrier for an individual to overcome. "School, it's harder now because I'm older, been long time since I was in class, so I gotta work on it every day. And the thing is, that makes it harder to get ahead [because of being out of a formal classroom for decades]" (Interview with Moore, May 9, 2012).

Other participants discussed how the courses that were offered were inappropriate for the skills they did have, or if they were interested in going back to school, they did not have the funds to take classes or take the accreditation exam at the end of the course. For instance, one participant said, "The classes inside, if they cover stuff that's going to help [out] here are general, like cover the same stuff. I like doing math, and I can do math, but I need help with using the right words [vocabulary], you know, and putting them together perfect like [grammar, punctuation, sentence structure]" (Field Notes, March 19, 2012). Another participant said, "I could have got my GED, I think, when I was inside, but it didn't happen, 'cuz after taking the classes, I didn't have the money to take the test. They [prison administrators] make it hard to get all the stuff done [paperwork and payment processing]. So now, I guess I gotta start from the start" (Field Notes, May 9, 2012).

Several participants argued that going to school after their release was hard because of the lack of direction and not having the money because of other priorities. "Everyone says go to school, but how? I got to feed my kids, when am I going to pay for school, and like, what am I supposed to take, what? Ain't no one got answers for that and there is no real help out here" (Field Notes, July 11, 2012). "Yeah, like I thought about getting my GED, but ain't never get it. I went up to Essex [Community College] and was there and took classes for a bit, but didn't finish. I need somebody to help me get started again and find a way to pay for those darn classes" (Field Notes, February 6, 2013).

Each one of these participants had a felony conviction in common, and although they were convicted of different types of crimes, and served different lengths of time in prison, having a felony attached to their public record became its own type of hurdle that had to be navigated. Making education a reality was hard due to the lack of social capital, not having someone who could walk each of them through the process of registering for and taking classes, but also because of limited financial resources and being ineligible for the main source of educational funds, Pell grants. The nonprofit organization provided some resources, but it was overwhelmed with the degree of need and did not have the funds to pay for a full-time instructor or provide one-on-one instruction. As a result, participants had to navigate their educational reentry on their own.

Current statistics demonstrate that the vast majority of individuals released from prison fail at reentering (i.e., they are re-arrested for a new crime or for a parole violation and are re-incarcerated). There are multiple reasons why men and women fail at reentry, but the loss of educational benefits and access to other public services and benefits, such as traditional welfare, suggests that individuals convicted of a felony are unlikely to be able to re-start their educational career without public assistance in the form of Pell grants. This is because most prisoners return home poor. Intuitively, men and women I interacted with knew that rehabilitation was not an integral part of their prison experiences; rather, participants unanimously contended that the educational programming offered inside prison had no useful application on the outside with regard to securing a job or housing, helping reunite with their family, or gaining educational accredited credits.

Overcrowding is among the reasons why prison does not prepare prisoners to reenter society in New Jersey; because of the increased costs of building new prisons in the state, prisons have had to transform recreational spaces, like indoor gyms, into dorm-style sleeping quarters with three-bunk bunk beds, and they are placing two prisoners in cells designed for one to accommodate new prisoners (DeVeaux 2013). The limited space means that there are more instances of conflict between prisoners and between prisoners and guards; as a result, male participants described spending a lot of time "locked down" and unable to attend classes. Participants shared their thoughts on why all of the "real" educational programs leading to diplomas or certificates valued on the outside were cut: "It's all related to the 'war on drugs,' the long sentences, racist politicians, it all comes down to punishment, ain't no rehab going on" (Field Notes, June 27, 2012).

For instance, after serving twenty-five years in various New Jersey prisons, Bradford returned to Newark without any resources; his parents had died while he was incarcerated and his extended family had moved out of the area. "He entered society with no family support, no legal work experience, and limited educational attainment" (Middlemass 2017, 67). Bradford was in a precarious position as he reentered society; once his time at the halfway house ended, he had no permanent place to live, no public financial support, and no means to support himself. Bradford made a decision to violate his parole to get sent back to prison rather than be homeless with no financial resources. Although not every participant purposely violates their parole, every single participant said they did not want to go back to prison, the way the criminal justice system is structured, successful prisoner reentry and rehabilitation are forgotten goals, which mean individuals will continue to recidivate at high rates after release. Bradford's experience of being homeless, family-less, and penniless was not unique; his experience is representative of what many hundreds of former prisoners experience upon reentering society (Middlemass 2017).

## Conclusion

The current system emphasizes retribution over rehabilitation, which means rehabilitation and community integration are difficult, and public policies, particularly as they relate to education, play a role in making reentry difficult. Some states are trying to tackle sentencing reform, and elected officials at the local, state, and federal levels are beginning to ask questions about the costs of incarceration, but for the most part, punitive policies continue to be supported by the public. Yet, 95% of all prisoners are eventually released (Travis 2005).

As a result of "tough on crime" politics and policies, prisoners and former prisoners are disenfranchised from accessing Pell grants, which would assist them in their reentry journey (Middlemass 2017, 2014). Such "tough on crime" policies extend well beyond the prison walls, and although prisoners have many of their rights forfeited while incarcerated, they never forfeit all of their rights of citizenship (e.g., right to religious expression, free speech, due process, and being free of cruel and unusual punishment). Men and women convicted of a felony are able to regain some of their rights upon release from prison and completion of their entire sentence (e.g., parole and/or probation, payment of fines), and should be able to regain all of their rights, such as attending institutions of higher learning while using Pell grants. Studies have shown that education reduces criminal propensity and future criminal activity, which increases the likelihood of securing legal employment, reducing individual recidivism, and would contribute to decreasing the cost of the criminal justice system (Burke and Tonry 2006; Chappell 2004; Ward 2009). To make this a reality, prisoners and individuals convicted of a felony need to be able to regain their right to access Pell grants.

    A prison sentence is designed as a consequence of engaging in serious criminal behavior, and that punishment should be sufficient, so the process of extending punishment beyond parole and probation becomes a second "secret sentence" (Chin and Holmes 2002). Studies have shown that low literacy rates lead to poor labor outcomes, and having a felony conviction and being African American practically guarantee that the process of securing a job will be very difficult, regardless of educational attainment (Pager 2007). In an ideal world, accredited educational programs would be taught by certified instructors inside prison, prison administrators would mandate prisoners to attend classes, and prisoners would be allowed to take the required tests so that they would leave prison with at least their GED and in many instances with accredited college courses that could be transferred to community colleges within the state. Although "perfect" rehabilitation is unrealistic and not every prisoner would pass officially recognized tests, that does not mean progress cannot be made; however, to make it possible for more individuals convicted of a felony to reenter society successfully, the barriers preventing them from gaining an education should be removed. Education is a proven tool that can change reentry outcomes, so at the very least, the current policy restrictions to access Pell grants while serving time and upon reentry should be lifted. Increasing access to education can serve as a legitimate policy choice to reduce future crimes and reduce recidivism rates, and these facts are supported by multiple studies (Burke and Tonry 2006; Ward 2009).

NOTE
1 Participants were assured of their anonymity; therefore, pseudonyms are used.

# 14

## Mercy-Oriented Reentry and Reintegration

*Lessons from Policy, Research, and Practice*

ALEXANDRA L. COX AND REGINALD DWAYNE BETTS

The theoretical claims about pathways into and out of offending, desistance, and the impact of incarceration on those serving time have largely been absent from discussions about the outcome of an individual criminal case. The adjudicatory process leaves little room for the theoretical when criminal defense teams act as a patched-together sieve for clients facing charges that lead many in the general public to view them with disdain and want to see them banished, without a thought about their futures. The system, as disparate and hydra-like as it is, provides few opportunities for its actors to understand, let alone access, the research that demonstrates why and how we came to incarcerate as frequently as we do. Or to grasp the critiques of the race, class, and gender inequities that abound within the system. Moreover, the adjudicatory process rarely invites the inclusion of a broad range of scholarship that could help to frame a crime. The process is a black hole that often only allows room for a single discussion about numbers: numbers of prison years, detention days, probation years, community service days, fines, fees, program months.

Drawing on the example of sentencing mitigation work and its role in contextualizing an individual's life in the context of their offense and pointing a way to their future, we argue that reentry scholarship must attend to the practicalities of the sentencing process and the collective knowledge and wisdom that is gathered through the life history investigation process. Additionally, we argue that the sentencing process itself must draw from the collective wisdom and knowledge not only about the pathways that lead to offending, but also those that lead individuals out of it. Finally, we argue that the practice of sentencing must examine the social context in which an individual lives, which is not limited to the range of services and institutions that can meet their needs, and those of the individuals who are victims of crime, but also to the *lack of* institutional supports and services that exist outside of prison. This process points to the need for all of us to support the expansion and strengthening of community-based social welfare institutions for people charged with crimes.

Criminal law is concerned with determining who should be arrested and who should be prosecuted and the punishment that is meted out after a conviction (Stuntz, 2004). Classical theories of punishment conceptualize the defendant as a rational individual who responds to punitive inducements to change, but also address a rational public, who may be deterred from offending as a result of their awareness of punitive policies (Hudson, 2003; von Hirsch and Ashworth, 2004). Deterrence-based sentencing practices aimed at the individual are focused on the future of the sentenced individual only inasmuch as they are focused on their *offending* future (von Hirsch and Ashworth, 2004). These practices view imprisonment as a suitable deterrent or inducement to future offending and fail to recognize the criminogenic features of imprisonment and the enduring power of the stigma of the criminal conviction. Incapacitation-based logics view imprisonment as a way of inhibiting an individual from offending and prevent any discussion about the future of the individual at the heart of the case (Bottoms and Brownsword, 1998). Rehabilitation-focused sentencing practices have also viewed the sentence itself as the crucible of change, rather than taking the long view in recognizing the sentence as merely a feature or factor in an individual's life and offending life (Lacey, 2013). More broadly speaking, most jurisdictions have moved toward a kind of "mixed" approach to penal theory in applying punishment (ibid.).

Yet, what remains central to the practice of punishment in contemporary American life is almost overwhelmingly the idea of a rational and responsible individual who lies at the center of the practice (Garland, 2001). Nicola Lacey has argued that "questions about the social causes and conditions of criminality—questions that play a central role in both criminological and political debate tend in penal philosophy (with the important but partial exception of rehabilitative theories) to drop out of view" (2013: 178). As she notes, the rehabilitative perspective has in part evolved toward an approach that largely abstracts the individual from their environment (180). As rehabilitative practices have evolved toward so-called risk-needs-responsivity models, the individual becomes more fully elevated as the centerpiece of the criminal case and intervention, as their "risk factors" (albeit some of them environmentally related ones) are intervened in with the goal of directly impacting on, and preventing, their future offending (Andrews, Bonta, and Wormith, 2006), seeking to turn offenders into citizens who are capable of regulating their own (future) risks (Robinson, 2008). This has meant that it has become more difficult to advance claims about the complex contours of an individual life in the context of data-driven risk management strategies.

In the context of contemporary punishment, we have also witnessed increased limitations on judicial discretion and the amplification of punishment. The "just deserts" movement, which gained traction in the United States in the 1970s and 1980s, forced the federal and state governments to reckon with the civil liberties and rights consequences of indeterminate sentencing and issues of penal parsimony (Garland, 2001). This resulted in a shift in many states toward determinate sentencing and the growth of longer and more severe sanctions (Lacey, 2013). The US Sentencing Commission's federal sentencing guidelines, implemented in 1984 partly in response to the movement to increase proportionality in sentencing and place checks on judicial discretion, have profoundly shaped the landscape of sentencing and punishment. Serious checks on the discretion of judges were implemented (Freed, 1992). Recognizing in part that the aims of punishment—those of deterrence, incapacitation, and rehabilitation—can be confused, conflated, and misapplied by judges, many states and the federal government sought to curb judicial discretion and impose tighter sentencing guidelines and practices.

It is in this context of harsher sentencing that some scholars have argued that there is very little room for a discussion about what leniency in sentencing should look like (Markel, 2004; Roberts, 2011). Some have recently argued that despite our robust knowledge about sentencing, we have spent very little time considering the place and principled and fair use of aggravation and mitigation in sentencing (Roberts, 2011). These and similar arguments led to challenges to the federal sentencing guidelines and their impact on judicial discretion and decision making. Federal sentencing guidelines were later made *advisory*, rather than mandatory, following the decision in the 2005 US Supreme Court case *United States v. Booker*, which held that the sentencing guidelines violated the Sixth Amendment jury trial rights of the criminally accused. Yet what remains is a varied set of sentencing policies and practices across the United States.

Despite the changes brought by *Booker*, neither judges nor prosecutors in the federal or state systems are tasked with envisioning what a person's life will look like after the case is over. This is true for people who must serve prison time and for people sentenced to probation. Prison sentences are consequential in a person's life, from their relationships, to their labor, to their health (National Research Council, 2014; Western and Pettit, 2010; Wildeman and Western, 2010). The stigma of a criminal arrest and conviction is enduring and deeply tied to race and class (Uggen et al., 2014; Pager, 2007; Lageson and Maruna, 2018). The broad consequences that follow a criminal conviction or completion of a criminal sentence controvert the very purpose of the sentence, in the sense that they have overwhelmingly been shown to lead to future criminal convictions (Kurlychek, Brame, and Bushway, 2006; Chiricos et al., 2007). And these future convictions have consequences not only for the person who has been convicted, but also for the victims of crimes, and for the broader set of individuals that are harmed through the effects of crime and punishment. Given what we know about these consequences, it is arguable that defense attorneys, prosecutors, and judges should always be envisioning what these effects mean in the context of the lives of the individuals they sentence. Yet many of those individuals believe that the fate of the individuals at the center of a criminal case is to reoffend.

Some scholars have recognized the critical need to integrate the social context of the individual's life into sentencing theory and practice. The criminologist Pat Carlen (1989) has argued that criminal legal systems, which are "predicated on an assumption of formal equality under the law" (309) and yet operate in a broader system of substantive *inequality*, must respond to the criminally accused as "socially situated individuals" in order to "help them create living conditions in which they will be more likely to choose to be law-abiding in the future" (322). Some scholars have advanced an alternative theory of punishment, one rooted in a critical communitarianism or social justice, arguing that:

> punishment which is not facilitative of some future good is unjustified; and that the "good" to be promoted and protected by criminal justice must be consistent with a general obligation of social policies and institutions to promote people's participation in society as free and equal citizens. (Hudson, 2003: 73)

The communitarian vision for punishment, Nicola Lacey argues, is rooted in the goal of facilitating *positive* freedom, or the "capacity to discover and develop ourselves as members of a community, including a capacity to act on and shape, at least within limits, our own environment" (2013: 186). This approach to punishment recognizes that "personal autonomy and welfare can only be realized in a social context" (187). A communitarian approach to punishment would express, symbolically, the community's judgment toward the person who offends and would be more broadly focused on reintegration into the community (ibid.).

Who assumes responsibility for the life of a person who leaves prison? In the criminal defense context, we are often guided by the desire to minimize the impact of the power of the state in a person's life. This often leads to seeking the least restrictive possible sentence, the lowest sentence under the law, or seeking out ways that a person can seek relief because of their age or other factors.

While many defense attorneys are under no illusion that parole "works," it is our experience that they often see the world of release as messy, complex, too human. In fact, although there is an increased engagement of "holistic" defense, in which clients' lives are placed more squarely at the center of defense practice (Giovanni, 2012; Lee et al., 2015), this kind of practice remains uncommon. Instead, if there is to be any focus on sentencing mitigation in the context of serious and violent crimes that involve mandatory imprisonment, much of that focus is on the etiology of the crime and its context. Are there places within the criminal court process where we may begin to carve out a vision for an individual to be understood as someone who has a life beyond bars? Are there institutions that can set an individual's life into motion and simultaneously compel court actors to recognize that they are persons beyond their crime?

## No Time for the Future

The social consequences and costs of incarceration have been well-documented and well-researched, yet they are arguably evacuated from the criminal court context. Risk assessment instruments are putatively aimed at assessing future risks, but cannot and do not attempt to assess the future *possibilities* of an individual, as measured by past training, work or education experiences, and family and community support systems. This makes the work of defense attorneys aimed at representing their clients holistically difficult; they must argue and provide the support that establishes their client's ability to thrive within a larger society that seems centrally focused on making coming home from jail and prison impossible.

For it is not simply the individual effects of punishment that are significant; punishment also has *social* effects. The forms of inequality that punishment creates by setting deep, intergenerational processes of marginality into motion are profound, and have effects on the lives of individuals and communities in ways that affect their health and well-being, their employment prospects, and their prospects for social inclusion (Western and Petit, 2010). Even if we stipulate that imprisonment is used simply as a form of incapacitation, that its use is in itself future-focused—that period of incapacitation, for most, will end. The judge determines how long that period will be (or sometimes, with the help of a risk assessment instrument or sentencing guidelines), with the explicit understanding that the individual who has been sentenced will be released after a period of time, that is deemed long enough to satisfy purposes such as public protection, or safety, or proportionality. If there is a focus on the future, to some extent it lies in the realm of risk assessment, which is largely concerned with *future dangerousness* as opposed to a flourishing future. And yet, where lies the opportunity within the court context to contend with the flourishing future?

Below, we analyze an avenue within the court context for this opportunity: sentencing mitigation. This is an imperfect avenue that is fraught with questions about the role of evidence, the ethical questions raised by conducting deep investigations into individual lives, what we know and what we don't know, and how and where we can attend to the formal requirements of the law, but it also arguably recognizes the role of one's future within the law. We analyze the role of sentencing mitigation in the court cases of individuals charged with serious and violent crimes who face prison sentences, where in that mitigation process it is possible to locate an opportunity to attend to a person's future while also analyzing their past.

## The Practice of Sentencing Mitigation

When guilt is not at issue, a defense team must find grounds to argue for leniency. Sensing room within the formal requirements of law in the sentencing process, some defense attorneys began to rely upon the human story of the individual accused of the crime as a way of rebutting the presumption of unworthiness. This kind of work began during the sentencing phase primarily in death penalty cases, when the defense can present mitigating factors that bear on the justification of the use of the death penalty. It involves the defense's presentation of evidence of the character, upbringing, human frailties and capacities of the accused in order to lessen the impact and exposure of their eventual sentence (Dudley and Leonard, 2008). The US Supreme Court has explicitly recognized the need to present mitigating evidence in death penalty cases in *Gregg v. Georgia*, *Lockett v. Ohio*, and *Walton v. Arizona* and the importance of such work in non-capital cases, such as in *Pepper v. United States*. A sentencing mitigation practice is also being developed in the non-capital sentencing world, where some have increasingly recognized the role that it can play in informing the sentencing process beyond a probation report or prosecutor-provided information (Gohara, 2013). The work is typically done by individuals with training in social work, mental health, and the law, although there is no specific degree requirement to conduct the work. There is, however, a national professional association (the National Alliance of Sentencing Advocates and Mitigation Specialists, NASAMS), ethical standards, and multiple institutions and organizations that conduct sentencing mitigation training.[1] Sentencing mitigation specialists may exist within public defenders' offices themselves, or they are hired on a case-by-base basis by defense attorneys. In the context of death penalty cases, Supreme Court jurisprudence requires that juries *consider* mitigating evidence, although this does not require death penalty attorneys to have a mitigation specialist on their team.

Several professional bodies have developed standards and guidelines about mitigation, including the American Bar Association (ABA). The ABA (2008) has issued guidelines on this matter, arguing that in death penalty cases, "the defense team should consist of no fewer than two attorneys . . . an investigator, and a mitigation specialist." There are multiple aims of a mitigation report: ameliorating a prison sentence or asking for an alternative to incarceration by provoking empathy in the judge and prosecutor, building a case for the context of the offense, and engaging the court in mitigation-related issues that are sometimes specifically rooted in Supreme Court jurisprudence or state statute, such as the youthfulness of the person accused of the crime.

Sentencing mitigation work sits in an uncomfortable space between the legal and the human (Cheng, 2010). It includes stories about a criminally accused individual's life, yet ones that advocate for a particular outcome, from life without parole, to a shorter sentence, to an alternative to incarceration. Although sentencing mitigation investigations differ from life history investigations done by qualitative researchers, particularly those studying the onset and desistance from offending—they may share some aims, seeking to understand how life histories may inform individual behavior and actions (see, e.g., Crewe, 2009; Goodey, 2000; Maruna, Wilson, and Curran, 2006; Tatum, 1999; Thomson et al., 2002; Young, 1999). Social science researchers have used individual's biographies to shed light on the relationship between agency and structure, for example Furlong and Cartmel (2007), as well as into the ways that individual identities reflect their social contexts (Crewe, 2007; McAdams, 2008). Mitigation reports draw more broadly from the individual's life story to shed light on how their individual actions in a criminal case are shaped by their social histories, key events in their lives, and the web of personal relationships and opportunities that may have played a role in their offending and desistance from crime. Typically, a "report" or memorandum is produced by a sentencing mitigation specialist in the context of a criminal case and submitted to a prosecutor for review in a pre-pleading context, or to a judge in a pre-sentencing context. This report can take on many forms, but a number of criminal defense sentencing mitigation practitioners choose to tell this story in a narrative-driven, life history format.[2]

In contrast to social science inquiries, though, sentencing mitigation documents also have a moral purpose: the appeal to mercy, the primary conduit to leniency linked to the law. This moral purpose to some extent transcends and challenges the quest for "fact" or "truth" about offending and re-offending at which social science inquiries are at least putatively aimed. Instead, these inquiries are, in their efforts at empathy, seeking to challenge the court to see the person as a person, not the crime they are accused of. They also more broadly fit in what Lacey (2013) would consider a communitarian approach to sentencing—ask the judge to consider the realities of the conditions of confinement and incarceration (as opposed to the *theoretical* intentions of punishment) as well as the evidence of the criminogenic effects of incarceration (Nagin, Cullen, and Jonson, 2009) and their potentially negative impact on the individual's ability to successfully reintegrate into their community.

The work of sentencing mitigation exists in a complex web of punitive realities and meanings and is both aspirational and hopeful, but also attempts to be realistically attuned to the limitations of social institutions in people's lives. In addition, it raises some considerable ethical questions: To what extent could a large-scale investigation into someone's life also result in net-widening, in that the investigation itself can produce information about that person's life that begs for *further* intervention? Can the practice in fact imbed the positivist connections between "risk factors" and offending of the penal welfarist agenda? Below, we illustrate the core components of a sentencing mitigation investigation that is aimed at producing the future flourishing of the individual at the center of the case, but also reveals the continuing challenges of sentencing practices that exist in a liberal individualist framework that fails to recognize the importance of strong social institutions in supporting individuals' lives. Although we have access to voluminous records, interviews, and "data" about individual lives that we have gathered through our work on criminal defense cases, both as an attorney (Betts) and as a mitigation specialist (Cox), as well as countless sentencing mitigation letters, we are not able to share the full stories of our clients' lives without jeopardizing the confidentiality of our clients. One of the ironies of sentencing mitigation and defense work is that it can involve access to intimate, extensive, and long-term knowledge about individual lives, particularly as they intersect with social systems and institutions. This knowledge is in some cases broader and more extensive than that which is acquired in the context of social science research studies given the ethical limitations of presenting identifying information about individuals' lives.

## Early Childhood

A sentencing mitigation investigation aims to gain an understanding of a person's early childhood from a range of different sources in the recognition that the story of their early life informs an analysis of their present actions. This work builds on collective knowledge about the history of trauma, the role of "Adverse Childhood Experiences" in individuals' lives, their cognitive and neurological development, and the significance of familial relationships in individual development and lives (Ashford and Kupferberg, 2013; Ardino, 2012). A mitigation specialist conducts a number of interviews with their client about significant events in their early life, from their earliest childhood memories, to their memory of traumatic incidents, to events that they view more positively. These interviews can often take place over a long period of time, often while a person is in custody. As in the case of social science research processes, the interviews must be understood analytically and contextually. For example, an individual may share that their earliest memory involved witnessing their father hitting their mother; the mitigation specialist might ask the person to talk about where they were when the incident happened, if it happened regularly, and whether their father was ever arrested or incarcerated. This information can contribute to a framing of an individual's early life trauma and its impact on their self-concept and identity through the narrative of their life (see also Dudley and Leonard, 2008; Goodey, 2000).

The mitigation investigation also involves collateral interviews with an individual's parents or other caregivers, their extended family members, and other people with whom they came into contact in their early lives, such as friends, teachers, and social workers. These interviews may not only provide the mitigation specialist with context about the birth of their client, and whether their mother experienced any difficulties in her pregnancy which may have led to adverse outcomes, but also in order to gain a broader sense about how the individual's childhood is narrated and framed. These interviews also provide important information about the conditions in which the person grew up (where and how did they live? How often did they move? Who was involved in their family's life in their early childhood?). As we know from our accumulated social science knowledge about childhood development, this information about the early life history, the social and familial context, the relationships and social support networks that existed in the individual's life matters a great deal in understanding their later life outcomes (Elder, 1998; Farrington, 2009); it is here where the complex questions arise about whether the deployment of this "evidence" embeds, for the prosecutors, judges, and jury members, positivist conceptions of criminality. For it is the danger of this kind work of that, without a broader attention to the *stories* of people's lives from their early childhoods which also speak to the complex and competing narratives that existed in those lives, the "truths" and untruths, and the importance of attending to the relationship between agency and structure in understanding offending, the picture presented of the individual remains incomplete. For example, a young person may have been removed from their mother when they were a child and placed with their grandparents because their mother suffered from a crack cocaine addiction, but they may have grown up to believe that their grandparents were their parents and their mother was their aunt. Yet they may later go on to learn about the real identity of their birth mother when they are diagnosed with Type 1 diabetes. This event may precipitate a crisis of identity as well as health that impacts on their decision-making capacities. The context in which the individual navigates that health condition—if they are living in deep poverty, for example, might also impact on adherence to their health regimen. Interviews with the individuals who exist in the client's broader orbit help to lay the groundwork for a holistic investigation of their life, and one that strongly influences an analysis of the emotional and psychological conditions of an individual's life that link up to the sociostructural obstacles and challenges they face.

These in-person interviews can then be triangulated with birth and hospital records (and an analysis of Apgar score and an investigation about the context of pregnancy and birth), to child welfare, to education, to shelters and housing. It might be reported by a mother, for example, that her child was exposed to lead poisoning and she no longer has access to the results; those records can be obtained and analyzed in the context of a child's performance in school, for example. But the presence of lead poisoning alone cannot simply be "read" as a process that informs criminality and offending; instead, the broader context in which the lead poisoning exposure may have happened, including the failures of the state to meaningfully provide safe living conditions for its citizens, can contribute to a structurally informed investigation.

The records also help to highlight inconsistencies and gaps in an individual's knowledge of their life history, their families' and friends' reporting of events, and also the limitations of social service bureaucracies in meeting identified needs of the child and family. The records can point to the intersecting sets of institutions that an individual may have come into contact with, from housing, to social welfare, to mental health, to education. They help to contextualize the role that those institutions play in the broader social context, as it is possible to frame the interventions in context. For example, if a scandal was erupting in the child welfare system in New York City shortly before a client was removed from their family which causes that institution to increase the number of removals they engage in, it is possible to raise questions about the context for the client's removal from their home. Social history records also help to raise questions for further investigation through interviews, such as a revelation of the existence of family members who may not have been identified in earlier interviews.

In comprehensive life history investigations, particularly in death penalty cases and those involving life without parole, sentencing mitigation investigators will often interview relatives from multiple generations of a family and will do extensive life history analysis. For example, an investigator might examine a family's history of forced migration or experience of wartime trauma and analyze the intergenerational effects of such experiences. This allows for an attention to intergenerational forms of trauma and violence, including and not limited to racialized violence and exposure to intergenerational incarceration (Nelson, 2006; Murray and Farrington, 2008; Stevenson, 2014; Wildeman and Western, 2010).

The early life history of an individual accused of a crime helps to shape and structure the broader story that it is possible to tell about an individual's pathway to offending. Yet these records and interviews are not a simple process of revealing or identifying so-called risk factors for offending, nor do they hew to the analytical frame offered by researchers from the psychological disciplines who analyze factors in individuals' lives that may lead them into particular pathways of offending (i.e., "life course persistent" or "adolescent limited") (Moffitt, 1993; Farrington, 2002). And, although it would seem that these investigations to some extent resonate with life course approaches (Elder, 1998), they also aim at assembling a comprehensive portrait of an individual's life as it has unfolded in a *holistic, narrative* approach, one that also draws from the power of storytelling to situate an individual's crime in context. While we acknowledge that it is the relatively unregulated nature of the profession of sentencing mitigation that makes a sociostructurally informed and narrative-driven approach difficult to standardize and enforce, we note here that this kind of approach is an aspirational one that addresses the limitations and challenges of penal-welfarist, individualizing endeavors.

Life history investigations are also used to understand some of the moments in that individual life where help could have been provided but wasn't, where institutional failures existed, and in identifying the social services gaps that may have existed in their life. For example, for an impoverished individual from a very isolated rural area whose parent suffered from a crack cocaine dependency, their parents' inability to access public transportation to get to a drug treatment facility, and their isolation from neighbors and other community members may have isolated them from the scrutiny of the child welfare system and impacted on the persistence of their addiction over the course of their child's young life. It is this attention to sociostructural failings that also allows the sentencing mitigation investigations to be future-focused, in that they also help to identify the opportunities for intervention where they may not have existed.

## Institutional Lives

A number of the individuals that we have represented had previously spent time in juvenile residential facilities or prisons, have had extensive contact with law enforcement, have been psychiatrically hospitalized, and excluded from schools. Their experiences and histories in those institutions reveal a great deal about their relationships to offending and criminalization but also about their future capacities to desist from offending. For many of these individuals, their experiences in and out of institutions, as well as their family members' experiences, have been extensive and defining. Thus, their relationships to institutionalization are, in many ways, intimately familiar ones. But these relationships are important to understand for their impact on individuals' adolescent growth and development, their intimate partnerships and friendships, their relationship and insight into their mental health and illness, their educational progress (or lack thereof), as well as their experiences of the pains and terrors of institutionalization and incarceration. Although we have extensive knowledge about the negative consequences of institutionalization in individuals' lives (National Research Council, 2014, 2012; Haney, 2003), the information obtained about individuals' lives as they have traveled through institutions sheds a great deal of light onto the precise ways that these institutions impact on selfhood, identity, and well-being.

An individual's criminal history records as well as their institutional history records, from school suspension records, juvenile facilities, and prisons to psychiatric hospitals, also helps to shed light on how system actors have viewed them. These systemic perspectives are not *labels* per se, but rather assessments and attributions that set certain kinds of interventions into motion. For example, a school suspension hearing record might reveal some of the ways that the young person has been understood at school, and when understood in the context of an undiagnosed learning disability, might reveal that the individual's seemingly obstreperous behavior in a classroom might be reflective of their efforts to distract teachers from their struggle to understand the class materials. These psychosocial dimensions of human life are critical in understanding how it unfolds, and also how these dimensions impact on offending (Gadd and Jefferson, 2007).

## Future Flourishing

The sentencing mitigation investigation is also increasingly focused on understanding the direction of an individual's life after incarceration (see also, e.g., Gohara, 2018). It lends itself to knowledge about an individual's life that points to a range of interventions that may be able to facilitate their growth and development. The records may also reveal a gap in understanding; for example, an individual may have had extensive behavioral problems at school and at home, yet their parents and teachers never referred them for an educational evaluation; this may have led the individual to leave school and to avoid employment because of their anxiety about reading and writing. They might get into fights with others because their frustration tolerance levels are low, leading to their arrest. The defense team may be able to reveal, for example, that this person suffers from severe developmental disabilities. They may then be able to find a placement at an organization that serves individuals with developmental disabilities and provides them with vocational training. However, all defense teams must also strike a balance between identifying interventions that help to facilitate a person's liberation from the system of punishment and those that continue to enmesh them in the criminal justice system, particularly in a context where "therapeutic jurisprudence" initiatives often link success in treatment to sentencing outcomes.

We have grown and developed extensive knowledge about the interactive links between agency and structure in individuals' lives in their processes of desisting from offending (Farrall, Bottoms, and Shapland, 2010). What this literature has helped us to understand are the complex ways that early life events and histories can impact on individuals' later life choices, relationships, and connections that have a significant impact on their socially structured abilities to desist from offending. The life history investigation is a unique site in which to explore an individual's capacity to change, and in fact what lies at the heart of the plea for mercy embedded in the sentencing mitigation document is a plea to recognize that very capacity in a sentencing decision. Increasingly, we also have gained rich knowledge about the ways that individuals' offending "lives" are limited (Kurlychek et al., 2006), and we have learned that age and maturity matter in desistance (Blumstein and Nakamura, 2009). This evidence helpfully frames a case for an individual's future life to be valued in the face of incarceration and can arguably be leveraged in the service of an argument for mercy that is attuned to an individual's capacity for change.

## The Role of Empirical Research in Sentencing Practice

The requirements of the law—to focus on the facts of the particular case—restrict the presentation of evidence to the individual (Dunn and Kaplan, 2009: 343). The law itself is organized around the principles of individualism, which militate against broader, sociostructural explanations (Dunn and Kaplan, 2009: 344; Lacey, 2013), although with the rise in determinate sentencing and sentencing guidelines, the opportunity for an individualized sentence is arguably increasingly constrained (Gohara, 2013: 4). As a result, the mitigation report itself is often limited to and dependent upon individualistic theories of offending in ways that restrict and limit the focus to the offense itself, to the individual causes and consequences of that offense, rather than the sociostructural conditions that may have given rise to it, and which also can help to facilitate a departure from it. And the potential downsides of an individualized approach to sentencing are clear: They have been used to justify harsh and moralistic approaches to sentencing and have arguably resulted in net widening and the deepening of punishment. In particular, this can result in sentences driven by racial animus or racialized assumptions about criminality, which can be particularly insidious in a "color-blind" society (Bonilla-Silva, 2003; Van Cleve and Mayes, 2015). The risks are particularly high in rural jurisdictions or places where there may only be a single judge. Yet, we propose that there is a space to argue for a more individualized approach that is deliberative, equitable, and constrained by due process (see also Lacey, 2013). It is rooted in an approach to discretion that is equitable and linked closely to the person's individual act (Markel, 2004), but in ways that is justified and tied to their possible future that meaningfully reflect the salience of the act as embedded in a social context; we can learn about this context through a sentencing mitigation investigation.

We argue that this is possible when we can allow sentencing practices to be more deeply informed by our social science knowledge about the effects of criminalization and punishment in individuals' lives. But we must also, as advocates for sentencing reform and as social science researchers, more adequately link and merge our work in ways that are properly attuned to the need to strengthen social support mechanisms and institutions.

Yet, so many of the researchers who have produced the valuable knowledge about the pathways into and out of offending have not had access to the full life history of the individual as a defense team does—or as full as it can get through access to records and interviews. However, even in the context of the mitigation process, that history is partial and particular. It is often only used to persuade a judge or prosecutor to decrease a sentence by a few years. To simply lessen the pain of imprisonment, just partially. We ask: Is there a fruitful place to collaborate and build on this shared knowledge of individual lives?

Sentencing policy more broadly is rarely informed by research evidence (Gottschalk, 2015). Furthermore, there are ethical and logical complexities involved in bringing group-level empirical data to bear on individual-level cases, and in educating the court about the hypothetical as opposed to the concrete facts of a case. This is particularly true in the context of the individualized approach to punishment. The research on the processes of desistance has been criticized for being too focused on the individuals and their agentic response to punishment, an approach that sometimes excludes arguments in favor of social justice and social change that impact on criminalization processes (McNeill, 2017). The presentation of sentencing mitigation evidence recognizes the immediate needs of the individual but leverages the broader experiences of the group and combats the criminalization and punishment process by offering evidence in support of mercy.

## Mitigation-Focused Reentry / Reentry-Focused Mitigation

Sentencing mitigation work focused on reentry is uniquely concerned not only with meeting a client's needs and tailoring services to their needs, but also to the prerogatives of judges and prosecutors—and their concerns about public safety in particular. This is a complex form of advocacy. On the one hand, it is eminently practical: It is focused on meeting the needs of an individual whose life will be deeply negatively impacted by a prison sentence, and who is likely socially marginalized and impoverished and thus in need of an array of services and opportunities. On the other hand, the reentry focus of a criminal defense case is also strategic—it is often aimed at persuading judges and prosecutors that an individual has the capacity to desist from offending if given the right services and opportunities in the community.

*Mitigation-focused reentry* work differs from traditional reentry work in that it draws from the comprehensive life history of an individual to effectively advocate for services tailored to meet those needs. This work involves an in-depth knowledge of programs and practices that exist in communities, and an everyday knowledge of what "works" and what doesn't "work," in ways that fall outside of evidence-based discourses. In resource-rich urban areas, for example, it is often possible to find reentry and alternatives to incarceration programs that offer a wider range of services and opportunities, such as rap-sheet cleanup services, job training programs, college entry advocacy, and mental health–specific programming and advocacy. But in rural areas, the array of services and programs can be extremely limited. And almost all of these programs have complex dynamics of punitiveness that sometimes complicate their ostensibly therapeutic aims (Miller and Stuart, 2017). Mitigation-focused reentry holds out the promise and possibility of recognizing the person at the center of the case, and in identifying services and programs in communities that "work" to facilitate desistance in ways that don't always fit in to neat categories of "what works" as established in the evidence base.

Mitigation-focused reentry practice could recognize that an individual's interests are primary but also that those interests are not simply about the primary needs for shelter, food, and social supports, but also for living a life without criminal justice system intervention. This view of reentry provision arguably acknowledges that individuals are vulnerable to re-arrest not just because of their "criminogenic risk factors" but also because they may be at high risk of being *criminalized*. Finally, it recognizes that the services provided to the individual serve to transform their life in ways that recognize the structural barriers to their reentry.

*Reentry-focused mitigation* acknowledges the presence of failure, of re-arrest, and re-incarceration, but nonetheless advocates for the individuals' potential to live their life free of criminal justice system involvement. It envisions an ideal package of services and opportunities for the individual given the realities of the collateral consequences of incarceration, the labor market, and the social welfare state. In this context, sentencers would consider the costs and criminogenic features of incarceration in their deliberative practice, but also would recognize the community and context that the individual will be reintegrated to, considering the range of opportunities available to them to do so *outside of* imprisonment. Yet it is a form of advocacy that fights against futility—in part rooted in an ethic of care and social responsibility toward the individual who is at the center of the case. We argue that if a judge is able to consider the possible reintegrative benefits of sentencing an individual in a manner that is not simply attuned to their past, but to their possibilities, then we may hope to see an improvement in the lives of the individuals who are sentenced.

## *Mitigation-Focused Sentencing Research and Reform*

Sentencing mitigation, while not focused on political economic change, approaches what legal scholar James Q. Whitman (2003) has argued is a legal approach that is rooted in the presumption of mercy; it is one that focuses on dignity rather than degradation. Whitman argues that America's harsh justice system embraces degradation at all stages of the system process. This has partially resulted, he argues, in our extraordinarily high sentence lengths and our appetite for punishment. Sentencing mitigation practice arguably presents the individual who is accused of a crime as in need of mercy rather than degradation, as someone who will be returning to a community rather than someone who deserves to be incapacitated (see also Gohara, 2013). It assumes that the extension of mercy also involves an assumed risk, yet one that should be focused on the sociostructural limitations rather than those of the individual. As sentencing advocates, we need to educate the judiciary about such sociostructural realities, but we cannot do so without the help of the social scientists who have enhanced our knowledge of these claims. There is an opportunity to fuse and reproduce our collective knowledge. This may also begin to contribute to our knowledge about the array of programs and services that are available to individuals in the community by drawing from our collective knowledge about what survival and flourishing look like in the context of the lives of individuals in their criminal case and sentence as well as through an understanding of their life history.

## Conclusion

Mitigation work that is informed by our knowledge about the forces that affect individual lives in their pathways into and out of crime is an intervention into a criminal justice system practice that raises significant questions about the role of mercy, hope, and justice in that system. Mitigation work is rare. Yet this considerably under-researched area of work is one that might contribute to our exploration of and advocacy for penal restraint.

This work also forces us to acknowledge that empirical considerations of reentry work should not be bifurcated from an awareness of the criminal case and court process. To do so risks us forgetting an essential component of the process of punishment and release—the one that typically focuses on the individual at the heart of the case and their crime, as opposed to their release. Yet, it is arguable that there are opportunities within this process to more effectively carve out space for pressing the boundaries of sentencing and release in a way that asks judges and prosecutors to consider the conditions of human growth and change more deeply than they do. Existing research and knowledge on the conditions for desistance highlight the individual's complex location in their social structure, the importance of age and maturity, the role of social and human capital, the profound role of relationships, and the importance of self-stories and narratives for change.

We argue that any form of advocacy that takes place at sentencing can and should consider the long view of someone's life. Looking beyond the particular case helps us to realize that even for those who some may consider worthless, there is worth and value in requiring that we attend to their future, in ways that do not expand the reach of punishment or widen the net, but rather focus on liberating individuals from the net of criminal justice control. In order to shift the system in this direction, we must take mitigation at sentencing seriously. We must more fully integrate a vision for sentencing and reentry that integrates our social-scientific knowledge with our sentencing realities, advocating for a sentencing framework that attends to social and community justice at its heart and understands the individual in their social context, but doesn't neglect to attend to the values of deliberation and due process, equity, and fairness (Lacey, 2013).

NOTES

1 NASAMS is part of the National Legal Aid and Defender Association. See "Who We Are," National Alliance of Sentencing Advocates and Mitigation Specialists, NLADA, www.nlada.org.

2 As a sentencing mitigation practitioner, Alexandra Cox has attended national and local sentencing mitigation trainings, organized statewide trainings in New York, and conducted trainings for law students, lawyers, and aspiring sentencing mitigation specialists. She also serves on the board of Advancing Real Change, Inc., a national organization that provides sentencing mitigation work in Life Without Parole and Death Penalty cases. Thus, she is regularly in contact with sentencing mitigation specialists who work in contexts around the United States and has written and read a significant number of life history reports. Although they take many different forms, the life history narrative format is the most common.

# Afterword

*Can the Rehabilitative Ideal Survive the Age of Trump?*

SHADD MARUNA

I am deeply honored to have the last word in this fascinating collection asking us to think "beyond recidivism" in discussions about the reentry of people from prison to the community. The diversity, rigor, and insight of the preceding chapters says a great deal about the vibrancy of work going on in this area across numerous fields in the United States and internationally. It was not always thus.

The fascinating work herein can be read as a sort of barometer of the health of what academics call the "rehabilitative ideal" in the United States. As documented by Tonry (2004), Enns (2016), and others, American thinking and policymaking around criminal justice has cycled through a series of shifts in focus over the past century—partially tracking changes in the crime rate with high crime periods leading to punitive overreactions and low crime periods opening up opportunities for investment in reintegration. For all of our pretentions of objectivity and political neutrality, academic research has not been removed from these political cycles, with very similar patterns found in academic publishing which is also following changes in research funding and popular opinion.

Indeed, when I started doing research with people released from prison in the early 1990s, the academic landscape was unrecognizable from the one in place today. In applying to graduate schools, I was repeatedly asked why I would want to focus on ex-prisoner issues when it was so obvious that rehabilitation was "dead." The story of the "decline of the rehabilitative ideal" in the late 1970s is well known (Allen, 1981), and the consequences for criminal justice policy were utterly staggering, with human warehousing at a scale that would have been unimaginable even a decade earlier. The backlash against rehabilitation was equally pronounced in academia, with both critical (Irwin, 1974) and conservative criminologists (Wilson, 1975) united in opposition. As the great Berkeley criminologist Richard Korn (1992: 4) wrote at exactly the same time I was pushing my idea for a study of people released from prison: "No one but an academic simpleton will even use the word 'rehabilitation' without apprehension."

Indeed, when I published my book *Making Good: How Ex-Convicts Reform and Rebuild Their Lives* on the basis of this PhD research in 2001, it was one of only a tiny number of books on the subject. That timing proved to be quite fortuitous for me, as Bill Clinton's National Institute of Justice had re-discovered the issue of reentry in the late 1990s, with Jeremy Travis's remarkably simple but hugely effective warning that we may want to "lock 'em up" (and in the wake of the crack epidemic of the 1980s, we certainly did in record numbers), "But they all come back" (Travis, 2000). A flood of (better, stronger) books soon followed my own (not least, Travis, 2005; but see also Laub and Sampson, 2003; Petersilia, 2003), kicking off what would become a revival of the rehabilitative ideal in the first decade of the twenty-first century.

Although actual policy change was slower to develop, eventually justice policy began to catch up with academic work on this issue. After decades of pursuing a disastrous punitiveness that nearly bankrupted state budgets across the country, American criminal justice policy between 2000 and 2016 had been characterized by limited but seemingly sincere efforts to reduce the overreach of the justice system. In particular, the political Left and Right appeared to be aligning around issues like prisoner reentry with genuine potential to make a difference (Green, 2013). In 2008, just as George W. Bush was winding up his presidency, criminologist Richard Rosenfeld (2008: 312) observed: "Make no mistake, rehabilitation is back; when a conservative President [George W. Bush] promotes prisoner reentry in his State of the Union address, the winds have changed."

At the same time, Rosenfeld acknowledged that this movement for evidence-based justice was a "battle hardened" version of the rehabilitative ideal characterized by "an overriding emphasis on public safety." That is, the issue of released prisoners could be discussed, but only if the focus was on recidivism (or else desistance). This was not a welfarist interest in whether former prisoners could lead "good lives"; this was a "risk model" of rehabilitation (see, in particular, Ward and Maruna, 2007). The *needs* of the returning person could only be considered if they were the "criminogenic" sort (i.e., dynamic risk factors).

As perfectly illustrated by the chapters in this book, this "hard edge" has given way to a much more humanistic approach to understanding the lives of the formerly incarcerated as human beings, not just potential risks. *Beyond Recidivism* challenges those of us in the research community to think more broadly and ambitiously about the reintegration of the formerly incarcerated in a way that perfectly captures the spirit of the moment. Indeed, the enormous social struggles faced by former prisoners to reintegrate (find housing, work, support networks) has gone from essentially a nontopic in the 1980s and 1990s to being possibly *the* hot topic in recent years, with high-profile treatment in work like Pager (2007), Western (2018), Harding, Morenoff, and Wyse (2019), and others. This shift can be understood by a number of factors, including the drop in violent crime, but unquestionably President Barack Obama deserves some credit for bringing attention to the issue (Horowitz and Uggen, 2019), not least via his National Institute of Justice under the leadership of desistance research pioneer John Laub.

Will this energy and creativity around reentry and desistance last through the tumultuous political moment of the Trump era? It is nearly impossible to predict as so much has changed on the American landscape. Indeed, to an outsider like me, the United States of America has been transformed almost beyond recognition in the short space of time between when this book was initiated (at an impactful National Science Foundation workshop hosted at Rutgers University, Newark in 2016) to when it will appear in print.

On the one hand, the Trump presidency has exemplified the ideal of "second chances." For instance, in the case of Supreme Court nominee Brett Kavanaugh, Republicans united around the idea that a person's life should not be "ruined" by even multiple allegations of serious crimes if they were committed in a youthful state. Trump and colleagues also very generously used his presidential pardon power to formally forgive conservative operators like Lewis "Scooter" Libby and Dinesh D'Souza of their less than youthful indiscretions. Indeed, symbolically, Trump used his first pardon to forgive America's self-styled "Toughest Sheriff"

Joe Arpaio, despite charges of widespread abuses of power, misuse of funds, and the worst pattern of racial profiling ever recorded by the US Department of Justice. Many predict that a slew of future pardons will be waiting for those working for Trump's own administration, family business, and Foundation pending the results of multiple investigations from Russian interference to misuse of charitable donations. Second chances for all!

On the other hand, this remarkable level of mercy and forgiveness does not appear to extend beyond those in Trump's gilded inner circle. Indeed, the most powerful symbol of the Trump presidency to date has been the mass caging of children (once called "dreamers"), forcibly separated from their parents and guilty only of being noncitizens in the new United States. We are seeing, in other words, the classic bifurcation that has poisoned the rehabilitative ideal from its origins: redemption for "us" (the middle and upper classes), condemnation for "them" (the poor minorities whom Sheriff Joe used to enjoy torturing in his infamous tent city jail). Poor, urban, minority members were never included under the umbrella of the redeemable in the revivals of modern-day Calvinism. No amount of praying and weeping ever earned forgiveness for those guilty of being "outsiders." Trump has only made this distinction obvious—it was always so.

After all, the Trump Era cannot possibly be blamed for America's tragic experiment with mass incarceration, as it started decades before the current administration. At the same time, there may be no other way to understand the Trump phenomenon without first recognizing the corrosive societal impact of locking up and stigmatizing generations of men and women in the name of an unwinnable "war" on drugs and crime. Thanks to work like *The New Jim Crow* (Alexander, 2010), future historians will not miss the link between the staggeringly disproportionate levels of minority confinement, widespread voter disenfranchisement, the use of prison industry to prop up the rural economy, and the rise of the authoritarian, race-baiting Trump regime. A nation of jails and jailers has become a full-fledged carceral state with the dehumanizing ethos and language of the prison somehow seeping into the political discourse. Seemingly daily, the president poses for another carefully staged photo shoot surrounded by burly, uniformed officers of one type or another, then tweets out dehumanizing attacks on immigrants, journalists, and political opponents as the "enemies" within. This is to say there is no coincidence that the chant most commonly heard at Trump rallies is "Lock her up" directed sometimes at Hillary Clinton, sometimes at Diane Feinstein or Alexandria Ocasio-Cortez, sometimes to no one in particular. It is the singular slogan of the Era, and it is a chilling one.

With an estimated 70 million Americans now saddled with a criminal record of some sort—as many Americans as have college degrees (Friedman, 2015)—mass incarceration has now reached the same stage as climate change. That is, as the contributions in this volume clearly demonstrate, the time for half measures is over. Like with the hurricanes and forest fires devastating America's landscape, we are already seeing the effects of mass incarceration on society, on civility, on notions of "one nation, indivisible," and they have been devastating. At this advanced stage of civic decline, only a dramatic reversal of course has any hope of saving the society.

What is needed in the Age of Trump is not yet another evidence-based recidivism reduction program, but rather a social movement—a social movement of the incarcerated and formerly incarcerated, of their families and supporters, of the millions on community supervision or struggling with a criminal record. Fortunately, such a movement is very much under way in the United States, aided by the efforts of several of the contributors to this volume. Evidence of this can be found in academic work (with the rise of so-called convict criminology), in criminal justice agencies (with "credible messengers," or "experts by experience" flourishing), and increasingly at the level of policymaking and politics (see Maruna, 2017). Such a social movement may not be enough to turn back the tide of the Trump Era, but history has shown—from civil rights to the LGBT movement—it is the only thing that possibly can.

ACKNOWLEDGMENTS

Our collaboration on this project began at a Racial, Democracy, Crime and Justice Network (RDCJN) Meeting. Then, in April 2016, we hosted a workshop at Rutgers University, Newark on "Prisoner Reentry and Reintegration: Improving Data Collection and Methodology to Advance Theory and Knowledge." The stimulating presentations and discussions at that workshop inspired this book project. Our workshop was supported by a grant through the National Science Foundation (SES 1535615) and Rutgers University School of Criminal Justice. We gratefully acknowledge RDCJN, NSF, and the workshop participants, many of whom are also contributors to this volume. In addition, we thank Adam Pittman for his excellent research assistance, NYU Press editor Ilene Kalish for shepherding this project from conceptualization through publication, production staff and editors for their meticulous editorial assistance, and the anonymous manuscript reviewers for their helpful feedback. Finally, we extend our heartfelt thanks to Ruth Peterson, Laurie Krivo, and Marjorie Zatz for their invaluable guidance, advice, support, and encouragement.

# REFERENCES

Abramson, Lyn Y., Martin E. P. Seligman, and John D. Teasdale. 1978. "Learned Helplessness in Humans: Critique and Reformulation." *Journal of Abnormal Psychology* 87 (1): 49–74.

Adler, Patricia A., and Peter Adler. 1987. *Membership in Roles in Field Research*. Vol. 6. Thousand Oaks, CA: Sage.

Advancement Project. 2010. "Test, Punish, and Push Out: How 'Zero Tolerance' and High-Stakes Testing Funnel Youth into the School-To-Prison Pipeline."

Ainsworth, James W., and Vincent J. Roscigno. 2005. "Stratification, School-Work Linkages and Vocational Education." *Social Forces* 84 (1): 257–84.

Ainsworth, Stephanie A., and Faye S. Taxman. 2013. "Creating Simulation Parameter Inputs with Existing Data Sources: Estimating Offender Risks, Needs and Recidivism." In *Simulation Strategies to Reduce Recidivism: Risk Need Responsivity (RNR) Modeling in the Criminal Justice System*, edited by Faye S. Taxman and April Pattavina. New York: Springer.

Alba, Richard. 2005. "Bright vs. Blurred Boundaries: Second-Generation Assimilation and Exclusion in France, Germany, and the United States." *Ethnic and Racial Studies* 28 (1): 20–49.

Aldrich, Howard E., and Roger Waldinger. 1990. "Ethnicity and Entrepreneurship." *Annual Review of Sociology* 16 (1): 111–35.

Alexander, Michelle. 2010. *The New Jim Crow: Mass Incarceration in the Age of Colorblindness*. New York: New Press.

Alicke, Mark D., and Oleysa Govorun. 2005. "The Better-than-Average Effect." In *The Self in Social Judgement*, edited by Mark D. Alicke, David Dunning, and Joachim Krueger, 85–106. New York: Psychology Press.

Allen, Francis A. 1981. *The Decline of the Rehabilitative Ideal: Penal Policy and Social Purpose*. New Haven, CT: Yale University Press.

Allen, Steve, Andy Barbee, Grace Call, Rachael Druckhammer, and Ben Shelor. 2017. "Justice Reinvestment in Missouri." Presented at the Missouri State Justice Reinvestment Task Force, Jefferson City, MO.

Alm, Steven S. 2016. "HOPE Probation: Fair Sanctions, Evidence-Based Principles, and Therapeutic Alliances." *Criminology and Public Policy* 15 (4): 1195–1214.

Alper, Mariel, Matthew R. Duros, and Joshua Markman. 2018. "2018 Update on Prisoner Recidivism: A 9-Year Follow-Up Period (2005–2014)." Special Report NCJ 250975. Washington, DC: US Department of Justice, Office of Justice Programs, Bureau of Justice Statistics.

American Bar Association. 2008. "Supplementary Guidelines for the Mitigation Function of Defense Teams in Death Penalty Cases." *Hofstra Law Review* 36 (3): 693–762.

Anderson, David. 1995. *Crime and the Politics of Hysteria: How the Willie Horton Story Changed American Justice.* New York: Time Books (Crown Publishing Group).

Andrews, Donald A., and James Bonta. 2010a. "Rehabilitating Criminal Justice Policy and Practice." *Psychology, Public Policy, and Law* 16: 39–55.

———. 2010b. *The Psychology of Criminal Conduct.* New York: Routledge.

Andrews, Donald A., Ivan Zinger, Robert D. Hoge, James Bonta, Paul Gendreau, and Francis T. Cullen. 1990. "Does Correctional Treatment Work? A Clinically Relevant and Psychologically Informed Meta-Analysis." *Criminology* 28 (3): 369–404.

Andrews, Donald Arthur, James Bonta, and Stephen Wormith. 2006. "The Recent Past and Near Future of Risk and/or Need Assessment." *Crime and Delinquency* 52 (1): 7–27.

Andrews, Frank M., and Stephen B. Withey. 1976. *Social Indicators of Well-Being.* New York: Plenum.

Aos, Steven, Marna Miller, and Elizabeth K. Drake. 2006a. *Evidence-Based Adult Corrections Programs: What Works and What Does Not.* Olympia: Washington State Institute of Public Policy.

———. 2006b. *Evidence-Based Public Policy Options to Reduce Future Prison Construction, Criminal Justice Costs, and Crime Rates.* Olympia: Washington State Institute of Public Policy.

Apel, Robert. 2016. "The Effects of Jail and Prison Confinement on Cohabitation and Marriage." *ANNALS of the American Academy of Political and Social Science* 665 (1): 103–26.

Ardino, Vittoria. 2012. "Offending Behaviour: The Role of Trauma and PTSD." *European Journal of Psychotraumatology* 3 (1): 1–4.

Arditti, Joyce A. 2005. "Families and Incarceration: An Ecological Approach." *Families in Society* 86 (2): 251–60.

Ashford, Jose, and Melissa Kupferberg. 2013. *Death Penalty Mitigation: A Handbook for Mitigation Specialists, Investigators, Social Scientists, and Lawyers.* New York: Oxford University Press.

Atkin, Ron. 1977. *Combinatorial Connectivities in Social Systems: An Application of Simplicial Complex Structures to the Study of Large Organizations.* Basel: Birkhäuser.

Avison, William R. 2010. "Incorporating Children's Lives into a Life Course Perspective on Stress and Mental Health." *Journal of Health and Social Behavior* 51 (4): 361–75.

"Background Checking—The Use of Criminal Background Checks in Hiring Decisions." 2012. www.shrm.org.

Baillargeon, Jacques, Ingrid A. Binswanger, Joseph V. Penn, Owen J. Murray, and Brie A. Williams. 2009. "Psychiatric Disorders and Repeat Incarcerations: The Revolving Prison Door." *American Journal of Psychiatry* 166 (1): 103–9.

Baillargeon, Jacques, Brie A. Williams, Jeff Mellow, Amy Jo Harzke, Steven K. Hoge, Gwen Baillargeon, and Robert B. Greifinger. 2009. "Parole Revocation among

Prison Inmates with Psychiatric and Substance Use Disorders." *Psychiatric Services* 60 (11): 1516–21.

Baldwin, Lucy. 2017. "Tainted Love: The Impact of Prison on Mothering Identity Explored Via Mothers' Post Prison Reflections." *Prison Service Journal* 233: 28–33.

Bales, William D., and L. Sergio Garduno. 2016. "Confinement in Local Jails: Institutions and Their Clients Neglected by Criminologists." In *Advancing Criminology and Criminal Justice Policy*, edited by Thomas G. Blomberg, Julie M. Brancale, Kevin M. Beaver, and William D. Bales. New York: Routledge.

Bales, William D., and Daniel P. Mears. 2008. "Inmate Social Ties and the Transition to Society." *Journal of Research in Crime and Delinquency* 45: 287–321.

Bales, William D., and Alex R. Piquero. 2012. "Racial and Ethnic Differentials in Sentencing to Incarceration." *Justice Quarterly* 29: 742–73.

Ball, W. David. 2010. "E Pluribus Unum: Data and Operations Integration in the California Criminal Justice System." *Stanford Law and Policy Review* 21 (277): 277–309.

Barry, Monica. 2007. "The Transitional Pathways of Young Female Offenders: Towards a Non-Offending Lifestyle." In *What Works with Women Offenders*, edited by Rosemary Sheehan, Gill McIvor, and Chris Trotter, 23–9. Cullompton, UK: Willan.

Bartos, Bradley J., and Charis E. Kubrin. 2018. "Can We Downsize Our Prisons and Jails Without Compromising Public Safety?" *Criminology and Public Policy* 17 (3): 693–715.

Bauer, Jack J., Dan P. McAdams, and Jennifer L. Pals. 2008. "Narrative Identity and Eudaimonic Well-Being." *Journal of Happiness Studies* 9 (1): 81–104.

Bazemore, Gordon. 1999. "After Shaming, Whither Reintegration: Restorative Justice and Relational Rehabilitation." In *Restorative Juvenile Justice: Repairing the Harm of Youth Crime*, edited by Gordon Bazemore and Lode Walgrave, 155–94. Monsey, NY: Criminal Justice Press.

Bechtold, Jordan, Kathryn Monahan, Sara Wakefield, and Elizabeth Cauffman. 2015. "The Role of Race in Probation Monitoring and Responses to Probation Violations among Juvenile Offenders in Two Jurisdictions." *Psychology, Public Policy, and Law* 21 (3): 323–37.

Becker, Howard. 1966. *Outsiders: Studies in the Sociology of Deviance*. London: Free Press.

Bellamy, Christine, and Charles Raab. 2005. "Joined Up Government and Privacy in the United Kingdom: Managing Tensions between Data Protection and Social Policy. Part II." *Public Administration* 83 (2): 393–415.

Berg, Mark T., and Beth M. Huebner. 2011. "Reentry and the Ties That Bind: An Examination of Social Ties, Employment, and Recidivism." *Justice Quarterly* 28 (2): 328–410.

Bidart, Claire, and Johanne Charbonneau. 2011. "How to Generate Personal Networks: Issues and Tools for a Sociological Perspective." *Field Methods* 23 (3): 266–86.

Binnall, James. 2009. "Sixteen Million Angry Men: Reviving a Dead Doctrine to Challenge the Constitutionality of Excluding Felons from Jury Service." *Virginia Journal of Society Policy and the Law* 17 (1): 1–42.

Binswanger, Ingrid A., Marc F. Stern, Richard A. Deyo, Patrick J. Heagerty, Allen Cheadle, Joann G. Elmore, and Thomas D. Koepsell. 2007. "Release from Prison—A High Risk of Death for Former Inmates." *The New England Journal of Medicine* 356 (2): 157–65.

Bishop, Donna M., and Michael J. Leiber. 2012. "Racial and Ethnic Differences in Delinquency and Justice System Responses." In *The Oxford Handbook of Juvenile Crime and Juvenile Justice*, edited by Barry C. Feld and Donna M. Bishop, 445–84. New York: Oxford University Press.

Blackburn, F. S. 1981. "The Relationship between Recidivism and Participation in a Community College Program for Incarcerated Offenders." *Journal of Correctional Education* 32 (3): 23–5.

Blomberg, Thomas G., William Bales, and Karen Reed. 1993. "Intermediate Punishment: Redistributing or Extending Social Control?" *Crime, Law, and Social Change* 19: 187–201.

Blumstein, Alfred, and Kiminori Nakamura. 2009. "Redemption in the Presence of Widespread Criminal Background Checks." *Criminology* 47 (2): 327–59.

Bobo, Lawrence D. 2017. "Racism in Trump's America: Reflections on Culture, Sociology, and the 2016 US Presidential Election." *British Journal of Sociology* 68 (S1): S85–104.

Bobo, Lawrence D., Camille L. Zubrinsky, James H. Johnson, Jr., and Melvin L. Oliver. 1995. "Work Orientation, Job Discrimination, and Ethnicity." *Research in the Sociology of Work* 5: 45–85.

Bolger, Niall, and Jean-Phillipe Laurenceau. 2013. *Intensive Longitudinal Methods: An Introduction to Diary and Experience Sampling Research*. New York: Guilford.

Boman, John H., and Thomas J. Mowen. 2017. "Building the Ties That Bind, Breaking the Ties That Don't: Family Support, Criminal Peers, and Reentry Success." *Criminology and Public Policy* 16 (3): 753–74.

Bonilla-Silva, Eduardo. 2003. *Racism without Racists: Color-Blind Racism and the Persistence of Racial Inequality in America*. Lanham, MD: Rowman & Littlefield.

Bonilla-Silva, Eduardo, and Tukufu Zuberi. 2008. "Toward a Definition of White Logic and White Methods." In *White Logic, White Methods: Racism and Methodology*, edited by Eduardo Bonilla-Silva and Tukufu Zuberi, 3–30. United Kingdom: Rowman & Littlefield.

Bonnar-Kidd, Kelly K. 2010. "Sexual Offender Laws and Prevention of Sexual Violence or Recidivism." *American Journal of Public Health* 100: 412–19.

Bonta, James, and D. A. Andrews. 2007. "Risk-Need-Responsivity Model for Offender Assessment and Treatment." User Report No. 2007-06. Ottawa, Ontario: Public Safety Canada.

———. 2017. *The Psychology of Criminal Conduct*. 6th ed. New York: Routledge.

Bonta, James, Suzanne Wallace-Capretta, and Jennifer Rooney. 2000. "A Quasi-Experimental Evaluation of an Intensive Rehabilitation Supervision Program." *Criminal Justice and Behavior* 27 (3): 312–29.

Borgatti, Stephen P., Martin G. Everett, and Jeffrey C. Johnson. 2013. *Analyzing Social Networks*. London: Sage.

Bosworth, Mary, Debi Campbell, Bonita Demby, Seth M. Ferranti, and Michael Santos. 2005. "Doing Prison Research: Views from Inside." *Qualitative Inquiry* 11 (2): 249–64.

Bottoms, Anthony, and Roger Brownsword. 1998. "Incapacitation and 'Vivid Danger.'" In *Principled Sentencing: Readings on Theory and Policy*, edited by Andreas von Hirsch, Andrew Ashworth, and Julian V. Roberts. Oxford: Hart Publishing.

Bottoms, Anthony, and Joanna Shapland. 2010. "Steps towards Desistance among Male Young Adult Recidivists." In *Escape Routes: Contemporary Perspectives on Life after Punishment*, edited by Stephen Farrall, Mike Hough, Shadd Maruna, and Richard Sparks. London: Routledge.

Boxer, Paul, Keesha Middlemass, and Tahlia Delorenzo. 2009. "Exposure to Violent Crime During Incarceration: Effects on Psychological Adjustment Following Release." *Criminal Justice and Behavior* 36: 793–807.

Braithwaite, D. O., B. W. Bach, L. A. Baxter, R. DiVerniero, J. R. Hammonds, A. M. Hosek, E. K. Willer, and B. M. Wolf. 2010. "Constructing Family: A Typology of Voluntary Kin." *Journal of Social and Personal Relationships* 27 (3): 388–407.

Braithwaite, John. 1989. *Crime, Shame, and Reintegration*. Cambridge: Cambridge University Press.

Braman, Donald. 2004. *Doing Time on the Outside: Incarceration and Family Life in Urban America*. Ann Arbor: University of Michigan Press.

Brame, Robert. 2016. "Static Risk Factors and Criminal Recidivism." In *Handbook of Corrections and Sentencing: Risk and Need Assessment—Theory and Practice*, edited by Faye S. Taxman. New York: Routledge.

Branscombe, Nyla R., and Naomi Ellemers. 1998. "Coping with Group-Based Discrimination: Individualistic Versus Group-Level Strategies." In *Prejudice: The Target's Perspective*, edited by Janet K. Swim and Charles Stangor, 234–66. New York: Academic Press.

Brett, Sharon. 2012. "No Contact Parole Restrictions: Unconstitutional and Counterproductive." *Michigan Journal of Gender and Law* 18 (2): 485–519.

Brewer, Devon D. 2000. "Forgetting in the Recall-Based Elicitation of Personal and Social Networks." *Social Networks* 22 (1): 29–43.

Britton, Dana M. 2003. *At Work in the Iron Cage*. New York: NYU Press.

Bromwich, Jonah E. 2017. "Meek Mill's Lawyer Says Judge Showed 'Enormous Bias' in Sentencing." *New York Times*, November 7. www.nytimes.com.

Bronson, Jennifer, Laura M. Maruschak, and Marcus Berzofsky. 2015a. "Indicators of Mental Health Problems Reported by Prisoners and Jail Inmates, 2011–2012." Washington, DC: Bureau of Justice Statistics. www.bjs.gov.

———. 2015b. "Indicators of Substance Use, Dependence and Abuse by Prisoners and Jail Inmates, 2007–2009." Washington, DC: Bureau of Justice Statistics. www.bjs.gov.

Bronte-Tinkew, Jacinta, Jennifer Carrano, Tiffany Allen, Lillian Bowie, Kassim Mbawa, and Gregory Matthews. 2007. "Elements of Promising Practice for Fatherhood Programs: Evidence-Based Research Findings on Programs for Fathers." Washington, DC: US Department of Health and Human Services.

Brown, Randall, Eric Killian, and William P. Evans. 2003. "Familial Functioning as a Support System for Adolescents' Postdetention Success." *International Journal of Offender Therapy and Comparative Criminology* 47 (5): 529–41.

Browning, Christopher R. 2009. "Illuminating the Downside of Social Capital: Negotiated Coexistence, Property Crime, and Disorder in Urban Neighborhoods." *American Behavioral Scientist* 52 (11): 1556–78.

Bruhn, John G. 2011. *The Sociology of Community Connections*. New York: Springer Science and Business Media.

Bruns, Angela. 2017. "Consequences of Partner Incarceration for Women's Employment." *Journal of Marriage and Family* 79 (5): 1331–52.

Buffard, Jeffrey A., and Faye S. Taxman. 2000. "Client Gender and the Implementation of Jail-Based Therapeutic Community Programs." *Journal of Drug Issues* 30 (4): 881–900.

Burke, Lisa, and James E. Vivian. 2001. "The Effect of College Programming on Recidivism Rates at the Hampden County House of Correction: A 5-Year Study." *Journal of Correctional Education* 52 (4): 160–62.

Burke, Peggy, and Michael Tonry. 2006. *Successful Transition and Reentry for Safer Communities: A Call to Action for Parole*. Silver Springs, MD: JEHT Foundation and Center for Effective Policy. www.cepp.com.

Burnett, Ros, and Shadd Maruna. 2004. "So 'Prison Works,' Does It? The Criminal Careers of 130 Men Released from Prison under Home Secretary, Michael Howard." *Howard Journal of Criminal Justice* 43: 390–404.

Burt, Ronald S. 1992. *Structural Holes: The Social Structure of Competition*. Cambridge, MA: Harvard University Press.

Cadora, Eric. n.d. "Justice Mapping." www.justicemapping.org/.

Calarco, Jessica McCrory. 2011. "'I Need Help!' Social Class and Children's Help-Seeking in Elementary School." *American Sociological Review* 76 (6): 862–82.

Calverley, Adam. 2013. *Cultures of Desistance: Rehabilitation, Reintegration and Ethnic Minorities*. London: Routledge.

Campbell, Christopher M. 2018. "Rethinking Conditional Release as an Assumption-Based Test of Offender Readiness." *Criminal Justice Review* 43 (2): 1–20.

Caplan, Gerald. 1982. "The Family as a Support System." In *Family Stress, Coping, and Social Support*, edited by Hamilton I. McCubbin, Elizabeth Cauble, and Joan Patterson. Sprinfield, IL: Charles C. Thomas.

Caplow, Theodore, and Jonathan Simon. 1999. "Understanding Prison Policy and Population Trends." *Crime and Justice* 26: 63–120.

Carlen, Pat. 1989. "Crime, Inequality and Sentencing." In *Paying for Crime*, edited by Pat Carlen and Dee Cook, 8–28. Milton Keynes: Open University Press.

Carsen, Dena. 2018. "Examining Racial and Ethnic Variations in Reasons for Leaving a Youth Gang." *Journal of Developmental and Life Course Criminology* 4: 449–72.

Carson, E. Ann. 2018. *Prisoners in 2016*. Washington, DC: Bureau of Justice Statistics.

Caudy, Michael, Liansheng Tang, Stephanie A. Ainsworth, Jennifer Lerch, and Faye S. Taxman. 2013. "Reducing Recidivism through Correctional Programming: Using Meta-Analyses to Inform the RNR Simulation Tool." In *Simulation Strategies to*

*Reduce Recidivism: Risk Need Responsivity (RNR) Modeling in the Criminal Justice System*, edited by Faye S. Taxman and April Pattavina. New York: Springer.

Celinska, Katarzyna, and Jane A. Siegel. 2010. "Mothers in Trouble: Coping with Actual or Pending Separation from Children Due to Incarceration." *Prison Journal* 90 (4): 447–74.

Chambliss, William. 2001. *Power, Politics, and Crime*. Boulder, CO: Westview Press.

Chammah, Maurice. 2013. "Hygiene Products Running Low in Prisons as State Contracts Lapse." *Texas Tribune*, January 30. www.texastribune.org.

Chappell, Cathryn. 2004. "Post-Secondary Correctional Education and Recidivism: A Meta-Analysis of Research Conducted, 1990–1999." *Journal of Correctional Education* 55 (2): 148–69.

Charles, Devon R., Karen M. Abram, Gary M. McClelland, and Linda A. Teplin. 2003. "Suicidal Ideation and Behavior among Women in Jail." *Journal of Contemporary Criminal Justice* 19: 65–81.

Chen, Elsa Y., and Ericka B. Adams. 2019. "'I've Risen Up from the Ashes That I Created': Record Clearance and Gendered Narratives of Self-Reinvention and Reintegration." *Feminist Criminology* 14 (2): 143–72.

Cheng, Jesse. 2009. "The Social History in Death Penalty Defense Advocacy." *Critical Criminology* 17 (2): 125–39.

———. 2010. "Frontloading Mitigation: The 'Legal' and the 'Human' in Death Penalty Defense." *Law and Social Inquiry* 35 (1): 39–65.

Chesney-Lind, Meda. 2002. "Imprisoning Women: The Unintended Victims of Mass Imprisonment." In *Invisible Punishment: The Collateral Consequences of Mass Imprisonment*, edited by Marc Mauer and Meda Chesney-Lind, 79–94. New York: Free Press.

Cheurprakobkit, Sutham. 2000. "Police-Citizen Contact and Police Performance: Attitudinal Differences Between Hispanics and Non-Hispanics." *Journal of Criminal Justice* 28 (4): 325–36.

Chin, Gabriel, and Richard Holmes. 2002. "Effective Assistance of Counsel and the Consequences of Guilty Pleas." *Cornell Law Review* 87 (3): 697–742.

Chiricos, Ted, Kelle Barrick, William Bales, and Stephanie Bontrager. 2007. "The Labeling of Convicted Felons and Its Consequences for Recidivism." *Criminology* 45 (3): 547–81.

Christian, Johnna. 2005. "Riding the Bus: Barriers to Prison Visitation and Family Management Strategies." *Journal of Contemporary Criminal Justice* 21 (1): 31–48.

Christian, Johnna, and Leslie W. Kennedy. 2011. "Secondary Narratives in the Aftermath of Crime: Defining Family Members' Relationships with Prisoners." *Punishment and Society* 13 (4): 379–402.

Clampet-Lundquist, Susan, Kathryn Edin, Jeffrey R. Kling, and Greg J. Duncan. 2011. "Moving Teenagers Out of High-Risk Neighborhoods: How Girls Fare Better Than Boys." *American Journal of Sociology* 116 (4): 1154–89.

Clear, Todd. 2007. *Imprisoning Communities: How Mass Incarceration Makes Disadvantaged Neighborhoods Worse*. New York: Oxford University Press.

Clear, Todd R., Elin Waring, and Kristen Scully. 2005. "Communities and Reentry: Concentrated Reentry Cycling." In *Prisoner Reentry and Crime in America*, edited by Jeremy Travis and Christy A. Visher, 179–208. New York: Cambridge University Press.

Cobb, Sidney. 1976. "Social Support as a Moderator of Life Stress." *Psychosomatic Medicine* 38 (5): 300–14.

———. 1982. "Social Support and Health Through the Life Course." In *Family Stress, Coping, and Social Support*, edited by Hamilton I. McCubbin, Elizabeth Cauble, and Joan Patterson. Sprinfield, IL: Charles C. Thomas.

Cobbina, Jennifer E. 2010. "Reintegration Success and Failure: Factors Impacting Reintegration Among Incarcerated and Formerly Incarcerated Women." *Journal of Offender Rehabilitation* 49 (3): 210–32.

Cochran, Joshua. 2014. "Breaches in the Wall: Imprisonment, Social Support, and Recidivism." *Journal of Research in Crime and Delinquency* 51 (2): 200–229.

Cochran, Joshua C., Daniel P. Mears, and William D. Bales. 2014. "Assessing the Effectiveness of Correctional Sanctions." *Journal of Quantitative Criminology* 30 (2): 317–47.

Cohen, Jacob. 1960. "A Coefficient of Agreement for Nominal Scales." *Educational and Psychological Measurement* 20 (1): 37–46.

Cohen, Jacob, Patricia Cohen, Stephen G. West, and Leona S. Aiken. 2003. *Applied Multiple Regression/Correlation Analysis for the Behavioral Sciences*. 3rd ed. Mahwah, NJ: Lawrence Erlbaum Associates.

Coleman, James. 1988. "Social Capital in the Creation of Human Capital." *American Journal of Sociology* 94: S95–120.

Coley, Richard, and Paul Barton. 2006. *Locked Up and Locked Out: An Educational Perspective on the US Prison Population*. Princeton, NJ: Educational Testing Service.

Collica, Kimberly. 2010. "Surviving Incarceration: Two Prison-Based Peer Programs Build Communities of Support for Female Offenders." *Deviant Behavior* 31 (4): 314–47.

Collica-Cox, Kimberly. 2018. "Female Offenders, HIV Peer Programs, and Attachment: The Importance of Prison-Based Civilian Staff in Creating Opportunities to Cultivate Prosocial Behaviors." *International Journal of Offender Therapy and Comparative Criminology* 62 (2): 524–50.

Collins, Susan E., Daniel K. Malone, and Seema L. Clifaselfi. 2013. "Housing Retention in Single-Site Housing First for Chronic Individuals with Severe Alcohol Problems." *American Journal of Public Health* 103 (2): S269–74.

Comfort, Megan. 2007. "Punishment Beyond the Legal Offender." *Annual Review of Law Social Science* 3: 271–96.

———. 2008. *Doing Time Together: Love and Family in the Shadow of the Prison*. Chicago: University of Chicago Press.

———. 2016. "'A Twenty-Hour-a-Day Job': The Impact of Frequent Low-Level Criminal Justice Involvement on Family Life." *ANNALS of the American Academy of Political and Social Science* 665 (1): 63–79.

Comfort, Megan, Andrea M. Lopez, Christina Powers, Alex H. Kral, and Jennifer Lorvick. 2015. "How Institutions Deprive: Ethnography, Social Work, and Interventionist Ethics Among the Hypermarginalized." *Russell Sage Foundation Journal of Social Sciences* 1 (1): 100–119.

"Computer Software." n.d. EgoWeb 2.0. http://github.com.

Converse, Jean M. 1984. "Strong Arguments and Weak Evidence: The Open/Closed Questioning Controversy of the 1940s." *Public Opinion Quarterly* 48: 267–82.

Copp, Jennifer E., and William D. Bales. 2018. "Jails and Local Justice System Reform: Overview and Recommendations." *Future of Children* 28 (1): 103–24.

Corda, Alessandro, and Michelle S. Phelps. 2017. "American Exceptionalism in Community Supervision." *American Probation and Parole Association (APPA)—Perspectives* Spring: 20–27.

Cortoni, Franca, Kevin Nunes, and Mark Latendresse. 2006. "An Examination of the Effectiveness of the Violence Prevention Program." Ottawa, Ontario: Correctional Services of Canada. www.csc-scc.gc.ca.

Council of State Governments Justice Center. 2014. "Reducing Recidivism: States Deliver Results." www.ncjrs.gov.

Cox, Alexandra. 2018. *Trapped in a Vice: The Consequences of Confinement for Young People*. New Brunswick, NJ: Rutgers University Press.

Coyne, James C., and Geraldine Downey. 1991. "Social Factors and Psychopathology: Stress, Social Support, and Coping Processes." *Annual Review of Psychology* 42: 401–25.

Crawley, Elaine, and Richard Sparks. 2005. "Older Men in Prison: Survival, Coping and Identity." In *The Effects of Imprisonment*, edited by Alison Liebling and Shadd Maruna, 343–65. New York: Routledge.

Crewe, Ben. 2007. "Power, Adaptation, and Resistance in a Late-Modern Men's Prison." *British Journal of Criminology* 47 (2): 256–75.

———. 2009. *The Prisoner Society: Power, Adaptation, and Social Life in an English Prison*. Oxford: Oxford University Press.

———. 2016. "The Sociology of Imprisonment." In *Handbook on Prisons*, edited by Y. Jewkes, J. Bennett, and B. Crewe, 77–100. New York: Routledge.

Crewe, Ben, Susie Hulley, and Serena Wright. 2017. "The Gendered Pains of Life Imprisonment." *British Journal of Criminology* 57 (6): 1359–78.

Crilly, John F., Eric D. Caine, J. Steven Lamberti, Theodore Brown, and Bruce Friedman. 2009. "Mental Health Services Use and Symptom Prevalence in a Cohort of Adults on Probation." *Psychiatric Services* 60 (4): 542–44.

Crites, Erin, and Faye S. Taxman. 2013. "The Responsivity Principle—Determining the Appropriate Program and Dosage to Match Risk and Needs." In *Simulation Strategies to Reduce Recidivism: Risk Need Responsivity (RNR) Modeling in the Criminal Justice System*, edited by Faye S. Taxman and April Pattavina. New York: Springer.

Crossley, Nick, Elisa Bellotti, Gemma Edwards, Martin G. Everett, Johan Koskinen, and Mark Tranmer. 2015. *Social Network Analysis for Ego-Nets*. London: Sage.

Culhane, Dennis P., John Fantuzzo, Heather L. Rouse, Vicky Tam, and Jonathan Lukens. 2010. "Connecting the Dots: The Promise of Integrated Data Systems for Policy Analysis and Systems Reform." *Intelligence of Social Policy* 1 (3): 1–22.

Cullen, Francis. 2013. "Rehabilitation: Beyond Nothing Works." *Crime and Justice* 42 (1): 299–376.

Cullen, Francis T., Cheryl L. Jonson, and Daniel P. Mears. 2017. "Reinventing Community Corrections." *Crime and Justice* 46: 27–93.

Culver, Leigh. 2004. "The Impact of New Immigration Patterns on the Provision of Police Services in Midwestern Communities." *Journal of Criminal Justice* 32 (4): 329–44.

Daly, Kathleen. 1994. *Gender, Crime and Punishment*. New Haven, CT: Yale University Press.

Daly, Kathleen, and Michael Tonry. 1997. "Race and Sentencing." *Crime and Justice* 22: 201–52.

David-Ferdon, Corrine, and Thomas R. Simon. 2014. "Preventing Youth Violence: Opportunities for Action." Atlanta, GA: Centers for Disease Control and Prevention. www.cdc.gov.

Davis, James F. 1991. *Who Is Black? One Nation's Definition*. University Park: Pennsylvania State University Press.

Davis, Lois, Robert Bozick, Jennifer Steele, Jessica Saunders, and Jeremy Miles. 2013. *Evaluating the Effectiveness of Correctional Education: A Meta-Analysis of Programs That Provide Education to Incarcerated Adults*. Santa Monica, CA: RAND Corporation. www.rand.org.

Davis, Robert C., and Edna Erez. 1998. "Immigrant Populations as Victims: Toward a Multicultural Criminal Justice System." Research in Brief NCJ 167571. Washington, DC: Office of Justice Programs, National Institute of Justice.

Deaton, Angus, and Darren Lubotsky. 2003. "Mortality, Inequality, and Race in American Cities and States." *Social Science and Medicine* 56: 1139–53.

De Castro, Arnold B., Kaori Fujishiro, Erica Sweitzer, and Jose Oliva. 2006. "How Immigrant Workers Experience Workplace Problems: A Qualitative Study." *Archives of Environmental and Occupational Health* 61 (6): 249–58.

DeHart, Dana, Cheri Shapiro, and James W. Hardin. 2017. "Impact of Incarceration on Families: A Single-Jurisdiction Pilot Study Using Triangulated Administrative Data and Qualitative Interviews." NCJ 250657. Washington, DC: National Criminal Justice Reference Service.

De Jong, Christina. 1997. "Survival Analysis and Specific Deterrence: Integrating Theoretical and Empirical Models of Recidivism." *Criminology* 35 (4): 561–75.

Department of Housing and Urban Development. 2016. *Office of General Counsel Guidance on Application of Fair Housing Act Standards to the Use of Criminal Records by Providers of Housing and Real Estate-Related Transactions*. Retrieved from http://portal.hud.gov.

Desmond, Matthew. 2012. "Disposable Ties and the Urban Poor." *American Journal of Sociology* 117 (5): 1295–1335.

DeVeaux, Mika'il. 2013. "The Trauma of the Incarcerated Experience." *Harvard Civil Rights-Civil Liberties Law Review* 48 (1): 257–77.
Dhami, Mandeep K., David R. Mandel, George Loewenstein, and Peter Ayton. 2006. "Prisoners' Positive Illusions of Their Post-Release Success." *Law and Human Behavior* 30: 631–47.
Digard, Leon. 2010. "When Legitimacy Is Denied: Offender Perceptions of the Prison Recall System." *Probation Journal* 57 (1): 43–61.
Dmitrieva, Julia, Kathryn C. Monahan, Elizabeth Cauffman, and Laurence Steinberg. 2012. "Arrested Development: The Effects of Incarceration on the Development of Psychosocial Maturity." *Development and Psychopathology* 24 (3): 1073–90.
Draine, Jeffrey, and Phyllis Solomon. 1994. "Jail Recidivism and the Intensity of Case Management Services among Homeless Persons with Mental Illness Leaving Jail." *Journal of Psychiatry and Law* 2: 245–62.
Duckworth, Angela. 2016. *Grit: Passion, Perseverance and the Science of Success*. New York: Random House.
Dudley, Richard G., and Pamela Leonard. 2008. "Getting It Right: Life History Investigation as the Foundation for a Reliable Mental Health Assessment." *Hofstra Law Review* 36: 963–88.
Duneier, Mitchell. 2000. "Race and Peeing on Sixth Avenue." In *Racing Research and Researching Race: Methodological Dilemmas in Critical Race Studies*, edited by France W. Twine and Jonathan W. Warren, 215–26. New York: New York University Press.
Dunn, Kerry, and Paul J. Kaplan. 2009. "The Ironies of Helping: Social Interventions and Executable Subjects." *Law & Society Review* 43 (2): 337–68.
Durose, Mattew R., Alexia D. Cooper, and Howard N. Snyder. 2014. "Recidivism of Prisoners Released in 30 States in 2005: Patterns from 2005 to 2010." NCJ 244205. Washington, DC: Department of Justice, Office of Justice Programs, Bureau of Justice Statistics.
Durrant, Gabriele B., and Julia D'Arrigo. 2014. "Doorsetp Interactions and Interviewer Effects on the Process Leading to Cooperation or Refusal." *Sociological Methods and Research* 3 (3): 490–518.
Duwe, Grant, and Valerie Clark. 2014. "The Effects of Prison-Based Educational Programming on Recidivism and Employment." *Prison Journal* 94 (4): 454–78.
Eason, John M. 2017. *Big House on the Prairie*. Chicago: University of Chicago Press.
Eddy, J. Mark, and Julie Poehlmann. 2010. "Multidisciplinary Perspectives on Research and Intervention with Children of Incarcerated Parents." In *Children of Incarcerated Parents: A Handbook for Researchers and Practitioners*, edited by Julie Poehlmann and J. Mark Eddy, 1–9. Washington, DC: Urban Institute.
Eddy, J. Mark, and John B. Reid. 2003. "The Adolescent Children of Incarcerated Parents: A Developmental Perspective." In *Prisoners Once Removed: The Impact of Incarceration and Reentry on Children, Families, and Communities*, edited by Jeremy Travis and Michelle Waul, 233–58. Washington, DC: Urban Institute.
Eder, Donna, and William Corsaro. 1999. "Ethnographic Studies of Children and Youth: Theoretical and Ethical Issues." *Journal of Contemporary Ethnography* 28 (5): 520–31.

Elder, Glen H. 1998. "The Life Course as Developmental Theory." *Child Development* 69 (1): 1–12.

Ellis, Albert. 1973. *Humanistic Psychology: The Rational-Emotive Approach*. New York: Julian Press.

Emerson, Robert, Rachel I. Fretz, and Linda L. Shaw. 2011. *Writing Ethnographic Fieldnotes*. 2nd ed. Chicago: University of Chicago Press.

Enns, Peter K. 2014. "The Public's Increasing Punitiveness and Its Influence on Mass Incarceration in the United States." *American Journal of Political Science* 58: 857–72.

———. 2016. *Incarceration Nation*. Cambridge: Cambridge University Press.

Enos, Sandra. 2001. *Mothering from the Inside: Parenting in a Women's Prison*. Albany: State University of New York Press.

Espino, Rodolfo, and Michael M. Franz. 2002. "Latino Phenotypic Discrimination Revisited: The Impact of Skin Color on Occupational Status." *Social Science Quarterly* 83 (2): 612–23.

Esterling, Beth A., and Ben Feldmeyer. 2017. "Race, Incarceration, and Motherhood: Spoiled Identity among Rural White Mothers in Prison." *Prison Journal* 97 (2): 143–65.

Evans, Douglas. 2014. *The Debt Penalty—Exposing the Financial Barriers to Offender Reintegration*. New York: Research and Evaluation Center, John Jay College of Criminal Justice, City University of New York.

Fader, Jamie J. 2013. *Falling Back: Incarceration and Transitions to Adulthood Among Urban Youth*. New Brunswick, NJ: Rutgers University Press.

———. 2016. "'Selling Smarter, Not Harder': Life Course Effects on Drug Sellers' Risk Perceptions and Management." *International Journal of Drug Policy* 36: 120–29.

Farrall, Stephen. 2002. *Rethinking What Works with Offenders: Probation, Social Context and Desistance from Crime*. Cullompton, UK: Willan.

Farrall, Stephen, Anthony Bottoms, and Joanna Shapland. 2010. "Social Structures and Desistance from Crime." *European Journal of Criminology* 7 (6): 546–70.

Farrall, Stephen, Ben Hunter, Gilly Sharpe, and Adam Calverley. 2014. *Criminal Careers in Transition: The Social Context of Desistance from Crime*. New York: Oxford University Press.

Farrington, David P. 2002. "Developmental Criminology and Risk-Focused Prevention." In *The Oxford Handbook of Criminology*, edited by Mike Maguire, Rod Morgan, and Robert Reiner, 3rd ed., 657–701. Oxford: Oxford University Press.

———. 2007. "Childhood Risk Factors and Risk Focused Prevention." In *The Oxford Handbook of Criminology*, 4th ed., edited by Mike Maguire, Rod Morgan, and Robert Reiner, 602–40. Oxford: Oxford University Press.

———. 2009. "Building Developmental and Life-Course Theories of Offending." In *Taking Stock: The Status of Criminological Theory*, edited by Francis T. Cullen, John Paul Wright, and Kristie Blevins, 2nd ed. New Brunswick, NJ: Transaction.

Fazel, Seena, and Jacques Baillargeon. 2011. "The Health of Prisoners." *Lancet* 377: 956–65.

Fazel, Seena, Parveen Bains, and Helen Doll. 2006. "Substance Abuse and Dependence in Prisoners: A Systematic Review." *Addiction* 101 (2): 181–91.

Fearn, Noelle E., Michael G. Vaughn, Erik J. Nelson, Christopher P. Salas-Wright, Matt DeLisi, and Zhengmin Qian. 2016. "Trends and Correlates of Substance Use Disorders among Probationers and Parolees in the United States, 2002–2014." *Drugs and Alcohol Dependence* 167: 128–39.

Federal Interagency Reentry Council. 2016. *A Record of Progress and a Roadmap for the Future: Final Report*. Washington, DC: US Department of Justice. https://cgsjusticecenter.org.

Feeley, Malcolm M., and Jonathan Simon. 1992. "The New Penology: Notes on the Emerging Strategy of Corrections and Its Implications." *Criminology* 30 (4): 447–74.

Feucht, Thomas, and Tammy Holt. 2016. "Does Cognitive Behavioral Therapy Work in Criminal Justice?" *NIJ Journal* 227: 1–8.

Fine, Michelle, Maria Elena Torre, Kathy Boudin, Iris Bowen, and Debora Upegui. 2001. *Changing Minds: The Impact of College in a Maximum-Security Prison*. Bedford Hills, NY: New York Department of Correctional Services. http://web.gc.cuny.edu.

Fishman, Laura T. 1990. *Women at the Wall: A Study of Prisoners' Wives Doing Time on the Outside*. Albany: State University of New York Press.

Flores, Jerry. 2016. *Caught Up: Girls, Surveillance, and Wraparound Incarceration*. Berkeley: University of California Press.

Flory, Julie Hail. 2016. "Washington University and United Way Join Forces on Gun Violence Prevention." *The Source*. https://source.wustl.edu.

Foster, Holly, and John Hagan. 2015. "Punishment Regimes and the Multilevel Effects of Paternal Incarceration: Intergenerational, Intersectional, and Interinstitutional Models of Social Inequality and Systemic Exclusion." *Annual Review of Sociology* 41: 135–58.

Fournier, Arthur M., and Daniel Herlihy. 2006. *The Zombie Curse: A Doctor's 25-Year Journey into the Heart of the AIDS Epidemic in Haiti*. Washington, DC: Joseph Henry Press.

Fox, Kathleen, Katheryn Zambrana, and Jodi Lane. 2011. "Getting In (and Staying In) When Everyone Else Wants to Get Out: 10 Lessons Learned from Conducting Research with Inmates." *Journal of Criminal Justice Education* 22 (2): 304–27.

Fox, Kathryn J. 2017. "Contextualizing the Policy and Pragmatics of Reintegrating Sex Offenders." *Sex Abuse: A Journal of Research and Treatment* 29 (1): 28–50.

Freed, Daniel J. 1992. "Federal Sentencing in the Wake of Guidelines: Unacceptable Limits on the Discretion of Sentencers." *Yale Law Journal* 101 (8): 1681–1754.

Friedman, Matthew. 2015. "Just Facts: As Many Americans Have Criminal Records as College Diplomas." *Brennan Center for Justice* (blog). November 17, 2015. www.brennancenter.org.

Furlong, Andy, and Fred Cartmel. 2007. *Young People and Social Change: New Perspectives*. Berkshire: Open University Press.

Gadd, David, and Tony Jefferson. 2007. *Psychosocial Criminology*. London: Sage.

Gainey, Randy R., Brian K. Payne, and Mike O'Toole. 2000. "The Relationships between Time in Jail, Time on Electronic Monitoring, and Recidivism: An Event History Analysis of a Jail-Based Program." *Justice Quarterly* 17 (4): 733–52.

Garcia, Janet. 2016. "The Importance of the Mentor-Mentee Relationship in Women's Desistance from Destructive Behaviors." *International Journal of Offender Therapy and Comparative Criminology* 60 (7): 808–27.

Garcia-Hallett, Janet. 2017. "The Navigation of Motherhood for African American, West Indian, and Hispanic Women in Reentry." PhD dissertation. Newark, NJ: Rutgers University.

Garland, David. 2001. *Culture of Control: Crime and Social Order in Contemporary Society*. Chicago: University of Chicago Press.

Geller, Amanda, Carey E. Cooper, Irwin Garfinkel, Ofira Schwartz-Soicher, and Ronald B. Mincy. 2012. "Beyond Absenteeism: Father Incarceration and Child Development. *Demography* 49 (1): 49–76.

Geer, John G. 1988. "What Do Open-Ended Questions Measure?" *Public Opinion Quarterly* 52: 365–71.

Giallombardo, Rose. 1966. *Society of Women: A Study of a Women's Prison*. New York: Wiley.

Giguere, Rachelle, and Lauren Dundes. 2002. "Help Wanted: A Survey of Employer Concerns About Hiring Ex-Convicts." *Criminal Justice Policy Review* 13 (4): 396–408.

Giordano, Peggy C., Stephen A. Cernkovich, and Jennifer L. Rudolph. 2002. "Gender, Crime, and Desistance: Toward a Theory of Cognitive Transformation." *American Journal of Sociology* 107 (4): 990–1064.

Giordano, Peggy C., Monica A. Longmore, Ryan D. Schroder, and Patrick M. Seffrin. 2008. "A Life-Course Perspective on Spirituality and Desistance from Crime." *Criminology* 46 (1): 99–132.

Giovanni, Thomas. 2012. *Community-Oriented Defense: Start Now*. New York: Brennan Center for Justice at New York University School of Law.

Giroux, Henry. 2009. *Youth in a Suspect Society: Democracy or Disposability*. New York: Palgrave MacMillan.

Glaser, Barney, and Anselm Strauss. 1967. *The Discovery of Grounded Theory: Strategies for Qualitative Research*. New Brunswick, NJ: Aldine.

Goffman, Alice. 2009. "On the Run: Wanted Men in a Philadelphia Ghetto." *American Sociological Review* 74: 339–57.

Goffman, Erving. 1961. *Asylums: Essays on the Social Situation of Mental Patients and Other Inmates*. New York: Anchor Books.

———. 1963. *Stigma: On the Management of Spoiled Identity*. Englewood Cliffs, NJ: Prentice-Hall.

Gohara, Miriam. 2013. "Grace Notes: A Case for Making Mitigation the Heart of Noncapital Sentencing." *American Journal of Criminal Law* 41: 41–89.

———. 2018. "In Defense of the Injured: How Trauma-Informed Criminal Defense Can Reform Sentencing." *American Journal of Criminal Law* 45 (1): 1–53.

Gonnerman, Jennifer. 2004. "The Neighborhood Costs of America's Prison Boom: Million-Dollar Blocks." *Village Voice Online*, November 16.

Goodey, Jo. 2000. "Biographical Lessons for Criminology." *Theoretical Criminology* 4 (4): 473–98.
Goodman, Philip, Joshua Page, and Michelle Phelps. 2015. "The Long Struggle: An Agonistic Perspective on Penal Development." *Theoretical Criminology* 19 (3): 315–35.
Goodstein, Lynne. 1984. "Determinate Sentencing and the Correctional Process: A Study of the Implementation and Impact of Sentencing Reform in Three States, Executive Summary." Washington, DC: National Institute of Justice, US Department of Justice.
Goodstein, Lynne, and James A. Hudack. 1982. "Importance to Prisoners of Predictability of Release: A Test of a Presumed Benefit of the Determinate Sentence." *Criminal Justice and Behavior* 9 (2): 217–28.
Gopaul-McNicol, Sharon. 1993. *Working with West Indian Families*. New York: Guilford.
Gottschalk, Marie. 2006. *The Prison and the Gallows: The Politics of Mass Incarceration in America*. New York: Cambridge University Press.
———. 2011. "The Past, Present, and Future of Mass Incarceration in the United States." *Criminology and Public Policy* 10: 483–504.
———. 2015. *Caught: The Prison State and the Lockdown of American Politics*. Princeton, NJ: Princeton University Press.
Governing. 2018. State Marijuana Laws in 2018 Map. www.governing.com.
Government Accounting Office (GAO). 2005. "Drug Offenders: Various Factors May Limit the Impacts of Federal Laws that Provide for Denial of Selected Benefits." www.gao.gov.
Graffam, Joseph, Alison J. Shinkfield, and Lesley Hardcastle. 2008. "The Perceived Employability of Ex-Prisoners and Offenders." *International Journal of Offender Therapy and Comparative Criminology* 52 (6): 673–85.
Granovetter, Mark. 1973. "The Strength of Weak Ties." *American Journal of Sociology* 78: 1360–80.
———. 1995. *Getting a Job: A Study of Contacts and Careers*. 2nd ed. Chicago: University of Chicago Press.
Green, David A. 2013. "Penal Optimism and Second Chances: The Legacies of American Protestantism and the Prospects for Penal Reform." *Punishment and Society* 15 (2): 123–46.
Greene, Judith, and Marc Mauer. 2010. *Downscaling Prisons: Lessons from Four States*. Washington, DC: Sentencing Project.
Greenfeld, Lawrence, and Tracy L. Snell. 1999. "Women Offenders." Bureau of Justice Statistics Special Report NCJ 175688. Washington, DC: Department of Justice, Office of Justice Programs.
Guetzkow, Harold. 1950. "Unitizing and Categorizing Problems in Coding Qualitative Data." *Journal of Clinical Psychology* 6 (1): 47–58.
Gunnison, Elaine, and Jacqueline B. Helfgott. 2013. *Offender Reentry: Beyond Crime and Punishment*. Boulder, CO: Lynne Rienner.

Hairston, Creasie Finney. 1988. "Family Ties during Imprisonment: Do They Influence Future Criminal Activity." *Federal Probation* 52 (1): 48–52.

Hallett, Michael. 2012. "Reentry to What? Theorizing Prisoner Reentry in the Jobless Future." *Critical Criminology* 20 (3): 213–28.

Halsey, Mark, Ruth Armstrong, and Serena Wright. 2017. "'F*ck It!': Matza and the Mood of Fatalism in the Desistance Process." *British Journal of Criminology* 57 (4): 1041–60.

Halsey, Mark, and Vandra Harris. 2011. "Prisoner Futures: Sensing the Signs of Generativity." *Australian and New Zealand Journal of Criminology* 44 (1): 74–93.

Halushka, John. 2016. "Work Wisdom: Teaching Former Prisoners How to Negotiate Workplace Interactions and Perform a Rehabilitated Self." *Ethnography* 17 (1): 72–91.

Hamilton, Zachary, Christopher M. Campbell, Jaqueline van Wormer, Alex Kigerl, and Brianne Posey. 2016. "Impact of Swift and Certain Sanctions: Evaluation of Washington State's Policy for Offenders on Community Supervision." *Criminology and Public Policy* 15 (4): 1009–72.

Haney, Craig. 2003. "The Psychological Impact of Incarceration: Implications for Post-Prison Adjustment." In *Prisoners Once Removed: The Impact of Incarceration and Reentry on Children, Families, and Communities*, edited by Jeremy Travis and Michelle Waul, 33–66. Washington, DC: Urban Institute.

Haney, Craig, Curtis Banks, and Philip Zimbardo. 1973. "Interpersonal Dynamics in a Simulated Prison." *International Journal of Criminology and Penology* 1: 69–97.

Harding, David J. 2003. "Jean Valjean's Dilemma: The Management of Ex-Convict Identity in the Search for Employment." *Deviant Behavior* 24: 571–95.

———. 2010. *Living the Drama: Community, Conflict, and Culture among Inner-City Boys*. Chicago: University of Chicago Press.

Harding, David J., Cheyney C. Dobson, Jessica J. B. Wyse, and Jeffrey D. Morenoff. 2016. "Narrative Change, Narrative Stability, and Structural Constraint: The Case of Prisoner Reentry Narratives." *American Journal of Cultural Sociology* 5 (1–2): 261–304.

Harding, David J., Jeffrey D. Morenoff, and Claire W. Herbert. 2013. "Home Is Hard to Find: Neighborhoods, Institutions, and the Residential Trajectories of Returning Prisoners." *ANNALS of the American Academy of Political and Social Science* 647 (1): 214–36.

Harding, David J., Jeffrey D. Morenoff, and Jessica J. B. Wyse. 2019. *On the Outside: Prisoner Reentry and Reintegration*. Chicago: University of Chicago Press.

Harding, David J., Jessica J. B. Wyse, Cheyney Dobson, and Jeffrey D. Morenoff. 2014. "Making Ends Meet after Prison." *Journal of Policy Analysis and Management* 33 (2): 440–70.

Harding, David, Jonah Siegel, and Jeffrey D. Morenoff. 2017. "Custodial Parole Sanctions and Earnings after Release from Prison." *Social Forces* 96 (2): 909–34.

Harding, Sandra. 1995. "Strong Objectivity: A Response to the New Objectivity Question." *Synthese* 104 (3): 331–49.

Harlow, Caroline Wolf. 2003. "Education and Correctional Populations." NCJ 195670. Washington, DC: Bureau of Justice Statistics.

Harris, Alexes. 2016. *A Pound of Flesh*. New York: Russell Sage Foundation.

Hartney, Christopher, and Fabiana Silva. 2007. *And Justice for Some: Differential Treatment of Minority Youth in the Justice System*. Oakland, CA: National Council on Crime and Delinquency.

Hartwell, Stephanie. 2004. "Comparison of Offenders with Mental Illness Only and Offenders with Dual Diagnoses." *Psychiatric Services* 55 (2): 145–50.

Harvey, Richard D. 2001. "Individual Differences in the Phenomenological Impact of Social Stigma." *Journal of Social Psychology* 141 (2): 174–89.

Haskins, Anna, and Kristin Turney. 2017. "The Demographic Landscape and Sociological Implications of Parental Incarceration for Childhood Inequality." In *When Parents Are Incarcerated: Interdisciplinary Research and Interventions to Support Children*, edited by Christopher Wildeman, Anna Haskins, and Julie Pohelmann-Tynan. Washington, DC: American Psychological Association Books.

Hassine, Victor. 2010. *Life Without Parole: Living and Dying in Prison Today*. Edited by R. Johnson and S. Tabriz. 5th ed. Oxford: Oxford University Press.

Hawken, Angela, and Mark Kleiman. 2009. *Managing Drug Involved Probationers with Swift and Certain Sanctions: Evaluating Hawaii's HOPE*. Washington, DC: National Institute of Justice.

Hayes, Kecia. 2006. "Constructing a Prison to School Pipeline: An Examination of the Educational Experiences of Incarcerated Youth." New York: City University of New York.

Hayes, Lindsay M., and Joseph R. Rowan. 1988. "National Study of Jail Suicides: Seven Years Later." Windsor Mill, MD: National Center for Institutions and Alternatives.

Haynie, Dana L. 2001. "Delinquent Peers Revisited: Does Network Structure Matter?" *American Journal of Sociology* 106 (4): 1013–57.

Haynie, Dana L., Corey Whichard, David R. Schaefer, Derek A. Kreager, and Sara Wakefield. 2018. "Social Networks and Health in a Prison Unit." *Journal of Health and Social Behavior* 59 (3): 318–34.

Healy, Deirdre. 2013. "Changing Fate? Agency and the Desistance Process." *Theoretical Criminology* 17 (4): 557–74.

Henning, Kris R., and B. Christopher Frueh. 1996. "Cognitive-Behavioral Treatment of Incarcerated Offenders: An Evaluation of the Vermont Department of Corrections' Cognitive Self-Change Program." *Criminal Justice and Behavior* 23 (4): 523–41.

Henrichson, Christian, Joshua Rinaldi, and Ruth Delaney. 2015. *The Price of Jails: Measuring the Taxpayer Cost of Local Incarceration*. New York: Vera Institute of Justice.

Hepburn, John R., and Marie Griffin. 2004. "An Analysis of Risk Factors Contributing to the Recidivism of Sex Offenders on Probation." NIJ 203905. Washington, DC: National Institute of Justice.

Herbert, Claire W., Jeffrey D. Morenoff, and David J. Harding. 2015. "Homelessness and Housing Insecurity Among Former Prisoners." *Russell Sage Foundation Journal of Social Sciences* 1 (2): 44–79.

Herbst, Leigh, and Samuel Walker. 2001. "Language Barriers in the Delivery of Police Services: A Study of Police and Hispanic Interactions in a Midwestern City." *Journal of Criminal Justice* 29: 329–40.

Higher Education Act of 1965. 1965 (November). Public Law No. 89-329 (89th Congress, H.R. 9567).

Hipp, John, Joan Petersilia, and Susan Turner. 2010. "Parolee Recidivism in California: The Effect of Neighborhood Context and Social Service Agency Characteristics." *Criminology* 48 (4): 947–79.

Hipp, John R., Jesse Jannetta, Rita Shah, and Susan Turner. 2009. "Parolees' Physical Closeness to Health Service Providers: A Study of California Parolees." *Health and Place* 15 (3): 679–88.

Hipp, John R., Susan Turner, and Jesse Jannetta. 2010. "Are Sex Offenders Moving into Social Disorganization? Analyzing the Residential Mobility of California Parolees." *Journal of Research in Crime and Delinquency* 47 (4): 558–90.

Hirschi, Travis. 1979. *Causes of Delinquency*. Berkeley: University of California Press.

Hlavka, Heather, Darren Wheelock, and Richard Jones. 2015. "Exoffender Accounts of Successful Reentry from Prison." *Journal of Offender Rehabilitation* 54 (6): 406–28.

Hogan, Bernie, Juana Antonio Carrasco, and Barry Wellman. 2007. "Visualizing Personal Networks: Working with Participant-Aided Sociograms." *Field Methods* 19 (2): 116–44.

Horney, Julie C., D. Wayne Osgood, and Ineke Haen Marshall. 1995. "Criminal Careers in the Short-Term: Intra-Individual Variability in Crime and Its Relation to Local Life Circumstances." *American Sociological Review* 60 (5): 655–73.

Horowitz, Ruth. 1986. "Remaining an Outsider: Membership as a Threat to Research Rapport." *Journal of Contemporary Ethnography* 14 (4): 409–30.

Horowitz, Veronica, and Christopher Uggen. 2019. "Consistency and Compensation in Mercy: Commutation in the Era of Mass Incarceration." *Social Forces* 97 (3): 1205–30.

House, James S., Debra Umberson, and Karl R. Landis. 1988. "Structures and Processes of Social Support." *Annual Review of Sociology* 14: 293–318.

Hudson, Barbara. 2003. *Understanding Justice: An Introduction to Ideas, Perspectives, and Controversies in Modern Penal Theory*. 2nd ed. Buckingham: Open University Press.

Huebner, Beth M. 2005. "The Effect of Incarceration on Marriage and Work Over the Life Course." *Justice Quarterly* 22 (3): 281–303.

Huebner, Beth M., and Timothy S. Bynum. 2006. "An Analysis of Parole Decision Making Using a Sample of Sex Offenders: A Focal Concerns Perspective." *Criminology* 44 (4): 961–91.

Huebner, Beth M., Christina De Jong, and Jennifer Cobbina. 2010. "Women Coming Home: Long-Term Patterns of Recidivism." *Justice Quarterly* 27 (2): 225–54.

Hunt, Kim Steven, and Robert Dumville. 2016. "Recidivism among Federal Offenders: A Comprehensive Overview." Washington, DC: US Sentencing Commission.

Hunter, Margaret. 2007. "The Persistent Problem of Colorism: Skin Tone, Status, and Inequality." *Sociology Compass* 1 (1): 237–57.

Huynh, Kim H., Brittany Hall, Mark A. Hurst, and Lynette H. Bikos. 2015. "Evaluation of the Positive Re-Entry in Corrections Program: A Positive Psychology Intervention with Prison Inmates." *International Journal of Offender Therapy and Comparative Criminology* 59 (9): 1006–23.

Hyatt, Jordan M., and Geoffrey C. Barnes. 2017. "An Experimental Evaluation of the Impact of Intensive Supervision on the Recidivism of High-Risk Probationers." *Crime and Delinquency* 63 (1): 33–38.

Inyang, Enobong J. 2010. "Reentry Experiences of Sex Offenders: A Phenomenology Study." Unpublished dissertation. Huntsville, TX: Sam Houston State University.

Institute for Criminal Policy Research (2018). World Prison Brief (online database). www.prisonstudies.org.

International Center for Prison Studies. 2018. www.prisonstudies.org.

Irwin, John. 1970. *The Felon*. Englewood Cliffs, NJ: Prentice-Hall.

———. 1974. "The Trouble with Rehabilitation." *Correctional Psychologist* 1 (2): 139–49.

———. 1980. *Prisons in Turmoil*. Boston: Little, Brown.

———. 1985. *The Jail: Managing the Underclass in American Society*. Berkeley: University of California Press.

———. 2005. *The Warehouse Prison: Disposal of the New Dangerous Class*. Los Angeles, CA: Roxbury.

Irwin, John, and Donald R. Cressey. 1962. "Thieves, Convicts and the Inmate Culture." *Social Problems* 10 (2): 142–55.

Irwin, John, and Barbara Owen. 2005. "Harm and the Contemporary Prison." In *The Effects of Imprisonment*, edited by Alison Liebling and Shadd Maruna, 94–117. New York: Routledge.

Jackson, Kelly. 2013. "The Biracial Black/White Experience." Mixed Heritage Center. www.mixedheritagecenter.org.

James, Angela. 2008. "Making Sense of Race and Racial Classification." In *White Logic, White Methods: Racism and Methodology*, edited by Tukufu Zuberi and Eduardo Bonilla-Silva, 31–46. United Kingdom: Rowman & Littlefield.

James, Doris J. 2004. *Profile of Jail Inmates, 2002*. Washington, DC: Bureau of Justice Statistics.

Janetta, Jesse, Justin Breaux, Helen Ho, and Jeremy Porter. 2014. *Examining Racial and Ethnic Disparities in Probation Revocation: Summary Findings and Implications from a Multistate Study*. Washington, DC: Urban Institute.

Jarrett, R. L., O. S. Bahar, and Ezella McPherson. 2015. "'Do What You Gotta Do': How Low-Income African American Mothers Manage Food Insecurity." In *Family Problems: Stress, Risk, and Resilience*, edited by Joyce Arditti, 101–16. West Sussex, UK: Wiley.

Jay-Z. 2017. "Jay-Z: The Criminal Justice System Stalks Black People Like Meek Mill." *New York Times*, November 17. www.nytimes.com.

Jean-Louis, Eustache, Janine Walker, Guy Apollon, Joel Piton, M. B. Antoine, Alfred Mombeleur, Marc Thelsimond, and Nicole César. 2001. "Drug and Alcohol Use Among Boston's Haitian Community: A Hidden Problem Unveiled by CCHER's

Enhanced Innovative Case Management Program." *Drugs and Society* 16 (1–2): 107–22.

Jenness, Valerie. 2010. "From Policy to Prisoners to People: A 'Soft Mixed Methods' Approach to Studying Transgender Prisoners." *Journal of Contemporary Ethnography* 39 (5): 517–53.

Jewkes, Yvonne, and Serena Wright. 2016. "Researching the Prison." In *The Handbook of Prisons*, edited by Yvonne Jewkes, Ben Crewe, and Jamie Bennett, 659. Oxon, UK: Routledge.

Johnson, Elizabeth I., and Beth Easterling. 2012. "Understanding the Unique Effects of Parental Incarceration on Children: Challenges, Progress, and Recommendation." *Journal of Marriage and Family* 74 (2): 342–56.

Johnson, Elmer H. 1971. "A Basic Error: Dealing with Inmates as Though They Were Abnormal." *Federal Probation* 35: 39–44.

Johnson, Jeffrey C., and Susan C. Weller. 2002. "Elicitation Techniques for Interviewing." In *Handbook of Interview Research: Context and Method*, edited by Jaber F. Gubrium and James A. Holstein, 491–514. Newbury Park, CA: Sage.

Jordan, Kathleen, William E. Schlenger, John A. Fairbank, and Justea M. Caddell. 1996. "Prevalence of Psychiatric Disorder among Incarcerated Women: Convicted Felons Entering Prison." *Archives of General Psychiatry* 53: 513–19.

Jost, John T., Diana Burgess, and Cristina O. Mosso. 2001. "Conflicts of Legitimation among Self, Group, and System: The Integrative Potential of System Justification Theory." In *The Psychology of Legitimacy: Emerging Perspectives on Ideology, Justice, and Intergroup Relations*, edited by John T. Jost and Brenda Major, 363–88. New York: Cambridge University Press.

Kadushin, Charles. 2012. *Understanding Social Networks: Theories, Concepts, and Findings*. Oxford: Oxford University Press.

Kaeble, Danielle, and Thomas P. Bonczar. 2016. *Probation and Parole in the United States, 2015*. Washington, DC: Bureau of Justice Statistics.

Kaeble, Danielle, and Mary Cowhig. 2018. *Correctional Populations in the United States, 2016*. Washington, DC: Bureau of Justice Statistics.

Kaeble, Danielle, and Lauren Glaze. 2016. *Correctional Populations in the United States, 2015*. Washington, DC: Bureau of Justice Statistics.

Kaeble, Danielle, Lauren Glaze, Anastasios Tsoutis, and Todd Minton. 2016. *Correctional Populations in the United States, 2014*. Washington, DC: Bureau of Justice Statistics.

Kent, Mary M. 2007. "Immigration and America's Black Population." *Population Bulletin* 62 (4). Washington, DC: Population Reference Bureau.

Kerrison, Erin M. 2017. "Risky Business, Risk Assessment, and Other Heteronormative Misnomers in Women's Community Corrections and Reentry Planning." *Punishment and Society* 20 (1): 134–51.

Kingsnorth, Rodney F., Randall C. MacIntosh, and Sandra Sutherland. 2002. "Criminal Charge or Probation Violation? Prosecutorial Discretion and Implications for Research in Criminal Court Proceeding." *Criminology* 40 (3): 553–78.

Kirk, David S. 2009. "A Natural Experiment of the Effect of Residential Change on Recidivism: Lessons from Hurricane Katrina." *American Sociological Review* 74 (3): 484–505.

———. 2012. "Residential Changes as a Turning Point in the Life Course of Crime: Desistance or Temporary Cessation?" *Criminology* 50 (2): 329–58.

Klas, Mary Ellen. 2017. "Florida Prisons Have Toilet Paper, But They're Not Supplying It to Some Inmates." *Miami Herald*, July 19. www.miamiherald.com.

Klein, Steven, Michelle Tolbert, Rosio Bugarian, Emily Forrest Cataldi, and Gina Tauschek. 2004. *Correctional Education: Assessing the Status of Prison Programs and Information Needs*. Washington, DC: US Department of Education.

Kleinman, Paula H., and Irving F. Lukoff. 1978. "Ethnic Differences in Factors Related to Drug Use." *Journal of Health and Social Behavior* 19 (2): 190–99.

Kleinstuber, Ross. 2016. "Attorneys' Use of Hegemonic Tales and Subversive Stories in the Presentation of Capital Mitigation." *Criminal Justice Review* 41 (1): 41–54.

Kohler-Hausmann, Issa. 2018. *Misdemeanorland: Criminal Courts and Social Control in an Age of Broken Windows Policing*. Princeton, NJ: Princeton University Press.

Korn, Richard. 1992. "Novum Organum: An Argument for a Fundamentally Different Curriculum in Criminal Justice." *Criminologist* 17 (2): 1–7.

Kornhauser, Ruth. 1978. *Social Sources of Delinquency*. Chicago: University of Chicago Press.

Kossinets, Gueorgi. 2006. "Effects of Missing Data in Social Networks." *Social Networks* 28 (3): 247–68.

Krauth, Barbara. 1997. "A Review of the Jail Function within State Unified Corrections Systems." https://nicic.gov.

Kreager, Derek A., Martin Bouchard, George De Leon, David R. Schaefer, Michaela Soyer, Jacob T. N. Young, and Gary Zajac. 2018. "A Life Course and Networks Approach to Prison Therapeutic Communities." In *Social Networks and the Life Course: Linking Human Lives and Social Relational Structures*, edited by Duane Alwin, Diane Felmlee, and Derek A. Kreager. New York: Springer.

Kreager, Derek A., and Candace Kruttschnitt. 2018. "Inmate Society in the Era of Mass Incarceration." *Annual Review of Criminology* 1: 261–83.

Kreager, Derek A., David R. Schaefer, Martin Bouchard, Dana L. Haynie, Sara Wakefield, Jacob Young, and Gary Zajac. 2016. "Toward a Criminology of Inmate Networks." *Justice Quarterly* 33 (6): 1000–28.

Kreager, Derek A., Jacob T. N. Young, Dana L. Haynie, Martin Bouchard, David R. Schaefer, and Gary Zajac. 2017. "Where 'Old Heads' Prevail: Inmate Hierarchy in a Men's Prison Unit." *American Sociological Review* 82 (4): 685–718.

Kruttschnitt, Candace, and Rosemary Gartner. 2005. *Making Time in the Golden State: Women's Imprisonment in California*. Cambridge: Cambridge University Press.

Kruttschnitt, Candace, and Jeanette Hussemann. 2008. "Micropolitics of Race and Ethnicity in Women's Prisons in Two Political Contexts." *British Journal of Sociology* 59 (4): 709–28.

Kubrin, Charis E., and Eric Stewart. 2006. "Predicting Who Reoffends: The Neglected Role of Neighborhood Context in Recidivism Studies." *Criminology* 44 (1): 165–95.

Kurlychek, Megan C., Robert Brame, and Shawn D. Bushway. 2006. "Scarlet Letters and Recidivism: Does an Old Criminal Record Predict Future Offending?" *Criminology and Public Policy* 5 (3): 483–504.

———. 2007. "Enduring Risk? Old Criminal Records and Predictions of Future Criminal Involvement." *Crime and Delinquency* 53 (1): 64–83.

Lacey, Nicola. 2013. "Penal Theory and Penal Practice: A Communitarian Approach." In *The Use of Punishment*, edited by Sean McConville, 175–98. Cullompton, UK: Willan.

Lageson, Sarah E. 2016. "Digital Punishment Tangled Web." *Contexts* 15 (1): 22–7.

Lageson, Sarah E., and Shadd Maruna. 2018. "Digital Degradation: Stigma Management in the Internet Age." *Punishment and Society* 20 (1): 113–33.

Landale, Nancy S., R. S. Oropesa, and Cristina Bradatan. 2006. "Hispanic Families in the United States: Family Structure and Process in an Era of Family Change." In *Hispanics and the Future of America*, edited by Marta Tienda and Faith Mitchell, 138–78. Washington, DC: National Academies Press.

Landenberg, Nana, and Mark Lipsey. 2006. "The Positive Effects of Cognitive-Behavioral Programs for Offenders: A Meta-Analysis of Factors Associated with Effective Treatments." *Journal of Experimental Criminology* 4: 451–76.

Lareau, Annette. 2003. *Unequal Childhoods: Class, Race, and Family Life*. Berkeley: University of California Press.

Latta, Rachel E., and Lisa A. Goodman. 2005. "Considering the Interplay of Cultural Context and Service Provision in Intimate Partner Violence: The Case of Haitian Immigrant Women." *Violence Against Women* 11 (11): 1441–64.

Lattimore, Pamela K., Doris Layton MacKenzie, Gary Zajac, Debbie Dawes, Elaine Arsenault, and Stephen Tueller. 2016. "Outcome Findings from the HOPE Demonstration Field Experiment: Is Swift, Certain, and Fair an Effective Supervision Strategy?" *Criminology and Public Policy* 15 (4): 1103–41.

Laub, John H., and Robert J. Sampson. 1993. "Turning Points in the Life Course: Why Change Matters to the Study of Crime." *Criminology* 31 (3): 301–25.

———. 2001. "Understanding Desistance from Crime." *Crime and Justice* 28: 1–69.

———. 2003. *Shared Beginnings, Divergent Lives: Delinquent Boys to Age 70*. Cambridge, MA: Harvard University Press.

Laumann, Edward O., John H. Gagnon, Robert T. Michael, and Stuart Michaels. 1994. *The Social Organization of Sexuality: Sexual Practices in the United States*. Chicago: University of Chicago Press.

La Vigne, Nancy, Lisa E. Brooks, and Tracey L. Shollenberger. 2009. *Women on the Outside: Understanding the Experiences of Female Prisoners Returning to Houston, Texas*. Washington, DC: Urban Institute.

La Vigne, Nancy G., and Cynthia A. Mamalian. 2004. *Prisoner Reentry in Georgia*. Washington, DC: Urban Institute.

La Vigne, Nancy G., Cynthia A. Mamalian, Jeremy Travis, and Christy Visher. 2003. "A Portrait of Prisoner Reentry in Illinois." Washington, DC: Urban Institute.

La Vigne, Nancy G., Tracey L. Shollenberger, and Sara Debus. 2009. *One Year Out: The Experiences of Male Returning Prisoners in Houston, Texas*. Washington, DC: Urban Institute.

La Vigne, Nancy G., Gillian L. Thompson, Christy Visher, Vera Kachnowski, and Jeremy Travis. 2003. *A Portrait of Prisoner Reentry in Ohio*. Washington, DC: Urban Institute.

La Vigne, Nancy G., Christy Visher, and Jennifer Castro. 2004. *Chicago Prisoners' Experiences Returning Home*. Washington, DC: Urban Institute.

LeBel, Thomas P. 2007. "An Examination of the Impact of Formerly Incarcerated Persons Helping Others." *Journal of Offender Rehabilitation* 46 (1–2): 1–24.

———. 2012. "Invisible Stripes? Formerly Incarcerated Persons' Perceptions of Stigma." *Deviant Behavior* 33: 89–107.

LeBel, Thomas P., Ros Burnett, Shadd Maruna, and Shawn Bushway. 2008. "The 'Chicken and Egg' of Subjective and Social Factors in Desistance from Crime." *European Journal of Criminology* 5: 130–58.

LeBel, Thomas P., Matt Richie, and Shadd Maruna. 2015. "Helping Others as a Response to Reconcile a Criminal Past: The Role of the Wounded Healer in Prisoner Reentry Programs." *Criminal Justice and Behavior* 42 (1): 108–20.

Lee, Cynthia G., Brian J. Ostrom, and Matthew Kleiman. 2014. "The Measure of Good Lawyering: Evaluating Holistic Defense in Practice." *Albany Law Review* 78: 1215–38.

Lee, Hedwig, Tyler McCormick, Margaret T. Hicken, and Christopher Wildeman. 2015. "Racial Inequalities in Connectedness to Imprisoned Individuals in the United States." *Du Bois Review: Social Science Research on Race* 12 (2): 269–82.

Leon, Chrysanthi S. 2011. *Sex Fiends, Perverts, Pedophiles: Understanding Sex Crime Policy in America*. New York: NYU Press.

Leonard, Pamela. 2002. "A New Profession for an Old Need: Why a Mitigation Specialist Must Be Included on the Capital Defense Team." *Hofstra Law Review* 31 (4): 1134–55.

Levenson, Jill S., and Andrea L. Hern. 2007. "Sex Offender Residence Restrictions: Unintended Consequences and Community Reentry." *Justice Research and Policy* 9 (1): 59–73.

Leverentz, Andrea. 2010. "People, Places, and Things: How Female Ex-Prisoners Negotiate Their Neighborhood Context." *Journal of Contemporary Ethnography* 39 (6): 646–81.

———. 2012. "Narratives of Crime and Criminals: How Places Socially Construct the Crime Problem." *Sociological Forum* 27 (2): 348–71.

———. 2014. *The Ex-Prisoner's Dilemma: How Women Negotiate Competing Narratives of Reentry and Desistance*. New Brunswick, NJ: Rutgers University Press.

———. 2018. "Churning Through the System: How People Engage with the Criminal Justice System When Faced with Short Sentences." *Studies in Law, Politics, and Society* 77: 123–43.

———. 2019. "Beyond Neighborhoods: Activity Spaces of Returning Prisoners." *Social Problems*. Online First.

Liebling, Alison, and Shadd Maruna. 2005. "Introduction: The Effects of Imprisonment Revisited." In *The Effects of Imprisonment*, edited by Alison Liebling and Shadd Maruna, 1–29. New York: Routledge.

Lin, Nan. 2002. *Social Capital: A Theory of Social Structure and Action*. Cambridge: Cambridge University Press.

Link, Bruce G. 1987. "Understanding Labeling Effects in the Area of Mental Disorders: An Assessment of the Effects of Expectations of Rejection." *American Sociological Review* 52: 96–112.

Link, Nathan Wong. 2017. "Paid Your Debt to Society? Legal Financial Obligations and Their Effects on Former Prisoners." PhD dissertation. Philadelphia, PA: Temple University.

Liu, Mingnan, and Kevin Stainback. 2013. "Interviewer Gender Effects on Survey Responses on Marriage-Related Questions." *Public Opinion Quarterly* 77 (2): 606–18.

Lloyd, Caleb D., and Ralph C. Serin. 2012. "Agency and Outcome Expectancies for Crime Desistance: Measuring Offenders' Personal Beliefs about Change." *Psychology, Crime, and Law* 6: 543–65.

Lofland, John, and Lyn Lofland. 1994. *Analyzing Social Settings: A Guide to Qualitative Observation and Analysis*. 3rd ed. Belmont, CA: Wadsworth.

Lopez-Aguado, Patrick. 2018. *Stick Together and Come Back Home: Racial Sorting and the Spillover of Carceral Identity*. Berkeley: University of California Press.

Lopoo, Leonard M., and Bruce Western. 2005. "Incarceration and the Formation and Stability of Marital Unions." *Journal of Marriage and Family* 67: 721–34.

Lowenkamp, Christopher, Marie Van Nostrand, and Alex Holsinger. 2013. *The Hidden Costs of Pretrial Detention*. New York: Arnold Foundation.

Lurigio, Arthur J. 2001. "Effective Services for Parolees with Mental Illnesses." *Crime and Delinquency* 47 (3): 446–61.

Lurigio, Arthur J., Young I. Cho, James A. Swartz, Timothy P. Johnson, Ingrid Graf, and Lillian Pickup. 2003. "Standardized Assessment of Substance-Related, Other Psychiatric, and Comorbid Disorders among Probationers." *International Journal of Offender Therapy and Comparative Criminology* 47 (6): 630–52.

Lynch, John, and William Sabol. 2001. *Prisoner Reentry in Perspective*. Washington, DC: Urban Institute.

MacDonald, John, and Steven Raphael. 2017. "An Analysis of Racial and Ethnic Disparities in Case Dispositions and Sentencing Outcomes for Criminal Cases Presented to and Processed by the Office of the San Francisco District Attorney." Unpublished manuscript, Goldman School of Public Policy, University of California, Berkeley.

Malik-Kane, Kamala, and Christy A. Visher. 2008. "Health and Prisoner Reentry: How Physical, Mental, and Substance Abuse Conditions Shape the Process of Reintegration." Washington, DC: Urban Institute Justice Policy Center.

Mallach, Alan. 2010. *Facing the Urban Challenge: The Federal Government and America's Older Distressed Cities*. Washington, DC: Urban Institute.

Maltz, Michael D. 1984. *Recidivism*. Orlando, FL: Academic Press.
ManpowerGroup. 2017. "ManpowerGroup Reports 4th Quarter and Full Year 2016 Results." Milwaukee, WI: ManpowerGroup. www.manpowergroup.com.
Manza, Jeff, and Christopher Uggen. 2008. *Locked Out: Felon Disenfranchisement and American Democracy*. New York: Oxford University Press.
Marable, Manning, Ian Steinberg, and Keesha Middlemass. 2007. *Racializing Justice, Disenfranchising Lives: The Racism, Criminal Justice and Law Reader*. New York: Palgrave MacMillan.
Markel, Dan. 2004. "Against Mercy." *Minnesota Law Review* 88 (6): 1421–80.
Marshall, Liam E., William L. Marshall, Yolanda M. Fernandez, Bruce Malcom, and Heather M. Moulden. 2008. "The Rockwood Preparatory Program for Sexual Offenders: Description and Preliminary Appraisal." *Sexual Abuse: A Journal of Research and Treatment* 20: 25–42.
Martin, Liam. 2013. "Reentry Within the Carceral: Foucault, Race and Prisoner Reentry." *Critical Criminology* 21 (4): 493–508.
Martinez, Damian. 2006. "Informal Helping Mechanisms: Conceptual Issues in Family Support of Reentry of Former Prisoners." *Journal of Offender Rehabilitation* 44 (1): 23–37.
Martinez, Damian J. 2004. "Felony Disenfranchisement and Voting Participation: Considerations in Latino Ex-Prisoner Reentry." *Columbia Human Rights Law Review* 36 (217): 217–40.
Martinez, Damian J., and Johnna Christian. 2009. "The Familial Relationships of Former Prisoners: Examining the Link between Residence and Informal Support Mechanisms." *Journal of Contemporary Ethnography* 38 (2): 201–24.
Martínez, Jr., Ramiro. 2002. *Latino Homicide: Immigration, Violence, and Community*. New York: Routledge.
———. 2003. "Moving Beyond Black and White Violence: African American, Haitian, and Latino Homicides in Miami." In *Violent Crime: Assessing Race and Ethnic Differences*, edited by Darnell F. Hawkins, 22–43. Cambridge: Cambridge University Press.
Martínez, Jr., Ramiro, Matthew T. Lee, and Amie L. Nielson. 2004. "Segmented Assimilation, Local Context and Determinants of Drug Violence in Miami and San Diego: Does Ethnicity and Immigration Matter?" *International Migration Review* 38 (1): 131–57.
Martínez, Jr., Ramiro, and Amie L. Nielson. 2006. "Extending Ethnicity and Violence Research in a Multiethnic City: Haitian, African American, and Latino Nonlethal Violence." In *The Many Colors of Crime: Inequalities of Race, Ethnicity, and Crime in America*, edited by Ruth Peterson, Lauren Krivo, and John Hagan, 108–21. New York: New York University Press.
Martinson, Robert. 1974. "What Works? Questions and Answers About Prison Reform." *Public Interest* 35 (Spring): 22–54.
Maruna, Shadd. 2001. *Making Good: How Ex-Convicts Reform and Rebuild Their Lives*. Washington, DC: American Psychological Association Books.

———. 2004. "Desistance from Crime and Explanatory Style: A New Direction in the Psychology of Reform." *Journal of Contemporary Criminal Justice* 20: 184–200.
———. 2017. "Desistance as a Social Movement." *Irish Probation Journal* 14: 5–20.
Maruna, Shadd, and Thomas P. LeBel. 2003. "Welcome Home? Examining the 'Reentry Court' Concept from a Strengths-Based Perspective." *Western Criminology Review* 4 (2): 91–107.
———. 2009. "Strengths-Based Approaches to Reentry: Extra Mileage Toward Reintegration and Destigmatization." *Japanese Journal of Sociological Criminology* 34: 59–80.
Maruna, Shadd, Louise Wilson, and Kathryn Curran. 2006. "Why God Is Often Found behind Bars: Prison Conversions and the Crisis of Self-Narrative." *Research in Human Development and Psychopathology* 32 (2–3): 161–84.
Massetti, Greta M., and Corrine David-Ferdon. 2016. "Preventing Violence Among High-Risk Youth and Communities with Economic, Policy, and Structural Strategies." Atlanta, GA: Centers for Disease Control and Prevention. www.cdc.gov.
Massoglia, Michael, Glenn Firebaugh, and Cody Warner. 2013. "Racial Variation in the Effect of Incarceration on Neighborhood Attainment." *American Sociological Review* 78 (1): 142–65.
Mauer, Marc. 2006. *Race to Incarcerate*. 2nd ed. Washington, DC: Sentencing Project.
Mauer, Marc, and Meda Chesney-Lind. 2002. *Invisible Punishment: The Collateral Consequences of Mass Imprisonment*. Washington, DC: Sentencing Project.
Mawby, B. I., and I. D. Batta. 1980. *Asians and Crime: The Bradford Experience*. Middlesex: Scope Communications.
May, David C., Brandon K. Applegate, Rick Ruddell, and Peter B. Wood. 2014. "Going to Jail Sucks (And It Really Doesn't Matter Who You Ask)." *American Journal of Criminal Justice* 39 (2): 250–66.
May, Reuben A. B. 2014. "When the Methodological Shoe Is on the Other Foot: African American Interviewer and White Interviewees." *Qualitative Sociology* 37 (1): 117–36.
May, Reuben A. B., and Mary Patillo-McCoy. 2000. "Do You See What I See? Examining a Collaborative Ethnography." *Qualitative Inquiry* 6 (1): 63–87.
Mayorga-Gallo, Sarah, and Elizabeth Hordge-Freeman. 2017. "Between Marginality and Privilege: Gaining Access and Navigating the Field in Multiethnic Settings." *Qualitative Research* 17 (4): 377–94.
Mazzei, Julie, and Erin E. O'Brien. 2008. "You Got It, So When Do You Flaunt It?" *Journal of Contemporary Ethnography* 38 (3): 358–83.
McAdams, Dan P. 2008. "The Life Story Interview." Foley Center for the Study of Lives. www.sesp.northwestern.edu.
———. 2012. "Exploring Psychological Themes Through Life-Narrative Accounts." In *Varieties of Narrative Analysis*, edited by James A. Holstein and Jaber F. Gubrium, 15–32. Los Angeles: Sage.
———. 2013. *The Redemptive Self*. New York: Oxford University Press.

McAdams, Dan P., Barry J. Hoffman, Rodney Day, and Elizabeth D. Mansfield. 1996. "Themes of Agency and Communion in Significant Autobiographical Scenes." *Personality* 64 (2): 229–77.

McAdams, Dan P., Jeffrey Reynolds, Martha Lewis, Allison Patton, and Phillip J. Bowman. 2001. "When Bad Things Turn Good and Good Things Turn Bad: Sequences of Redemption and Contamination in Life Narratives and Their Relation to Psychosocial Adaptation in Midlife Adults and in Students." *Personality and Social Psychology Bulletin* 27 (4): 474–85.

McCarty, Christopher, Peter D. Killworth, and James Rennell. 2007. "Impact of Methods for Reducing Respondent Burden on Personal Network Structural Measures." *Social Networks* 29 (2): 300–315.

McCorkel, Jill A. 2013. *Breaking Women: Gender, Race, and the New Politics of Imprisonment*. New York: New York University Press.

McCorkel, Jill A., and Kristen Myers. 2003. "What Difference Does Difference Make? Position and Privilege in the Field." *Qualitative Sociology* 26 (2): 199–231.

McCorkle, Richard, and John P. Crank. 1996. "Meet the New Boss: Institutional Change and Loose Coupling in Parole and Probation." *American Journal of Criminal Justice* 21 (1): 1–25.

McCoy, Candace, and Patrick McManimon, Jr. 2004. *New Jersey's "No Early Release Act": Its Impact on Prosecution, Sentencing, Corrections, and Victim Satisfaction. Final Report Grant #98-CE-VX-0007*. Washington, DC: National Institute of Justice.

McGloin, Jean Marie, and David S. Kirk. 2010. "Social Network Analysis." In *Handbook of Quantitative Criminology*, edited by Alex Piquero and David Weisburd, 209–24. New York: Springer.

McLaughlin, Diane K., and C. Shannon Stokes. 2002. "Income Inequality and Mortality in US Counties: Does Minority Racial Concentration Matter?" *American Journal of Public Health* 92: 99–104.

McNeil, Dale E., Renee L. Binder, and Jo C. Robinson. 2005. "Incarceration Associated with Homelessness, Mental Disorder, and Co-Occurring Substance Abuse." *Psychiatric Services* 56 (7): 840–46.

McNeill, Fergus. 2017. "Punishment, Rehabilitation, and Reintegration." *Discovering Desistance* (blog). http://blogs.iriss.org.uk.

McNeill, Fergus, and Shadd Maruna. 2007. "Giving Up and Giving Back: Desistance, Generativity and Social Work with Offenders." In *Developments in Social Work with Offenders*, edited by Gill McIvor and Peter Raynor, 224–39. London: Jessica Kingsley.

Mears, Daniel P., Xia Wang, Carter Hay, and William D. Bales. 2008. "Social Ecology and Recidivism: Implications for Prisoner Reentry." *Criminology* 46 (2): 301–40.

Mehl, Matthias R., and Tamlin S. Conner, eds. 2012. *Handbook of Research Methods for Studying Daily Life*. New York: Guilford.

Mendenhall, Ruby, Kathryn Edin, Susan Crowley, Jennifer Sykes, Laura Tach, Katrin Kriz, and Jeffrey R. Kling. 2012. "The Role of Earned Income Tax Credit in the Budgets of Low-Income Households." *Social Service Review* 86 (3): 367–400.

Menjívar, Cecilia, and Cynthia L. Bejarano. 2004. "Latino Immigrants' Perceptions of Crime and Police Authorities in the United States: A Case Study from the Phoenix Metropolitan Area." *Ethnic and Racial Studies* 27 (1): 120–48.

Mercado, Cynthia Calkins, Shea Alvarez, and Jill Levenson. 2008. "The Impact of Specialized Sex Offender Legislation on Community Reentry." *Sexual Abuse: A Journal of Research and Treatment* 20 (2): 188–205.

Merton, Robert K. 1938. "Social Structure and Anomie." *American Sociological Review* 3 (5): 672–82.

Middlemass, Keesha. 2014. "War as Metaphor: The Convergence of the War on Poverty and The War on Drugs." In *The War on Poverty: A Retrospective*, edited by Kyle Farmbry, 85–104. Lanham, MD: Lexington Books.

———. 2017. *Convicted and Condemned: The Politics and Policies of Prisoner Reentry*. New York: New York University Press.

Middlemass, Keesha, and Calvin John Smiley. 2016. "Doing a Bid: The Construction of Time as Punishment." *Prison Journal* 96 (6): 793–813.

Mijs, Jonathan JB. 2016. "The Missing Organizational Dimension of Prisoner Reentry: An Ethnography of the Road to Reentry at a Nonprofit Service Provider." *Sociological Forum* 31 (2): 291–309.

Miller, Holly V., and J. Mitchell Miller. 2010. "Community In-Reach Through Jail Reentry: Findings from a Quasi-Experimental Design." *Justice Quarterly* 27 (6): 898–910.

Miller, Jody. 2001. *One of the Guys: Girls, Gangs, and Gender*. New York: Oxford University Press.

Miller, Reuben J. 2014. "Devolving the Carceral State: Race, Prisoner Reentry, and the Micro-Politics of Urban Poverty Management." *Punishment and Society* 16 (3): 305–35.

Miller, Reuben J., and Forrest Stuart. 2017. "Carceral Citizenship: Race, Rights, and Responsibility in the Age of Mass Supervision." *Theoretical Criminology* 21 (4): 532–48.

Miller, Riane N., Brandon K. Applegate, and William R. King. 2013. "May We Help You? Applying Organizational Theory to Predict Jails' Human Service Orientation." Paper presented at the Academy of Criminal Justice Sciences, Dallas, TX.

Mills, Alice, and Helen Codd. 2008. "Prisoners' Families and Offender Management: Mobilizing Social Capital." *Probation Journal* 55 (1): 9–24.

Minton, Todd D. 2013. "Jail Inmates at Midyear 2012—Statistical Tables." Bureau of Justice Statistical Tables NCJ 241264. Washington, DC: Department of Justice, Office of Justice Programs.

Minton, Todd D., and Zhen Zeng. 2016. *Jail Inmates in 2015*. Washington, DC: Bureau of Justice Statistics.

Missouri Board of Probation and Parole. 2017. *2016 Annual Report*. Jefferson City: Missouri Department of Corrections. https://doc.mo.gov.

Missouri Department of Mental Health. 2014. *Status on Health and Mental Health, 2013–2014*. Columbus. https://dmh.mo.gov.

Mitchell, Ojmarrh. 2005. "A Meta-Analysis of Race and Sentencing Research: Explaining the Inconsistencies." *Journal of Quantitative Criminology* 21: 439–66.

Model, Suzanne. 1995. "West Indian Prosperity: Fact or Fiction?" *Social Problems* 42 (4): 535–53.

Moffitt, Terrie E. 1993. "Adolescence-Limited and Life-Course-Persistent Antisocial Behavior: A Developmental Taxonomy." *Psychological Review* 100 (4): 647–701.

Moore, L., D. Youngs, and B. Ritter. 2006. "Statewide Data Warehouse Design: A Case Study on the Statewide Homeless Assistance Data Online Warehouse (SHADoW)." 2006. www.dropbox.com.

Morash, Merry. 2010. *Women on Probation and Parole: A Feminist Critique of Community Programs and Services*. Boston: Northeastern University Press.

Morenoff, Jeffrey D., and Avraham Astor. 2006. "Immigrant Assimilation and Crime: Generational Differences in Youth Violence in Chicago." In *Immigration and Crime*, edited by Ramiro Martínez, Jr. and Abel Valenzuela, Jr., 36–63. New York: New York University Press.

Morenoff, Jeffrey D., and David J. Harding. 2014. "Incarceration, Prisoner Reentry, and Communities." *Annual Review of Sociology* 40: 411–29.

Morris, Norval. 1977. *Future of Imprisonment*. Chicago: University of Chicago Press.

Mowen, Thomas J., Eric J. Wodahl, John H. Boman, and Brett E. Garland. 2015. "Responding to Probation and Parole Violations: Are Jail Sanctions More Effective than Community-Based Graduated Sanctions?" *Journal of Criminal Justice* 43 (3): 242–50.

Mowen, Thomas J., Eric J. Wodahl, John J. Brent, and Brett E. Garland. 2018. "The Role of Sanctions and Incentives in Promoting Successful Reentry: Evidence from the SVORI Data." *Criminal Justice and Behavior* 45 (8): 1288–1307.

Mumola, Christopher J. 2000. "Incarcerated Parents and Their Children." Bureau of Justice Statistics Special Report NCJ 182335. Washington, DC: Department of Justice, Office of Justice Programs.

Mumola, Christopher J., and Jennifer C. Karberg. 2006. "Drug Use and Dependence, State and Federal Prisoners, 2004." Washington, DC: US Department of Justice.

Muñoz, Ed A., Barbara J. McMorris, and Matt J. DeLisi. 2004. "Misdemeanor Criminal Justice: Contextualizing Effects of Latino Ethnicity, Gender, and Immigrant Status." *Race, Gender, and Class* 11 (4): 1112–34.

Murguia, Edward, and Edward E. Telles. 1996. "Phenotype and Schooling among Mexican Americans." *Sociology of Education* 69 (4): 276–89.

Murray, Joseph, and David P. Farrington. 2008. "Parental Imprisonment: Long-Lasting Effects on Boys' Internalizing Problems through the Life Course." *Development and Psychopathology* 20 (1): 273–90.

Murray, Joseph, David P. Farrington, and Ivana Sekol. 2012. "Children's Antisocial Behavior, Mental Health, Drug Use, and Educational Performance After Parental Incarceration: A Systematic Review and Meta-Analysis." *Psychological Bulletin* 138 (2): 175–210.

Nagin, Dan, Francis Cullen, and Cheryl Jonson. 2009. "Imprisonment and Reoffending." In *Crime and Justice: An Annual Review of Research*, edited by Michael Tonry. Chicago: University of Chicago Press.

Nagin, Daniel S. 2016. "Project HOPE: Does It Work?" *Criminology and Public Policy* 15 (4): 1005–7.

Nally, John, Susan Lockwood, Katie Knutson, and Taiping Ho. 2012. "An Evaluation of the Effect of Correctional Education Programs on Post-Release Recidivism and Employment: An Empirical Study in Indiana." *Journal of Correctional Education* 63 (1): 69–89.

Naples, Nancy A. 1996. "A Feminist Revisiting of the Insider/Outsider Debate: The 'Outsider Phenomenon' in Rural Iowa." *Qualitative Sociology* 19 (1): 83–106.

Naser, Rebecca L., and Nancy La Vigne. 2006. "Family Support in the Prisoner Reentry Process: Expectations and Realities." *Journal of Offender Rehabilitation* 43 (1): 93–106.

Naser, Rebecca L., and Christy A. Visher. 2006. "Family Members' Experiences with Incarceration and Reentry." *Western Criminology Review* 7 (2): 20–31.

National Household Survey on Drug Use and Health (2016). Indicators as measured through the 2015 National Survey on Drug Use and Health, the National Survey of Substance Abuse Treatment Services, and the Uniform Reporting System. https://store.samhsa.gov.

National Institute of Corrections. 2012. *Motivational Interviewing in Corrections: A Comprehensive Guide to Implementing MI in Corrections*. Washington, DC.

National Research Council. 2012. "Reforming Juvenile Justice: A Developmental Approach." Washington, DC: National Academies Press.

———. 2014. "The Growth of Incarceration in the United States: Exploring Causes and Consequences." Washington, DC: National Academies Press.

Nelson, Camille A. 2006. "Of Egg-Shells and Thin-Skulls: A Consideration of Racism-Related Mental Illness Affecting Black Women." *International Journal of Law and Psychiatry* 29 (2): 112–36.

Nelson, Marta, Perry Deess, and Charlotte Allen. 1999. "The First Month Out." New York: Vera Institute of Justice.

Nesmith, Ande, and Ebony Ruhland. 2008. "Children of Incarcerated Parents: Challenges and Resiliency, In Their Own Words." *Children and Youth Services Review* 30 (10): 1119–30.

Nurse, Anne. 2002. *Fatherhood Arrested: Parenting from Within the Juvenile Justice System*. Nashville, TN: Vanderbilt University Press.

O'Connell, Daniel J., John J. Brent, and Christy A. Visher. 2016. "Decide Your Time: A Randomized Trial of a Drug Testing and Graduated Sanctions Program for Probationers." *Criminology and Public Policy* 15 (4): 1073–1102.

Office of Justice Programs. 2017. "Diagnostic Analysis for the City of St. Louis, Missouri: Opportunities for Evidence-Based Technical Assistance." Washington, DC: Department of Justice.

Olusanya, Olaoluwa, and Jeffrey M. Cancino. 2012. "Cross-Examining the Race-Neutral Frameworks of Prisoner Re-Entry." *Critical Criminology* 20 (4): 345–58.

Orrico, Laura A. 2015. "'Doing Intimacy' in a Public Market: How the Gendered Experience of Ethnography Reveals Situated Social Dynamics." *Qualitative Research* 15 (4): 473–88.

Osher, Fred, Henry J. Steadman, and Heather Barr. 2003. "A Best Practice Approach to Community Reentry from Jails for Inmates with Co-Occurring Disorders: The APIC Model." *Crime and Delinquency* 49 (1): 79–96.

Owen, Barbara. 1998. *"In the Mix" Struggle and Survival in a Women's Prison*. Albany: State University of New York Press.

———. 2005. "Gendered Harm in the Contemporary Prison." In *The Warehouse Prison*, edited by John Irwin, 240–60. Los Angeles: Roxbury.

Owen, Barbara, James Wells, and Joycelyn Pollock. 2017. *In Search of Safety: Confronting Inequality in Women's Imprisonment*. Oakland: University of California Press.

Padgett, Kathy, William D. Bales, and Thomas Blomberg. 2006. "Under Surveillance: An Empirical Test of the Effectiveness and Consequences of Electronic Monitoring." *Criminology and Public Policy* 5: 61–91.

Pager, Devah. 2006. "Evidence for Successful Prisoner Reentry." *Criminology and Public Policy* 5: 505–14.

———. 2007. *Marked: Race, Crime, and Finding Work in an Era of Mass Incarceration*. Chicago: University of Chicago Press.

Pager, Devah, Bruce Western, and Naomi Sugie. 2009. "Sequencing Disadvantage: Barriers to Employment Facing Young Black and White Men with Criminal Records." *ANNALS of the American Academy of Political and Social Science* 623 (1): 195–213.

Painter, Matthew A., Malcom D. Holmes, and Jenna Bateman. 2016. "Skin Tone, Race/Ethnicity, and Wealth Inequality Among New Immigrants." *Social Forces* 94 (3): 1153–85.

Papachristos, Andrew. 2014. "The Network Structure of Crime." *Sociology Compass* 8 (4): 347–57.

Parisi, Nicolette. 1982. *Coping with Imprisonment*. Thousand Oaks, CA: Sage.

Paternoster, Ray, Ronet Bachman, Erin Kerrison, Daniel O'Connell, and Lionel Smith. 2016. "Desistance from Crime and Identity: An Empirical Test with Survival Time." *Criminal Justice and Behavior* 43 (9): 1204–24.

Paternoster, Ray, and Shawn Bushway. 2009. "Desistance and the 'Feared Self': Toward an Identity Theory of Criminal Desistance." *Journal of Criminal Law and Criminology* 99 (4): 1103–56.

Patillo, Mary, David F. Weiman, and Bruce Western. 2004. *Imprisoning America: The Social Effects of Mass Incarceration*. New York: Russell Sage Foundation.

Patillo-McCoy, Mary. 1999. *Black Picket Fences: Privilege and Peril in the Black Middle Class*. Chicago: University of Chicago Press.

Patterson, Joan. 2002. "Integrating Family Resilience and Family Stress Theory." *Journal of Marriage and Family* 64 (2): 349–60.

Patton, Michael Quinn. 1990. *Qualitative Evaluation and Research Methods*. Newbury Park, CA: Sage.

Payne, Yasser Arafat. 2011. "Site of Resilience: A Reconceptualization of Resiliency and Resilience in Street Life-Oriented Black Men." *Journal of Black Psychology* 37 (4): 426–51.

Pearlin, Leonard I. 1989. "The Sociological Study of Stress." *Journal of Health and Social Behavior* 30 (3): 241–56.

Petersilia, Joan. 1999. "A Decade of Experimenting with Intermediate Sanctions: What Have We Learned?" *Justice Research and Policy* 1: 9–23.

———. 2003. *When Prisoners Come Home: Parole and Prisoner Reentry*. New York: Oxford University Press.

———. 2012. "Looking Back to See the Future of Prison Downsizing in America." Keynote Address presented at the National Institute of Justice Conference. http://nij.ncjrs.gov.

Peterson, Ruth, Lauren Krivo, and John Hagan. 2006. "Introduction: Inequalities of Race, Ethnicity, and Crime in America." In *The Many Colors of Crime: Inequalities of Race, Ethnicity, and Crime in America*, edited by Ruth Peterson, Lauren Krivo, and John Hagan, 1–7. New York: New York University Press.

Pettit, Becky. 2012. *Invisible Men: Mass Incarceration and the Myth of Black Progress*. New York: Russell Sage Foundation.

Pettit, Becky, and Bruce Western. 2004. "Mass Imprisonment in the Life Course." *American Sociological Review* 69 (4): 151–69.

Pew Center on the States. 2009. *One in 31: The Long Reach of American Corrections*. Washington, DC: Pew Charitable Trusts.

———. 2011a. *The Impact of Arizona's Probation Reforms*. Washington, DC: Pew Charitable Trusts.

———. 2011b. State of Recidivism: The Revolving Door of America's Prisons. Retrieved from www.ncjrs.gov.

Pfaff, John. 2017. *Locked In: The True Causes of Mass Incarceration and How to Achieve Real Reform*. New York: Basic Books.

Phelps, Michelle S. 2011. "Rehabilitation in the Punitive Era: The Gap Between Rhetoric and Reality in US Prison Programs." *Law and Society Review* 45 (1): 33–68.

———. 2013. "The Paradox of Probation: Community Supervision in the Age of Mass Incarceration." *Law and Policy* 35 (1–2): 51–80.

———. 2017. "Discourses of Mass Probation: From Managing Risk to Ending Human Warehousing in Michigan." *British Journal of Criminology* 58 (5): 1–20.

Phelps, Michelle S., and Devah Pager. 2016. "Inequality and Punishment: A Turning Point for Mass Incarceration?" *ANNALS of the American Academy of Political and Social Science* 663 (1): 185–203.

Piehl, Anne M., David M. Kennedy, and Anthony A. Braga. 2000. "Problem Solving and Youth Violence: An Evaluation of the Boston Gun Project." *American Law and Economics Association* 2 (1): 58–106.

Pini, Barbara. 2005. "Interviewing Men: Gender and the Collection and Interpretation of Qualitative Data." *Journal of Sociology* 41 (2): 201–16.

Piquero, Alex R. 2015. "Understanding Race/Ethnicity Differences in Offending Across the Life Course: Gaps and Opportunities." *Journal of Developmental and Life-Course Criminology* 1: 21–32.

Poe-Yamagata, Eileen. 2009. *And Justice for Some: Differential Treatment of Minority Youth in the Justice System*. Darby, PA: DIANE Publishing.

Portes, Alejandro, Luis Eduardo Guarnizo, and William J. Haller. 2002. "Transnational Entrepreneurs: An Alternative Form of Immigrant Economic Adaptation." *American Sociological Review* 67 (2): 278–98.

Portes, Alejandro, and Rubén G. Rumbaut. 2014. *Immigrant America: A Portrait*. 4th ed. Berkeley: University of California Press.

Putnam, Robert. 2000. *Bowling Alone: The Collapse and Revival of American Community*. New York: Simon & Schuster.

Redcross, Cindy, Megan Millenky, Timothy Rudd, and Valerie Levshin. 2012. "More Than a Job: Final Results from the Evaluation of the Center for Employment Opportunities (CEO) Transitional Jobs Program." New York: MDRC.

Repak, Terry A. 2010. *Waiting on Washington: Central American Workers in the Nation's Capital*. Philadelphia, PA: Temple University Press.

Richards, Stephen C., and Jeffrey I. Ross. 2001. "Introducing the New School of Convict Criminology." *Social Justice* 28 (1): 177–90.

Robbers, Monica L. P. 2009. "Lifers on the Outside: Sex Offenders and Disintegrative Shaming." *International Journal of Offender Therapy and Comparative Criminology* 53 (1): 5–28.

Roberts, Julian V. (ed.). 2011 *Mitigation and Aggravation at Sentencing*. Cambridge: Cambridge University Press.

Roberts, Margaret E., Brandom M. Stewart, Dustin Tingley, Christopher Lucas, Jetson Leder-Luis, Shana Gadarian Kushner, Bethany Albertson, and David G. Rand. 2014. "Structural Topic Models for Open-Ended Survey Responses." *American Journal of Political Science* 58 (4): 1064–82.

Robins, Garry. 2015. *Doing Social Network Research: Network-Based Research Design for Social Scientists*. London: Sage.

Robinson, Gwen. 2008. "Late-Modern Rehabilitation: The Evolution of a Penal Strategy." *Punishment and Society* 10 (4): 429–45.

Rodríguez, Clara E. 2000. *Changing Race: Latinos, the Census, and the History of Ethnicity in the United States*. New York: New York University Press.

Rodriguez, Michelle, and Maurice Emsellem. 2011. *65 Million Need Not Apply: The Case for Reforming Criminal Background Checks for Employment*. New York: National Employment Law Project.

Rodriguez, Nancy, and Vincent J. Webb. 2007. "Probation Violations, Revocations, and Imprisonment: The Decisions of Probation Officers, Prosecutors, and Judges Pre- and Post-Mandatory Drug Treatment." *Criminal Justice Policy Review* 18 (1): 3–30.

Román, Ediberto. 1997. "Common Ground: Perspectives on Latino-Latina Diversity." *Harvard Latino Law Review* 2: 483–94.

Rondilla, Joanne, and Paul Spickard. 2007. *Is Lighter Better?* Lanham, MD: Rowman & Littlefield.

Rooney, Shannon. 2015. "What Does It Cost to Rent a One-Bedroom in Philadelphia?" *Philadelphia Inquirer*, August 3. www.philly.com.

Root, Maria P. 1996. *The Multiracial Experience: Racial Borders as the New Frontier*. Thousand Oaks, CA: Sage.

Rose, Dina R., and Todd R. Clear. 1998. "Incarceration, Social Capital, and Crime: Implications for Social Disorganization Theory." *Criminology* 36 (3): 441–80.

Rose, Susan J., and Thomas P. LeBel. 2017. "Incarcerated Mothers of Minor Children: Physical Health, Substance Use, and Mental Health Needs." *Women and Criminal Justice* 27 (3): 170–90.

Rosenberg, Morris. 1965. *Society and the Adolescent Self-Image*. Princeton, NJ: Princeton University Press.

Rosenberg, Morris, and Timothy J. Owens. 2001. "Low Self-Esteem People: A Collective Portrait." In *Extending Self-Esteem Theory and Research: Sociological and Psychological Currents*, edited by Timothy J. Owens, Sheldon Stryker, and Norman Goodman, 400–436. Cambridge: Cambridge University Press.

Rosenfeld, Richard. 2008. "Recidivism and Its Discontents." *Criminology and Public Policy* 7 (2): 311–17.

———. 2016. *Firearm Assault in St. Louis: Preliminary Overview*. Unpublished manuscript. Department of Criminology and Criminal Justice, University of Missouri St. Louis.

Rosenmerkel, Sean, Matthew Durose, and Donald Farole Jr. 2009. "Felony Sentences in State Courts, 2006—Statistical Tables." NCJ 226846. Washington, DC: Department of Justice, Office of Justice Programs, Bureau of Justice Statistics.

Rosenthal, Carolyn J. 1985. "Kinkeeping in the Familial Division of Labor." *Journal of Marriage and Family* 47 (4): 965–74.

Ross, Jeffrey I., and Stephen C. Richards. 2003. *Convict Criminology*. Belmont, CA: Wadsworth.

Rucker, Lila. 1994. "Coercive Versus Cooperative Environments: The Collateral Effects in Prisons." *Prison Journal* 73 (1): 73–92.

Rumbaut, Rubén G., Roberto G. Gonzales, Golnaz Komaie, Charlie V. Morgan, and Rosaura Tafoya-Estrada. 2006. "Immigration and Incarceration: Patterns and Predictors of Imprisonment among First- and Second-Generation Young Adults." In *Immigration and Crime*, edited by Ramiro Martínez, Jr. and Abel Valenzuela, Jr., 64–89. New York: New York University Press.

Rumgay, Judith. 2004. "Scripts for Safer Survival: Pathways Out of Female Crime." *Howard Journal of Criminal Justice* 43 (4): 405–19.

Russell, Gemma, Fred Seymour, and Ian Lambie. 2013. "Community Reintegration of Sex Offenders of Children in New Zealand." *International Journal of Offender Therapy and Comparative Criminology* 57 (1): 55–70.

Russell, Katheryn, and Dragan Milovanovic. 2001. *Petit Apartheid in the US Criminal Justice System: The Dark Figure of Racism*. Durham, NC: Carolina Academic Press.

Russell-Brown, Katheryn. 2004. *Underground Codes: Race, Crime, and Related Fires*. New York: New York University Press.

Ryan, Tracey, and Kimberly McCabe. 1994. "Mandatory vs Voluntary Prison Education and Academic Achievement." *Prison Journal* 74 (4): 450–61.

Salganik, Matthew J., and Karen E. C. Levy. 2015. "Wiki Surveys: Open and Quantifiable Social Data Collection." *PLoS ONE* 10 (5).

Sampson, Robert J. 2011. "The Incarceration Ledger." *Criminology and Public Policy* 10 (3): 819–28.

Sampson, Robert J., and John H. Laub. 1993. *Crime in the Making: Pathways and Turning Points through Life*. Cambridge, MA: Harvard University Press.

Sanders, Jimy M. 2002. "Ethnic Boundaries and Identity in Plural Societies." *Annual Review of Sociology* 28: 327–57.

Sarchiapone, M., N. Jovanovic, A. Roy, A. Podlesek, V. Carli, M. Amore, M. Mancini, and A. Marusic. 2009. "Relationship of Psychological Characteristics to Suicide Behavior: Results from a Large Sample of Male Prisoners." *Personality and Individual Differences* 47 (4): 250–55.

Schaefer, David R., Martin Bouchard, Jacob T. N. Young, and Derek A. Kreager. 2017. "Friends in Locked Places: An Investigation of Prison Inmate Network Structure." *Social Networks* 51: 88–103.

Schaeffer, Nora Cate. 1980. "Evaluating Race-of-Interviewer Effects in a National Survey." *Sociological Methods and Research* 8 (4): 400–419.

Schiraldi, Vincent. 2018. "The Pennsylvania Community Corrections Story." Columbia Justice Lab. http://justicelab.iserp.columbia.edu.

Schlosser, Jennifer A. 2008. "Issues in Inmate Interviewing: Navigating the Methodological Landmines of Prison Research." *Qualitative Inquiry* 14 (8): 1500–25.

Schneider, Meghan. 2010. "From Criminal Confinement to Social Confinement: Helping Ex-Offenders Obtain Public Housing with a Certificate of Rehabilitation." *New England Journal on Criminal and Civil Confinement* 36 (2): 355–58.

Schnittker, Jason. 2013. "The Psychological Dimensions and the Social Consequences of Incarceration." *ANNALS of the American Academy of Political and Social Science* 651 (1): 122–38.

Schnittker, Jason, and Andrea John. 2016. "Enduring Stigma: The Long-Term Effects of Incarceration on Health." *Journal of Health and Social Behavior* 48 (2): 115–30.

Schnittker, Jason, Michael Massoglia, and Christopher Uggen. 2011. "Incarceration and the Health of the African American Community." *Du Bois Review: Social Science Research on Race* 8 (1): 133–41.

Schnittker, Jason, Christopher Uggen, Sarah K. S. Shannon, and Suzy M. McElrath. 2015. "The Institutional Effects of Incarceration: Spillovers from Criminal Justice to Health Care." *Milbank Quarterly* 93 (3): 516–60.

Schoenfeld, Heather. 2018. *Building the Prison State: Race and the Politics of Mass Incarceration*. Chicago: University of Chicago Press.

Schuman, Howard. 1966. "The Random Probe: A Technique for Evaluating the Validity of Closed Questions." *American Sociological Review* 31 (2): 218–22.

Schuman, Howard, and Stanley Presser. 1979. "The Open and Closed Question." *American Sociological Review* 44 (5): 692–712.

Schwartz-Soicher, Ofira, Amanda Geller, and Irwin Garfinkle. 2011. "The Effect of Paternal Incarceration on Material Hardship." *Social Service Review* 85 (3): 447–73.

Serin, Ralph, Nick Chadwick, and Caleb D. Lloyd. 2016. "Dynamic Risk and Protective Factors." *Psychology, Crime, and Law* 22 (1): 1–44.

Shapiro, Carol, and Meryl Schwartz. 2001. "Coming Home: Building on Family Connections." *Corrections Management Quarterly* 5 (3): 52–61.

Sharkey, Patrick. 2006. "Navigating Dangerous Streets: The Sources and Consequences of Street Efficacy." *American Sociological Review* 71 (5): 826–46.

Sharkey, Patrick, and Robert J. Sampson. 2010. "Destination Effects; Residential Mobility and Trajectories of Adolescent Violence in a Stratified Metropolis." *Criminology* 48 (3): 639–81.

Sharpe, Gilly. 2017. "Sociological Stalking? Methods, Ethics and Power in Longitudinal Criminological Research." *Criminology and Criminal Justice* 17 (3): 233–47.

Shaw, Clifford R. 1930. *The Jack-Roller: A Delinquent Boy's Own Story*. Chicago: University of Chicago Press.

Shaw, Clifford R., and Henry D. McKay. 1972. *Juvenile Delinquency and Urban Areas*. Chicago: University of Chicago Press.

Sherman, Laurence W., Denise C. Gottfredson, Doris L. MacKenzie, John Eck, Peter Reuter, and Shawn D. Bushway. 1997. "Preventing Crime: What Works, What Doesn't, What's Promising." Washington, DC: National Institute of Justice.

Shih, Johanna. 2002. ". . . 'Yeah, I Could Hire This One, but I Know It's Gonna Be a Problem': How Race, Nativity and Gender Affect Employers' Perceptions of the Manageability of Job Seekers." *Ethnic and Racial Studies* 25 (1): 99–119.

Shinkfield, Alison J., and Joseph Graffam. 2009. "Community Reintegration of Ex-Prisoners: Type and Degree of Change in Variables Influencing Successful Reintegration." *International Journal of Offender Therapy and Comparative Criminology* 53 (1): 29–42.

Shollenberger, Tracey L. 2009. "When Relatives Return: Interviews with Family Members of Returning Prisoners in Houston, Texas." Washington, DC: Urban Institute Justice Policy Center.

Siegel, Jane. 2011. *Disrupted Childhoods: Children of Women in Prison*. New Brunswick, NJ: Rutgers University Press.

Simes, Jessica T. 2018. "Place After Prison: Neighborhood Attainment and Attachment During Reentry." *Journal of Urban Affairs* 16 (1): 1–21.

Simon, Jonathan. 2007. *Governing Through Crime: How the War on Crime Transformed American Democracy and Created a Culture of Fear*. New York: Oxford University Press.

Skarbeck, David. 2012. "Prison Gangs, Norms, and Organizations." *Journal of Economic Behavior and Organization* 82 (1): 96–109.

Smith, Jeffrey A., and James Moody. 2013. "Structural Effects of Network Sampling Coverage I: Nodes Missing at Random." *Social Networks* 35 (4): 652–68.

Smoyer, Amy B., Kim M. Blankenship, and Brandis Belt. 2009. "Compensation for Incarcerated Research Participants: Diverse State Policies Suggest a New Research Agenda." *American Journal of Public Health* 99 (10): 1746–52.

Snodgrass, Jon. 1982. *The Jack-Roller at Seventy: A Fifty-Year Follow-Up*. Lexington, MA: Lexington Books.

Snyder, Howard N., and Melissa Sickmund. 1999. "Minorities in the Juvenile Justice System." 1999 National Report Series NCJ 178257. Washington, DC: Office of Juvenile Justice and Delinquency Prevention.

Solomon, Amy L., Jenny W. L. Osborne, Stefan F. LoBuglio, Jeff Mellow, and Debbie A. Mukamal. 2008. *Life After Lockup: Improving Reentry from Jail to the Community*. Washington, DC: Urban Institute.

Soyer, Michaela. 2014. "Off the Corner and Into the Kitchen: Entering a Male-Dominated Research Setting as a Woman." *Qualitative Research* 14 (4): 459–72.

———. 2016. *A Dream Denied: Incarceration, Recidivism, and Young Minority Men in America*. Berkeley: University of California Press.

Srivastava, Prachi, and Nick Hopwood. 2009. "A Practical Iterative Framework for Qualitative Data Analysis." *International Journal of Qualitative Methods* 8 (1): 76–84.

Stack, Carol B. 1974. *All Our Kin: Strategies for Survival in a Black Community*. New York: Harper & Row.

State of New York Department of Correctional Services. 2009. *2004 Releases: Three Year Post Release Follow-Up*. Albany: State of New York Department of Correctional Services.

Steffensmeier, Darrell, and Stephen Demuth. 2000. "Ethnicity and Sentencing Outcomes in US Federal Courts: Who Is Punished More Harshly?" *American Sociological Review* 65: 705–29.

Steffensmeier, Darrell, Ben Feldmeyer, Casey T. Harris, and Jeffrey T. Ulmer. 2011. "Reassessing Trends in Black Violent Crime, 1980–2008: Sorting Out the 'Hispanic Effect' in Uniform Crime Reports Arrests, National Crime Victimization Survey Offender Estimates, and US Prisoner Counts." *Criminology* 49 (1): 197–251.

Steffensmeier, Darrell J. 1986. *The Fence: In the Shadow of Two Worlds*. Totowa, NJ: Rowman & Littlefield.

Steffensmeier, Darrell J., and Jeffrey T. Ulmer. 2005. *Confessions of a Dying Thief: Understanding Criminal Careers and Illegal Enterprise*. New Brunswick: Aldine de Gruyter.

Steffensmeier, Darrell, Jeffrey T. Ulmer, Ben Feldmeyer, and Casey T. Harris. 2010. "Scope and Conceptual Issues in Testing the Race-Crime Invariance Thesis: Black, White, and Hispanic Comparisons." *Criminology* 48 (4): 1133–69.

Stephan, James. 2008. "Census of State and Federal Correctional Facilities, 2005." NCJ 222182. Washington, DC: US Department of Justice, Office of Justice Programs, Bureau of Justice Statistics.

Stevenson, Bryan. 2014. *Just Mercy: A Story of Justice and Redemption*. New York: Spiegel and Grau.

Stinson, Jill D., and Michael D. Clark. 2017. *Motivational Interviewing with Offenders: Engagement, Rehabilitation, and Reentry.* New York: Guilford.

Stoll, Adam. 2006. *Higher Education Act Reauthorization: A Comparison of Current Law and Major Proposals.* Washington, DC: CRS Report for Congress (RL33415, May 2). www.finaid.org.

Stone, Arthur, Saul Shiffman, Audie Atienza, and Linda Nebeling. 2007. *The Science of Real-Time Data Capture: Self-Reports in Health Research.* New York: Oxford University Press.

Stone, Rebecca, Merry Morash, Marva Goodson, Sandi W. Smith, and Jennifer Cobbina. 2018. "Women on Parole, Identity Processes, and Primary Desistance." *Feminist Criminology* 13 (4): 382–403.

Stuart, Forrest. 2016. *Down, Out, and Under Arrest: Policing and Everyday Life in Skid Row.* Chicago: University of Chicago Press.

Stuntz, William. 2001. "The Pathological Politics of Criminal Law." *Michigan Law Review* 100: 505–600.

Stuntz, William J. 2004. "Plea Bargaining and Criminal Law's Disappearing Shadow." *Harvard Law Review* 117 (8): 2548–69.

Subramanian, Ram, Ruth Delaney, Stephen Roberts, Nancy Fishman, and Peggy McGarry. 2015. *Incarceration's Front Door: The Misuse of Jails in America.* New York: Vera Institute of Justice.

Sugie, Naomi F. 2018. "Utilizing Smartphones to Study Disadvantaged and Hard-to-Reach Groups." *Sociological Methods and Research* 47 (3): 458–91.

Suldo, Shannon M., and Scott E. Huebner. 2004. "Does Life Satisfaction Moderate the Effects of Stressful Life Events on Psychopathological Behavior During Adolescence?" *School Psychology Quarterly* 19 (2): 93–105.

Sykes, Gresham M. 1958. *The Society of Captives.* Princeton, NJ: Princeton University Press.

Tabachnik, Naomi, Jennifer Crocker, and Lauren B. Alloy. 1983. "Depression, Social Comparison, and the False-Consensus Effect." *Journal of Personality and Social Psychology* 45 (3): 688–99.

Tafoya, Sonya, Ryken Grattet, and Mia Bird. 2014. "Corrections Realignment and Data Collection in California. San Francisco, CA: Public Policy Institute of California." Public Policy Institute of California. www.ppic.org.

Tajfel, Henri. 1982. "Social Psychology of Intergroup Relations." *Annual Review of Psychology* 33: 1–39.

Tatum, Beverly. 1999. *Why Are All the Black Kids Sitting Together in the Cafeteria?* New York: Basic Books.

Taxman, Faye S. 2008. "No Illusions: Offender and Organization Change in Maryland's Proactive Community Supervision Efforts." *Criminology and Public Policy* 7 (2): 275–302.

———. 2014. "Second Generation of RNR: The Importance of Systemic Responsivity in Expanding Core Principles of Responsivity." *Federal Probation* 78 (2). www.uscourts.gov.

———. 2018a. "Are You Asking Me to Change My Friends?" *Criminology and Public Policy* 16 (3): 775–82.

———. 2018b. "The Partially Clothed Emperor: Evidence-Based Practices." *Journal of Contemporary Criminal Justice* 34 (1): 97–114.

Taxman, Faye S., and Michael Caudy. 2015. "Risk Tells Us Who, but Not What or How: Empirical Assessment of the Complexity of Criminogenic Needs to Inform Correctional Programming." *Criminology and Public Policy* 14 (1): 71–103.

Taxman, Faye S., and April Pattavina, eds. 2013. *Stimulation Strategies to Reduce Recidivism: Risk Need Responsivity (RNR) Modeling for the Criminal Justice System*. New York: Springer.

Taxman, Faye S., Matthew Perdoni, and Michael Caudy. 2013. "The Plight of Providing Appropriate Substance Abuse Treatment Services to Offenders: Modeling the Gaps in Service Delivery." *Victims and Offenders* 8 (1): 70–93.

Taxman, Faye S., Douglas Young, and James M. Byrne. 2003. "Transforming Offender Reentry into Public Safety: Lessons from OJP's Reentry Partnership Initiative." *Justice Research and Policy* 5: 101–28.

Taxman, Faye S., Francis Zelphi, and Alex Breno. 2017. "Systemic Responsivity in St. Louis, Missouri: Service Gaps to Reduce Violence." St. Louis, Missouri: United Way and Washington University.

Taylor, Shelley E., and Jonathan D. Brown. 1988. "Illusion and Well-Being: A Social Psychological Perspective on Mental Health." *Psychological Bulletin* 103 (2): 193–210.

———. 1994. "Positive Illusions and Well-Being Revisited: Separating Fact from Fiction." *Psychological Bulletin* 116 (1): 21–27.

Telles, Edward E., and Edward Murguia. 1990. "Phenotypic Discrimination and Income Differences among Mexican Americans." *Social Science Quarterly* 71 (4): 682–96.

Teplin, Linda A., Karen M. Abram, and Gary M. McClelland. 1996. "Prevalence of Psychiatric Disorders among Incarcerated Women: Pretrial Jail Detainees." *Archives of General Psychiatry* 53: 505–12.

Tewksbury, Richard, and Heith Copes. 2012. "Incarcerated Sex Offenders' Expectations for Reentry." *Prison Journal* 9 (1): 102–22.

Tewksbury, Richard, and Matthew Lees. 2006. "Perceptions of Sex Offender Registration: Collateral Consequences and Community Experiences." *Sociological Spectrum* 26 (3): 309–34.

The Sentencing Project (2010). State Recidivism Studies (online database). Retrieved from www.prisonpolicy.org.

Thomas, James C., and Elizabeth Torrone. 2006. "Incarceration as Forced Migration: Effects on Health Outcomes." *American Journal of Public Health* 96 (10): 1762–65.

Thompson, Anthony C. 2008. *Releasing Prisoners, Redeeming Communities: Reentry, Race, and Politics*. New York: New York University Press.

Thomson, Rachel, Robert Bell, Janet Holland, Sheila Henderson, Sheena McGrellis, and Sue Sharpe. 2002. "Critical Moments: Choice, Chance and Opportunity in Young People's Narratives of Transition." *Sociology* 36 (2): 335–54.

Thorne, Barrie. 1987. "Re-Visioning Women and Social Change: Where Are the Children?" *Gender and Society* 1 (1): 85–109.
Toch, Hans. 1977. *Living in Prison: The Ecology of Survival*. New Brunswick, NJ: Transaction.
———. 2005. "Reinventing Prisons." In *The Effects of Imprisonment*, edited by Alison Liebling and Shadd Maruna, 465–73. New York: Routledge.
Tonry, Michael. 2004. *Thinking about Crime: Sense and Sensibility in American Penal Culture*. New York: Oxford University Press.
———. 2011. *Punishing Race*. New York: Oxford University Press.
Torelli, Nicola, and Ugo Trivellato. 1993. "Modelling Inaccuracies in Job-Search Duration Data." *Journal of Econometrics* 59 (1): 187–211.
Travis, Jeremy. 2000. *But They All Come Back: Rethinking Prisoner Reentry*. Washington, DC: US Department of Justice, Office of Justice Programs, National Institute of Justice.
———. 2002. "Invisible Punishment: An Instrument of Social Exclusion." In *Invisible Punishment: The Collateral Consequences of Mass Imprisonment*, edited by Marc Mauer and Meda Chesney-Lind, 15–36. New York: Norton.
———. 2005. *But They All Come Back: Facing the Challenges of Prisoner Reentry*. Washington, DC: Urban Institute.
Travis, Jeremy, Amy L. Solomon, and Michelle Waul. 2001. *From Prison to Home: The Dimensions and Consequences of Prisoner Reentry*. Washington, DC: Urban Institute.
Travis, Jeremy, Bruce Western, and F. Stevens Redburn. 2014. *The Growth of Incarceration in the United States: Exploring Causes and Consequence*. Washington, DC: National Academies Press.
Turanovic, Jillian J., Nancy Rodriguez, and Travis C. Pratt. 2012. "The Collateral Consequences of Incarceration Revisited: A Qualitative Analysis of the Effects on Caregivers of Children of Incarcerated Parents." *Criminology* 50 (4): 913–59.
Turney, Kristin. 2014a. "Stress Proliferation Across Generations? Examining the Relationship Between Parental Incarceration and Childhood Health." *Journal of Health and Social Behavior* 55 (3): 302–19.
———. 2014b. "The Consequences of Paternal Incarceration for Maternal Neglect and Harsh Parenting." *Social Forces* 92 (4): 1607–36.
———. 2014c. "The Intergenerational Consequences of Mass Incarceration: Implications for Children's Co-Residence and Contact with Grandparent." *Social Forces* 93 (1): 299–327.
———. 2015. "Hopelessly Devoted? Relationship Quality During and After Incarceration." *Journal of Marriage and Family* 77 (2): 480–95.
———. 2017. "The Unequal Consequences of Mass Incarceration for Children." *Demography* 54 (1): 361–89.
Turney, Kristin, Britni L. Adams, Emma Conner, Rebecca Goodsell, and Janet Muñiz. 2017. "Challenges and Opportunities for Conducting Research on Children of Incarcerated Fathers." *Sociological Studies of Children and Youth* 22: 199–221.

Turney, Kristin, and Emma Conner. 2019. "Jail Incarceration: A Common and Consequential Form of Criminal Justice Contact." *Annual Review of Criminology* 2: 265–90.

Turney, Kristin, and Rebecca Goodsell. 2018. "Parental Incarceration and Children's Wellbeing." *Future of Children* 28 (1): 147–64.

Turney, Kristin, and Anna Haskins. 2014. "Falling Behind? Children's Early Grade Retention After Paternal Incarceration." *Sociology of Education* 87 (4): 241–58.

Turney, Kristin, Jason Schnittker, and Christopher Wildeman. 2012. "Those They Leave Behind: Paternal Incarceration and Maternal Instrumental Support." *Journal of Marriage and Family* 74 (5): 1149–65.

Turney, Kristin, and Christopher Wildeman. 2013. "Redefining Relationships: Explaining the Countervailing Consequences of Paternal Incarceration for Parenting." *American Sociological Review* 78 (6): 949–79.

Twine, France W., and Jonathan W. Warren. 2000. *Racing Research, Researching Race: Methodological Dilemmas in Critical Race Studies*. New York: NYU Press.

Uggen, Christopher, Jeff Manza, and Angela Behrens. 2004. "The Growth of Incarceration in the United States: Exploring Causes and Consequences." In *After Crime and Punishment: Pathways to Offender Reintegration*, edited by Shadd Maruna and Russ Immarigeon, 261–93. Cullompton, UK: Willan.

Uggen, Christopher, Mike Vuolo, Sarah Lageson, Ebony Ruhland, and Hilary Whitham. 2014. "The Edge of Stigma: An Experimental Audit of the Effects of Low-Level Criminal Records on Employment." *Criminology* 52 (4): 627–54.

Uggen, Christopher, Sara Wakefield, and Bruce Western. 2005. "Work and Family Perspectives on Reentry." In *Prisoner Reentry and Crime in America*, edited by Jeremy Travis and Christy Visher, 209–43. Cambridge: Cambridge University Press.

US Census. 2016. Quick Facts: Missouri. www.census.gov.

US Census Bureau. 2016. *2016 American Community Survey 1-Year Estimates* (S0201). Generated using American FactFinder, http://factfinder2.census.gov.

US Department of Justice. 2013. *Prisoners and Prisoner Re-Entry*. Washington, DC: US Department of Justice, Office of Justice Programs. www.justice.gov.

US Department of Justice, Federal Bureau of Investigation. 2016. *Uniform Crime Reporting: UCR*. https://crime-data-explorer.fr.cloud.gov.

Van Cleve, Nicole Gonzalez, and Lauren Mayes. 2015. "Criminal Justice Through 'Colorblind' Lenses: A Call to Examine the Mutual Constitution of Race and Criminal Justice." *Law and Social Inquiry* 40 (2): 406–32.

Van Dijk, Jan, John van Kesteren, and Paul Smit. 2007. "Criminal Victimization in International Perspective: Key Findings from the 2004–2005 ICVS and EU ICS." http://repository.tudelft.nl.

Van Ginneken, Esther F.J.C. 2016. "Making Sense of Imprisonment: Narratives of Posttraumatic Growth among Female Prisoners." *International Journal of Offender Therapy and Comparative Criminology* 60 (2): 208–27.

Van Olphen, Julian, Michele Eliason, Nicholas Freudenberg, and Marilyn Barnes. 2009. "Nowhere to Go: How Stigma Limits the Options of Female Drug Users After Release from Jail." *Substance Abuse Treatment, Prevention, and Policy* 4 (10): 1–10.

Van Tilburg, Theo. 1998. "Interviewer Effects in the Measurement of Personal Network Size: A Nonexperimental Study." *Sociological Methods and Research* 26 (3): 300–28.

Van Voorhis, Patricia, and Emily J. Salisbury. 2016. "Cognitive Therapies." In *Correctional Counseling and Rehabilitation*, edited by Patricia Van Voorhis and Emily J. Salisbury, 9th ed., 171–95. New York: Routledge.

Vega, William A. 1995. "Latino Families: Conceptual Approaches and Overview." In *Understanding Latino Families: Scholarship, Policy, and Practice*, edited by Ruth E. Zambrana, 3–17. Thousand Oaks, CA: Sage.

Vélez, María. 2006. "Toward an Understanding of the Lower Rates of Homicide in Latino versus Black Neighborhoods: A Look at Chicago." In *The Many Colors of Crime: Inequalities of Race, Ethnicity, and Crime in America*, edited by Ruth Peterson, Lauren Krivo, and John Hagan, 91–107. New York: New York University Press.

Verrecchia, P. J., and Eric Ling. 2013. "The Effects of Legal and Extralegal Factors on Probation Revocation Decisions." *International Journal of Criminology and Sociology* 2: 13–19.

Vidales, Guadalupe, Kristen M. Day, and Michael Powe. 2009. "Police and Immigration Enforcement: Impacts on Latino(a) Residents' Perceptions of Police." *Policing: An International Journal of Police Strategies and Management* 32 (4): 631–53.

Visher, Christy A. 1983. "Gender, Police Arrest Decisions, and Notions of Chivalry." *Criminology* 21 (1): 5–28.

Visher, Christy A., and Nicholas W. Bakken. 2014. "Reentry Challenges Facing Women with Mental Health Problems." *Women and Health* 54 (8): 768–80.

Visher, Christy A., Nicholas W. Bakken, and Whitney D. Gunter. 2013. "Fatherhood, Community Reintegration, and Successful Outcomes." *Journal of Offender Rehabilitation* 52: 451–469.

Visher, Christy A., and Shannon M. E. Courtney. 2007. *One Year Out: Experiences of Prisoners Returning to Cleveland*. Washington, DC: Urban Institute.

Visher, Christy A., Carly R. Knight, Aaron Chalfin, and John K. Roman. 2009. *The Impact of Marital and Relationship Status on Social Outcomes for Returning Prisoners*. Washington, DC: Urban Institute.

Visher, Christy A., Nancy La Vigne, and Jeremy Travis. 2004. "Returning Home: Understanding the Challenges of Prisoner Reentry: Maryland Pilot Study: Findings from Baltimore." Washington, DC: Urban Institute.

Visher, Christy A., and Daniel J. O'Connell. 2012. "Incarceration and Inmates' Perceptions about Returning Home." *Journal of Criminal Justice* 40: 386–93.

Visher, Christy A., and Jeremy Travis. 2003. "Transitions from Prison to Community: Understanding Individual Pathways." *Annual Review of Sociology* 29: 89–113.

Von Hirsch, Andreas, and Andrew Ashworth. 2004. *Principled Sentencing: Readings on Theory and Policy*. Oxford: Hart.

Von Hirsch, Andreas, Anthony Bottoms, Elizabeth Burney, and Per Olof Wikstron. 1999. *Criminal Deterrence and Sentence Severity: An Analysis of Recent Research*. Oxford: Hart.

Vuolo, Mike, Sarah Lageson, and Christopher Uggen. 2017. "Criminal Record Questions in the Era of 'Ban the Box.'" *Criminology and Public Policy* 16 (1): 139–65.

Wacquant, Loïc. 2010. "Prisoner Reentry as Myth and Ceremony." *Dialectical Anthropology* 34 (4): 605–20.

Wagner, Peter, and Bernadette Rabuy. 2016. *Mass Incarceration: The Whole Pie 2016*. Prison Policy Initiative. www.prisonpolicy.org.

———. 2017. *Mass Incarceration: The Whole Pie 2017*. Northampton, MA: Prison Policy Initiative.

Wagner, Peter, and Wendy Sawyer. 2018. *Mass Incarceration: The Whole Pie 2018*. Prison Policy Initiative. www.prisonpolicy.org.

Wakefield, Sara, and Janet Garcia-Hallett. 2017. "Incarceration Effects on Families." In *Oxford Research Encyclopedia of Criminology*. http://oxfordre.com.

Wakefield, Sara, and Christopher Uggen. 2010. "Incarceration and Stratification." *Annual Review of Sociology* 36: 387–406.

Wakefield, Sara, and Christopher Wildeman. 2013. *Children of the Prison Boom: Mass Incarceration and the Future of American Inequality*. New York: Oxford University Press.

Walker, Michael L. 2016. "Race Making in a Penal Institution." *American Journal of Sociology* 121 (4): 1051–78.

Walmsley, Roy. 2013. *World Prison Population List*. London: International Centre for Prison Studies.

Wang, Emily A, Gefei A. Zhu, Linda Evans, Amy Carroll-Scott, Rani Desai, and Lynn E. Fiellin. 2013. "A Pilot Study Examining Food Insecurity and HIV Risk Behaviors among Individuals Recently Released from Prison." *AIDS Education and Prevention* 25 (2): 112–23.

Ward, Shakoor. 2009. "Career and Technical Education in the United States Prisons: What Have We Learned?" *Journal of Correctional Education* 60 (3): 191–200.

Ward, Tony, and Clare-Ann Fortune. 2013. "The Good Lives Model: Aligning Risk Reduction with Promoting Offenders' Personal Goals." *European Journal of Probation* 5 (2): 29–46.

Ward, Tony, and Shadd Maruna. 2007. *Rehabilitation* New York. Routledge.

Warr, Jason. 2017. "Quid Pro Quo in Prison Research." *Comparative Penology* (blog). www.compen.crim.cam.ac.uk.

Wasserman, Stanley, and Katherine Faust. 1994. *Social Network Analysis: Methods and Applications*. Cambridge: Cambridge University Press.

Waters, Mary C. 1999. *Black Identities: West Indian Immigrant Dreams and American Realities*. Cambridge, MA: Harvard University Press.

Waters, Mary C., and Philip Kasinitz. 2010. "Discrimination, Race Relations, and the Second Generation." *Social Research* 77 (1): 101–32.

Watson, Jamie, Amy Solomon, Nancy La Vigne, and Jeremy Travis. 2004. "A Portrait of Prisoner Reentry in Texas." Washington, DC: Urban Institute.

Webster, Colin. 1997. "The Construction of British 'Asian' Criminality." *International Journal of the Sociology of Law* 25 (1): 65–86.

Weiss, Robert. 1994. *Learning from Strangers: The Art and Method of Qualitative Interviewing*. New York: Free Press.
West, Heather, and William Sabol. 2011. "Prisoners in 2009." NCJ 231675. Washington, DC: US Department of Justice, Office of Justice Programs, Bureau of Justice Statistics. www.bjs.gov.
Western, Bruce. 2006. *Punishment and Inequality in America*. New York: Russell Sage Foundation.
———. 2018. *Homeward: Life in the Year after Prison*. New York: Russell Sage Foundation.
Western, Bruce, Anthony A. Braga, Jaclyn Davis, and Catherine Sirois. 2015. "Stress and Hardship After Prison." *American Journal of Sociology* 120 (5): 1512–47.
Western, Bruce, Anthony Braga, David Hureau, and Catherine Sirois. 2016. "Study Retention as Bias Reduction in a Hard-to-Reach Population." *Proceedings of the National Academy of Sciences* 113 (20): 5477–85.
Western, Bruce, Jeffrey R. Kling, and David F. Weiman. 2001. "The Labor Market Consequences of Incarceration." *Crime and Delinquency* 47: 410–27.
Western, Bruce, and Becky Pettit. 2005. "Black-White Wage Inequality, Employment Rates, and Incarceration." *American Journal of Sociology* 111 (2): 553–78.
———. 2010. "Incarceration and Social Inequality." *Daedalus* 139 (3): 8–19.
Western, Bruce, and Catherine Sirois. 2019. "Racialized Re-Entry: Labor Market Inequality After Incarceration." *Social Forces* 97 (4): 1517–42.
Western, Bruce, and Christopher Wildeman. 2009. "The Black Family and Mass Incarceration." *ANNALS of the American Academy of Political and Social Science* 621 (1): 221–42.
Wheeler, Ladd, Harry Reis, and John B. Nezlek. 1983. "Loneliness, Social Interaction, and Sex Roles." *Journal of Personality and Social Psychology* 45 (4): 943–53.
Whitman, James Q. 2003. *Harsh Justice: Criminal Punishment and the Widening Divide between America and Europe*. New York: Oxford University Press.
Wildeman, Christopher. 2009. "Parental Imprisonment, the Prison Boom, and the Concentration of Childhood Advantage." *Demography* 46 (2): 265–80.
———. 2010. "Paternal Incarceration and Children's Physically Aggressive Behaviors: Evidence from the Fragile Families and Child Wellbeing Study." *Social Forces* 89 (1): 285–309.
Wildeman, Christopher, and Christopher Muller. 2012. "Mass Imprisonment and Inequality in Health and Family Life." *Annual Review of Law and Social Science* 8: 11–30.
Wildeman, Christopher, Jason Schnittker, and Kristin Turney. 2012. "Despair by Association? The Mental Health Mothers with Children by Recently Incarcerated Fathers." *American Sociological Review* 77 (2): 216–43.
Wildeman, Christopher, and Kristin Turney. 2014. "Positive, Negative, or Null? The Effects of Maternal Incarceration on Children's Behavioral Problems." *Demography* 51 (3): 1041–68.

Wildeman, Christopher, Kristin Turney, and Youngmin Yi. 2016. "Paternal Incarceration and Family Functioning: Variation Across Federal, State, and Local Facilities." *ANNALS of the American Academy of Political and Social Science* 665 (1): 80–97.

Wildeman, Christopher, Sarah Wakefield, and Kristin Turney. 2013. "Misidentifying the Effects of Parental Imprisonment? A Comment on Johnson and Easterling." *Journal of Marriage and Family* 75 (1): 252–8.

Wildeman, Christopher, and Bruce Western. 2010. "Incarceration in Fragile Families." *Future of Children* 20 (2): 157–77.

Wills, Thomas A. 1981. "Downward Comparison Principles in Social Psychology." *Psychological Bulletin* 90 (2): 245–71.

Wills, Thomas A., and Ori Shinar. 2000. "Measuring Perceived and Received Social Support." In *Social Support Measurement and Intervention: A Guide for Health and Social Scientists*, edited by Sheldon Cohen, Lynn G. Underwood, and Benjamin H. Gottlieb, 86–135. New York: Oxford University Press.

Wilson, James Q. 1975. *Thinking about Crime*. New York: Basic Books.

Winters, Georgia M., Elizabeth L. Jeglic, Cynthia Calkins, and Brandy L. Blasko. 2017. "Sex Offender Legislation and Social Control: An Examination of Sex Offenders' Expectations Prior to Release." *Criminal Justice Studies* 30 (2): 202–22.

Wodahl, Eric J., John H. Boman, and Brett Garland. 2015. "Responding to Probation and Parole Violations: Are Jail Sanctions More Effective Than Community-Based Graduated Sanctions." *Journal of Criminal Justice* 43 (3): 242–50.

Wodahl, Eric J., and Brett Garland. 2009. "The Evolution of Community Corrections: The Enduring Influence of the Prison." *Prison Journal* 89: 81S–104S.

Woldgabreal, Yilma A., Andrew Day, and Tony Ward. 2016. "Linking Positive Psychology to Offender Supervision Outcomes: The Mediating Role of Psychological Flexibility, General Self-Efficacy, Optimism, and Hope." *Criminal Justice and Behavior* 43 (6): 1–25.

Wolff, Nancy, and Jeffrey Draine. 2004. "The Dynamics of Social Capital of Prisoners and Community Reentry: Ties That Bind?" *Journal of Correctional Health Care* 10 (3): 457–90.

Wooditch, Alese, Liansheng Tang, and Faye S. Taxman. 2014. "Which Criminogenic Need Changes Are Most Important in Promoting Desistance from Crime and Substance Use?" *Criminal Justice and Behavior* 41 (3): 276–99.

Wright, Emily, Dana D. DeHart, Barbara A. Koons-Witt, and Courtney A. Crittenden. 2013. "Buffers Against Crime? Exploring the Roles and Limitations of Positive Relationships among Women in Prison." *Punishment and Society* 15 (1): 71–95.

Wyse, Jessica J. B., David J. Harding, and Jeffrey D. Morenoff. 2014. "Romantic Relationships and Criminal Desistance: Pathways and Processes." *Sociological Forum* 29 (2): 365–85.

Young, Alford. 1999. "The (Non) Accumulation of Capital: Explicating the Relationship of Structure and Agency in the Lives of Poor Black Men." *Sociological Theory* 17 (2): 201–27.

Zatz, Marjorie S., and Nancy Rodriguez. 2006. "Conceptualizing Race and Ethnicity in Studies of Crime and Criminal Justice." In *The Many Colors of Crime: Inequalities of Race, Ethnicity, and Crime in America*, edited by Ruth Peterson, Lauren Krivo, and John Hagan, 39–53. New York: New York University Press.

Zeng, Zhen. 2018. *Jail Inmates in 2016*. Washington, DC: Bureau of Justice Statistics, US Department of Justice.

## ABOUT THE EDITORS

Andrea Leverentz is Associate Professor of Sociology at the University of Massachusetts, Boston. She is the author of *The Ex-Prisoner's Dilemma: How Women Negotiate Competing Narratives of Reentry and Desistance*. Her current work looks at short-term incarceration, how returning prisoners navigate neighborhood and place, and how residents perceive crime and disorder in their neighborhoods.

Elsa Y. Chen is Professor of Political Science and Vice Provost for Academic Affairs at Santa Clara University. Her current research studies the de-escalation of mass incarceration and prisoner reintegration into society. Her published work has appeared in journals including *Justice Quarterly*, *Punishment and Society*, *Social Science Quarterly*, the *Journal of Contemporary Criminal Justice*, *Feminist Criminology*, and the *Journal of Ethnicity in Criminal Justice*.

Johnna Christian is Associate Professor at the School of Criminal Justice at Rutgers University, Newark. Her research examines family visitation at prisons, the social and economic implications of maintaining ties to incarcerated people, and reentry and reintegration after incarceration. She is co-editor of the book *How Offenders Transform Their Lives* and has published work in *Punishment and Society*, *Journal of Offender Rehabilitation*, and *Journal of Contemporary Ethnography*.

## ABOUT THE CONTRIBUTORS

Elizabeth A. Adams is a doctoral student in the School of Criminal Justice at Michigan State University. Her research focuses on advancing correctional research by incorporating frameworks from fields including communication and social psychology. She is particularly interested in the gendered challenges faced by justice-involved women, as well as how communication and social support can be employed within correctional settings to improve women's circumstances. She co-authored and presented a top paper at the International Communication Association's annual conference in 2016, and her work appears in *British Journal of Criminology* and *Journal of Criminal Justice and Behavior*.

Dallas Augustine is a doctoral candidate in the Department of Criminology, Law, and Society at the University of California, Irvine. She is fellow of the Economic Self-Sufficiency Policy Research Institute and was recognized as the 2018 Emerging Scholar for the University of California Center at Sacramento. Her current work examines the intersection of punishment and the labor market, looking at experiences of coercive work while on community supervision and highlighting the ways in which formerly incarcerated people overcome barriers to employment at reentry.

Reginald Dwayne Betts is a doctoral candidate at Yale Law School. He is the author of *A Question of Freedom: A Memoir of Learning, Survival and Coming of Age in Prison*, and two poetry collections, *Bastards of the Reagan Era* and *Shahid Reads His Own Palm*. He has published his scholarly work in the *Yale Law Journal* and *Valparaiso Law Review*.

Jennifer E. Cobbina is Associate Professor in the School of Criminal Justice at Michigan State University. Her research interests focus on gender and prisoner reentry, desistance, and recidivism. Her work also examines the intersection of gender, race, class, and crime. Her work has appeared in *Criminology, Justice Quarterly, Crime and Delinquency, Deviant Behavior,* and *Race and Justice.*

Alexandra L. Cox is a Lecturer in Sociology at the University of Essex. She is the author of *Trapped in a Vice: The Consequences of Confinement for Young People* and has published her work in *Punishment & Society, Theoretical Criminology, Social Justice,* and the *Journal of Youth Studies,* among other outlets.

Jamie J. Fader is Associate Professor in the Department of Criminal Justice at Temple University. Her research interests lie at the intersection of crime, justice, social inequalities, and the life course. Her book, *Falling Back: Incarceration and Transitions to Adulthood Among Urban Youth,* won the 2016 Michael J. Hindelang award.

Janet Garcia-Hallett is Assistant Professor at the University of Missouri, Kansas City in the Department of Criminal Justice and Criminology, and an affiliate faculty member of the Latinx and Latin American Studies Program. Her research is focused primarily on social justice issues across race/ethnicity and gender—particularly on the impact of incarceration on families and communities of color, the obstacles women face post-incarceration, as well as the racial-ethnic differences in policing strategies. Janet has received numerous awards for her work, including the Rutgers Dissertation Fellowship, the American Society of Criminology Graduate Fellowship for Ethnic Minorities, as well as the Racial/Ethnic Minority Graduate Scholarship from the Society for the Study of Social Problems. She has recently published her work in *Feminist Criminology, Sociology Compass,* and the *International Journal of Offender Therapy and Comparative Criminology.*

Marva V. Goodson is a doctoral candidate at Michigan State University in the School of Criminal Justice. Her research focuses on female offenders' experiences surrounding seeking supervision-related resource support, with emphasis on personal support network characteristics. She is a Ford Foundation Fellow, King-Chavez-Parks Future Faculty Fellow, and recipient of the National Science Foundation Dissertation Research Improvement Grant. Marva has published research articles in *Feminist Criminology* and *Criminal Justice and Behavior.*

Abigail R. Henson is a doctoral candidate in the Department of Criminal Justice at Temple University. Her dissertation work examines parenting strategies among black fathers in a heavily policed community.

Beth M. Huebner is Professor in the Department of Criminology and Criminal Justice at the University of Missouri, St. Louis. Her principal research interests include the collateral consequences of incarceration, racial and gender disparities in the criminal justice system, and public policy. She is currently serving as co-principal investigator for the St. Louis County MacArthur Safety + Justice Challenge and is collaborating on a study of monetary sanctions in Missouri with funding from the Arnold Foundation. She is the current chair of the Division on Corrections and Sentencing for the American Society of Criminology. She earned her PhD in Criminal Justice from Michigan State University in 2003.

Kashea P. Kovacs is a PhD student in the School of Criminal Justice at Rutgers, The State University of New Jersey. Her research interests are police-community relations, youth violence, and prisoner reentry. Her work appears in *City & Community* and *Justice Quarterly*.

Derek A. Kreager is Professor of Criminology, Sociology, and Demography at Pennsylvania State University. He is Principal Investigator of the PINS projects, which include network data collections in men's and women's prison units and a prison-based therapeutic community.

Thomas P. LeBel is Associate Professor in the Department of Criminal Justice in the University of Wisconsin, Milwaukee's Helen Bader School of Social Welfare. His research focuses on prisoner reintegration, desistance from crime, the stigma of incarceration, drug treatment courts, and interventions for criminal justice involved women with drug and alcohol problems.

Shadd Maruna is Professor of Criminology at Queen's University Belfast in Northern Ireland. Previously, he was the Dean of the Rutgers School of Criminal Justice (USA) and has worked at the University of Cambridge, the State University of New York, Albany, and the University of Manchester. His research focuses on prisoner reentry. His book, *Making Good: How Ex-Convicts Reform and Rebuild Their Lives*, was named the Outstanding Contribution to Criminology in 2001. He also received the inaugural Research Medal from the Howard League for Penal Reform for the impact of his research on prison reform.

Morgan McGuirk is a PhD student in Criminology and Criminal Justice at the University of Missouri, St. Louis (UMSL). Her research interests include prisoner reentry and the collateral consequences of punishment. Additionally, she is interested in procedural justice within the criminal court system. She is currently working on a research project that examines the needs of pretrial detainees and individuals who are jailed for a probation violation and a project exploring defendant court debt.

Sophie E. Meyer recently completed a MS degree at the University of Oxford. During her undergraduate career, she was an honors student studying political science, French language, and urban education at Santa Clara University. Her research interests include criminal justice, housing, homelessness, and education policy reform.

Keesha Middlemass is Associate Professor in the Department of Political Science at Howard University. Her book, *Convicted & Condemned: The Politics and Policies of Prisoner Reentry*, was published in 2017. Currently, Professor Middlemass is studying food insecurity and prisoner reentry. Her previous research is published in *Aggressive Behavior*, *Criminal Justice & Behavior*, *Prison Journal*, and *Punishment & Society*. Professor Middlemass is a former Andrew Mellon Post-Doctoral Fellow on Race, Crime and Justice at the Vera Institute of Justice in New York City and a former American Political Science Association Congressional Fellow.

Merry Morash is Professor in the School of Criminal Justice at Michigan State University. Her research focuses on gender and justice, with special emphasis on women and girls in correctional programs and violence against US and South Asian women. She is a fellow of the American Society of Criminology and a recipient of the Mentoring awards from both the American Society of Criminology and the Academy of Criminal Justice Sciences. Most recently she has completed a six-year study of slightly more than 400 women on probation and parole that integrates communication and criminological theories.

Matt Richie is Assistant Professor of Criminal Justice at the University of Wisconsin, Oshkosh. His current research focuses on the process of desistance, risk assessment validation, program evaluation, as well as jail reentry in non-metropolitan areas. He earned a PhD in Criminal Justice from the University of Wisconsin, Milwaukee.

Naomi F. Sugie is Assistant Professor in the Criminology, Law and Society Department at the University of California, Irvine. Her research engages with issues of punishment, families, inequality, and new technologies for research with hard-to-reach groups. Her work has been published in journals such as *American Journal of Sociology*, *American Sociological Review*, *Demography*, *Social Forces*, and *Social Problems*, and has been supported by agencies such as the *National Institutes of Health*, *National Institute of Justice*, and *National Science Foundation*. Sugie earned a PhD in Sociology and Social Policy, as well as a specialization in Demography, from Princeton University.

Faye S. Taxman is University Professor in the Criminology, Law and Socicty Department and Director of the Center for Advancing Correctional Excellence at George Mason University. She is a health service criminologist and has worked to develop seamless systems-of-care models that link the criminal justice system with other healthcare and other service delivery systems and reengineering probation and parole supervision services. She has conducted experiments to examine different processes to improve treatment access and retention, to assess new models of probation supervision consistent with RNR frameworks, and to test new interventions. She has active "laboratories" with numerous agencies including Maryland Department of Public Safety and Correctional Services, Virginia Department of Corrections, Alameda County Probation Department (CA), Hidalgo County Community Corrections Department (TX), North Carolina Department of Corrections, and Delaware Department of Corrections. She developed the translational RNR Simulation Tool (www.gmuace.org/tools) to assist agencies to advance practice. Dr. Taxman is author of numerous books and articles, including *Implementing Evidence-Based Community Corrections and Addiction Treatment* (with Steven Belenko). She is co-editor of *Health & Justice* and *Perspectives* (a publication of the American Probation and Parole Association). The American Society of Criminology's Division of Sentencing and Corrections has recognized her as Distinguished Scholar twice, and she has also received the Rita Warren and Ted Palmer Differential Intervention Treatment award. She received the Joan McCord Award in 2017 from the Division of Experimental Criminology. In 2018, she was appointed a Fellow of the American Society of Criminology. She has received numerous awards from practitioner organizations such as the American Probation and Parole Association and Caron Foundation. She has a PhD from Rutgers University's School of Criminal Justice.

Kristin Turney is Associate Professor in the Department of Sociology at the University of California, Irvine. Her research investigates the complex and dynamic role of families in creating and exacerbating social inequalities. Existing research examines the consequences of criminal justice contact for individuals, families, and children. In the related ongoing Jail & Family Life Study, she is interviewing jailed fathers and their family members—including current and former romantic partners, children, and mothers—during incarceration and after release. These substantive interests are accompanied by a methodological interest in causal inference.

Sara Wakefield is Associate Professor of Criminal Justice at Rutgers University, Newark. Her research interests focus on the consequences of mass imprisonment for the family, with an emphasis on childhood well-being and racial inequality. More recently, her work on the PINS and R-PINS projects leverage a variety of methods to understand how social ties influence the conditions of confinement, community reintegration, and social inequality among former prisoners and their families.

Corey Whichard is Assistant Professor of Criminal Justice at the State University of New York, Albany. His research interests include prisoner reentry, social network analysis, and life course studies. He served as an interviewer for the PINS projects and is a co-investigator for the R-PINS project.

# INDEX

Anti-Drug Abuse Act of 1986, 279, 284
arrested development, 241–42

black/white dichotomy: and colorism, 146–47; and implications for research, 147–49; and implications for policy, 149–50; limitations of, 137; reinforcing of, 138–39

cognitive behavioral therapy (CBT), 41, 192
cognitive transformation theory, 153, 155–58, 165–67
correctional staff cooperation in research, 67, 70–72, 79–80n7, 94–96, 99n8, 105–6, 108
criminogenic needs, 42–43, 44, 47–52, 54, 316–17

data integration, 18–20, 30–33, 38; obstacles to, 20–21, 33–36
desistance, 152–55, 168–70, 172–74; role of hope in, 174–75, 191–93
deterrence, 168, 265–67, 294
disposable (social) ties, 223
drug offenses, 17

EgoWeb 2.0, 88–89
electronic monitoring, 235, 265, 270
employment discrimination, 136, 149
ethics, 99n1, 116, 129, 301–2, 309; and data security, 19; Institutional Review Board (IRB) review, 70–71, 86; and subject recruitment, 85, 112

evidence-based practices, 40–41, 53–56
experience sampling method, 204–5; limitations of, 216

identity theory of desistance, 174–75

Jail and Family Life Study, 60–61, 65–66; challenges of, 70–73, 77–78; design of, 66–70; recruitment to, 66–68, 74–77
"just deserts" movement, 295

life story interviewing, 159–61
longitudinal research, 100–103; and case studies, 238–39; challenges in, 101, 109, 122–29; design of, 104–6; and researcher attrition, 119–20; recruitment to, 106–8; and social media, 112; strategies for retention, 110–17, 120–22, 128–29

Meek Mill, 259

name-generator design, 88–90
narrative identity theory, 152–53, 155–58, 164–65
Newark Smartphone Reentry Project (NSRP), 203–6

Oceanside Sheriff's Department (OSD), 66–67, 70–75, 79–80n7
offender-funded justice, 251, 254

parole, 17, 297; for sex offenders, 242–46; technical violations of, 15, 243–44
Pell grants, 280–84, 289–91

379

380 | INDEX

Prison Inmate Networks Study (PINS). *See* social network research
prison realignment, 66
privacy laws, 19, 33–34
probation, 260–62; and changes to policy, 265–67, 272–74; scope of, 259; technical violations of, 259–60, 267–69, 271–73
Project HOPE, 266–67

qualitative research: and audio recording, 22, 72, 79–80n7, 106, 130n8, 225, 277; design of, 21–22, 66–70, 104–13, 158–59, 203–6, 224–25, 238–39, 277–78; and interviewer effects, 117–22; in prison, 66–74, 105–8; in reentry, 109–113, 158–161, 203–7, 224–25, 238–39, 277–78; therapeutic potential of, 114–15, 120

rabble class, 102, 122–29
racial disparities, 135–36
rearrest, 12–15
recidivism: definitions of, 13–17, 23–24, 37, 39–40; and education, 283; and gender, 28; and immigration, 28–29; measures of, 14–18, 21–22, 24–30, 37–40; and probation violation, 271; and race, 16; scope of, 13, 265, 281; and social capital, 55–56, 81–82, 221–23
reconviction, 15
reentry: challenges to, 2–5, 59–60, 219–20, 275–76, 281–82; and drug addiction, 100–103, 122–25; and education, 276–76, 282–92; evaluating success in, 13–14, 20, 37–38; and family, 59–60, 63–65, 77–79, 126–27, 139–41, 149–50, 176–77, 208–12, 215, 219–22, 225–34, 276; and immigration, 141–42; and language, 142–43; and negative social relationships, 198, 201–2, 209–10, 212, 214–15, 227, 232–33; and neighborhood context, 103, 142–44, 176, 189, 275–76; and race, 135–37, 139, 150; and residential instability, 122–25; and social capital, 141–42, 222–23; and stereotypes, 136, 145–47; and stigma, 174–77, 188, 190–91, 235–37
Reentry Prison Inmate Networks Study (R-PINS). *See* social network research
reformed lifers, 287
rehabilitation, 3–4, 37–38, 214, 260, 278, 290–91, 294–95; politics of, 315–19
reincarceration, 15–16
Risk-Need-Responsivity (RNR) model, 41–42, 53–54, 269, 272, 295; case study of, 46–53; and human frailty, 43–44, 54–55; and place, 44–45, 55–56; revision of, 42–44, 55–56

sentencing mitigation, 297, 299, 308–9, 312; and early childhood, 302–5; guidelines for, 300; and incarceration history, 305–6; and life after incarceration 306–7; limitations of 301–2; and mercy, 311; procedure of, 300–301; and reentry, 309–11
sex offenders, 235–37, 241–42, 253–56; and employment, 248–51; and housing, 246–48; and parole, 242–45
social control theories, 139
social disorganization, 143
social network research, 81–83, 97–98; administration of, 90–96; and audio recording, 87; challenges in, 85–86, 90–91, 93, 96, 99n6; design of, 87–90; elements of, 83–84; and gender, 91–92, 99n7; recruitment to, 92–93
social support, 197–99, 216–17, 219–20, 225–34; changes in, 203, 212–13, 215; and reciprocity, 200–201, 214, 234; sources of, 202, 210–12, 220–24, 251–53; types of, 197, 199–201, 207–9, 213–14
St. Louis Area Violence Prevention Collaborative (STLVPC), 46–47
St. Louis County Probation Violation Program, 269–71; outcomes of, 271–72
stigma: theories on, 172–74
swift-and-certain (SAC) programs, 266–67

"tough on crime" politics, 1, 53, 279–82, 290–91
Trump administration, 317–19
typical former prisoner (identity), 172–73, 175–77, 193; policy implications of, 191–92; psychological and behavioral outcomes of 186–87, 190–91; sources of, 185–86, 188–89

unified correctional systems, 15–16

Violent Crime Control and aw Enforcement Act of 1994, 280–81

"what works" movement. *See* evidence-based practices
Willie Horton commercial, 280